Dr. Ela Sharma's

SAT Math
Manual and Workbook
For the New SAT

ISBN: 9798334700697

Published in the United States of America.
Copyright © 2024 Dr. Ela Sharma
All rights reserved.
Version SE4.03

No part of this book may be reproduced or distributed in any form or means.
Volume discounts are available for schools, teachers, tutors, and learning agencies.
Email: tutorhubllc@gmail.com.

Additional resources and information on this book, including errata, are available at www.tutorhubllc.com.

Disclaimers:
The author of this book has made best effort to provide accurate and complete content and assumes no liability for errors and inaccuracies that may occur.

*SAT is a registered trademark of the College Board, which is not affiliated in the publication of, and does not endorse this book.

Preface and Acknowledgments

Teaching, especially in mathematics, has been my passion since I was a teen. Over the course of years, I have helped many students achieve their target scores on the SAT and ACT math sections.

It wasn't until it hit home that I recognized the stress, and the anxiety high school students go through the college admission process. My daughter was preparing for the SAT a few years ago. She was struggling with how to get started, which math books to buy, and which math websites to subscribe to (even though mom taught math!). That is when I decided to write a book on SAT math with the mission to provide students like her with a complete resource that would enable them to achieve their target score while maximizing study time.

To my excitement, my daughter provided encouragement and support throughout the writing process and studied the content as I wrote.

I am grateful to Rob Pollak and Jeff Eisenberg for proofreading various sections of this book, and to all the students who have provided insightful feedback!

I wish good luck to all the students using this book to prepare for the SAT math!

Getting Started!

Fourth Edition: Without the Answer Section

This fourth edition of the SAT Math Manual and Workbook, <u>without the answer section</u>, is published for tutors and schoolteachers who prefer that students work through the practice questions with focus and understanding rather than go straight to the answer solutions.

Hundreds of Examples and Practice Questions

The 800+ practice questions and 200+ examples are created for students to master the required math skills and knowledge and achieve their target scores on the SAT math.

To avoid confusing students with multiple approaches (except leveraging Desmos) to solving a question, examples in this book showcase the shortest and most consistent stepwise approach that always works to solve a question type.

The Desmos Graphing Calculator

The 50+ Desmos graphing calculator examples (40 with Desmos graph) are opportunities for students to learn how to leverage the Desmos graphing calculator to minimize errors and maximize time for more challenging questions. These examples are identified by an asterisk (*).

Desmos is best learnt by experience. If your lesson plans incorporate leveraging the Desmos graphing calculator, then either have students open it and follow the steps from the Desmos graphing calculator examples in this book or assign these examples as homework. Students can continue to hone Desmos skills with the practice questions marked as "Desmos".

Categories and Sections for a Tailored Lesson Plan

As the book is divided into 87 small, manageable, and independent categories logically arranged in 14 sections, creating a tailored lesson plan or curriculum for students is easy.

Tutors can assess a student's skill by having a student take any two practice tests, and based on the results, select the sections or categories that require improvement. Likewise, schoolteachers can construct a custom curriculum based on their requirements or syllabus.

Each category contains 3 sections:

- **Key Points**: These provide students with an enhanced understanding of the math concepts required to solve the questions in that category. They are presented as bullet points to avoid overwhelming students with long and confusing explanations. They are also great as a quick study reference.
- **How to Solve**: Each category has 1 to 4 examples that demonstrate the application of the Key Points. The examples accompanied by Desmos graphing calculator solution show the solution after the stepwise approach.
- **Practice Questions**: Examples are followed by a variety of easy, medium, and hard practice questions that are representative of the questions on the SAT math.

The **section review practice questions** at the end of each section are a great tool for tutors and schoolteachers to assess progress in that section!

Table of Contents

Introduction to the Digital SAT...7

Introduction to the Desmos Graphing Calculator...9

Commonly Used Terminology..11

Section 1 – Variables and Expressions in Linear Equations...12

Category 1 – Solve Variables and Expressions in Linear Equations..13

Section 2 – Lines and Linear Functions..19

Category 2 – Slope-Intercept Form Equation of a Line...20

Category 3 – Standard Form Equation of a Line...27

Category 4 – Points on a Line with Unknown Coordinates...30

Category 5 – Slope of Parallel Lines..32

Category 6 – Slope of Perpendicular Lines..35

Category 7 – Linear Functions...38

Category 8 – Graph Transformations of Linear Functions..41

Section 2 – Review Questions..45

Section 3 – Systems of Linear Equations and Inequalities...49

Category 9 – Systems of Linear Equations and Number of Solutions...50

Category 10 – Systems of Linear Equations with No Solution..54

Category 11 – Systems of Linear Equations with Infinite Solutions..56

Category 12 – System of Linear Equations with One Solution..58

Category 13 – Systems of Linear Inequalities..62

Category 14 – Equivalent and Nonequivalent Linear Expressions..67

Section 3 – Review Questions..70

Section 4 – Word Problems on Linear Equations and Inequalities...73

Category 15 – Word Problems on Linear Equations with One Variable..74

Category 16 – Word Problems on Linear Equations with Two Variables..78

Category 17 – Word Problems on Interpretation of Linear Equations...80

Category 18 – Word Problems on Linear System of Equations...83

Category 19 – Word Problems on Linear Inequalities...88

Category 20 – Word Problems on Linear System of Inequalities..91

Category 21 – Word Problems on Equal Variables in Linear Equations..93

Section 4 – Review Questions..96

Section 5 – Polynomial and Undefined Functions..100

Category 22 – Standard Form Polynomial Functions..101

Category 23 – Tables and Graphs of Polynomial Functions..104

Category 24 – Nested Polynomial Functions...107

Category 25 – Zeros, Factors, and Factored Form Polynomial Functions.......................................110

Category 26 – Graph Transformations of Polynomial Functions...113

Category 27 – Remainders in Polynomial Functions...115

Category 28 – Undefined Functions...118
Section 5 – Review Questions..120

Section 6 – Quadratic Equations and Parabola..123
Category 29 – Quadratic Equations and Factors..124
Category 30 – Quadratic Equations and Number of Roots..127
Category 31 – Sum and Product of Quadratic Roots..129
Category 32 – Standard Form Equation of a Parabola...131
Category 33 – Vertex Form Equation of a Parabola..137
Category 34 – Factored Form Equation of a Parabola...141
Category 35 – Equivalent Equations of a Parabola..143
Category 36 – Parabola Intersections and Systems of Equations...145
Category 37 – Graph Transformations of a Parabola...149
Category 38 – Equivalent Quadratic Expressions..152
Section 6 – Review Questions...155

Section 7 – Absolute Value..159
Category 39 – Absolute Value and Linear Equations..160
Category 40 – Absolute Value and Linear Inequalities...163
Category 41 – Absolute Value and Functions...167
Section 7 – Review Questions...171

Section 8 – Ratios, Proportions, and Rates..173
Category 42 – Ratios and Proportions...174
Category 43 – Rates...178
Section 8 – Review Questions...182

Section 9 – Percentages...184
Category 44 – Percentages of a Number and Percent Increase/Decrease..185
Category 45 – The Original Number before a Percent Increase/Decrease..189
Category 46 – A Number Percent of Another Number...191
Category 47 – Percent Change..193
Section 9 – Review Questions...195

Section 10 – Exponents and Exponential Functions..197
Category 48 – Exponents...198
Category 49 – Linear Versus Exponential Growth and Decay..202
Category 50 – Exponential Growth and Decay...204
Category 51 – Graphs of Exponential Growth and Decay Functions..208
Section 10 – Review Questions...210

Section 11 – Manipulate Expressions and Equations..212
Category 52 – Fractions with Expressions in the Denominator...213
Category 53 – Rearrange Variables in an Equation..216
Category 54 – Combine or Factor Like Terms..218

Category 55 – Expressions with Square Root..219
Section 11 – Review Questions...222

Section 12 – Data Analysis and Interpretation..224
Category 56 – Probability...225
Category 57 – Graphs with Line Segments and Curves..228
Category 58 – Scatter Plots and Lines of Best Fit...232
Category 59 – Bar Graphs...237
Category 60 – Histograms and Dot Plots..240
Category 61 – Mean..243
Category 62 – Histograms, Dot Plots, and Mean..246
Category 63 – Median...249
Category 64 – Histograms, Dot Plots, Bar Graphs, and Median..252
Category 65 – Box Plots and Median...256
Category 66 – Mode..259
Category 67 – Standard Deviation and Range..260
Category 68 – Compare Mean, Median, Mode, SD, and Range..262
Category 69 – Interpretation of Sample Data in Studies and Surveys...266
Section 12 – Review Questions...269

Section 13 – Geometry..274
Category 70 – Area and Angles of a Circle..275
Category 71 – Circumference and Arc of a Circle...280
Category 72 – Equation of a Circle..283
Category 73 – Parallel and Intersecting Lines..287
Category 74 – Polygons..291
Category 75 – Angles, Sides, and Area of a Triangle...294
Category 76 – Similar Triangles...300
Category 77 – Squares and Cubes..303
Category 78 – Rectangles and Right Rectangular Prisms..305
Category 79 – Trapezoids and Parallelograms...307
Category 80 – Volume of Cylinders, Spheres, Cones, Pyramids, Prisms..309
Category 81 – Mass, Volume, and Density Relationship...313
Category 82 – Combined Geometric Figures...314
Category 83 – Geometric Figures in the xy-plane...319
Category 84 – Geometric Figures and Percent...321
Category 85 – Ratio of Linear Side Length to Area or Volume..323
Section 13 – Review Questions...324

Section 14 – Trigonometry...328
Category 86 – Right Triangles and Trigonometry...329
Category 87 – Unit Circle and Trigonometry..335

Introduction to the Digital SAT

The full SAT Suite of Assessments is administered digitally. Students at international test centers have been taking the digital SAT since March 2023. In U.S., students have been taking the digital SAT since March 2024.

The digital SAT continues to measure the same skills and knowledge as the paper and pencil test and continues to be scored on the same scale as the paper and pencil test. The Reading and Writing section is scored on a scale of 200-800, and the Math section is scored on a scale of 200-800.

Each section of the digital SAT has two parts, known as modules.

Digital administration

Students will take the SAT on a laptop or tablet using a custom-built digital testing application, known as the Bluebook™. Students are responsible for downloading the Bluebook™ testing app and setting it up before the test day. Students will be provided with scratch paper and can bring a pen or pencil.

The digital testing application starts with the first module of the Reading and Writing section and moves to the second module after the time runs out on the first module. There is a 10-minute break at the end of the Reading and Writing section. After the break the testing application moves to the first module of the Math section, followed by the second module after the time runs out on the first module.

Students can move back and forth among questions in a module before time runs out.

Information on additional topics such as device requirements, device lending, accommodations, and what to bring on test day can be obtained by visiting https://satsuite.collegeboard.org/digital and selecting the submenu of interest.

Adaptive test design

The second module of each section is adaptive.

Students begin each test section by answering the questions in the first module. This module contains a mix of easy, medium, and hard questions. The questions in the second module are based on the performance of a student in the first module. The better a student performs on the first module, the harder are the questions on the second module.

Number of questions and duration

	Reading and Writing Section	**Math Section**
Number of questions per module	1st module: 25 operational questions and 2 pretest questions 2nd module: 25 operational questions and 2 pretest questions	1st module: 20 operational questions and 2 pretest questions 2nd module: 20 operational questions and 2 pretest questions
Time per module	1st module: 32 minutes 2nd module: 32 minutes	1st module: 35 minutes 2nd module: 35 minutes
Total number of questions	54 questions	44 questions
Total time allocated	64 minutes	70 minutes
Question type(s)	Four-option multiple choice	Four-option multiple choice approximately 75%, and student-produced responses approximately 25%

Only operational questions count towards the score. Pretest questions are included to aid the College Board with the test development process and do not count towards the score. Since it is not possible to identify pretest questions on the test, students should treat all questions equally important.

Digital SAT practice tests

Six full-length digital adaptive practice tests are available in the Bluebook™ testing app. These tests mimic the actual digital adaptive test interface, format, and scoring system. They are a valuable resource to familiarize students with the digital platform interface and the adaptive nature of the test. Students can download the Bluebook™ testing app and sign-in using the College Board account to access these practice tests.

Additionally, pdf versions of six linear (nonadaptive) tests are available at the College Board website. Though they are not adaptive and not taken digitally, they provide students with an additional resource for the digital test format and type of questions.

Digital SAT math section

The four math content domains for the digital SAT along with the required skills and question distribution are shown in the table below. Mapping of sections in this book to the four math content domains is included.

Content Domain	Skill/Knowledge Required	Operation Question Distribution	Section in this Book
Algebra	Linear equations in one variable. Linear equations in two variables. Linear functions. Systems of two linear equations in two variables. Linear inequalities in one or two variables.	Approximately 35% with 13-15 questions	1, 2, 3, 4
Advanced Math	Equivalent expressions. Nonlinear equations in one variable and systems of equations in two variables. Nonlinear functions.	Approximately 35% with 13-15 questions	5, 6, 7, 10, 11
Problem-Solving and Data Analysis	Ratios, rates, proportional relationships, and units. Percentages. One-variable data: distributions and measures of center and spread. Two-variable data: models and scatterplots. Probability and conditional probability. Inference from sample statistics and margin of error. Evaluating statistical claims: observational studies and experiments.	Approximately 15% with 5-7 questions	8, 9, 12
Geometry and Trigonometry	Area and volume. Lines, angles, and triangles. Right triangles and trigonometry. Circles.	Approximately 15% with 5-7 questions	13, 14

The four-option multiple choice and student-produced response questions are distributed throughout each math module.

Calculators are allowed for all the math questions. Students may use their own approved calculator on test day or utilize the Desmos graphing calculator embedded in the Bluebook™ testing app.

The availability of the Desmos graphing calculator is an advantage. Several math questions on the SAT, a few seemingly hard, can be solved within seconds with the Desmos graphing calculator. Students not familiar with the graphing calculator do not need to stress. This book contains examples of several questions that can be solved using basic features of the Desmos graphing calculator.

Disclaimers:

* *The information on digital adaptive SAT summarized above is taken from the College Board website.*

Introduction to the Desmos Graphing Calculator

The Desmos graphing calculator can graph a variety of equations, inequalities, and data sets. It is a free online tool.

The figure below shows the Desmos graphing calculator interface. The section to the left of the graph is the Expression List section. Equations, tables, and data sets are entered here.

This book displays the graphs in black and white. However, Desmos displays points and graphs in color.

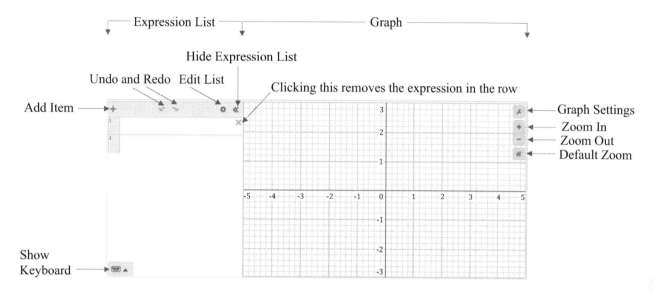

- Add Item: Clicking this opens a drop-down menu. Selecting table from the drop-down menu will create a two-column table to enter x- and y-coordinates of a point.
- Hide Expression List: Clicking this will hide the expression list giving more area to view the graph.
- X: Clicking this will clear the expression in that row.
- Show Keyboard: Clicking this will display the calculator keyboard.
- Zoom In: Clicking this will zoom in the graph. Use this to accurately read points on the graph.
- Zoom Out: Clicking this will zoom out the graph. Use this to view the points or graphs that are farther from each other or not visible on the default zoom of the graph.
- Default Zoom: Clicking this will reset to the default zoom of the graph. This is the zoom at the opening of the Desmos graphing calculator.

A graph can be manually moved up, down, left, or right using the track pad. Use this to view the points that are farther from the origin.

Few considerations when using the Desmos graphing calculator

- Using the Desmos graphing calculator requires basic understanding of its features and interface. How efficiently a student can manipulate it depends on the student's experience and proficiency with the graphing calculator.
- In the Bluebook™ testing app, the graphing calculator can be invoked from an icon. It opens in a small screen partially overlaying the screen occupied by a question and may require adjustment with its size and position.
- The graphing calculator only recognizes x and y variables. For example, to solve for a in the equation $4(3 + a) = 3a - 8$, a must be substituted by x or y before entering the equation in the graphing calculator.
- Points are displayed as decimals on a Desmos graph. When answer choices are given as fractions or square roots, type them in Desmos, one at a time, to convert to a decimal and match.
- It is important to zoom in and out at the right level. For example, zoom in to accurately view the points on graphs, and zoom out to view graphs that are not visible at the default zoom.
- Some of the questions may be solved faster using scratch paper or a regular calculator. For example, in the equation $4x - 5 = 11$, the value of x can be solved quickly using mental math, or scratch paper. It is for a student to decide which approach to use.

Enter an equation

Type an equation in the Expression List section. See below.

Upon entering an equation, the corresponding graph is displayed. The graph below shows the solution to the equation $2(x - 4) = 3x - 14$. As seen in the graph, the equation is of a line, and the value of x is 3. (Note that if the equation was $2(y - 4) = 3y - 14$, then the graph would display a line at $y = 3$.)

When an equation is typed a colored circle appears to the left of the equation, as seen below. The color of the line matches the color of the circle. (Note that this book only utilizes black and white color.)

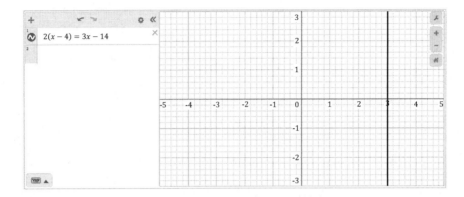

The above equation can be typed using the device keyboard. Use the graphing calculator keyboard to enter an inequality operator, an absolute value, a square root, or an exponent in equations.

Create a table

Click on the Add Item and select table from the dropdown. Type the x- and y-coordinates of a point in the respective columns. See below for a point $(-2, 1)$. To enter another point, click the cell below and enter the point.

Note that the Desmos graphing calculator will always have x and y column labels with subscript. The first table created after opening the graphing calculator will label x and y columns as the x_1 and y_1, respectively. The second table created without clearing the first table will label x and y columns as the x_2 and y_2, respectively, and so on.

The color of the circle that appears to the left of the y column label matches the color of the points on the graph.

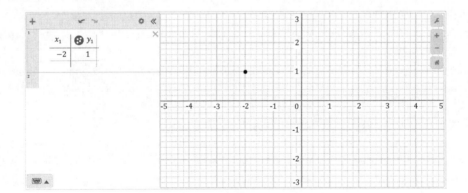

Disclaimers:

* *Desmos graphing calculator is a product of Desmos Studio.*

* *This book does not provide an in-depth tutorial on Desmos graphing calculator. Numerous tutorials are available on Desmos website.*

* *Desmos graphs in this book are the best attempt of the author to mimic the Desmos graphing calculator interface on a laptop. The author assumes no liability for errors and inaccuracies that may occur.*

Commonly Used Terminology

xy-plane and ordered pair

xy-plane refers to a coordinate system that has a horizontal *x*-axis and a vertical *y*-axis. See the figure below. The axes are perpendicular to each other and intersect at a point known as the origin.

Each point in the coordinate system has a coordinate on the *x*-axis and a coordinate on the *y*-axis, collectively known as the ordered pair (x, y). For example, in the figure below, the *x*-coordinate of point A is 3, and the *y*-coordinate is 1. The ordered pair is (3, 1).

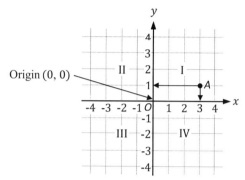

Quadrant

The four sections formed by the intersecting *x*- and *y*-axes in the *xy*-plane are known as quadrants. See the figure above. They are numbered 1 to 4 in the counterclockwise direction starting from the upper right quadrant. The quadrant numbers are denoted by Roman numerals.

Line segment

A line segment is a part of a line that has distinct and finite end points. For example, the sides of a triangle or a square or any other geometric figure that has distinct end points.

Variable

A variable is a placeholder for a numerical value. It is denoted by a letter. For example, in $5x - 7$, x is a variable. The value given to x will determine the value of $5x - 7$.

Constant

A constant is a static number in an equation. For example, in the equation $y = x - 7$, 7 is a constant. Its value will not change in the equation. A question that denotes a letter as a constant will specifically call out the constant. For example, in the equation $y = x - a$, a is a constant.

Coefficient

A coefficient is a constant that is multiplied by a variable. For example, in the equation $2y = 5x - 7$, 2 is the coefficient of the variable y and 5 is the coefficient of the variable x.

Every variable has a coefficient. If a number is not given in front of the variable, then the implicit value of the variable is 1. For example, in the equation $2y = x - 7$, the coefficient of the variable x is 1.

Term

A term refers to a number, a variable, several variables multiplied together, or a number and several variables multiplied together. For example, in the equation $2xy + x + 7 = 3y - 2x$, the terms on the left-side of the equation are $2xy$, x, and 7, and the terms on the right-side of the equation are $3y$ and $2x$.

Expression vs. Equation

The terms on either side of an equation are collectively known as an expression. For example, in the equation $2xy + x + 7 = 3y - 2x$, the two expressions are $2xy + x + 7$ and $3y - 2x$.

Section 1 – Variables and Expressions in Linear Equations

Category 1 – Solve Variables and Expressions in Linear Equations

Category 1 – Solve Variables and Expressions in Linear Equations

Key Points

- Moving a term from one side of the equation to the other side of the equation reverses the operator. A positive term becomes negative, and a negative term becomes positive. Similarly, multiplication becomes division, and division becomes multiplication. For example, in the equation $4x - 1 = 2x + 5$, $2x$ moved to the left-side is $-2x$ and -1 moved to the right-side is 1.

$$4x - 1 = 2x + 5 \rightarrow 4x - 2x = 5 + 1 \rightarrow 2x = 6$$

  2 from $2x$ (2 multiplied by x) on the left-side of the equation can be removed by dividing the right-side by 2.

$$2x = 6 \rightarrow x = \frac{6}{2}$$

- See the following when solving equations with fractions:
  - Moving a fraction from one side of the equation to the other side of the equation reverses the addition and subtraction operators, same as above. See below.

$$\frac{5x}{3} = \frac{1}{5} + \frac{x}{3} \rightarrow \frac{5x}{3} - \frac{x}{3} = \frac{1}{5}$$

  - Fractions with the same denominator can be added or subtracted by adding/subtracting the numerators. See below.

$$\frac{5x}{3} - \frac{x}{3} = \frac{1}{5} \rightarrow \frac{5x - x}{3} = \frac{1}{5} \rightarrow \frac{4x}{3} = \frac{1}{5}$$

  - Fractions that do not have the same denominator can be added or subtracted after creating the same denominator in the fractions.
  - Multiplying the numerator of the fraction on one side of the equation with the denominator of the fraction on the other side of the equation (cross multiplication) clears the fraction. See below.

$$\frac{4x}{3} = \frac{1}{5} \rightarrow \frac{4x}{3} \bowtie \frac{1}{5} \rightarrow 4x \times 5 = 1 \times 3 \rightarrow 20x = 3 \rightarrow x = \frac{3}{20}$$

- Expressions within parentheses can be simplified by multiplying each term within the parentheses by the outside term. For example, in the expression $3a(x + b)$, x and b can be individually multiplied by $3a$ and then added. See below.

$$3a(x + b) = (3a \times x) + (3a \times b) = 3ax + 3ab$$

- Each term within the parentheses must be multiplied by the entire outside term. For example, in the expression $-3a(x - b)$, both x and b must be multiplied by $-3a$ not $3a$. See below.

$$-3a(x - b) = (-3a \times x) - (-3a \times b) = -3ax + 3ab$$

- Identical expressions in an equation can be added or subtracted as a unit. For example, in the equation $3(4x + 1) - 2(4x + 1) = 9$, $(4x + 1)$ can be considered as a unit. 3 units − 2 units is 1 unit. See below.

$$3(4x + 1) - 2(4x + 1) = 9 \rightarrow (4x + 1) = 9$$

How to Solve

*Most questions in this category that contain one variable can be solved using the Desmos graphing calculator. Note that some of the questions, such as $3x - 18 = x$, can be just as quickly solved using the mental math or a hand-held calculator.

Example 1:

What value of x satisfies the equation $3(x - 2) = x + 2$?

Step 1: Simplify the expression within parentheses
$$3(x - 2) = x + 2 \;\rightarrow\; (3 \times x) - (3 \times 2) = x + 2 \;\rightarrow\; 3x - 6 = x + 2$$

Step 2: Isolate variables on one side of the equation and solve
$$3x - 6 = x + 2 \;\rightarrow\; 3x - x = 2 + 6 \;\rightarrow\; 2x = 8 \;\rightarrow\; x = \frac{8}{2} = 4$$

The correct answer is **4**.

Desmos Graphing Calculator Solution

Type the equation and read the value of x where the graph of the equation passes through the x-axis. See the vertical line in the graph below. The value of x is 4.

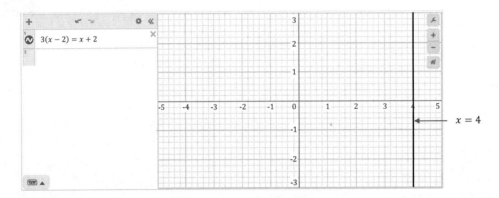

Example 2:

$$\frac{\left(\frac{x}{3}\right)}{5} = 8$$

What value of x is the solution to the given equation?

A) $\frac{5}{3}$

B) $\frac{5}{8}$

C) 40

D) 120

Step 1: Simplify the fraction

In the above fraction, $\frac{x}{3}$ is the numerator (evident by the parentheses) and 5 is the denominator. This is same as $\frac{x}{3} \div 5$.

$$\frac{\left(\frac{x}{3}\right)}{5} = 8 \;\rightarrow\; \frac{x}{3} \div 5 = 8 \;\rightarrow\; \frac{x}{3} \times \frac{1}{5} = 8 \;\rightarrow\; \frac{x}{15} = 8$$

Step 2: Cross multiply and solve
$$\frac{x}{15} = 8 \;\rightarrow\; x = 8 \times 15 = 120$$

The correct answer choice is **D**.

*Desmos Graphing Calculator Solution

Type the equation and read the value of x where the graph of the equation passes through the x-axis. See the vertical line in the graph below. Make sure to put parentheses in the numerator fraction so the graphing calculator knows that x divided by 3 is the numerator of the fraction.

Since the line is not visible at the default zoom, zoom out to view the line. See the vertical line in the graph below. The value of x is 120.

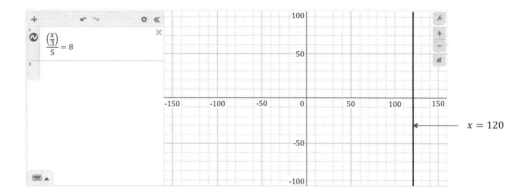

*Example 3:

If n satisfies the equation $5(n + 3) - 16 = 3(n + 3)$, what is the value of $n + 3$?

Step 1: Isolate all terms of the identical expression on one side of the equation and solve

$$5(n + 3) - 16 = 3(n + 3) \rightarrow 5(n + 3) - 3(n + 3) = 16 \rightarrow 2(n + 3) = 16 \rightarrow n + 3 = 8$$

The correct answer is **8**.

*Desmos Graphing Calculator Solution

When entering the equation, change n to x or y. In this example n is changed to y. Type the equation and read the value of y where the graph of the equation passes through the y-axis. See the horizontal line in the graph below. The value of y is 5. Hence, $n = 5$.

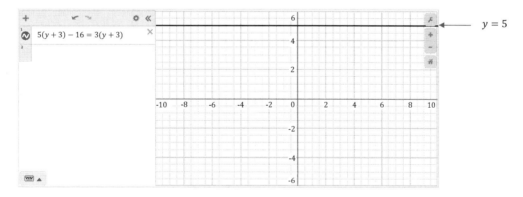

$n + 3 = 5 + 3 = 8$.

Digital SAT Math Manual and Workbook

Example 4:

In the equation $\frac{2p}{5} = \frac{3q}{4}$, what is the value of $\frac{q}{p}$?

A) $\frac{6}{20}$

B) $\frac{8}{15}$

C) $\frac{18}{20}$

D) $\frac{15}{8}$

Step 1: Cross multiply
$$2p \times 4 = 3q \times 5 \rightarrow 8p = 15q$$

Step 2: Isolate $\frac{q}{p}$ on one side of the equation
$$8 = \frac{15q}{p} \rightarrow \frac{8}{15} = \frac{q}{p} \rightarrow \frac{q}{p} = \frac{8}{15}$$

The correct answer choice is **B**.

Example 5:

2 times of a number 18 is equal to x plus 7.

Question 1:
What is the value of x?

Step 1: Determine the equation

2 times 18 is 2×18.

x plus 7 is $x + 7$.

Since 2×18 is equal to $x + 7$, the equation is
$$2 \times 18 = x + 7 \rightarrow 36 = x + 7$$

Step 2: Isolate variables on one side of the equation and solve
$$x = 36 - 7 = 29$$

The correct answer is **29**.

Question 2:
Which of the following expressions represents the value of x?

A) $(2)(18) + 7$

B) $(2)(18) - 7$

C) $(11) - 7$

D) $(2)(11)$

Step 1: Determine the equation

See Step 1 above. The equation $2 \times 18 = x + 7$ is same as
$$(2)(18) = x + 7$$

Step 2: Isolate variables on one side of the equation
$$x = (2)(18) - 7$$

The correct answer choice is **B**.

Digital SAT Math Manual and Workbook

Category 1 – Practice Questions

1 Desmos

$$4(x - 3) = 3x - 4$$

What value of x satisfies the equation above?

A) 2
B) 3
C) 8
D) 16

2 Desmos

In the equation $y + 1 = -3(y - 3)$, what is the value of y?

A) 1
B) 2
C) 4
D) 9

3 Desmos

$$b - 3b + 2b - b + 3 - 5 = b$$

What is the solution to the given equation?

A) 5
B) 3
C) 0
D) −1

4 Desmos

In the equation $\frac{3a+2a+a}{5} = 2$, what is the value of a?

A) $\frac{2}{5}$
B) $\frac{6}{5}$
C) $\frac{5}{3}$
D) $\frac{9}{5}$

5

11 more than a number a is 5 times of 9. What is the value of a?

A) 24
B) 34
C) 64
D) 144

6 Desmos

$$\frac{x}{2} - \frac{2}{5} = \frac{3x}{10}$$

What is the value of x in the above equation?

A) $\frac{3}{5}$
B) $\frac{2}{3}$
C) 2
D) 3

7 Desmos

What is the value of x in the equation $3xy - 10x = 14$, when $y = 4$?

A) 4
B) 7
C) 10
D) 14

8

If $\frac{3x}{y} = \frac{4}{7}$, what is the value of $\frac{4y}{3x}$?

A) $\frac{3}{7}$
B) $\frac{12}{7}$
C) $\frac{21}{4}$
D) 7

Digital SAT Math Manual and Workbook

9

$$\frac{\left(\frac{x}{7}\right)}{3} = y$$

In the given equation, what is the value of $\frac{y}{x}$?

A) $\frac{1}{21}$

B) $\frac{1}{10}$

C) $\frac{3}{7}$

D) $\frac{7}{3}$

10

Which equation has the same solution as the equation $x + 8 = 11$?

A) $x = -3$

B) $3x = 6$

C) $4x = 12$

D) $11x = 8$

11 Desmos

If $9m + 24 = 15m$, what is the value of $3m$?

A) 4

B) 9

C) 12

D) 24

12

8 added to 14 times of a number c is equal to 96. Which equation represents this situation?

A) $(8)(14) = 96c$

B) $(8)(14)c = 96$

C) $8c + 14 = 96$

D) $14c + 8 = 96$

13 Desmos

If n satisfies the equation $4(n + 5) - 38 = 3(n + 5)$, what is the value of $3(n + 5)$?

A) 9

B) 38

C) 114

D) 152

14 Desmos

$$\frac{2x}{3} = \frac{x}{5} + \frac{7}{5}$$

What value of x is the solution to the given equation?

A) 7

B) 3

C) $\frac{3}{5}$

D) $\frac{1}{3}$

15 Desmos

If $\frac{5}{8}(x - 3) - 42 = \frac{3}{8}(x - 3)$, what is the value of $x - 3$?

A) 21

B) 42

C) 102

D) 168

16

In the equation $a = \frac{b}{n}$, n is a constant. If $a = 12$ when $b = m$, what is the value of a when $b = 3m$?

Section 2 – Lines and Linear Functions

Category 2 – Slope-Intercept Form Equation of a Line
Category 3 – Standard Form Equation of a Line
Category 4 – Points on a Line with Unknown Coordinates
Category 5 – Slope of Parallel Lines
Category 6 – Slope of Perpendicular Lines
Category 7 – Linear Functions
Category 8 – Graph Transformations of Linear Functions
Section 2 – Review Questions

Category 2 – Slope-Intercept Form Equation of a Line

Key Points
- The slope-intercept form of a line equation is $y = mx + b$, where m is the slope of the line, b is the y-coordinate of the y-intercept of the line, and x and y are the coordinates of any point on the line.
- The slope of a line can be negative or positive. On a graph, a line with a positive slope slant upward from left to right (Fig. 1). A line with a negative slope slant downward from left to right (Fig. 2).
- The slope of a line can also be written as $\frac{\text{rise}}{\text{run}} = \frac{\text{change in } y}{\text{change in } x}$ (Fig. 3).
  - For example, in the equation $y = \frac{2}{3}x + 5$, slope $= \frac{2}{3} = \frac{\text{rise}}{\text{run}}$.
- For any two points on a line, the slope can be determined using the slope formula, $m = \frac{y_2 - y_1}{x_2 - x_1}$, where m is the slope and (x_1, y_1) and (x_2, y_2) are the two points.
- The slope between any two points on a line is the same.
- The slope of a horizontal line is 0 as the difference in the y-values of any two points on a horizontal line is 0.
$$m = \frac{y_2 - y_1}{x_2 - x_1} = \frac{0}{x_2 - x_1} = 0$$
- The slope of a vertical line is undefined as the difference in the x-values of any two points on a vertical line is 0.
$$m = \frac{y_2 - y_1}{x_2 - x_1} = \frac{y_2 - y_1}{0} = \text{undefined}$$
- The y-intercept of a line is the point where the line intersects the y-axis (Fig. 1 and Fig. 2). At the y-intercept, $x = 0$. The coordinates of the y-intercept are $(0, y)$, where y is the y-coordinate of the y-intercept.
- The x-intercept of a line is the point where the line intersects the x-axis (Fig. 1 and Fig. 2). At the x-intercept, $y = 0$. The coordinates of the x-intercept are $(x, 0)$, where x is the x-coordinate of the x-intercept.
- A line passing through the origin passes through the point $(0, 0)$ (Fig. 3).

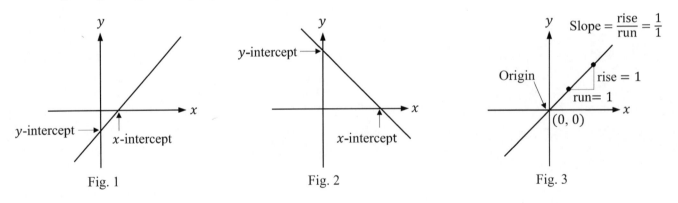

Fig. 1 Fig. 2 Fig. 3

How to Solve
Remember the following when not using the Desmos graphing calculator:
- If an equation is given where y is negative or has a constant, then it should be converted to the $y = mx + b$ form before determining the slope. For example, to determine the slope from the equation $-2y = 6x + 10$ divide it by -2. This gives $y = -3x - 5$. The slope is -3.
- The slope will be the same irrespective of whether a slope equation is set up as $\frac{y_2 - y_1}{x_2 - x_1}$ or $\frac{y_1 - y_2}{x_1 - x_2}$.

*Several questions in this category can be solved using the Desmos graphing calculator. Note that the linear regression equation $y_1 \sim mx_1 + b$ can be typed in Desmos to determine the slope and y-intercept of a line when two or more points on the line are given. Additional knowledge of linear regression is not required to solve these questions.

Example 1:

In the xy-plane, line l passes through the point $(0, 5)$ and has a slope of 2. Which of the following could represent the equation of line l?

A) $y = x + 1$
B) $y = 2x + 5$
C) $y = 2x + 9$
D) $y = 5x + 2$

Step 1: Determine the slope

It is given that the slope of the line is 2. This eliminates answer choices A and D. The slope in answer choice A is 1, and the slope in answer choice D is 5.

Step 2: Determine the y-coordinate of the y-intercept

The line passes through the point $(0, 5)$. Hence, $b = 5$. This eliminates answer choice C.

The correct answer choice is **B**.

*The slope and y-coordinate of the y-intercept are given to determine the equation of the line. Using the Desmos graphing calculator for this type of question does not save time.

Example 2:

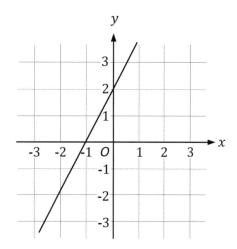

In the xy-plane, the graph of a line is shown above. Which of the following could be an equation of the line?

A) $y = -2x$
B) $y = -x + 2$
C) $y = 2x - 1$
D) $y = 2x + 2$

Step 1: Determine the slope

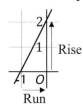

See a portion of the graph in the left figure.

$$\frac{\text{rise}}{\text{run}} = \frac{2}{1} = 2$$

Since the line slants upward from left to right, the slope of the line is positive. This eliminates answer choices A and B.

Step 2: Determine the y-coordinate of the y-intercept

The y-coordinate of the y-intercept can be read from the graph as 2. This eliminates answer choice C.

The correct answer choice is **D**.

*This question can be solved using the Desmos graphing calculator by typing the equation from each answer and matching the corresponding graph with the given graph. In this example, the above approach may be quicker.

*Example 3:

In the xy-plane, line n passes through the points $(2, 5)$ and $(4, 7)$. Which equation defines line n?

A) $y = x + 1$
B) $y = 2x + 3$
C) $2y = 2x + 6$
D) $2y = 6x + 7$

Step 1: Determine the slope

Set up a slope equation using the points $(2, 5)$ and $(4, 7)$.

$$\frac{y_2 - y_1}{x_2 - x_1} = \frac{7 - 5}{4 - 2} = \frac{2}{2} = 1$$

Note that the answer choices C and D have y with 2 as a constant. Divide the equations by 2. Now, answer choice C is $y = x + 3$, and answer choice D is $y = 3x + 3.5$.

This eliminates answer choices B and D. The slope in answer choice B is 2, and the slope in answer choice D is 3.

Step 2: Determine the y-coordinate of the y-intercept

Plug in the point $(2, 5)$ and slope $= 1$ in the $y = mx + b$ equation. Note that the same result will be obtained using the point $(4, 7)$.

$$5 = (1 \times 2) + b \quad \rightarrow \quad 5 = 2 + b \quad \rightarrow \quad b = 3$$

This eliminates answer choice A that has $b = 1$.

The correct answer choice is **C**.

*Desmos Graphing Calculator Solution**

Type the equation from each answer and determine if the line corresponding to each equation passes through the points $(2, 5)$ and $(4, 7)$. Stop when the correct answer choice is determined. No need to proceed with the remaining answer choices.

See the graph below of equations from the four answer choices. Only the line corresponding to the equation $2y = 2x + 6$ passes through both these points. Zoom in or move the graph, as needed.

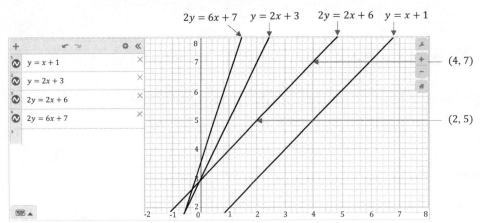

Note that in the Desmos graphing calculator each line will be a different color and this color will match with the color of the circle to the left of the typed equation.

*Example 4:

In the xy-plane, the slope of line m is $\frac{3}{2}$, and the y-intercept is $(0, -6)$. What is the x-coordinate of the x-intercept of line m?

A) -3
B) 0
C) 4
D) 6

Step 1: Determine the equation

Plug in slope $= \frac{3}{2}$ and y-coordinate of the y-intercept $= -6$ in the $y = mx + b$ equation.

$$y = \frac{3}{2}x - 6$$

Step 2: Determine the x-coordinate of the x-intercept

Since $y = 0$ at the x-intercept, plug in $y = 0$ in the equation and solve for x.

$$0 = \frac{3}{2}x - 6 \quad \rightarrow \quad \frac{3}{2}x = 6 \quad \rightarrow \quad 3x = 6 \times 2 \quad \rightarrow \quad 3x = 12 \quad \rightarrow \quad x = 4$$

The correct answer choice is **C**.

*Desmos Graphing Calculator Solution

For $m = \frac{3}{2}$ and $b = -6$, a slope-intercept equation is $y = \frac{3}{2}x - 6$. Type this equation and read the value of x where the line intersects the x-axis. This value is 4.

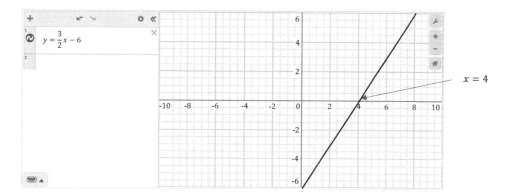

*Example 5:

What is the x-coordinate of the x-intercept of a line passing through the points $(4, 4)$ and $(6, 8)$?

Step 1: Determine the x-coordinate of the x-intercept

When the slope of a line are not given, the quickest approach is as shown below.

Let the x-intercept of the line $= (x, 0)$. (Remember $y = 0$ at the x-intercept).

Since the slope between any two points on a line is the same, set up two slope equations and equate them.

Set up one slope equation using the points $(4, 4)$ and $(6, 8)$. This will give the slope of the line. Set up the second slope equation using the points $(x, 0)$ and $(4, 4)$.

$$\frac{8-4}{6-4} = \frac{4-0}{4-x} \quad \rightarrow \quad \frac{4}{2} = \frac{4}{4-x} \quad \rightarrow \quad 2 = \frac{4}{4-x} \quad \rightarrow$$

$$2(4-x) = 4 \quad \rightarrow \quad 8 - 2x = 4 \quad \rightarrow \quad 2x = 8 - 4 \quad \rightarrow \quad 2x = 4 \quad \rightarrow \quad x = 2$$

The correct answer is **2**.

*Desmos Graphing Calculator Solution

Since the slope and y-intercept of the line are not given, graph a line using the two given points as shown below.

Create a table and type the two given points (4, 4) and (6, 8) in the table. In the next row, type $y_1 \sim mx_1 + b$. This graphs the corresponding line. Read the value of x where the line intersects the x-axis. This value is 2.

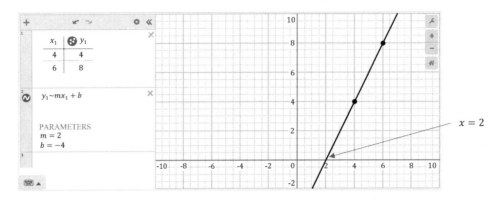

Note that typing $y_1 \sim mx_1 + b$ also displays the slope and y-coordinate of the y-intercept of the line. As seen above, the line graphed by the two points has slope $= m = 2$ and y-coordinate of the y-intercept $= b = -4$. (Additional statistical information is also displayed. However, it is not shown as it is not required to answer the questions on the SAT.)

*Example 6:

The equation of line p in the xy-plane is $y = \frac{1}{2}x + 1$. Which of the following point passes through line p?

A) $(-2, 1)$
B) $(-2, 0)$
C) $(2, 1)$
D) $(4, 2)$

Step 1: Plug the points from the answer choices in the given equation

For a point that is on the line, both sides of the equation will be the same.

Plug in point $(-2, 1)$ from choice A: $(1) = \frac{1}{2}(-2) + 1 \rightarrow 1 = -1 + 1 \rightarrow 1 = 0$. This eliminates answer choice A.

Plug in point $(-2, 0)$ from choice B: $(0) = \frac{1}{2}(-2) + 1 \rightarrow 0 = -1 + 1 \rightarrow 0 = 0$. Since both sides of the equation are the same, the point $(-2, 0)$ is a point the line p. Answer choice B is correct.

The correct answer choice is **B**.

*Desmos Graphing Calculator Solution

Type the equation and determine the point from the answer choices that is on the line. See below. Only point $(-2, 0)$ is on the line.

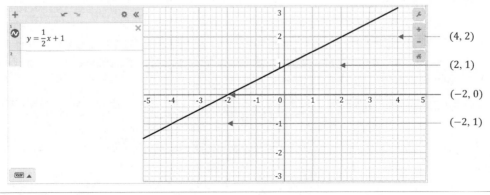

Digital SAT Math Manual and Workbook

Category 2 – Practice Questions

1 — Desmos

Line k, in the xy-plane, passes through the point $(2, 5)$. For every 3 units increase of x from left to right, y increases by 2 units up. Which of the following could be an equation of line k?

A) $y = -\frac{2}{3}x + 5$

B) $y = \frac{2}{3}x - \frac{3}{5}$

C) $y = \frac{2}{3}x + \frac{11}{3}$

D) $y = \frac{3}{2}x + 8$

2 — Desmos

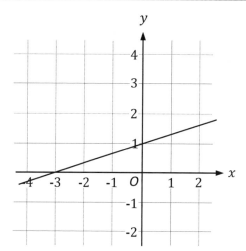

In the xy-plane, the graph of a line is shown above. Which of the following is an equation of the line?

A) $y = \frac{1}{3}x - 1$

B) $y = -x + 1$

C) $3y = -x + 1$

D) $3y = x + 3$

3 — Desmos

In the xy-plane, line s passes through the points $(-1, 2)$ and $(1, 6)$. Which equations defines line s?

A) $y = -2x + 4$

B) $y = 2x + 4$

C) $y = 2x + 6$

D) $y = 3x - 2$

4

$$y = 2x + 4$$

The equation of line l, in the xy-plane, is shown above. Line p passes through the point $(0, 2)$ and has a slope 3 times that of line l. Which of the following could be an equation of line p?

A) $y = 2x + 2$

B) $y = 3x + 4$

C) $y = 6x + 2$

D) $y = 6x + 4$

5 — Desmos

$$y = \frac{2x + 24}{4} - 3$$

In the xy-plane, what is the x-coordinate of the x-intercept of the line defined by the given equation?

A) -7

B) -6

C) 1

D) 3

6

The equation of line q in the xy-plane can be written in the form $ay = -2ax + ab$, where a and b are constants and $b > 1$. Which of the following could be the graph of line q?

A)

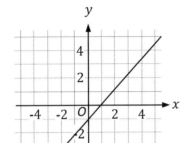

B)

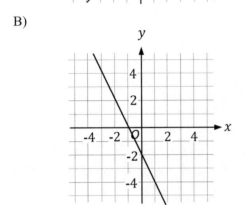

C)

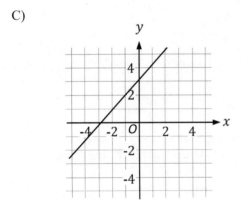

D)

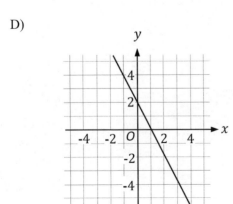

7 Desmos

In the xy-plane, line p passes through the origin and point $(2, 6)$. Which of the following equations defines line p?

A) $2y = 3x$
B) $2y = 6x$
C) $2y = 3x + 1$
D) $2y = 6x + 4$

8 Desmos

In the xy-plane, what is the slope of the graph of $y = \frac{1}{5}(42x + 19) - 5x$?

9 Desmos

What is the x-coordinate of the x-intercept of a line passing through the points $(0, -3.5)$ and $(4.5, 7)$?

10 Desmos

In the xy-plane, line n has a slope of -3 and passes through the point $(3, -5)$. What is the y-coordinate of the y-intercept of line n?

11 Desmos

Line p passes through the point $(3, 11)$, and intersects the x-axis at -8. What is the slope of line p?

Category 3 – Standard Form Equation of a Line

Key Points
- The standard form of a line equation is $Ax + By = C$, where A, B, and C are constants, and x and y are the coordinates of any point on the line. Constants that appear before x and y are also known as coefficients. A is the coefficient of x and B is the coefficient of y.
  - The slope of a line is $-\frac{A}{B}$.
  - The y-coordinate of the y-intercept of a line is $\frac{C}{B}$.
- The standard form equation can be converted to the slope-intercept form equation by rearranging the equation and vice versa. For example, $8x + 2y = 6 \rightarrow 2y = -8x + 6 \rightarrow y = -4x + 3$.

How to Solve
The following tip is helpful to remember when evaluating slope as $-\frac{A}{B}$.
- When both A and B are negative $\left(-\frac{-A}{-B} = -\frac{A}{B}\right)$ or both are positive $\left(-\frac{A}{B} = -\frac{A}{B}\right)$, the slope of the line is negative.
- When either A or B is negative $\left(-\frac{-A}{B} = -\frac{A}{B}\right)$ or $\left(-\frac{A}{-B} = -\frac{A}{B}\right)$, the slope of the line is positive.

*Several questions in this category can be solved using the Desmos graphing calculator.

Example 1:

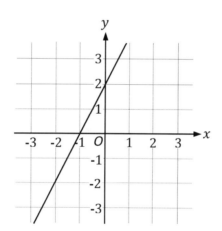

In the xy-plane, what is an equation of the graph above?
A) $-4x + 2y = 4$
B) $-2x + y = 4$
C) $x + 2y = 4$
D) $4x + 2y = 2$

Step 1: Determine the slope from the graph
Since the line slants upward from left to right, the slope of the line is positive.
$$\frac{\text{rise}}{\text{run}} = \frac{2}{1} = 2$$

Since the equations in the answer choices are given in the standard form, look for the equation where $-\frac{A}{B} = 2$. This eliminates answer choices C and D. See calculations below.

Answer choice A: $-\frac{A}{B} = -\frac{-4}{2} = 2$. Answer choice B: $-\frac{A}{B} = -\frac{-2}{1} = 2$.

Answer choice C: $-\frac{A}{B} = -\frac{1}{2}$. Answer choice D: $-\frac{A}{B} = -\frac{4}{2} = -2$.

Step 2: Determine the y-coordinate of the y-intercept

Answer choice A: $\frac{C}{B} = \frac{4}{2} = 2$.

Answer choice B: $\frac{C}{B} = \frac{4}{1} = 4$.

The y-coordinate of the y-intercept can be read from the graph as 2. This eliminates answer choice B.

The correct answer choice is **A**.

*This question can be solved using the Desmos graphing calculator by typing the equation from each answer and matching the corresponding graph with the given graph. However, the above shown approach may be quicker.

*Example 2:

Line k passes through the points $(-3, 2)$ and $(3, -1)$. Which of the following could be an equation of line k?

A) $-x - 2y = -1$
B) $-2x + 2y = -1$
C) $3x + 6y = 10$
D) $6x + 3y = 6$

Step 1: Determine the slope

Set up a slope equation using the points $(-3, 2)$ and $(3, -1)$.

$$\frac{y_2 - y_1}{x_2 - x_1} = \frac{-1 - 2}{3 - (-3)} = \frac{-3}{6} = -\frac{1}{2}$$

Since the equations in the answer choices are given in the standard form, look for the equation where $-\frac{A}{B} = -\frac{1}{2}$.

This eliminates answer choices B and D. In answer choice B, $-\frac{A}{B} = -\frac{-2}{2} = 1$. In answer choice D, $-\frac{A}{B} = -\frac{6}{3} = -2$.

Step 2: Determine the y-coordinate of the y-intercept

Plug in the point $(-3, 2)$ and slope $= -\frac{1}{2}$ in the $y = mx + b$ equation. (Same results will be obtained with $(3, -1)$.)

$$2 = \left(-\frac{1}{2} \times -3\right) + b \rightarrow 2 = \frac{3}{2} + b \rightarrow b = 2 - \frac{3}{2} = \frac{1}{2}$$

This eliminates answer choice C that has the y-coordinate of the y-intercept $= \frac{C}{B} = \frac{10}{6}$.

The y-coordinate of the y-intercept in answer choice A $= \frac{C}{B} = \frac{-1}{-2} = \frac{1}{2}$.

The correct answer choice is **A**.

*Desmos Graphing Calculator Solution

Type the equation from each answer and determine if the line corresponding to each equation passes through the given points. Stop after the correct answer choice is determined. See the graph below of equations from the four answer choices. Only the line corresponding to the equation $-x - 2y = -1$ passes through both these points. Zoom in as needed.

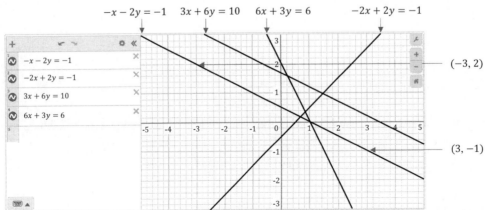

Category 3 – Practice Questions

Students comfortable with the slider feature can solve question 5 using the Desmos graphing calculator

1 — Desmos

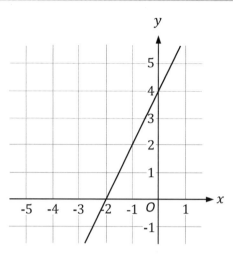

Which equation defines the above graph?

A) $6x - 3y = -12$
B) $3x - 6y = -12$
C) $6x + 3y = 12$
D) $2x + 5y = 6$

2 — Desmos

$$6x - 2y = -5$$

What is the y-coordinate of the y-intercept of a line in the xy-plane, defined by the above equation?

A) $\frac{1}{2}$
B) $\frac{5}{2}$
C) 2
D) 5

3 — Desmos

$$2x + 3y = 4c$$

An equation of a line in the xy-plane is shown above, where c is a constant. What are the (x, y) coordinates of the point at which the line crosses the x-axis?

A) $(-c, 0)$
B) $(c, 0)$
C) $(2c, 0)$
D) $(4c, 0)$

4 — Desmos

Line t, in the xy-plane, has a slope of $-\frac{3}{2}$ and intersects the x-axis at 4. Which of the following could be an equation of line t?

A) $3x - 2y = 12$
B) $3x + 2y = 8$
C) $2x + 3y = 8$
D) $3x + 2y = 12$

5

$$x - ay = a$$

An equation of line r, in the xy-plane, is shown above, where a is a constant. If line r passes through the point $(4, 1)$, which of the following can be the value of a?

A) 1
B) 2
C) 4
D) 6

Digital SAT Math Manual and Workbook

Category 4 – Points on a Line with Unknown Coordinates

Key Points
- The slope of any two points on a line is the same.
- For any two points on a line, the slope can be determined using the slope formula, $m = \frac{y_2 - y_1}{x_2 - x_1}$, where m is the slope and (x_1, y_1) and (x_2, y_2) are the two points.
- Any three points on a line can be equated in two slope equations. For example, $\frac{y_2 - y_1}{x_2 - x_1} = \frac{y_3 - y_2}{x_3 - x_2}$, where (x_1, y_1), (x_2, y_2), and (x_3, y_3) are the three points.
    - The result will be the same irrespective of which two points are used to set up a slope equation. For example, $\frac{y_2 - y_1}{x_2 - x_1} = \frac{y_3 - y_2}{x_3 - x_2}$ is same as $\frac{y_2 - y_1}{x_2 - x_1} = \frac{y_3 - y_1}{x_3 - x_1}$.
- The coordinates of the x-intercept are $(x, 0)$, and the coordinates of the y-intercept are $(0, y)$.

How to Solve

A question may be given where the coordinates of one or more points on a line are unknown. The unknown coordinates can be determined by setting up one or two slope equations, depending on the question.

If the slope is given or can be determined, then one slope equation can be set up and equated to the slope.

If the slope is not given, then two slope equations may be required to solve for the missing coordinate(s).

Example 1:
In the xy-plane, a line passes through the points $(0, b)$, $(3, 2b)$, and $(6, 9)$. What is the value of b, where b is a constant?

A) 0
B) 3
C) 6
D) 9

Step 1: Set up two slope equations

Since the slope is not given, set up two slope equations.

Set up a slope equation using the points $(0, b)$ and $(3, 2b)$.

$$\frac{2b - b}{3 - 0}$$

Set up a slope equation using the points $(3, 2b)$ and $(6, 9)$.

$$\frac{9 - 2b}{6 - 3}$$

Note that the results will be the same irrespective of the points used in a slope equation.

Step 2: Equate the two equations and solve

$$\frac{2b - b}{3 - 0} = \frac{9 - 2b}{6 - 3} \rightarrow \frac{b}{3} = \frac{9 - 2b}{3} \rightarrow$$
$$b = 9 - 2b \rightarrow 3b = 9 \rightarrow b = 3$$

The correct answer choice is **B**.

Digital SAT Math Manual and Workbook

Category 4 – Practice Questions
Students comfortable with the slider feature can solve the following questions using the Desmos graphing calculator

1

Line l passes through the points $(2, 2p)$ and $(5, p-1)$ in the xy-plane, and has a slope of -2. What is the value of $p-1$?

A) 4
B) 5
C) 7
D) 10

2

In the xy-plane, the points $(1, 4)$, $(5, m)$, and $(n, 7)$ lie on a line p. The slope of line p is 3. What is the value of $m + n$?

A) 12
B) 14
C) 17
D) 18

3

In the xy-plane, a line passes through the points $(1, 3)$, $(4, a)$, and $(7, a + b)$. What is the value of $a - b$?

A) -1
B) 0
C) 3
D) 11

4

x	1	s	5
y	2	6	10

A line, in the xy-plane, passes through the (x, y) coordinates shown in the table above. What is the value of s?

A) 2
B) 3
C) 5
D) 8

5

Line l has a slope of 3 and passes through the origin and point $(3, 3a)$ in the xy-plane. Which of the following is the point $(3, 3a)$?

A) $(1, 3)$
B) $(3, 1)$
C) $(3, 3)$
D) $(3, 9)$

6

In the xy-plane, a line of slope $-\frac{1}{2}$ passes through the points $(0, 2)$ and $(x, -2)$. What is the value of x?

Digital SAT Math Manual and Workbook

Category 5 – Slope of Parallel Lines

Key Points

- Non-vertical parallel lines have the same slope but different y-intercepts. See the figure below of two parallel lines, a and b. Vertical parallel lines are excluded since the slope of vertical lines is undefined.
- For any two points on a line, the slope can be determined using the slope formula, $m = \frac{y_2 - y_1}{x_2 - x_1}$, where m is the slope and (x_1, y_1) and (x_2, y_2) are the two points.
- The coordinates of the x-intercept are $(x, 0)$, and the coordinates of the y-intercept are $(0, y)$.

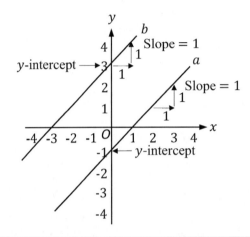

How to Solve

If the slope of one parallel line is given, then the slope of another parallel line is the same.

*Several questions in this category can be solved using the Desmos graphing calculator.

*Example 1:

In the xy-plane, line r passes through the points $(2, 3)$ and $(3, 5)$. Line s is parallel to line r and passes through the point $(1, 9)$. What is an equation of line s?

A) $y = x + 2$
B) $y = 2x + 1$
C) $y = 2x + 7$
D) $y = 4x + 5$

Step 1: Determine the slope

Set up a slope equation for line r using the points $(2, 3)$ and $(3, 5)$.

$$\frac{y_2 - y_1}{x_2 - x_1} = \frac{5 - 3}{3 - 2} = \frac{2}{1} = 2$$

Since line s is parallel to line r, the slope of line $s = 2$. This eliminates answer choices A and D.

Step 2: Determine the y-coordinate of the y-intercept of line s

Plug in the given point $(1, 9)$ and slope $= 2$ in the $y = mx + b$ equation.

$$9 = (2 \times 1) + b \quad \rightarrow \quad 9 = 2 + b \quad \rightarrow \quad b = 7$$

This eliminates answer choice B.

The correct answer choice is **C**.

*Desmos Graphing Calculator Solution

Determine the slope of line r:

Create a table and type the two given points. In the next row (2nd row), type $y_1 \sim mx_1 + b$. See below. Read the slope. Slope = $m = 2$. (Note that students comfortable with mental math can calculate slope in this example mentally and go straight to the next step.)

Determine the y-coordinate of the y-intercept of line s:

Since line s is parallel to line r, the slope of line s is also 2.

In the next row (3rd row), create a table for line s and type the given point $(1, 9)$. Note that since this is the 2nd table created, the column labels are x_2 and y_2.

In the next row (4th row), substituting $m = 2$, type $y_2 \sim 2x_2 + b$ and read the y-coordinate of the y-intercept = b. (Remember that the subscripts of the x- and y-column labels of a table must match the subscripts of the corresponding linear regression equation.)

$b = 7$.

Hence, an equation of line s is $y = 2x + 7$.

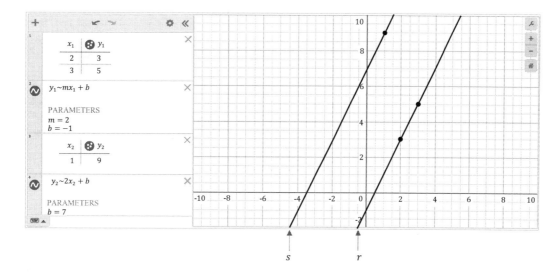

Digital SAT Math Manual and Workbook

Category 5 – Practice Questions
Students comfortable with the slider feature can solve question 4 using the Desmos graphing calculator

1 — Desmos

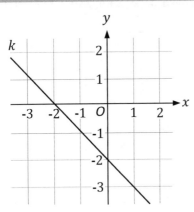

In the xy-plane, lines k and l are parallel lines. A partial graph of line k is shown above. Line l (not shown) passes through the point $(6, -4)$. What is an equation of line l?

A) $y = -x - 2$
B) $y = -x + 2$
C) $y = x - 2$
D) $y = 3x + 2$

2 — Desmos

$$6x + 3y = 5$$

An equation of line a is given above. Which of the following could be a possible equation of a parallel line b?

A) $-3x + 2y = 1$
B) $8x - 4y = 2$
C) $3x + 2y = 1$
D) $8x + 4y = 2$

3 — Desmos

In the xy-plane, line s has a slope of 4. Line t is parallel to line s and passes through the point $(3, 5)$. What are the (x, y) coordinates of the y-intercept of line t?

A) $(0, -12)$
B) $(0, -7)$
C) $(0, 3)$
D) $(4, 5)$

4

Line m in the xy-plane passes through the points $(c, 3)$ and $(6, 5)$. Line n is parallel to line m and passes through the points $(c, 1)$ and $(8, 4)$. Which of the following is the value of c?

A) 2
B) 4
C) 5
D) 8

5 — Desmos

$$\frac{2a}{3}x - \frac{b}{7}y = 51$$

Line p is defined by the above equation. In the xy-plane, which of the following could be an equation of a line parallel to line p, where a and b are constants, and $a \neq 0$, and $b \neq 0$?

A) $-\frac{4a}{3}x - \frac{2b}{7}y = 35$
B) $\frac{2a}{7}x - \frac{2b}{3}y = 35$
C) $\frac{7a}{3}x - \frac{b}{2}y = \frac{1}{42}$
D) $\frac{a}{4}x + \frac{b}{5}y = \frac{1}{51}$

Digital SAT Math Manual and Workbook

Category 6 – Slope of Perpendicular Lines

Key Points
- Perpendicular lines have negative reciprocal slope. See the figure below of two perpendicular lines, a and b.
- For any two points on a line, the slope can be determined using the slope formula, $m = \frac{y_2 - y_1}{x_2 - x_1}$, where m is the slope and (x_1, y_1) and (x_2, y_2) are the two points.
- The coordinates of the x-intercept are $(x, 0)$, and the coordinates of the y-intercept are $(0, y)$.

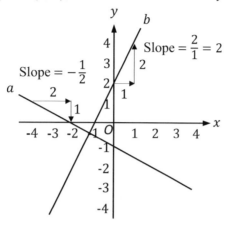

How to Solve
If the slope of a line is given, then the slope of a perpendicular line is the negative reciprocal.
*Several questions in this category can be solved using the Desmos graphing calculator.

*Example 1:
In the xy-plane, line p passes through the points $(2, 3)$ and $(4, 6)$. Line q is perpendicular to line p and intersects the x-axis at -3. Which of the following could define line q?

A) $y = -\frac{2}{3}x - 3$

B) $y = -\frac{2}{3}x - 2$

C) $y = \frac{3}{2}x + 1$

D) $y = 3x + 2$

Step 1: Determine the slope

Set up a slope equation for line p using the points $(2, 3)$ and $(4, 6)$.

$$\frac{y_2 - y_1}{x_2 - x_1} = \frac{6 - 3}{4 - 2} = \frac{3}{2}$$

Since line q is perpendicular to line p, the slope of line $q = -\frac{2}{3}$. This eliminates answer choices C and D.

Step 2: Determine the y-coordinate of the y-intercept of line q

Since line q intersects the x-axis at -3, point $(-3, 0)$ is the x-intercept of the line.

Plug in the point $(-3, 0)$ and slope $= -\frac{2}{3}$ in the $y = mx + b$ equation.

$$0 = \left(-\frac{2}{3} \times -3\right) + b \rightarrow 0 = 2 + b \rightarrow b = -2$$

This eliminates answer choice A.

The correct answer choice is **B**.

***Desmos Graphing Calculator Solution**

Determine the slope of line p:

Create a table and type the two given points. In the next row (2nd row), type $y_1 \sim mx_1 + b$. See below. Read the slope.

Slope $= m = 1.5 = \frac{3}{2}$.

Determine the y-coordinate of the y-intercept of line q:

Since line q is perpendicular to line p, the slope of line q is $-\frac{2}{3}$.

In the next row (3rd row), create a table for line q and type the point $(-3, 0)$. Note that since this is the 2nd table created, the column labels are x_2 and y_2.

In the next row (4th row), substituting $m = -\frac{2}{3}$, type $y_2 \sim -\frac{2}{3} x_2 + b$ and read the y-coordinate of the y-intercept $= b$. (Remember that the subscripts of the x- and y-column labels of a table must match the subscripts of the corresponding linear regression equation.)

$b = -2$.

Hence, an equation of line q is $y = -\frac{2}{3}x - 2$.

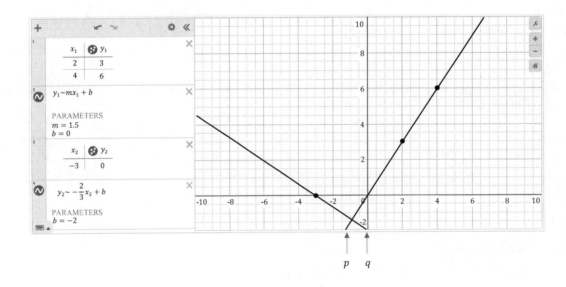

Category 6 – Practice Questions

1 — Desmos

Line p in the xy-plane has a slope of 3. Line q is perpendicular to line p and passes through the point $(0, -4)$. Which of the following equations defines line q?

A) $y = -\frac{1}{3}x - 4$

B) $y = -\frac{2}{3}x - 1$

C) $y = -\frac{1}{3}x + 4$

D) $y = \frac{2}{3}x + 1$

2 — Desmos

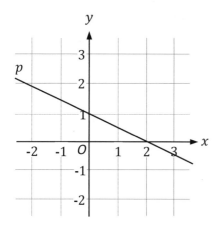

In the xy-plane, the partial graph of line p is shown above. Line t (not shown) is perpendicular to line p and passes through the point $(1, 4)$. What is the x-coordinate of the x-intercept of line t?

A) -2

B) -1

C) 1

D) 2

3 — Desmos

The points $(-1, 3)$ and $(3, 1)$ are the end points of line segment l in the xy-plane. Which of the following could be an equation of a perpendicular line h passing through line segment l?

A) $y = -\frac{1}{2}x + 2$

B) $y = \frac{1}{2}x + 5$

C) $y = 2x - 2$

D) $y = 2x + 7$

4 — Desmos

What are the coordinates of the y-intercept of a line that passes through the point $(-2, 5)$ and perpendicular to the graph of $9y + 3x = 3$, in the xy-plane?

A) $(0, -11)$

B) $(0, -3)$

C) $(0, 9)$

D) $(0, 11)$

5 — Desmos

In the xy-plane, line m passes through the points $(3, 7)$ and $(4, 9)$. Line n is perpendicular to line m and passes through the origin. What is an equation of line n?

A) $y = -\frac{1}{2}x - 3$

B) $y = -x + 3$

C) $2y = -x$

D) $4y = x$

Digital SAT Math Manual and Workbook

Category 7 – Linear Functions

Key Points
- In the xy-plane, a linear function graphs a line.
- A linear function is written in the form $f(x) = mx + b$.
  - $f(x)$ is the output value of a function for an input value of x. For example, if $x = 2$, then $f(2) = (m \times 2) + b =$ output value. Each input and output value pair of a function is a point. Collectively, these points graph a line.
  - For any (x, y) point on a line, $f(x) = mx + b$ is same as $y = mx + b$, where $f(x)$ is the value of y.
- A function can be given any name. For example, $g(x)$ or $h(x)$ or $t(x)$.
- For any two points on the graph of a linear function, the slope can be determined using the slope formula, $m = \frac{y_2 - y_1}{x_2 - x_1}$, where m is the slope and (x_1, y_1) and (x_2, y_2) are the two points.
- The coordinates of the x-intercept are $(x, 0)$, and the coordinates of the y-intercept are $(0, y)$.

How to Solve
Remember that $y = f(x)$ on the graph of a linear function f. For example, $f(4)$ is the value of y when $x = 4$.
*Several questions in this category can be solved using the Desmos graphing calculator.

*Example 1:
In the xy-plane, the points $(-2, -1)$ and $(4, 2)$ lie on the graph of a linear function f. Which of the following could define the function f?

A) $f(x) = \frac{1}{2}x$

B) $f(x) = \frac{1}{2} + 1$

C) $f(x) = 2x + 3$

D) $f(x) = 3x + 4$

Step 1: Determine the slope
Set up a slope equation using the points $(-2, -1)$ and $(4, 2)$.
$$\frac{2 - (-1)}{4 - (-2)} = \frac{3}{6} = \frac{1}{2}$$
This eliminates answer choices C and D.

Step 2: Determine the y-coordinate of the y-intercept
Plug in the point $(4, 2)$ and slope $= \frac{1}{2}$ in the $y = mx + b$ equation.
$$2 = \left(\frac{1}{2} \times 4\right) + b \rightarrow$$
$$2 = 2 + b \rightarrow b = 2 - 2 = 0$$
This eliminates answer choice B.
Note that the same result will be obtained by using the point $(-2, -1)$.
The correct answer choice is **A**.

*Desmos Graphing Calculator Solution

Create a table and type the two given points $(-2, -1)$ and $(4, 2)$ in the table. In the next row, type $y_1 \sim mx_1 + b$. This graphs the corresponding line and displays the slope and y-coordinate of the y-intercept of the line. See below. Read the slope = m and y-coordinate of the y-intercept = b.

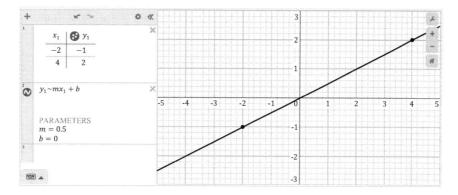

$m = 0.5$ and $b = 0$. Slope-intercept equation of the line is $y = 0.5x + 0$, or $y = \frac{1}{2}x$. The function that graphs this line is answer choice A, $f(x) = \frac{1}{2}x$.

*Example 2:

x	-4	0	4
$g(x)$	5	-3	-11

The above table shows three values of x and their corresponding values of $g(x)$ for the linear function g, where $y = g(x)$. What is the value of $g(-9)$?

Step 1: Set up slope equations

The question asks for the value of y when $x = -9$. This point is not given in the table. Let this point be $(-9, y)$.

Set up two slope equations and equate them. Below equations are set up using the points $(-4, 5)$ and $(0, -3)$ and the points $(0, -3)$ and $(-9, y)$.

$$\frac{-3 - 5}{0 - (-4)} = \frac{y - (-3)}{-9 - 0} \rightarrow \frac{-8}{4} = \frac{y + 3}{-9} \rightarrow -2 = \frac{y + 3}{-9} \rightarrow$$

$$-2 \times -9 = y + 3 \rightarrow 18 = y + 3 \rightarrow y = 18 - 3 = 15$$

Hence, $y = g(-9) = 15$.
The correct answer is **15**.

*Desmos Graphing Calculator Solution

Create a table and type any of the two given points. Points $(-4, 5)$ and $(0, -3)$ are used below. In the next row, type $y_1 \sim mx_1 + b$. This graphs the corresponding line. See below. Read the y-value on the line for $x = -9$. The value is 15.

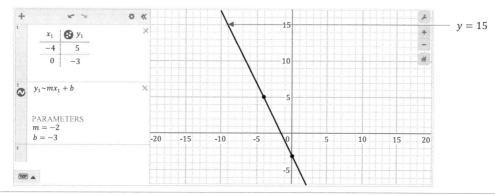

Digital SAT Math Manual and Workbook

Category 7 – Practice Questions

1 — Desmos

In the xy-plane, the graph of a linear function f passes through the points $(-2, -5)$ and $(2, 3)$. Which equation defines function f?

A) $f(x) = -x - 1$
B) $f(x) = 2x - 1$
C) $f(x) = 2x + 11$
D) $f(x) = 3x + 1$

2

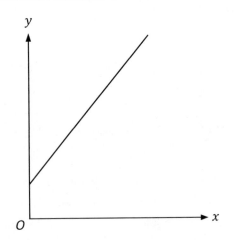

Bella bought a used car that had a certain number of miles on the odometer. The graph of $y = f(x)$ shown above models the total miles on the odometer x months after Bella bought the car. What is the best interpretation of the slope of the graph?

A) The number of miles when Bella bought the car.
B) The number of miles Bella drives in x months.
C) The average number of miles Bella drives per month.
D) The average number of days Bella drives the car each month.

3 — Desmos

The graph of $y = g(x)$ in the xy-plane passes through the point $(1, 4)$, and has a slope of 3. Which of the following is the value of $g(-2)$?

A) -5
B) -1
C) 2
D) 4

4 — Desmos

In the xy-plane, the points $(-2, 6)$ and $(3, -4)$ lie on the graph of a linear function f, where $y = f(x)$. What is the value of $f(1)$?

A) -1
B) 0
C) 1
D) 4

5 — Desmos

x	$g(x)$
2	6
4	9
6	12

The table above shows three values of x and their corresponding values of $g(x)$ for a linear function g. In the xy-plane, which of the following is the y-intercept of the graph of $y = g(x)$?

A) $(-2, -6)$
B) $(0, -1)$
C) $(0, 0)$
D) $(0, 3)$

Category 8 – Graph Transformations of Linear Functions

Key Points
- Graph transformations could be horizontal (left or right) or vertical (up or down) shifts, or reflections across the x-axis or y-axis. Horizontal and vertical shifts are also known as translations.
- See the horizontal and vertical transformation rules below for a line defined by $f(x) = x + 1$, where $y = f(x)$ and c is the units by which a horizontal or a vertical translation occurs.
    - Left horizontal translation by c units is $f(x) = (x + c) + 1$.
        - This will shift the x-intercept of the line left by c units.
    - Right horizontal translation by c units is $f(x) = (x - c) + 1$.
        - This will shift the x-intercept of the line right by c units.
    - Upward vertical translation by c units is $f(x) = x + 1 + c$.
        - This will shift the y-intercept of the line up by c units.
    - Downward vertical translation by c units is $f(x) = x + 1 - c$.
        - This will shift the y-intercept of the line down by c units.
- See the reflection rules below for a line defined by the slope-intercept equation $y = x + 1$.
    - Reflection across the x-axis does not change the x-values, but the y-values change to the opposite plus/minus operator. $f(x) = x + 1$ will become $-f(x) = x + 1$ → $f(x) = -(x + 1)$.
    - Reflection across the y-axis does not change the y-values, but the x-values change to the opposite plus/minus operator. $f(x) = x + 1$ will become $f(x) = -x + 1$.
- An equation of a line in the standard form $ax + by = c$ can be converted to the slope-intercept form $y = mx + b$ to apply the above transformation rules.

How to Solve
See example below of line a reflected across the x-axis and y-axis. The dashed line is the reflected line.
- Reflection across the x-axis is shown in Fig. 1. The x-coordinates of the points on the reflected line remain the same but the y-coordinates have the reverse plus/minus operator. For example, $(2, 2) \rightarrow (2, -2)$ and $(-4, -1) \rightarrow (-4, 1)$.
- Reflection across the y-axis is shown in Fig. 2. The y-coordinates of the points on the reflected line remain the same but the x-coordinates have the reverse plus/minus operator. For example, $(2, 2) \rightarrow (-2, 2)$ and $(-4, -1) \rightarrow (4, -1)$.

Equation of line a:
$$y = \frac{1}{2}x + 1$$

Equation of line a reflected across the x-axis:
$$y = -\left(\frac{1}{2}x + 1\right)$$

Equation of line a reflected across the y-axis:
$$y = -\frac{1}{2}x + 1$$

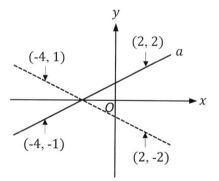

Fig. 1 Reflection of line a across x-axis

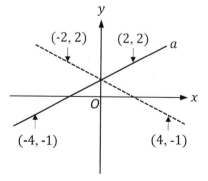

Fig. 2 Reflection of line a across y-axis

*Some of the questions in this category can be solved quicker using the Desmos graphing calculator.

Example 1:

$$f(x) = 3x + 5$$

The linear function f is defined above. Which of the following equations represents the translation of the graph of the function f left 4 units in the xy-plane?

A) $f(x) = 3x + 9$
B) $f(x) = 3x + 1$
C) $f(x) = 3(x - 4) + 5$
D) $f(x) = 3(x + 4) + 5$

Step 1: Determine the translation rule

Since the translation is 4 units left, the value of x is $(x + 4)$.

Note the significance of parentheses. 4 is added within the parentheses such that the equation is $f(x) = 3(x + 4) + 5$ not $f(x) = 3x + 4 + 5 = 3x + 9$.

The correct answer choice is **D**.

*This question can be solved using the Desmos graphing calculator by typing the given equation in the first row and the equation from each answer in the next row, one at a time, and determining which equation from the answer choice graphs a line that is 4 units left.

Example 2:

$$y = 2x - 3$$

In the xy-plane, the graph of the linear equation shown above is reflected across the x-axis. Which of the following could represent the reflected graph?

A)
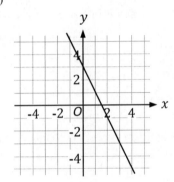

B)
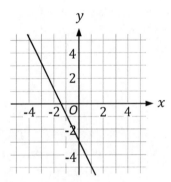

C)
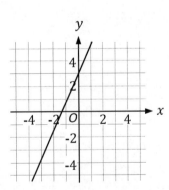

D)
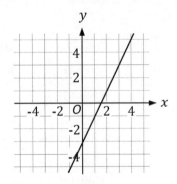

Step 1: Determine the transformation rule

The reflection across the x-axis will result in the following transformation.

$$y = -(2x - 3) \quad \rightarrow \quad y = -2x + 3$$

The transformed equation has negative slope and positive y-intercept. This eliminates answer choices B, C, and D. Answer choices C and D have positive slope. Answer choice B has negative y-intercept.

The correct answer choice is **A**.

*Example 3:

Line p passes through the points (15, 72) and (31, 152) in the xy-plane. Line q is a result of translating line p up 7 units. What is the x-coordinate of the x-intercept of line q?

A) $-\frac{2}{7}$

B) $-\frac{4}{5}$

C) $\frac{3}{5}$

D) $\frac{8}{11}$

Step 1: Determine the equation of line p

$$\frac{y_2 - y_1}{x_2 - x_1} = \frac{152 - 72}{31 - 15} = \frac{80}{16} = 5$$

Plug in the point (15, 72) and slope = 5 in the $y = mx + b$ equation to determine the y-coordinate of the y-intercept. Note that the same results will be obtained using the point (31, 152).

$$72 = (5 \times 15) + b \quad \rightarrow \quad 72 = 75 + b \quad \rightarrow \quad b = 72 - 75 = -3$$

Plug in the slope and y-coordinate of the y-intercept in $y = mx + b$ equation to determine the equation of line p.

$$y = mx + b \quad \rightarrow \quad y = 5x - 3$$

Step 2: Determine the equation of line q

Since line q is a result of translating line p up 7 units, the y-intercept of line q is 7 units up than line p. Hence,

$$y = 5x - 3 + 7 \quad \rightarrow \quad y = 5x + 4$$

Step 3: Determine the x-coordinate of the x-intercept of line q

Since $y = 0$ at the x-intercept, plug in $y = 0$ in the equation of line q and solve for x.

$$0 = 5x + 4 \quad \rightarrow \quad 5x = -4 \quad \rightarrow \quad x = -\frac{4}{5}$$

The correct answer choice is **B**.

*Desmos Graphing Calculator Solution

Line p: Create a table and type the two given points. In the next row, type $y_1 \sim mx_1 + b$. See below. Read the slope = m and y-coordinate of the y-intercept = b.
$m = 5$ and $b = -3$. Hence, a slope-intercept equation of line p is $y = 5x - 3$.

Line q: Since line q is a result of translating line p up 7 units, equation of line q is $y = 5x - 3 + 7$. Type this equation in the next row and read the x-intercept. See below.

x-coordinate of the x-intercept $= -0.8 = -\frac{4}{5}$. Make sure to zoom in to read -0.8 accurately.

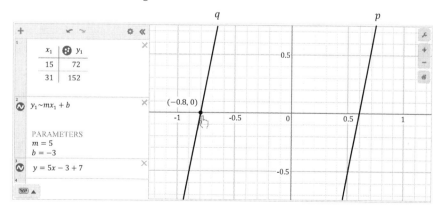

Category 8 – Practice Questions

1   Desmos

x	12	17	19
$f(x)$	114	149	184

The above table shows three values of x and their corresponding values of $f(x)$ for the linear function f, where $y = f(x)$. The graph of a linear function $g(x)$ is a result of translating the graph of $f(x)$ down 10 units in the xy-plane. What is the x-intercept of $y = g(x)$?

A) $\left(-\frac{40}{7}, 0\right)$

B) $\left(-\frac{30}{7}, 0\right)$

C) $\left(-\frac{20}{7}, 0\right)$

D) $\left(-\frac{10}{8}, 0\right)$

2   Desmos

$$f(x) = 2x - 4$$

An equation of a linear function f, in the xy-plane, is given above. Which of the following equations represents the translation of the graph of function f 3 units left and 2 unit up?

A) $f(x) = 2(x - 1) + 4$

B) $f(x) = 2(x + 1) - 4$

C) $f(x) = 2(x + 3) - 2$

D) $f(x) = 2(x + 3) + 2$

3   Desmos

$$y = 4x + 1$$

Which of the following equations represents the reflection of the graph of the above equation across the x-axis, in the xy-plane?

A) $y = -4x - 1$

B) $y = -4x + 1$

C) $y = 4x - 1$

D) $y = 4x + 1$

4   Desmos

$$f(x) = x + 2$$

In the xy-plane, which of the following graphs is the reflection of the above function across the y-axis?

A)
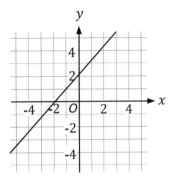

B)
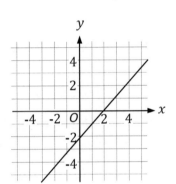

C)
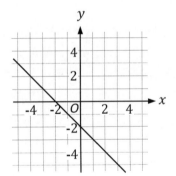

D)
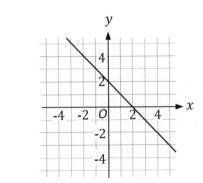

Digital SAT Math Manual and Workbook

Section 2 – Review Questions

Students comfortable with the slider feature can solve questions 11, 18, 21, and 22 using the Desmos graphing calculator

1

In the xy-plane, line k has a slope of 1. Line l is parallel to line k. What could be an equation of line l?

A) $4x - 4y = 12$
B) $8x - 4y = 12$
C) $4x + 4y = 12$
D) $6x + 3y = 12$

2 Desmos

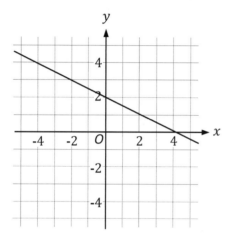

Which of the following could be an equation of the above graph in the xy-plane?

A) $y = -\frac{1}{2}x - 2$
B) $y = -\frac{1}{2}x + 2$
C) $y = \frac{1}{2}x - 2$
D) $y = \frac{1}{2}x + 2$

3 Desmos

$$f(x) = 5x - 2$$

In the xy-plane, the function f defined above graphs a line. If the line is translated and the equation of the translated line is $f(x) = 5(x - 2) + 2$, which of the following statements is true about the translation of the line?

A) Left 4 units and down 2 units.
B) Right 2 units and down 2 units.
C) Left 2 units and up 2 units.
D) Right 2 units and up 4 units.

4 Desmos

Which of the following is an equation of line p that passes through the points $(0, -2)$ and $(-2, -5)$ in the xy-plane?

A) $y = -\frac{3}{2}x - 2$
B) $y = -\frac{3}{2}x + 2$
C) $2y = 3x - 4$
D) $2y = 3x + 4$

5

In the xy-plane, the y-coordinate of the y-intercept of line s is -6. If $ax - by = 4$ is an equation of line s, where a and b are constants, what is the value of b?

A) $-\frac{1}{2}$
B) $-\frac{2}{3}$
C) $\frac{2}{3}$
D) 4

6

The slope of line p is undefined. Which of the following could be an equation of line p?

A) $x = 3$
B) $x = -y$
C) $x = y$
D) $y = 2$

7 Desmos

What of the following is an equation of the given graph?

A) $-x + 5y = 5$
B) $x + 5y = 5$
C) $2x - 5y = 20$
D) $2x + 5y = 20$

8 Desmos

x	$f(x)$
-1	-4
-2	-2
-3	0

The table above shows three values of x and their corresponding values of $y = f(x)$ for the linear function f. What is the value of $f(-6)$?

A) -8
B) -4
C) 6
D) 10

9 Desmos

$$g(x) = 3x + 5$$

The equation for the graph of a linear function $y = g(x)$, in the xy-plane, is given above. The graph of a linear function $y = f(x)$ is parallel to the graph of the function g and passes through the point $(3, 3)$. What is the value of $f(1)$?

A) -6
B) -3
C) 2
D) 8

10 Desmos

Two perpendicular lines m and n intersect at the point $(2, 4)$. Line m passes through the origin and line n intersects the x-axis at point P. Which of the following is the x-coordinate of point P?

A) 2
B) 4
C) 8
D) 10

11

x	$h(x)$
0	$2k$
3	$3k$
6	$4k$
9	$5k$

For the linear function h, the table above gives four values of x and their corresponding values of $h(x)$, where k is a constant and $y = h(x)$. Which equation defines h?

A) $h(x) = \frac{k}{3}x + k$
B) $h(x) = \frac{k}{3}x + 2k$
C) $h(x) = x - k$
D) $h(x) = x + 1$

12 Desmos

$$4x + 2y + 5 = 0$$

An equation of line s is given above. Line t is perpendicular to line s and passes through the point $(4, 5)$. What is the x-intercept and y-intercept of line t in the xy-plane?

A) x-intercept is $(-6, 0)$ and y-intercept is $(0, 3)$
B) x-intercept is $(6, 0)$ and y-intercept is $(0, 3)$
C) x-intercept is $(4, 0)$ and y-intercept is $(0, 2)$
D) x-intercept is $(4, 0)$ and y-intercept is $(0, -4)$

13 Desmos

Number of classes	Monthly cost ($)
4	44.95
8	84.95
12	124.95

A gym charges each member a monthly flat fee, in dollars, for attending yoga classes plus a fixed dollar charge for each yoga class attended. The table above shows the linear relationship between the number of yoga classes attended in a month and the total monthly cost, in dollars. Which of the following functions can be used to determine the total monthly cost, $f(x)$, in dollars, for attending x yoga classes in a month?

A) $f(x) = 4x$
B) $f(x) = x + 4$
C) $f(x) = 10x + 4.95$
D) $f(x) = 20x + 10.95$

14 Desmos

In the xy-plane, the point $(-1, -1)$ is on the graph of line l defined by $y = 2x + 1$. Which of the following points is also on the graph of line l?

A) $(-1, 0)$
B) $(0, -1)$
C) $(0, 2)$
D) $(1, 3)$

15 Desmos

Line k intersects with a perpendicular line l at the point $(-2, 5)$. The slope of line k is 2. What is the x-intercept of line p resulting from translating line l up 2.5 units in the xy-plane?

A) $(-4.5, 0)$
B) $(6.5, 0)$
C) $(13, 0)$
D) $(15, 0)$

16 Desmos

$$2x + 4y = 11$$

Line p is defined by the given equation. Line r is perpendicular to line p and is formed by joining two endpoints M and N. Which of the following could be the coordinates of the points M and N?

A) $M = (1, -2)$. $N = (3, -4)$.
B) $M = (1, 2)$. $N = (2, -4)$.
C) $M = (1, 2)$. $N = (2, 8)$.
D) $M = (1, 2)$. $N = (4, 8)$.

17 Desmos

$$2y = 5x - 15$$

The equation of a line is given above. In the xy-plane, what is the x-coordinate of the x-intercept of the line?

A) -3
B) 3
C) 5
D) 10

18

$$\frac{a}{4}x - \frac{3}{5}y = \frac{1}{2}$$

Line d is defined by the above equation. In the xy-plane, which of the following could be an equation of a line perpendicular to line d, where a is a constant and $a \neq 0$?

A) $-\frac{3}{4}x - \frac{3}{5a}y = -\frac{1}{2}$

B) $-\frac{3}{5a}x - \frac{1}{4}y = -\frac{1}{2}$

C) $-\frac{4}{a}x + \frac{5}{3}y = \frac{1}{3}$

D) $\frac{1}{4}x + \frac{3}{5a}y = \frac{1}{3}$

19 Desmos

$$y = -\frac{3}{10}x + 2$$

Line q is defined by the above equation. Which of the following could be an equation of a line perpendicular to line q?

A) $y = -\frac{3}{10}x - 2$

B) $y = -\frac{10}{3}x - 2$

C) $y = \frac{3}{10}x + 12$

D) $y = \frac{10}{3}x + 12$

20 Desmos

x	-4	0	8
y	-16	10	62

For line m, the table above shows three values of x and their corresponding values of y. Line n is a result of translating line m down 4.5 units in the xy-plane. Which is an equation of line n?

A) $-6.5x - y = -10$

B) $-6.5x + y = 5.5$

C) $6.5x + y = -10$

D) $6.5x + y = 14.5$

21

x	1	4	7	a
$h(x)$	3	b	9	10

The table above shows four values of x and their corresponding values of $h(x)$, for a linear function h. What is the value of $a + b$?

22

The slope of a line p is $-\frac{1}{2}$. Line l is perpendicular to line p and passes through the points $(-2, -2)$ and $(2, k)$. What is the value of k?

23 Desmos

The function g defined by $g(b) = \frac{4}{5}b$. For what value of b does $g(b) = 76$?

Section 3 – Systems of Linear Equations and Inequalities

Category 9 – Systems of Linear Equations and Number of Solutions
Category 10 – Systems of Linear Equations with No Solution
Category 11 – Systems of Linear Equations with Infinite Solutions
Category 12 – Systems of Linear Equations with One Solution
Category 13 – Systems of Linear Inequalities
Category 14 – Equivalent and Nonequivalent Linear Expressions
Section 3 – Review Questions

Category 9 – Systems of Linear Equations and Number of Solutions

Key Points
- A system of linear equations is comprised of two or more linear equations.
- A system of linear equations may have no (zero) solution, exactly one solution, or infinite solutions.
  - A system has no solution when the lines graphed by the equations in a system are parallel lines with the same slope and different y-intercepts.
  - A system has exactly one solution when the lines graphed by the equations in a system intersect at exactly one point (x, y).
  - A system has infinite solutions when the lines graphed by the equations in a system are the same line.
- When two linear equations in a system are compared in the standard form $Ax + By = C$, where A, B, and C are constants, the ratio of each respective constant in the two equations determine the number of solutions. The following rules apply for two equations $a_1 x + b_1 y = c_1$ and $a_2 x + b_2 y = c_2$.
  - If $\frac{a_1}{a_2}$, $\frac{b_1}{b_2}$, and $\frac{c_1}{c_2}$ are the same, then the system has infinite solutions.
  - If $\frac{a_1}{a_2}$ and $\frac{b_1}{b_2}$ are the same but $\frac{c_1}{c_2}$ is different, then the system has no solution.
  - If $\frac{a_1}{a_2}$ and $\frac{b_1}{b_2}$ are different, then the system has one solution. The ratio of c does not matter.
- A system of more than two linear equations has one solution when all the lines intersect at exactly one point (x, y). The system has no solution when some, but not all, of the lines intersect at one point or none of the lines intersect. For example, if in a system of three lines, l, m, and n, lines m and n intersect at one point and lines l and n intersect at one point but all three lines do not intersect at a common point, then the system has no solution.

How to Solve
As most of the questions have at least one equation in the standard form, this book focuses on evaluating the ratios of A, B, and C of the two equations, as described in the Key Points. An alternate approach is to convert the equations to slope-intercept form and evaluate the slope and y-intercept.

*Several questions in this category can be solved using the Desmos graphing calculator. A few considerations are:
- When the equations in the system are the same line, the graph will show a single line. Click on each equation to ensure that the same line is highlighted.
- When the equations in the system graph lines that intersect at one point, zoom in or out, as needed, to verify the intersection point.
- When the two equations are for parallel lines, it is important to zoom out to ensure that the lines do not intersect at all.

*Example 1:

$$-2x + 3y = 10$$
$$4x - 6y = -4$$

How many solutions does the above system of equations have?

A) Zero
B) Exactly one
C) Exactly two
D) Infinitely many

Step 1: Evaluate the ratios

Top equation: $a_1 = -2$. $b_1 = 3$. $c_1 = 10$.

Bottom equation: $a_2 = 4$. $b_2 = -6$. $c_2 = -4$.

$$\frac{a_1}{a_2} = \frac{-2}{4} = -\frac{1}{2}$$

$$\frac{b_1}{b_2} = \frac{3}{-6} = -\frac{1}{2}$$

$$\frac{c_1}{c_2} = \frac{10}{-4} = -\frac{5}{2}$$

The ratios of a and b are the same but different than the ratio of c. Hence, the system of equations has no solution. The correct answer choice is **A**.

*Desmos Graphing Calculator Solution

Type the two equations and determine the number of solutions. See below. The equations graph parallel lines. It can be observed from the two graphs that rise/run = slope is the same for both the lines.

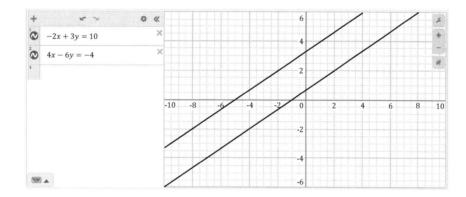

Digital SAT Math Manual and Workbook

*Example 2:

$$3x + 2y = 6$$
$$\frac{2}{3}y + \frac{1}{2} = -\frac{1}{2}x + \frac{3}{2} + \frac{1}{3}y$$

How many solutions does the above system of equations have?

A) Zero
B) Exactly one
C) Exactly two
D) Infinitely many

Step 1: Convert the equations to standard form

Bottom equation:

$$\frac{1}{2}x + \frac{2}{3}y - \frac{1}{3}y = \frac{3}{2} - \frac{1}{2} \rightarrow \frac{1}{2}x + \frac{1}{3}y = 1$$

Step 2: Evaluate the ratios

Top equation: $a_1 = 3$. $b_1 = 2$. $c_1 = 6$.

Bottom equation: $a_2 = \frac{1}{2}$. $b_2 = \frac{1}{3}$. $c_2 = 1$.

$$\frac{a_1}{a_2} = \left(3 \div \frac{1}{2}\right) = 3 \times 2 = 6$$

$$\frac{b_1}{b_2} = \left(2 \div \frac{1}{3}\right) = 2 \times 3 = 6$$

$$\frac{c_1}{c_2} = \frac{6}{1} = 6$$

The ratios of a, b, and c are the same. Hence, the system of equations has infinitely many solutions.

The correct answer choice is **D**.

*Desmos Graphing Calculator Solution

Type the two equations and determine the number of solutions. See below. The two equations graph the same line. Click on each equation to ensure the same line highlights.

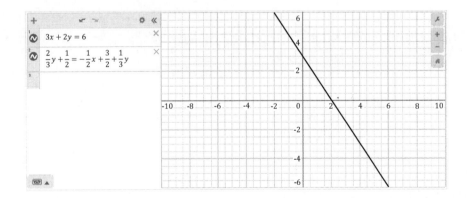

Digital SAT Math Manual and Workbook

Category 9 – Practice Questions

1 — Desmos

$$2x - 3y = -4$$
$$-6x + 9y = 12$$

How many solutions exist for the above system of equations?

A) Zero
B) Exactly one
C) Exactly two
D) Infinitely many

2

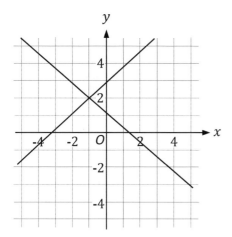

In the xy-plane, the graph of two lines in a system of equations is shown above. If a third line defined by $y = -1$ is added to the system, how many solutions will the system have?

A) Zero
B) Exactly one
C) Exactly two
D) Infinitely many

3 — Desmos

$$3x = y + 2$$
$$-y = 3x + 1$$

How many solutions does the above system of equations have?

A) Zero
B) Exactly one
C) Exactly two
D) Infinitely many

4 — Desmos

$$\frac{17}{4}x + \frac{10}{3}y - \frac{10}{3} = \frac{1}{4}x + \frac{1}{3}y - \frac{1}{3}$$
$$\frac{1}{3}x + \frac{1}{4}y = \frac{1}{2}$$

How many solutions does the above system of equations have?

A) Zero
B) Exactly one
C) Exactly two
D) Infinitely many

5 — Desmos

$$\frac{1}{4}x + y = -c$$
$$x + 4y = -4c$$

How many solutions does the above system of equations have, where c is a constant?

A) Zero
B) Exactly one
C) Exactly two
D) Infinitely many

Category 10 – Systems of Linear Equations with No Solution

Key Points
- A system of linear equations has no solution when the lines graphed by the equations are parallel lines with the same slope but different y-intercepts.
- When a system of equations is compared in the standard form $Ax + By = C$, where A, B, and C are constants, the following rule applies for two equations $a_1x + b_1y = c_1$ and $a_2x + b_2y = c_2$ to have no solution.
  - If $\frac{a_1}{a_2}$ and $\frac{b_1}{b_2}$ are the same but $\frac{c_1}{c_2}$ is different, then the system has no solution.

How to Solve
A question may give equations with one or more unknown constants. To determine the value of a constant, equate the ratios. A constant should be given a value that will make the ratios of a and b the same but different than that of c.

* Questions in this category can be solved using the slider feature of the Desmos graphing calculator. This requires careful manipulation especially when the correct answer is a decimal. Students proficient with this feature can try it out.

Example 1:
$$2nx + y = 3$$
$$x + \frac{1}{4}y = 1$$

In the system of equations above, n is a constant. For what value of n does the system have no solution?

Step 1: Equate the ratios

$2n$ is the value of a in the top equation. For the system to have no solution, the ratios of a and b must be the same. Determine the value of n that will result in the same a and b ratios.

$$\frac{a_1}{a_2} = \frac{b_1}{b_2} \rightarrow \frac{2n}{1} = \left(1 \div \frac{1}{4}\right) \rightarrow 2n = 4 \rightarrow n = 2$$

When $n = 2$, the ratios of a and b are the same. Hence, the system has no solution.

The correct answer is **2**.

Example 2:
$$3x + 2y = k$$
$$9x + 6y = 3$$

If the above system of equations has no solution, which of the following can NOT be the value of the constant k?

A) -3
B) 0
C) 1
D) 9

Step 1: Equate the ratios

k is the value of c in the top equation. For the system to have no solution, the value of k cannot result in the ratio of c to be same as the ratios of a and b. (Since the system has no solution, the ratios of a and b are the same.)

Equate the ratio of a or b with c and determine the value of k that makes the ratios same. See ratios of a and c below.

$$\frac{a_1}{a_2} = \frac{c_1}{c_2} \rightarrow \frac{3}{9} = \frac{k}{3} \rightarrow \frac{1}{3} = \frac{k}{3} \rightarrow k = 1$$

If $k = 1$, then all the ratios will be the same. For the system to have no solution, $k \neq 1$.

The correct answer choice is **C**.

Category 10 – Practice Questions

Students comfortable with the slider feature can solve the following questions using the Desmos graphing calculator

1

$$2x + 12y = 5$$
$$\frac{1}{6}x + \frac{1}{b}y = 12$$

In the system of equations above, for which of the following values of b does the system have no solution, where b is a constant?

A) -6
B) -1
C) 1
D) 8

2

$$y = 4x + 10$$
$$-ax = -4y + 14$$

In the xy-plane, the graphs of the equations above are parallel lines. Which of the following can be the value of the constant a?

A) -1
B) 4
C) 12
D) 16

3

$$3x + 2y = k$$
$$9x + 6y = 12$$

In the xy-plane, the equations of two parallel lines are given above. Which of the following can NOT be the value of the constant k?

A) 1
B) 3
C) 4
D) 9

4

$$-\frac{4}{3}x + \frac{2}{3}y = \frac{3}{5} - \frac{1}{3}y$$
$$ky - \frac{2}{3}x = \frac{8}{3}x + \frac{5}{3}$$

In the given system of equations, k is a constant. If the system has no solution, what is the value of k?

A) $-\frac{1}{3}$
B) $-\frac{4}{3}$
C) $\frac{2}{5}$
D) $\frac{5}{2}$

5

$$2x + my = n$$
$$5x + 10y = 15$$

The above system of equations has no solution, where m and n are constants. Which of the following could be the possible values of m and n?

A) $m = 2$ and $n = 1$
B) $m = 2$ and $n = 6$
C) $m = 4$ and $n = 6$
D) $m = 4$ and $n = 8$

6

$$0.2x + 0.3y = 0.1$$
$$ax + 0.6y = 0.3$$

For the above system of equations to have no solution, what is the value of a, where a is a constant?

A) 0.2
B) 0.4
C) 2.0
D) 3.1

Digital SAT Math Manual and Workbook

Category 11 – Systems of Linear Equations with Infinite Solutions

Key Points
- A system of linear equations has infinite solutions when the lines graphed by the equations are the same.
- When a system of equations is compared in the standard form $Ax + By = C$, where A, B, and C are constants, the following rule applies for two equations $a_1x + b_1y = c_1$ and $a_2x + b_2y = c_2$ to have infinite solutions.
  - If $\frac{a_1}{a_2}$, $\frac{b_1}{b_2}$, and $\frac{c_1}{c_2}$ are the same, then the system has infinite solutions.

How to Solve

A question may give equations with one or more unknown constants. To determine the value of a constant, equate the ratios. A constant should be given a value that will make all three ratios the same.

* Questions in this category can be solved using the slider feature of the Desmos graphing calculator. This requires careful manipulation especially when the correct answer is a decimal. Students proficient with this feature can try it out.

Example 1:

$$ax + 6y = c$$
$$3y = 1 - 4x + y$$

If the system of equations shown above is true for all values of x, what is the value of ac, where a and c are constants?

Step 1: Equate the ratios

Convert the bottom equation to the standard form before equating the ratios.

$$4x + 3y - y = 1 \quad \rightarrow \quad 4x + 2y = 1$$

For the system to have infinitely many solutions, the ratios of a, b, and c must be the same.

$$\frac{a_1}{a_2} = \frac{b_1}{b_2} = \frac{c_1}{c_2} \quad \rightarrow \quad \frac{a}{4} = \frac{6}{2} = \frac{c}{1} \quad \rightarrow \quad \frac{a}{4} = 3 = c$$

Since the ratio of b is 3, it can be equated with a and c to determine their values, respectively.

$$\frac{a}{4} = 3 \quad \rightarrow \quad a = 12$$
$$c = 3$$

Determine ac: $12 \times 3 = 36$.

The correct answer is **36**.

Category 11 – Practice Questions

Students comfortable with the slider feature can solve the following questions using the Desmos graphing calculator

1

$$kx - 10y = c$$
$$\frac{1}{2}x - \frac{1}{3}y = 2$$

If the given system has infinitely many solutions, what is the value of $c - k$, where c and k are constants?

A) 6
B) 15
C) 30
D) 45

2

$$mx + 6.25y = 13.75$$
$$nx + 1.25y = 2.75$$

The system of equations above has infinitely many solutions. What is the value of $\frac{m}{n}$, where m and n are constants?

A) 2
B) 5
C) 8
D) 9

3

$$x + ky = 2$$
$$kx + ty = 2k$$

The above system of equations has infinitely many solutions. Which of the following can NOT be true for the values of k and t, where k and t are constants?

I. $k = 1$ and $t = 1$
II. $k = 2$ and $t = 4$
III. $k = 3$ and $t = 6$

A) I only
B) II only
C) III only
D) I and II only

4

$$ax + 5y = 5$$
$$x + y = b$$

The above system of equations has infinitely many solutions. What is the value of $a + b$, where a and b are constants?

5

$$x\sqrt{k} + y = 2$$
$$2x + cy = \sqrt{k}$$

In the system of equations above, c and k are positive constants. If the system is true for all values of x, what is the value of c?

Digital SAT Math Manual and Workbook

Category 12 – Systems of Linear Equations with One Solution

Key Points
- A system of linear equations has one solution when the lines graphed by the equations intersect at one point (x, y).
  - The intersection point is the solution to the system and can be solved for the values of x and y.
- When a system of equations is compared in the standard form $Ax + By = C$, where A, B, and C are constants, the following rule applies for two equations $a_1 x + b_1 y = c_1$ and $a_2 x + b_2 y = c_2$ to have one solution.
  - If $\frac{a_1}{a_2}$ and $\frac{b_1}{b_2}$ are different, then the system has one solution. The ratio of c does not matter.

How to Solve

A question may give equations with an unknown constant for the value of a or b. A constant should be given a value that will make the ratios of a and b different.

A question may ask for combined values of x and y. For example, $x + y$, $x - y$, or $20x + 20y$. In such questions, it is likely that the answer can be obtained without solving for x or y by simply adding or subtracting the equations.

Remember the following when solving for the x- and y-values of the intersection point without the Desmos graphing calculator.
- When two equations are given in the slope-intercept form, they can be equated to solve for x. The value of y can be determined by plugging x into either of the equations. Note that in this situation the slope-intercept form equations must be in the $y = mx + b$ format. If y is negative or has a constant, it must be removed before equating.
- If the equations are given in a mixed form, such as one equation is in the slope-intercept form and the other is in standard form, convert them to one form.

*Several questions in this category can be solved using the Desmos graphing calculator.

Example 1:

$$2x + 3y = 5$$
$$kx + 15y = 8$$

The system of equations above intersects at one point (x, y). Which of the following can NOT be the value of k, where k is a constant?

A) 3
B) 8
C) 10
D) 15

Step 1: Equate the ratios

For the system to have one solution, the ratios of a and b must not be the same. Equate the ratios of a and b and determine the value of k that makes the ratios the same. This cannot be the value of k.

$$\frac{a_1}{a_2} = \frac{b_1}{b_2} \rightarrow \frac{2}{k} = \frac{3}{15} \rightarrow \frac{2}{k} = \frac{1}{5} \rightarrow k = 2 \times 5 = 10$$

If $k = 10$, then the ratios of a and b will be the same. For the system to have one solution $k \neq 10$.

The correct answer choice is **C**.

*This question can be solved using the slider feature of the Desmos graphing calculator. Students proficient in the slider feature can try it out.

***Example 2:**

$$2x + 7y = 9$$
$$5y = -3x - 3$$

Which of the following is the (x, y) solution to the given system of equations?

A) $(-6, 3)$
B) $(-3, 3)$
C) $(3, -5)$
D) $(6, -3)$

Step 1: Determine the approach

Convert $5y = -3x - 3$ to the standard form.

$$5y = -3x - 3 \quad \rightarrow \quad 3x + 5y = -3$$

Make one of the variables the same in both the equations. It is best to start with the variable that has smaller numbers.

If the equation $2x + 7y = 9$ is multiplied by 3 and the equation $3x + 5y = -3$ is multiplied by 2, then both the equations will have $6x$. (Note that to make the variable y same in both the equations, $2x + 7y = 9$ will be multiplied by 5 and $3x + 5y = -3$ will be multiplied by 7. This will overall result in larger numbers to work with.)

Equation 1: $(2x + 7y = 9) \times 3 \quad \rightarrow \quad 6x + 21y = 27$

Equation 2: $(3x + 5y = -3) \times 2 \quad \rightarrow \quad 6x + 10y = -6$

Step 2: Determine the value of one of the variables

Subtract Equation 2 from Equation 1 to cancel $6x$ and determine the value of y.

$$\begin{array}{c} 6x + 21y = 27 \\ -(6x + 10y = -6) \end{array} \quad \longrightarrow \quad \begin{array}{c} \cancel{6x} + 21y = 27 \\ -\cancel{6x} - 10y = 6 \\ \hline 11y = 33 \quad \rightarrow \quad y = 3 \end{array}$$

This eliminates answer choices C and D.

Step 3: Determine the value of the second variable

Substitute $y = 3$ in any of the given equations.

$$5y = -3x - 3 \quad \rightarrow \quad (5 \times 3) = -3x - 3 \quad \rightarrow \quad 15 = -3x - 3 \quad \rightarrow$$
$$3x = -3 - 15 = -18 \quad \rightarrow \quad x = -6$$

This eliminates answer choice B.

The correct answer choice is **A**.

*Desmos Graphing Calculator Solution

Type the two equations and read the x- and y-values of the intersection point. See below. It is important to click on the dot at the intersection point to read it accurately. Zoom in as needed. The intersection point (x, y) is $(-6, 3)$.

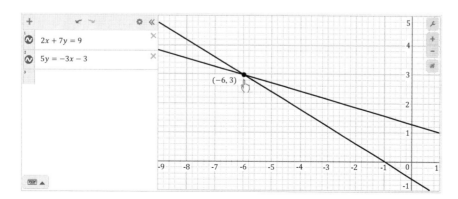

Digital SAT Math Manual and Workbook

Example 3:

$$y = -6x$$
$$2x - 3y = 100$$

In the above system of equations, what is the value of $\frac{x}{5}$?

A) 1
B) 2
C) 5
D) 20

Step 1: Determine the approach

Since it is given that $y = -6x$, the easiest approach is to substitute $-6x$ for y in the equation $2x - 3y = 100$ and solve for x.

Step 2: Solve x

$$2x - 3(-6x) = 100 \rightarrow 2x + 18x = 100 \rightarrow 20x = 100 \rightarrow x = 5$$

Step 3: Solve $\frac{x}{5}$

Substitute the value of x in $\frac{x}{5}$.

$$\frac{x}{5} = \frac{5}{5} = 1$$

The correct answer choice is **A**.

*The value of x can be determined using the Desmos graphing calculator by typing the two equations and reading the value of x at the intersection point. The value of $\frac{x}{5}$ can be determined thereafter.

Example 4:

$$-3x + 7y = 2$$
$$8x - 6y = 4$$

The solution to the above system of equation is (x, y). What is the value of $50x + 10y$?

Step 1: Determine the approach

Adding both the equations will give the value of $5x + y$. Multiplying this by 10 will give the value of $50x + 10y$. There is no need to individually solve for x and y to determine the value of $50x + 10y$.

Step 2: Solve

$$-3x + 7y = 2$$
$$8x - 6y = 4$$
$$\overline{5x + y = 6}$$

Multiply the equation by 10.

$$(5x + y = 6) \times 10$$
$$50x + 10y = 60$$

The correct answer is **60**.

*The value of (x, y) can be determined using the Desmos graphing calculator by typing the two equations and reading the (x, y) at the intersection point. The value of $50x + 10y$ can be determined thereafter. The above approach may be quicker.

Category 12 – Practice Questions

Students comfortable with the slider feature can solve question 3 using the Desmos graphing calculator

1 — Desmos

$$x = 4y$$
$$-5x + 2y = -54$$

In the above system of equations, what is the value of $7y$?

A) -5
B) -3
C) 3
D) 21

2

$$4x + y = 7$$
$$4x - 3y = 12$$

The solution to the above system of equation is (x, y). What is the value of $80x - 20y$?

A) 19
B) 84
C) 120
D) 190

3

$$\frac{1}{4}x - by = 7 - \frac{15}{4}x$$
$$-x + 6y = 2 + 7x$$

In the xy-plane, the lines graphed by the system of equations above intersect at one point. Which of the following could be a value of b, where b is a constant?

I. -3
II. 3

A) I only
B) II only
C) I and II
D) Neither I nor II

4

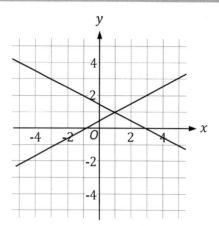

In the xy-plane, the graph of two lines in a system of equations is shown above. Which of the following (x, y) is a solution to the system?

A) $(-1, 1)$
B) $(1, -1)$
C) $(1, 1)$
D) $(2, 2)$

5 — Desmos

$$2x - 3y = 4$$
$$3x - 2y = 6$$

Which of the following is the solution to the above system of equations?

A) $(1, 0)$
B) $(1, 1)$
C) $(2, 0)$
D) $(4, 1)$

6 — Desmos

$$2y = -2x + 6$$
$$y = \frac{2}{3}x - 2$$

In the xy-plane, the graph of lines corresponding to the above system of equations intersect at a point (j, k). What is the value of $j + k$?

Digital SAT Math Manual and Workbook

Category 13 – Systems of Linear Inequalities

Key Points

- The four inequality symbols are less than (<), less than or equal to (≤), greater than (>), and greater than or equal to (≥).
- The inequality symbols determine where the solution set to an inequality lies on a graph in the xy-plane (Fig. 1, Fig. 2, Fig. 3, and Fig. 4).
    - The solution set of $y > x$ will be all the values above the line of the inequality (Fig. 1).
    - The solution set of $y \geq x$ will be all the values on and above the line of the inequality (Fig. 2).
    - The solution set of $y < x$ will be all the values below the line of the inequality (Fig. 3).
    - The solution set of $y \leq x$ will be all the values on and below the line of the inequality (Fig. 4).
- The inequalities with ≥ or ≤ symbols have a solid line on the graph, and the inequalities with > or < symbols have a dashed line on the graph.
- The solution to a system of two inequalities is the region where the solution set of the two inequalities overlaps.

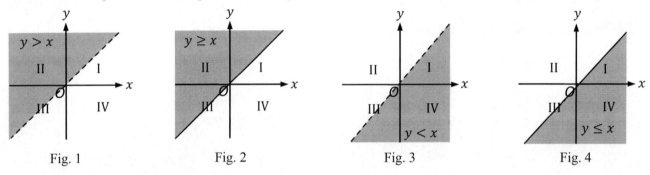

Fig. 1   Fig. 2   Fig. 3   Fig. 4

How to Solve

*Questions in this category can be solved using the Desmos graphing calculator. Use the Desmos graphing calculator keyboard to type the ≥ or ≤ inequality symbol.

Note that the Desmos graphing calculator displays the inequalities in a system in separate colors. The solution set (the overlapping graph) is a blend of colors. In this book, the graphs of inequalities are in different shades of gray. The overlapping graph of the inequalities, the solution set, is the darkest shade of gray.

*Example 1:

$$y \geq -x + 8$$
$$y \geq 2x + 2$$

In the xy-plane, which of the following point lies within the solution set of the above system of inequalities?

A) $(-4, 6)$
B) $(1, 10)$
C) $(4, 0)$
D) $(8, 6)$

The solution below is based on plugging points from the answer choices in the inequalities. Both inequalities will evaluate true for the correct point. Both inequalities must be checked to be sure.

Step 1: Select an answer choice and plug it in the inequalities

Answer choice A: Plug in the point $(-4, 6)$ in one of the inequalities.

Check $y \geq -x + 8$:

$$6 \geq -(-4) + 8 \;\rightarrow\; 6 \geq 4 + 8 \;\rightarrow\; 6 \geq 12$$

Since this evaluation is false, answer choice A can be eliminated.

Step 2: Select another answer choice and plug it in the inequalities

Answer choice B: Plug in the point $(1, 10)$ in one of the inequalities.

Check $y \geq -x + 8$:

$$10 \geq -(1) + 9 \;\rightarrow\; 10 \geq -1 + 9 \;\rightarrow\; 10 \geq 8$$

This evaluation is true. Check the second inequality with the point $(1, 10)$.

Check $y \geq 2x + 2$:

$$10 \geq (2 \times 1) + 2 \;\rightarrow\; 10 \geq 2 + 2 \;\rightarrow\; 10 \geq 4$$

This evaluation is true.

The correct answer choice is **B**.

Note that the points from answer choices C and D will evaluate false.

***Desmos Graphing Calculator Solution**

Type the two inequalities and determine which point from the answer choices is in the overlapping graph of the two inequalities. See below. Zoom in to view the points clearly. The graph below has been moved.

The point $(-4, 6)$ from answer choice A is only on the graph of $y \geq 2x + 2$. The point $(1, 10)$ from answer choice B is in the overlapping graph, hence, lies within the solution set of the system. The point $(4, 0)$ from answer choice C is not on the graph of either inequality. The point $(8, 6)$ from answer choice D is only on the graph of $y \geq -x + 8$.

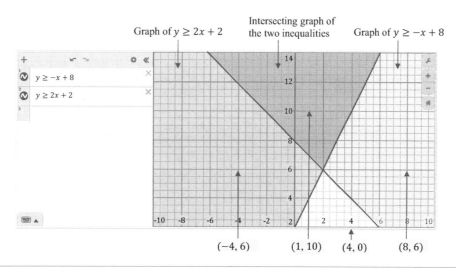

Digital SAT Math Manual and Workbook

*Example 2:

$$y > x + 2$$
$$y \leq -2x - 4$$

In the xy-plane, which of the quadrants contain(s) the solution to the above system of inequalities?

A) I only
B) II and III only
C) I, II, and III only
D) II, III, and IV only

Step 1: Evaluate the slope, the y-intercept, and the inequality symbol

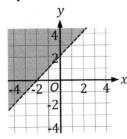

$y > x + 2$:

Since the slope is positive, the line will have an upward slant from left to right. Since the y-intercept is $(0, 2)$, the graph will pass through 2 on the y-axis.

Since the inequality symbol is $>$, the solution set will be above the line. See the figure on left.

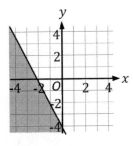

$y \leq -2x - 4$:

Since the slope is negative, the line will have a downward slant from left to right. Since the y-intercept is $(0, -4)$, the graph will pass through -4 on the y-axis.

Since the inequality symbol is $\leq$, the solution set will be on or below the line. See the figure on left.

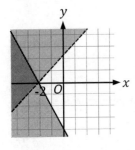

The region on the graph containing the overlapping shaded area is the solution to the system of inequalities. It spans quadrants II and III. See the figure on left.

The correct answer choice is **B**.

*Desmos Graphing Calculator Solution

Type the two inequalities and determine which quadrants contain the overlapping graph of the two inequalities. See below. The overlapping graph is in quadrant II and quadrant III.

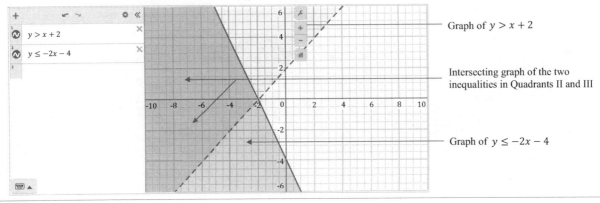

Digital SAT Math Manual and Workbook

*Example 3:

$$2y \geq 3x + 2$$
$$-y \leq 2x - 1$$

Which of the following graphs, in the xy-plane, could be the solution of the above system of inequalities?

A)
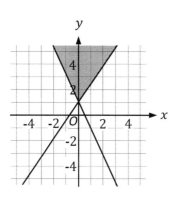

B)
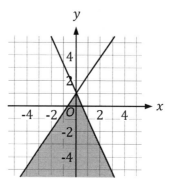

C)
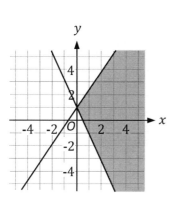

D)
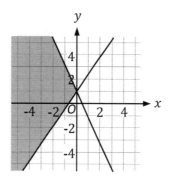

Step 1: Compare the slope, the y-intercept, and the inequality symbol

The value of y cannot be negative or contain a coefficient. Both the equations must be converted to the correct format.

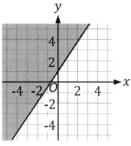

Equation $2y \geq 3x + 2$: Divide both sides by 2.

$$\frac{2}{2}y \geq \frac{3}{2}x + \frac{2}{2} \rightarrow y \geq 1.5x + 1$$

Since the slope is positive, the line will have an upward slant from left to right. Since the inequality symbol is $\geq$, the solution set will be on and above the line. Since the y-intercept is (0, 1), the graph will pass through 1 on the y-axis. See the figure on the left. This eliminates answer choices B and C that have a line with a positive slope but the solution below the line.

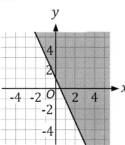

Equation $-y \leq 2x - 1$: Divide both sides by -1 to remove the negative sign from y. When an inequality is divided by a negative sign, the inequality symbol is flipped.
$$-y \leq 2x - 1 \rightarrow y \geq -2x + 1$$

Since the slope is negative, the line will have a downward slant from left to right. Since the inequality symbol is $\geq$, the solution set will be on and above the line. Since the y-intercept is (0, 1), the graph will pass through 1 on the y-axis. See the figure on the left. This eliminates answer choice D that has a line with a negative slope but the solution below the line.

The correct answer choice is **A**.

*Desmos Graphing Calculator Solution

Type the two inequalities and match the overlapping region on the graph with the graphs in the answer choices.

Category 13 – Practice Questions

1 — Desmos

$$y \geq x - 1$$
$$y < -2x + 2$$

Which of the following graphs represents the solution set of the above system of inequalities in the xy-plane?

A)
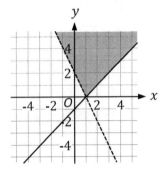

B)
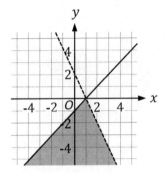

C)
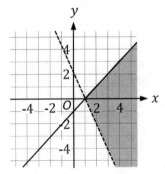

D)
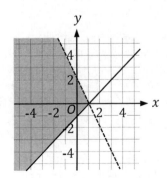

2 — Desmos

$$y > x + 2$$
$$y \leq -2x - 3$$

In the xy-plane, which of the following quadrants contain the solution set of the above system of inequalities?

A) I and II only
B) II and III only
C) II, III, and IV only
D) I, II, III, and IV

3 — Desmos

$$y > -2x + 4$$
$$y < 3x + 1$$

Which of the following (x, y) points satisfies the above system of inequalities?

A) $(-3, 4)$
B) $(1, -2)$
C) $(1, 3)$
D) $(2, 8)$

4 — Desmos

$$y > \frac{x}{4} - 2$$
$$3x + 15y < 18$$

In the xy-plane, the point $(-10, y)$ is a solution to the above system of inequalities. Which of the following can NOT be a possible value of y?

A) 4
B) 3
C) 0
D) -4

Digital SAT Math Manual and Workbook

Category 14 – Equivalent and Nonequivalent Linear Expressions

Key Points

- Two linear expressions in the form $ax + c$, where a is the coefficient of x and c is a constant, may or may not be equivalent depending on the values of the coefficients and constants in the two expressions. For example, the equation $3x + 2 = kx + p$ has expressions in the form $ax + c$ on both sides of the equation, where the values of k and p are not known. If $k = 3$ and $p = 2$, the equation will be $3x + 2 = 3x + 2$, and the expressions on both sides of the equation will be equal.
- The following rules apply for a linear equation $a_1x + c_1 = a_2x + c_2$, where a_1 is the coefficient of x and c_1 is a constant in the linear expression $a_1x + c_1$, and a_2 is the coefficient of x and c_2 is a constant in the linear expression $a_2x + c_2$.
    - An equation has infinite solutions when the coefficients of x and the constants are the same in the two expressions. In the xy-plane, the two expressions graph the same line.
    - An equation has no solution when the coefficients of x are the same and the constants are different in the two expressions. In the xy-plane, the two expressions graph parallel lines with different y-intercepts.
    - An equation has one solution when the coefficients of x are different in the two expressions. In the xy-plane, the graphs of the two expressions intersect at one point.

How to Solve

Remember that when an equation has a variable only in one of the expressions, then the coefficient of that variable equates to 0. For example, in the equation $ax + 2x + 7 = 5$, the coefficient of x in the left-side expression is $(a + 2)x \rightarrow a + 2$. However, there is no variable x in the right-side expression. Hence, $a + 2 = 0 \rightarrow a = -2$.

If an equation is not given in the $a_1x + c_1 = a_2x + c_2$ form mentioned above, then rearrange it to this form.

*Questions on number of solutions in this category can be solved using the Desmos graphing calculator by typing each expression in a separate row and evaluating the number of solutions in the xy-plane based on the above criteria.

Questions that ask for the value of a coefficient or constant in this category can be solved using the slider feature of the Desmos graphing calculator. This requires careful manipulation especially when the correct answer is a decimal. Students proficient with this feature can try it out.

*Example 1:

$$5(3x + 22) = -3(32 - 5x)$$

How many solutions does the above equation have?

A) None
B) Exactly one
C) Exactly two
D) Infinitely many

Step 1: Evaluate the coefficients and constants in both the expressions

Simplify the expressions on both sides of the equation.

$$15x + 110 = -96 + 15x \rightarrow 15x + 110 = 15x - 96$$

The coefficients of x are the same in both the equations, but the constants are different. Hence, the equation has no solution.

The correct answer choice is **A**.

***Desmos Graphing Calculator Solution**

Type the left-side expression $5(3x + 22)$ in the first row. Type the right-side expression $-3(32 - 5x)$ in the next row. See the graph below. The two expressions graph parallel lines with different y-intercepts. Hence, the equation has no solution.

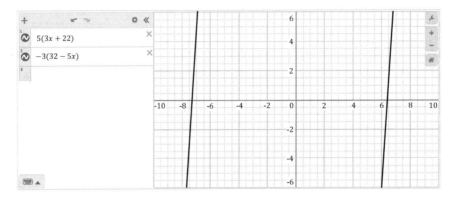

Example 2:

The equation $5bx + 3x + 7 = 18x + 4$ has no solution, where b is a constant. What is the value of b?

Step 1: Equate the coefficients of both the expressions

Note that the constants are not equal in the two expressions. For the equation to have no solution, the coefficient of x in the two expressions must be equal. Equate the coefficients of the two expressions to determine the value of b that makes them equal.

Before equating, factor all terms of x. See below the corresponding coefficients and constants of the two expressions enclosed in matching shape types (rectangular and oval, respectively).

$$\boxed{(5b + 3)}x + \widehat{7} = \boxed{18}x + \widehat{4}$$

Equate the coefficients of x.

$$5b + 3 = 18 \quad \rightarrow \quad 5b = 15 \quad \rightarrow \quad b = 3$$

The correct answer is **3**.

Example 3:

$$cx + 2(2bx + 3) + 1 = 10x + c + 1$$

If the given equation has infinitely many solutions, what is the value of b, where b and c are constants?

Step 1: Equate the coefficients and constants of both the expressions

For the equation to have infinitely many solutions, the coefficients of x and constants in the two expressions must be equal. Equate the coefficients and constants of the two expressions.

Before equating the coefficients and constants, simplify the parentheses, factor all x terms, and group the constants. See below the corresponding coefficients and constants of the two expressions enclosed in matching shape types (rectangular and oval, respectively).

$$cx + 4bx + 6 + 1 = 10x + c + 1$$
$$\boxed{(c + 4b)}x + \widehat{7} = \boxed{10}x + \widehat{c + 1}$$

First determine the value of c by equating the constants. Then substitute it in the coefficient of the left-side expression.

Equate the constants.

$$7 = c + 1 \quad \rightarrow \quad c = 6$$

Equate the coefficients of x and substitute $c = 6$.

$$c + 4b = 10 \quad \rightarrow \quad 6 + 4b = 10 \quad \rightarrow \quad 4b = 10 - 6 = 4 \quad \rightarrow \quad b = 1$$

The correct answer is **1**.

Category 14 – Practice Questions

Students comfortable with the slider feature can solve questions 1, 2, 4, 5, 6, and 7 using the Desmos graphing calculator

1

$$5(ax - 1) - 2 = 1.25x - 7$$

The equation above is true for all values of x. What is the value of a, where a is a constant?

A) 0.15
B) 0.25
C) 1.25
D) 5.50

2

$$3(bx + 3) + 2 = 8 + c$$

If the above equation has infinitely many solutions, what is the value of b, where b and c are constants and $b \neq c$?

A) 0
B) 3
C) 5
D) 9

3   Desmos

$$-18(12x - 5) = 12(7.5 - 18x)$$

How many solutions does the above equation have?

A) None
B) Exactly one
C) Exactly two
D) Infinitely many

4

$$0.2kx = \frac{x + 9}{5}$$

For what value of k, where k is a constant, does the given equation have no solution?

A) 0
B) 1
C) 9
D) 18

5

$$5x - 40kx = 90$$

In the above equation, k is a constant. For what value of k the equation has no solution?

A) 0
B) $\frac{4}{9}$
C) $\frac{1}{8}$
D) $\frac{1}{40}$

6

$$5(x + 1) + 3a + 1 = 5x + 18$$

If the above equation has infinitely many solutions, what is the value of the constant a?

7

$$1 = -14ax + 56x$$

The given equation has no solution, where a is a constant. What is the value of a?

Digital SAT Math Manual and Workbook

Section 3 – Review Questions

Students comfortable with the slider feature can solve questions 1, 4, 6, 7, 9, 16, and 18 using the Desmos graphing calculator

1

$$x - 4y = 4$$
$$4x - m = 16y$$

In the xy-plane, the equations of two parallel lines are shown above. Which of the following can NOT be the value of m, where m is a constant?

A) -4
B) -1
C) 4
D) 16

2 Desmos

$$2y = 3x + 5$$
$$y - \frac{3}{2}x = 5$$

How many solutions exist for the above system of equations?

A) Zero
B) Exactly one
C) Exactly two
D) Infinitely many

3

$$2(2x + 3kx) + x + 6 = 3(x + cx) + 2c$$

If the above equation has infinitely many solutions, what is the value of k, where c and k are constants and $c \neq k$?

A) -1
B) 0
C) $\frac{1}{2}$
D) $\frac{7}{6}$

4

$$11x + 50 = 4x + (k-3)x$$

If the above equation has no solution, what is the value of k, where k is a constant?

A) 10
B) 14
C) 18
D) 50

5

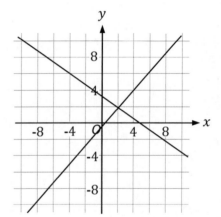

In the xy-plane, the graph of two lines in a system of equations is shown above. If a new graph is created using the system of equations above and the equation $2x - y = 2$, how many solutions (x, y) will the resulting system of three equations have?

A) Zero
B) Exactly one
C) Exactly two
D) Infinitely many

6

$$x - y = n$$
$$-mx + 2y = 12$$

In the above system of equations, m and n are constants. For which of the following values of m and n does the above system have no solution?

I. $m = -2$ and $n = 2$
II. $m = 2$ and $n = -6$
III. $m = 2$ and $n = 6$

A) I only
B) II only
C) III only
D) None of the above

7

$$\frac{b}{5}x = 4 + 2y$$
$$3x - 12y = 7$$

If the above equation has no solution, what is the value of b, where b is a constant?

A) 2.5
B) 3.0
C) 3.5
D) 5.0

8

$$2ax + y = b$$
$$4x - 2y = a$$

If the above system of equations is true for all values of x, and a and b are constants, what is the value of b?

A) -2
B) -1
C) $\frac{1}{4}$
D) $\frac{1}{2}$

9

$$5x + 3y = a + 3x$$
$$-\frac{4}{3}x - \frac{a}{6} = -\frac{1}{2}y - \frac{5}{3}x$$

In the xy-plane, which of the following must be true about the lines graphed by the above system of equations, where a is a constant?

A) They are perpendicular lines that intersect at one point.
B) They are parallel lines with different y-intercepts.
C) They are the same lines.
D) The information given is inconclusive.

10 Desmos

$$2x - 5y = 11$$
$$6x - 3y = 9$$

The solution to the above system of equation is (x, y). What is the value of $x - y$?

11

$$(a + 4)x + 4y = 4$$
$$3x + by = 3$$

The system of equations shown above has infinitely many solutions, where a and b are constants. What is the value of $a + b$?

12 Desmos

$$3(x + 5) + 5(y - 2) = 455$$
$$3(x + 5) - 5(y - 2) = -427$$

The solution to the given system is (x, y). What is the value of $24(x + 5)$?

13 Desmos

$$y < -x + 7$$
$$y < 3x + 4$$

In the xy-plane, a point P is contained on the graph of the solution set of the system of inequalities shown above. Which of the following could be point $P\ (x, y)$?

A) $(-3, -2)$
B) $(-2, -1)$
C) $(0, 2)$
D) $(1, 8)$

14 Desmos

$$y > -2x + 4$$
$$y < 3x + 2$$

In the xy-plane, which of the following quadrants do NOT contain the solution of the above system of inequalities?

A) I only
B) II only
C) I and II only
D) II and III only

15 Desmos

$$3x - 4y = 5$$
$$3y + 4x = -5$$

What is the value of y in the system of equations given above?

A) -5
B) $-\frac{7}{5}$
C) $\frac{1}{5}$
D) $\frac{1}{2}$

16

$$4(ax + 1) + 3ax + 2 = 6$$

The given equation has infinitely many solutions, where a is a constant. What is the value of a?

A) 0
B) 2
C) 3
D) 6

17 Desmos

$$5y = -x + 3$$
$$2x + 3y = -8$$

What is the solution (x, y) to the above system of equations?

A) $(-8, -2)$
B) $(-7, -2)$
C) $(-7, 2)$
D) $(1, 2)$

18

In the xy-plane, which of the following systems of equations graph perpendicular lines, where a and b are constants?

A) $-\frac{9}{7a}x - \frac{3}{14b}y = 75$
   $-\frac{2a}{3}x - by = -14$

B) $-\frac{9}{7a}x + \frac{3}{14b}y = -75$
   $\frac{2a}{3}x + by = -14$

C) $\frac{9}{7a}x - \frac{3}{14b}y = 75$
   $\frac{2a}{3}x + 4by = 14$

D) $\frac{9}{7a}x + \frac{3}{14b}y = 75$
   $\frac{2a}{3}x + 4by = 14$

Section 4 – Word Problems on Linear Equations and Inequalities

Category 15 – Word Problems on Linear Equations with One Variable
Category 16 – Word Problems on Linear Equations with Two Variables
Category 17 – Word Problems on Interpretation of Linear Equations
Category 18 – Word Problems on Linear System of Equations
Category 19 – Word Problems on Linear Inequalities
Category 20 – Word Problems on Linear System of Inequalities
Category 21 – Word Problems on Equal Variables in Linear Equations
Section 4 – Review Questions

Category 15 – Word Problems on Linear Equations with One Variable

Key Points
- A word problem may be given that contains a known number and an unknown number.
  - The known number is a constant. For example, a one-time fee, or an initial number.
  - The unknown number is comprised of a fixed number and an associated variable. For example, $4h$, where h is the variable and 4 is the fixed number. The value given to the variable h determines the value of $4h$.
- The sum of the constant and unknown number is the ending number.
- The constant, unknown number, and ending number form a linear equation.

How to Solve
Determine the constant and the unknown number from the word problem.

Example 1:
A yoga club charges an annual membership fee of $25 and $20 for each yoga class attended by members. Which of the following equations represents the total cost, C, in dollars, of attending p yoga classes in a year?

A) $C = 25 + p$
B) $C = 20 + 25p$
C) $C = 25 + 20p$
D) $C = 50 + 25p$

Step 1: Determine the constant
The value of the annual membership fee of $25 does not change in a year. Hence, it is a constant. This eliminates answer choice B that has 20 as the constant and answer choice D that has 50 as the constant.

Step 2: Determine the unknown number
The cost of p yoga classes is the unknown number.
The number of yoga classes in a year = p. Cost of each yoga class = $20.
$$\text{cost of } p \text{ classes} = 20p$$
This eliminates answer choice A that has p as the unknown number.
The correct answer choice is **C**.

Example 2:
A yoga club charges an annual membership fee of $25 and $20 for each yoga class attended by members. What is the total cost, in dollars, of attending 5 yoga classes in a year (ignore the dollar sign)?

Step 1: Determine the constant
The value of the annual membership fee of $25 does not change in a year. Hence, it is a constant.

Step 2: Determine the unknown number
The number of yoga classes in a year = 5. Cost of each yoga class = $20.
$$\text{cost of 5 yoga classes} = 20 \times 5 = \$100$$

Step 3: Determine the ending number:
$$\text{total cost} = \text{constant} + \text{unknown number} = 25 + 100 = \$125$$

The correct answer is **125**.

Digital SAT Math Manual and Workbook

Example 3:

Katie has access to 38 eBooks through an online bookstore. She plans to sign up for a program with the online bookstore that will give her access to 4 new eBooks each week. Which of the following is the total number of eBooks Katie will have access to 7 weeks after signing up for the program?

A) 28
B) 38
C) 54
D) 66

Step 1: Determine the constant

It is given that Katie has access to 38 eBooks at the beginning of the program. In this example, the constant is the initial number.

Step 2: Determine the unknown number

$$4 \text{ eBooks per week for 7 weeks} = 4 \times 7 = 28$$

Step 3: Determine the ending number

$$\text{total eBooks} = \text{constant} + \text{unknown number}$$
$$38 + 28 = 66$$

The correct answer choice is **D**.

Example 4:

Tim plans to complete 50 online quizzes in a month. Each quiz takes approximately 45 minutes to complete. If Tim has completed x quizzes in the month, which of the following expressions most closely represent the number of hours required to complete the remaining quizzes?

A) $\frac{1}{4}(30x)$

B) $\frac{3}{4}(50 - x)$

C) $50x$

D) $45(50 - x)$

Step 1: Determine the constant

It is given that Tim has 50 quizzes to complete. In this example, the constant is the initial number.

Step 2: Determine the unknown number

The unknown number = number of quizzes completed × 45 minutes.

Step 3: Determine the ending number

If Tim completed x quizzes out of 50, then the remaining number of quizzes is $(50 - x)$.
The number of minutes required to complete $(50 - x)$ quizzes is

$$(50 - x) \times 45 \text{ minutes}$$

Since the question asks for the number of hours, divide by 60 to convert minutes to hours.

$$\frac{(50 - x) \times 45}{60} = \frac{(50 - x) \times 3}{4} = \frac{3}{4}(50 - x)$$

The correct answer choice is **B**.

Category 15 – Practice Questions

1

For each visit, a roller-skating ring charges an entry fee of $10 and $5 per hour to roller skate. Which of the following equations gives the total cost, A, in dollars, for each visit to the roller-skating ring for h hours?

A) $A = 10 + 5h$
B) $A = 10 + 10h$
C) $A = 15 + 5h$
D) $A = 5h$

2

Robert rented a power washer from a local hardware store for t hours. He was charged a one-time fee of $25 and $20 per hour as the rental fee. Which of the following equations can determine the total cost, c, in dollars, for renting the power washer for t hours?

A) $c = 20t + 20$
B) $c = 20t + 25$
C) $c = 25t + 20$
D) $c = 45t + 25$

3

Jamie opened a savings account with d dollars. Starting next month, he will make a monthly deposit of $100 to this account for m months. Which of the following equations represents the amount, S, in dollars, Jamie will have saved in his account after m months, assuming no withdrawals or interest payments are made during m months?

A) $S = 100m$
B) $S = d + m$
C) $S = m + 100d$
D) $S = d + 100m$

4

For each job, a plumber charges a fixed service fee of s dollars in addition to p dollars for each hour spent on the job. For a 3 hour job, the plumber charged $360. Which of the following equations represents the relationship between p and s?

A) $s = 120 - p$
B) $s = 360 - p$
C) $s = 360 - 3p$
D) $s = 360 + 3p$

5

A car rental company charges a one-time fee of $75 in addition to $55 for each day the car is rented. Which of the following is the total cost of car rental, in dollars, for 4 days?

A) $75
B) $130
C) $220
D) $295

6

A teacher is grading 30 research papers. Each research paper takes 40 minutes to grade. If the teacher has completed grading r research papers, which of the following expressions can determine the number of hours required to grade the remaining research papers?

A) $40(30 - r)$
B) $120 - r$
C) $\frac{2}{3}(r)$
D) $\frac{2}{3}(30 - r)$

Digital SAT Math Manual and Workbook

7

A theater has x tickets to sell in 5 days. On the first day, 400 tickets are sold. If the theater wants to evenly sell the remaining tickets in the next 4 days, which of the following equations represents the number of tickets, T, that must be sold on each of the 4 days?

A) $T = \frac{x}{5} - 80$

B) $T = \frac{x}{4} - 100$

C) $T = \frac{x+4}{5}$

D) $T = \frac{x}{4}$

8

Samir wants to buy a computer that costs $1,500. He has d dollars saved and plans to save $150 per month. Which of the following equations represents the number of months, m, Samir will have to save before he can buy the computer?

A) $m = \frac{1,500}{d-150}$

B) $m = 10 - \frac{d}{150}$

C) $m = 1,500 - d$

D) $m = 1,200 + d$

9

The relationship between the height, g, of a plant, in centimeters and number of hours, h, the plant is exposed to sunlight can be modeled by the equation, $g = 0.003h + 0.2$. Which of the following is closest to the height of the plant, in centimeters, after 20 hours of exposure to sunlight?

A) 0.26

B) 0.28

C) 0.50

D) 0.60

10

A school administrator is responsible for maintaining the inventory of notebooks at a certain school. Currently, the inventory consists of 255 notebooks, and the school administrator estimates that each following week the inventory will have 15 less notebooks. Based on this estimate, in how many weeks will the inventory reach 75 notebooks?

A) 5

B) 8

C) 12

D) 15

11

Tatiana has $35 to spend on the entrance fee and tickets for rides at a local fair. The entrance fee is $8 and each ride ticket costs $1.50. Which of the following equations can solve for the number of rides, r?

A) $35 = 1.50 + r$

B) $35 = 1.50 + 8r$

C) $35 = 8 + r$

D) $35 = 8 + 1.50r$

12

A metro card has an initial value of $80. After 7 metro rides of the same value, the remaining balance on the metro card is $53.75. What is the cost of each metro ride?

A) $1.50

B) $3.75

C) $7.65

D) $11.42

Digital SAT Math Manual and Workbook

Category 16 – Word Problems on Linear Equations with Two Variables

Key Points
- A word problem may be given that contains two unknown numbers, each with a separate variable. The two unknown numbers and their sum form a linear equation.
- If the word problem asks to solve for one of the unknown numbers, then sufficient information will be provided to solve the other unknown number. For example, if $2m + 3n = 15$, then the value of m will be given to solve for n.

How to Solve
Determine the two unknown numbers from the word problem.

Example 1:
A bakery owner hires staff on hourly wages. The bakery owner pays each staff member $15 per hour and an additional $2.50 for each cake sold. Which of the following equations represents the total earnings, E, in dollars, of a staff member working for h hours and selling c cakes?

A) $E = 15 + 2.5c$
B) $E = 15h + 2.5$
C) $E = 15h + 2.5c$
D) $E = 15c + 2.5h$

Step 1: Determine the unknown numbers

Unknown number 1: The number of hours = h. A staff member is paid $15 for each hour of work.

$$\text{earnings for } h \text{ hours} = 15h$$

This eliminates answer choice A that does not have a variable h and answer choice D that has $2.5h$ as an unknown number.

Unknown number 2: The number of cakes = c. A staff member is paid $2.50 for each cake sold.

$$\text{earnings from selling } c \text{ cakes} = 2.5c$$

This eliminates answer choice B that does not have a variable c.

The correct answer choice is **C**.

Example 2:
Jimena and her friends bought 13 bags of pretzels and 10 bottles of sparkling water for a total of $40.50. If the cost of each bag of pretzels is $1.50, what is the cost of each bottle of sparkling water in dollars (ignore the dollar sign)?

Step 1: Determine the unknown numbers

In this example, information is given to determine the value of one of the unknown numbers, the cost of pretzels.

Unknown number 1: Number of bags of pretzels = 13. The cost of each bag of pretzel = $1.50.

$$\text{cost of 13 bags of pretzels} = 13 \times 1.50 = \$19.50$$

Unknown number 2: Number of sparkling water bottles = 10. Let the cost of each bottle of sparkling water = b.

$$\text{cost of 10 sparkling water bottles} = 10b$$

Step 2: Determine the value of b

$$\text{total cost} = \text{cost of 13 bags of pretzels} + \text{cost of 10 bottles of sparkling water}$$

$$40.50 = 19.50 + 10b$$

$$10b = 40.50 - 19.50 \rightarrow 10b = 21 \rightarrow b = 2.1 = \$2.10$$

The correct answer is **2.1 or 2.10**.

Digital SAT Math Manual and Workbook

Category 16 – Practice Questions

1

Jessica works two shifts per day at her job. She gets paid $15 per hour for the morning shift and $25 per hour for the night shift. Which of the following expressions represents the amount, in dollars, that Jessica earns per day working m hours in the morning shift and n hours in the night shift?

A) $15m + 25n$

B) $15n + 25m$

C) $15m + 40n$

D) $40m + 40n$

2

Sam works at a restaurant during the day for some hours and is paid $20 per hour. In the night, he works at a hotel for some hours and is paid $35 per hour. If on a certain day, Sam worked at the restaurant for x hours and at the hotel for 5 hours, which of the following equations represents his total earnings, E, in dollars, for that day?

A) $E = 35x + 20$

B) $E = 35x + 175$

C) $E = 20x + 35$

D) $E = 20x + 175$

3

An ice cream truck sells snow cones for c dollars each and frozen yogurt for $c + 1$ dollars each. Casey and her friends spent $40 altogether on snow cones and frozen yogurt. If they bought 4 snow cones and 7 frozen yogurts, which of the following is the value of c?

A) $2

B) $3

C) $10

D) $11

4

The equation $m + n = 1,277$ represents the pounds of paper, m, and pounds of aluminum cans, n, a company recycles every month. Last month, the company recycled 582 pounds of aluminum cans. How many pounds of paper did the company recycle last month?

A) 485

B) 582

C) 695

D) 705

5

Crane A and Crane B work individually to lift boxes. Crane A can lift 100 boxes per hour and Crane B can lift 75 boxes per hour. If on Friday, Crane A worked for 2 hours and together both the cranes lifted 500 boxes, how many hours did Crane B work?

6

A contractor works as a painter at an hourly rate of $80 and as a landscaper at an hourly rate of $50. On a certain day, the contractor earned a total of $470 working as a painter for 4 hours and as a landscaper for a hours. What is the value of a?

Digital SAT Math Manual and Workbook

Category 17 – Word Problems on Interpretation of Linear Equations

Key Points

Linear Equations with One Variable:

- A word problem may ask for the interpretation of the initial number (constant), the unknown number, or the ending number in a linear equation. For example, in the equation $C = 90 + 150h$, 90 is the one-time fee (constant) for a plumber to come to a job site, $150h$ is the cost of working h hours (unknown number) at an hourly rate of $150 (constant associated with the unknown number), and C is the total cost (ending number) determined by the number of hours, h, the plumber works.

- There may be a word problem that only has two components: an unknown number and an ending number. In the above example, if the plumber does not charge a one-time fee (constant), then the equation is $C = 150h$.

- When a linear equation models a change in the initial number over a period, the variable associated with the unknown number is an average increase/decrease of the initial number over the period. For example, in the equation $P = 2,254 + 45t$, 45 (constant associated with the unknown number) is the average annual increase in the initial population of 2,254 (initial number) resulting in population, P, (ending number) in t years.

  The reason it is "average" is because there is no guarantee that each year the increase will be exactly 45. It could be 42 one year and 47 the following year, and so on. Hence, it is the predicted, estimated, approximate, or plausible average increase modeled by the linear equation.

- The above also applies to a linear function. For example, in the linear function $f(t) = 2,254 + 45t$, the value of $f(t)$ is the ending number determined by the value given to the variable t.

Linear Equations with Two Variables:

- A word problem may ask for the interpretation of either of the two unknown numbers. For example, in the equation $c = 3.5n + 1.5p$, $3.5n$ is the total cost of purchasing n notebooks, $1.5p$ is the total cost of purchasing p pens, and c is the total cost of purchasing n notebooks and p pens.

How to Solve

Determine the components of the equation from the word problem and select the correct answer accordingly.

Example 1:

$$4,200 = 2,900 + 130t$$

In 1998, the population of crickets in a certain rain forest was 2,900. The above equation models the population of crickets t years after 1998. Which of the following is the best interpretation of 130 in the equation?

A) The population of crickets in the rain forest before 1998.

B) The total increase in the population of crickets in the rain forest after 1998 for t years.

C) The difference in the population of crickets in the rain forest from 1998 till present.

D) The average increase in the population of crickets in the rain forest each year after 1998 for t years.

Step 1: Determine the components of the equation

130 = Average increase in the population each year after 1998 for t years.

$2,900$ = Initial population in 1998.

$4,200$ = Ending population in t years from 1998.

The correct answer choice is **D**.

(Note that if the equation was $2,900 = 4,200 - 130t$, then 4,200 would be the initial population in 1998, 130 would be the average decrease in the population each year after 1998 for t years, and 2,900 would be the ending population in t years after 1998.)

Digital SAT Math Manual and Workbook

Example 2:

The equation $s = 6.7 + 0.5583m$ approximates the tusk size s, in inches, of an elephant for m months after turning one year old. Which of the following statements is consistent with the equation?

A) The average increase in the tusk size, in inches, of an elephant for m months after turning one year old is $\frac{1}{0.5583}$.

B) The average increase in the tusk size, in inches, of an elephant for m months after turning one year old is 0.5583.

C) The average increase in the tusk size, in inches, of an elephant for m months after turning one year old is 6.7.

D) The average increase in the tusk size, in inches, of an elephant for m months after turning one year old is 7.2583.

Step 1: Determine the components of the equation

$0.5583 = $ Average increase in the tusk size, in inches, of an elephant for m months after turning one year old.

$6.7 = $ Tusk size, in inches, of an elephant at turning one year old (initial number).

$s = $ Tusk size, in inches, of an elephant in m months after turning one year old (ending number).

The correct answer choice is **B**.

Example 3:

A gym bought b yoga balls and m yoga mats for a total of 485.40. The equation $8.99b + 15.28m = 485.40$ represents the situation in context. What is the interpretation of $15.28m$ in this context?

A) The number of yoga balls the gym bought.

B) The cost, in dollars, of each yoga mat the gym bought.

C) The total cost, in dollars, of b yoga balls the gym bought.

D) The total cost, in dollars, of m yoga mats the gym bought.

Step 1: Determine the components of the equation

$8.99 = $ The cost, in dollars, of each yoga ball.

$8.99b = $ The total cost, in dollars, of b yoga balls.

$15.28 = $ The cost, in dollars, of each yoga mat.

$15.28m = $ The total cost, in dollars, of m yoga mats.

$485.40 = $ The total cost, in dollars, of b yoga balls and m yoga mats.

The correct answer choice is **D**.

Category 17 – Practice Questions

1

$$R = 58 - 2d$$

Anika is a research assistant at a university. At the beginning of each month, she receives a fixed number of research papers to review during the month. At the end of each day, she can estimate the number of research papers left to review in a month by the above equation, where R is the number of research papers left to review and d is the number of days elapsed in a month. What is the meaning of 2 in this context?

A) Anika receives 2 research papers each day.

B) Anika completes the review of 2 research papers each week.

C) Anika works for 2 weeks as research assistant.

D) Anika reviews an average of 2 research papers each day.

2

$$g(h) = 15 + 0.0054h$$

A scientist conducted an experiment to study the effect of sunlight on the growth of a certain plant. The function above models the growth of the plant, in inches, exposed to h hours of sunlight. Which of the following statements best interprets 0.0054 in this context?

A) For each 1 hour increase in the exposure to sunlight, the plant grew by an average of 0.0054 inches.

B) For each 1 hour increase in the exposure to sunlight, the plant grew by an average of 1 inch.

C) For each 1 hour increase in the exposure to sunlight, the plant grew by an average of 5.4 inches.

D) For each 1 hour increase in the exposure to sunlight, the plant grew by 15.0054 inches.

3

The total weight, in pounds, of 5-pound boxes, a, and 12-pound boxes, b, is represented by the equation $5a + 12b = 451$. What is the best interpretation of $a + b$ in this context?

A) The number of 5-pound boxes.

B) The difference in the weight, in pounds, of 5-pound and 12-pound boxes.

C) The total weight, in pounds, of 5-pound and 12-pound boxes.

D) The total number of 5-pound and 12-pound boxes.

4

$$685 = 305 + 7.6t$$

The equation above models the population of certain insects, in thousands, in a rain forest for t years after 1970. Which of the following is the best interpretation of 7.6 in this context?

A) The number of years for the insect population to increase from 305 to 685, in thousands.

B) The plausible growth rate of the insects each year after 1970 for t years.

C) The plausible average increase in the population of insects, in thousands, each year after 1970 for t years.

D) The population of insects in 7.6 years.

5

A camp counselor bought a feet of rope to make b jump ropes for kids at a camp. The equation $a = 9b + 8$ represents the relationship between the total feet of rope the counselor bought and number of jump ropes the counselor made. What is the best interpretation of 8 in this context?

A) The camp counselor bought 8 feet of rope.

B) The camp counselor made 8 jump ropes.

C) The camp counselor bought 8 feet more rope than needed to make b jump ropes.

D) The camp counselor bought 8 feet less rope than needed to make b jump ropes.

Category 18 – Word Problems on Linear System of Equations

Key Points
- A word problem may be given that contains two unknown numbers, each with a separate variable, but the value of neither variable is given. A single equation cannot solve the value of both variables. For example, $x + y = 8$ cannot give the values of the two variables x and y. The word problem will contain information to set up two related equations (system of equations) that can together solve for the variables.

How to Solve
A word problem may either ask to identify the system of equations from the answer choices based on the given information or may require creating two equations to solve for the variables.

*Several questions in this category can be partially solved using the Desmos graphing calculator. After the system of equations has been identified from a word problem, the Desmos graphing calculator can be used to solve the intersection point.

Example 1:
A gardener ordered a total of 12 butterfly and rose bushes from a garden nursery. The cost of each butterfly bush is $35, and the cost of each rose bush is $55. If the gardener ordered x butterfly bushes and y rose bushes for $520, which of the following systems can determine the number of rose bushes the gardener ordered?

A) $x + y = 12$
   $35x + 55y = 520$

B) $x + y = 12$
   $55x + 35y = 520$

C) $x - y = 12$
   $35x + 55y = 520$

D) $x - y = 12$
   $55x + 35y = 520$

Step 1: Identify the two variables

Variable 1: Number of butterfly bushes = x.
Variable 2: Number of rose bushes = y.

Step 2: Determine the system of equations

Equation 1: It is given that the total number of bushes = 12.
$$x + y = 12$$
This eliminates answer choices C and D.

Equation 2: It is given that the total cost of x butterfly bushes and y rose bushes = $520.
$$(\text{cost of each butterfly bush} \times x) + (\text{cost of each rose bush} \times y) = 520$$
$$35x + 55y = 520$$
This eliminates answer choice B.

The correct answer choice is **A**.

Digital SAT Math Manual and Workbook

*Example 2:

An office manager placed an order for 5 boxes of pens and 10 notepads for a total cost of $54.95. The office manager placed a second order for 15 boxes of the same pens and 18 of the same notepads for a total cost of $128.85. What is the cost of 1 box of pens and 1 notepad, given that the cost of a box of pens and a notepad was the same in both the orders and no sales tax was collected?

A) $3.00
B) $4.25
C) $5.99
D) $7.99

Step 1: Identify the two variables

Variable 1: Let the cost of one box of pens = x.
Variable 2: Let the cost of one notebook = y.

Step 2: Determine the system of equations

Equation 1: It is given that in the first order the cost of 5 boxes of pens and 10 notepads = $54.95.

$$(\text{cost of each box of pens} \times 5) + (\text{cost of each notepad} \times 10) = 54.95$$
$$5x + 10y = 54.95$$

Equation 2: It is given that in the second order the cost of 15 boxes of pens and 18 notepads = $128.85.

$$(\text{cost of each box of pens} \times 15) + (\text{cost of each notepad} \times 18) = 128.85$$
$$15x + 18y = 128.85$$

Step 3: Solve the system of equations

Multiply the equation 1 by 3, and subtract equation 2 from equation 1. This will cancel $15x$ from both the equations.

Equation 1: $3(5x + 10y = 54.95)$ → $\cancel{15x} + 30y = 164.85$
Equation 2: $-(15x + 18y = 128.85)$ → $-\cancel{15x} - 18y = -128.85$

$$12y = 36 \rightarrow y = 3$$

Determine the value of x by substituting $y = 3$ in any of the equations.

$$5x + (10 \times 3) = 54.95 \rightarrow 5x + 30 = 54.95 \rightarrow 5x = 24.95 \rightarrow x = 4.99$$

One box of pens + one notebook = $x + y = 4.99 + 3 = 7.99$.
The correct answer choice is **D**.

Desmos Graphing Calculator Solution for Step 3: Solve the system of equations

Type the two equations and read the intersection point. See below. It is important to place the cursor over the dot at the intersection point to read it accurately. Zoom in as needed. The intersection point is (4.99, 3).

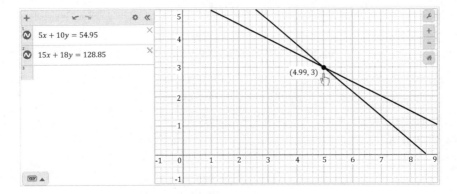

One box of pens + one notebook = $x + y = 4.99 + 3 = 7.99$.

Digital SAT Math Manual and Workbook

*Example 3:

84 passengers must be seated in an airplane in rows of 2 seats and rows of 3 seats. There is a total of 35 rows. If each seat is occupied by a passenger and all passengers have a seat, how many passengers are seated in rows of 3 seats?

Step 1: Identify the two variables

Variable 1: Let the number 2 seat rows $= x$.

Variable 2: Let the number of 3 seat rows $= y$.

Step 2: Determine the system of equations

Equation 1: It is given that the total number of rows $= 35$.
$$x + y = 35$$
Equation 2: It is given that the total number of passengers seated in x rows and y rows $= 84$.

Each x seats 2 passengers and each y seats 3 passengers. Hence,
$$2x + 3y = 84$$

Step 3: Solve the system of equations

Multiply equation 1 by 2, and subtract it from equation 2. This will cancel $2x$ from both the equations.

Equation 2: $\qquad 2x + 3y = 84 \qquad \longrightarrow \qquad 2x + 3y = 84$

Equation 1: $\qquad -2(x + y = 35) \qquad\qquad\qquad -2x - 2y = -70$

$$y = 14$$

Hence, there are 14 rows of 3 seats. The total passengers in these seats $= 14 \times 3 = 42$.

The correct answer is **42**.

*Desmos Graphing Calculator Solution for Step 3: Solve the system of equations

Type the two equations and read the intersection point. See below. It is important to place the cursor over the dot at the intersection point to read it accurately. Zoom in as needed. The intersection point is (21, 14).

Note that this graph is moved to the right and down to view the intersection point.

$y = $ number of rows with 3 seats $= 14$.

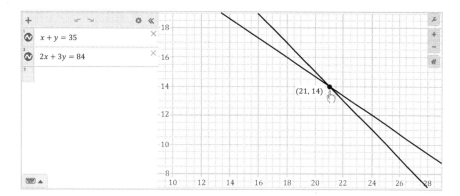

Since there are 14 rows with 3 seats, the total number of passengers in rows of 3 seats $= 14 \times 3 = 42$.

Digital SAT Math Manual and Workbook

Category 18 – Practice Questions

After the equations in the system are determined, the Desmos graphing calculator can be used to solve the intersection point in questions 4, 5, 7, 8, 9, 10, 11, and 12

1

At a movie theater, the cost of admission for ages 12 and below is $10, and for ages 13 and above is $14. On the opening day of a blockbuster movie, the theater sold 400 tickets and collected a total of $4,600 from the ticket sales. If c represents the number of tickets sold to ages 12 and below, and a represents the number of tickets sold to ages 13 and above, which of the following systems of equations can be used to determine the values of a and c?

A) $a + c = 400$
$14a + 10c = 4,600$

B) $a + c = 400$
$10a + 14c = 4,600$

C) $a + c = 4,600$
$14a + 10c = 4,600$

D) $a + c = 4,600$
$10a + 14c = 4,600$

2

A teacher is planning to buy a total of 78 spiral notebooks and pocket folders for her class. Each spiral notebook costs $3 and each pocket folder costs $0.50. The teacher has a budget of $164. Which of the following systems of equations can the teacher use to determine the number of spiral notebooks, n, and pocket folders, p, that the teacher can buy, assuming no sales tax is collected?

A) $n + p = 78$
$0.5n + 3p = 164$

B) $n + p = 78$
$3n + 0.5p = 164$

C) $n + p = 164$
$0.5n + 3p = 78$

D) $n + p = 164$
$3n + 0.5p = 78$

3

Maddie bought s shirts and h hats for $140. Each shirt costs $20 and each hat costs half the price of a shirt. If Maddie bought a total of 10 hats and shirts, which of the following systems can be used to determine the number of shirts Maddie bought (assuming there is no sales tax)?

A) $8s + 2h = 2(10)$
$20h + 10s = 140$

B) $s + 8h = 2(10)$
$20h + 20s = 140$

C) $s + h = 10$
$20h + 20s = 140$

D) $s + h = 10$
$20s + 10h = 140$

4

A group of 125 students from a certain high school went on an out-of-town overnight trip. The school reserved a total of 55 rooms in a hotel for the students. The rooms either had 2 beds or 3 beds. Given that all the beds were occupied, and every student got 1 bed, how many rooms had 3 beds?

A) 10
B) 11
C) 15
D) 25

5

At the present time, the sum of Shannon's and Tina's ages is 42. Three years ago, Tina was twice as old as Shannon. What is Shannon's present age?

Digital SAT Math Manual and Workbook

6

A furniture company hired a truck driver to deliver furniture from a warehouse to a retail store. The truck driver drove through the back roads for b hours at an average speed of 25 miles per hour and on the highway for h hours at an average speed of 65 miles per hour. The truck driver drove a total distance of 205 miles in 5 hours. Which of the following equations can be used with $b + h = 5$ to determine the distance, in miles, the truck driver drove through the backroads?

A) $b + 5h = 90$
B) $5b + 25h = 90$
C) $65b + 25h = 205$
D) $25b + 65h = 205$

7

A group of friends went to a taco shop and bought a total of 14 fish tacos and chicken tacos for $72. Each fish taco costs $6 and each chicken taco costs $4. How many fish tacos did the group buy?

A) 5
B) 6
C) 8
D) 12

8

A teacher bought 6 boxes of crayons and 4 boxes of pencils for $16. The following week, the teacher bought 3 more boxes of crayons and 7 more boxes of pencils for $13. Which of the following is the price of 1 one box of pencils, assuming the teacher bought the same boxes of crayons and pencils at the same cost and no sales tax was collected?

A) $1.00
B) $1.45
C) $2.00
D) $3.70

9

	20-ounce	50-ounce
Cost	$20	$42

A hair salon sells a certain brand of shampoo in 20-ounce and 50-ounce bottles. The table above shows the cost for each 20-ounce bottle and each 50-ounce bottle sold by the salon. If a total of 90 shampoo bottles were sold, and between $2,900 and $3,120 was collected in sales, which of the following could be the number of 50-ounce bottles sold?

A) 20
B) 42
C) 48
D) 54

10

The sum of two different numbers a and b is 110, and the sum of $3a$ and b is 170. What is number a?

11

Jamal has 40 coins comprised of quarters and dimes in his piggy bank. The total value of the coins in the piggy bank is $7.60. How many quarters does Jamal have in his piggy bank?

12

Rita bought a trays of muffins and b trays of cupcakes for a total of $148. If Rita bought a total of 18 trays of muffins and cupcakes, and each tray of muffin costs $10 and each tray of cupcake costs $6, what is the value of a?

Category 19 – Word Problems on Linear Inequalities

Key Points
- A word problem may be given that evaluates a conditional relationship between two or more numbers, where at least one number is unknown. The unknown number contains a variable that evaluates the condition. For example, $700 \leq 55a$. The value given to the variable a must result in the value of $55a$ equal to or greater than 700.
- When a condition evaluates "greater than", the inequality symbol is $>$. For example, x is greater than y is written as $x > y$.
- When a condition evaluates "less than", the inequality symbol is $<$. For example, x is less than y is written as $x < y$.
- When a condition evaluates "greater than or equal to" (or minimum or at least), the inequality symbol is $\geq$. For example, x is at least y is written as $x \geq y$.
- When a condition evaluates "less than or equal to" (or maximum or at the most), the inequality symbol is $\leq$. For example, x is at the most y is written as $x \leq y$.

How to Solve
Identify the conditional variables from the word problem and form an inequality based on the conditions.

Example 1:
A lemonade stand owner sells each cup of lemonade for $1.50. The daily cost of the renting the lemonade stand is $83, and the cost of making each cup of lemonade is $0.15.

Question 1
Which of the following inequalities can determine the minimum number of lemonade cups, c, that must be sold each day to cover the daily cost of renting the stand and making lemonade cups?

A) $c \leq \frac{83}{1.35}$

B) $c \geq \frac{83}{1.35}$

C) $c \leq \frac{83}{1.50}$

D) $c \geq \frac{83}{1.50}$

Step 1: Determine the variables
Number of lemonade cups $= c$.

Step 2: Determine the conditional relationship
Cost of daily rental $= 83$.
Cost of making c lemonade cups $= 0.15c$.
Earnings from c lemonade cups $= 1.50c$.
Cost of daily rental + cost of making c lemonade cups must be less than or equal to earnings from c lemonade cups.
$$83 + 0.15c \leq 1.50c \quad \rightarrow \quad 83 \leq 1.50c - 0.15c \quad \rightarrow \quad 83 \leq 1.35c \quad \rightarrow$$
$$\frac{83}{1.35} \leq c \quad \rightarrow \quad c \geq \frac{83}{1.35}$$

The correct answer choice is **B**.

Question 2

What is the minimum number of lemonade cups that must be sold each day to cover the daily costs?

Proceed from Step 2 of Question 1. Solve for c.

$$c \geq \frac{83}{1.35} \rightarrow c \geq 61.48$$

The minimum number of lemonade cups = 62.

Note that 61.48 cannot be rounded down to 61 as 61 cups will not cover the cost. To cover the cost, the number of cups must be equal to greater than 61.48. Since the number of cups is an integer, the next integer is 62.

The correct answer is **62**.

Example 2:

A landscaper has less than $200 to buy x bags of topsoil and y bags of potting soil. Each bag of topsoil costs $1.95 and each bag of potting soil costs $9.99. Which of the following inequalities represents the situation in context?

A) $200 > 1.95x + 9.99y$

B) $200 < 1.95x + 9.99y$

C) $200 \geq 9.99x + 1.95y$

D) $200 \leq 9.99x + 1.95y$

Step 1: Determine the variables

Number of topsoil bags = x.

Number of potting soil bags = y.

Step 2: Determine the conditional relationship

Cost of x bags = $1.95x$.

Cost of y bags = $9.99y$.

Total cost = $1.95x + 9.99y$ should be less than $200.

$$1.95x + 9.99y < 200 \rightarrow 200 > 1.95x + 9.99y$$

The correct answer choice is **A**.

Example 3:

Betty bought a 16 ounce bottle of sparkling water. She drank x ounces and accidently spilled y ounces. If there is at least 7 ounces of sparkling water left in the bottle, which of the following inequalities represents the plausible amount of sparkling water left in the bottle, in ounces?

A) $16 + x + y > 7$

B) $16 - x - y > 7$

C) $16 + x + y \geq 7$

D) $16 - x - y \geq 7$

Step 1: Determine the variables

Water drank = x.

Water spilled = y.

Step 2: Determine the conditional relationship

Total water removed from bottle = drank + spilled = $x + y$.

The ounces of water left after drinking and spilling = $16 - (x + y)$.

The ounces of water left after drinking and spilling is at least 7 ounces (same as greater than or equal to). Hence,

$$16 - (x + y) \geq 7 \rightarrow 16 - x - y \geq 7$$

The correct answer choice is **D**.

Category 19 – Practice Questions

1

Niya runs a hot dog stand. Each day, she rents the stand for $68 and sells hot dogs for $4 each. The cost of making each hot dog is $1.50. Which of the following inequalities can determine the least number of hot dogs, d, Niya must sell each day to cover the costs of renting the stand and making hot dogs?

A) $68 \leq 4d$

B) $68 \leq 2.50d$

C) $68 \geq 4d$

D) $68 \geq 2.50d$

2

Zhang has 15 baseball cards. After he gives a cards to his brother and b cards to his sister, he has at least 5 baseball cards left. Which of the following inequalities represents the possible number of baseball cards Zhang has after giving those cards to his brother and sister?

A) $15 - a - b \geq 5$

B) $15 + a + b \leq 5$

C) $15 - a - b > 5$

D) $15 + a + b < 5$

3

Joe can spend a maximum of $200 to buy soft pretzels and water bottles for an event. If each soft pretzel costs $3 and each water bottle costs $2, which of the following inequalities can determine the number of soft pretzels and water bottles Joe can buy?

A) $200 \leq 3p + 2b$

B) $200 \leq 3b + 2p$

C) $200 \geq 3p + 2b$

D) $200 \geq 3b + 2p$

4

A farmer sells cherry tomatoes and potatoes every day of the week during the summer. To cover the costs of growing and harvesting, the farmer must sell greater than 12 pounds of cherry tomatoes and potatoes combined each day. Which of the following inequalities determines the least number of cherry tomatoes, c, in pounds, and potatoes, p, in pounds, the farmer must sell per week during the summer?

A) $c + p \geq 12$

B) $c + p \geq 84$

C) $c + p > 12$

D) $c + p > 84$

5

Gary's cell phone plan charges a fixed fee of $17.99 per month and $0.16 for each call. If Gary cannot spend more than $25 per month, which of the following is the maximum number of calls Gary can make within a month?

A) 25

B) 42

C) 43

D) 44

6

A party planner can spend a maximum of $24 to buy napkins and candles. Each napkin costs $2 and each candle costs $1.50. If the party planner buys 7 napkins, what is the maximum number of candles the party planner can buy, assuming there is no sales tax?

Category 20 – Word Problems on Linear System of Inequalities

Key Points
- A word problem may be given that evaluates a conditional relationship between two sets of unknown variables. A single inequality, such as $x + y > 18$, cannot evaluate the conditional relationship between the variables x and y. The word problem will contain information to set up two or more inequalities (system of inequalities) that together can evaluate the conditional relationship.

How to Solve
Identify the conditional variables from the word problem and form the system of inequalities based on the conditions.

Example 1:
A restaurant manager wants to order a combination of at least 96 small and large size plates. The manager does not want to spend more than $550 but wants to buy at least 50 large plates. The cost of each small size plate is $4, and the cost of each large size plate is $6. If the manager decides to order x small size plates and y large size plates, which of the following systems of inequalities represents the situation in context?

A) $x + y \geq 96$
   $4x + 6y \leq 550$
   $x \leq 50$

B) $x + y \geq 96$
   $4x + 6y \leq 550$
   $y \geq 50$

C) $x + y \leq 96$
   $4x + 6y \geq 550$
   $x \leq 50$

D) $6x + 4y \leq 96$
   $x + y \leq 550$
   $y \leq 50$

Step 1: Identify the two variables
Variable 1: Number of small size plates $= x$.
Variable 2: Number of large size plates $= y$.

Step 2: Determine the conditional relationship in the system of inequalities
Inequality 1: The total number of small size plates x and large size plates y must be greater than or equal to 96.
$$x + y \geq 96$$
This eliminates answer choices C and D.

Inequality 2: The cost of each $x = \$4$, and the cost of each $y = \$6$. The total cost must be less than or equal to $550.
$$4x + 6y \leq 550$$

Inequality 3: It is given that the number of large plates must be at least 50.
$$y \geq 50$$
This eliminates answer choice A.

The correct answer choice is **B**.

Category 20 – Practice Questions

1

A truck is loaded with boxes that weigh either 20 pounds or 40 pounds. The truck can carry a maximum of 55 boxes with a total weight of 1,850 pounds or less. Which of the following systems of inequalities represents the allowed capacity of the truck, where m is the number of boxes that weigh 20 pounds and n is the number of boxes that weigh 40 pounds?

A) $m + n \geq 55$
$20m + 40n \geq 1,850$

B) $m + n \leq 55$
$20m + 40n \leq 1,850$

C) $m + n \geq 55$
$40m + 20n \geq 1,850$

D) $m + n \leq 55$
$40m + 20n \leq 1,850$

2

A library has allocated a budget of $680 or less to buy no more than 50 fiction and non-fiction books, combined. The cost of each fiction book, c, is $12, and the cost of each non-fiction book, k, is $15. Which of the following systems of inequalities represents the constraints on c and k?

A) $c + k \geq 50$
$15c + 12k \geq 680$

B) $c + k \geq 50$
$12c + 15k \geq 680$

C) $c + k \leq 50$
$15c + 12k \leq 680$

D) $c + k \leq 50$
$12c + 15k \leq 680$

3

Emma works as a part-time tutor. Each week, she provides l hours of on-line tutoring and h hours of in-home tutoring. Emma charges $25 per hour for on-line tutoring and $45 per hour for in-home tutoring. Her schedule does not permit her to provide tutoring for more than 20 hours per week. If Emma must earn at least $600 per week and provide at least 10 hours of in-home tutoring per week, which of the following systems of inequalities represents the weekly constraints on l and h?

A) $l + h \leq 20$
$45l + 25h \leq 600$
$h \geq 20$

B) $l + h \leq 20$
$25l + 45h \geq 600$
$h \leq 10$

C) $l + h \geq 20$
$45l + 25h \leq 600$
$10 \leq h \leq 20$

D) $l + h \leq 20$
$25l + 45h \geq 600$
$10 \leq h \leq 20$

4

A gym owner has allocated a maximum budget of $28,000 to buy at least 12 new treadmills and exercise bikes. Each treadmill costs $2,600 and each exercise bike costs $1,800. If the gym owner wants to buy t treadmills and b exercise bikes, which of the following systems of inequalities accurately represents the situation in context?

A) $b + t \geq 12$
$1,800b + 2,600t \leq 28,000$

B) $b + t \leq 12$
$1,800b + 2,600t \geq 28,000$

C) $b + t \geq 12$
$1,800t + 2,600b \leq 28,000$

D) $b + t \leq 12$
$1,800b + 2,600t \geq 28,0$

Category 21 – Word Problems on Equal Variables in Linear Equations

Key Points
- A word problem may be given that contains two linear equations that are equal for some value of a common variable for a certain duration. For example, a product price for which cost is equal to profit for d days after New Year's Day, or a product quantity for which the supply is equal to the demand for w weeks after product launch, or product price at which the sales of one item equal to the sales of another item for w weeks after a promotion.

How to Solve
Equate the two given equations and solve for the variable that makes them equal.

If the equations are not given, then form wo equations based on the information in the word problem and equate them.

*Several questions in this category can be partially solved using the Desmos graphing calculator. After the two equations are identified from a word problem, they can be equated and typed in Desmos graphing calculator to solve for the variable.

Example 1:

$$S = 122 - \frac{1}{4}P$$

$$D = \frac{1}{2}P + 59$$

In the equations above, S is the number of coffee machines manufactured by a certain manufacturer and D is the number of the coffee machines ordered by customers, from January 2021 to April 2021. At what price P, in dollars, is the number of coffee machines manufactured equal to the number of coffee machines ordered by the customers from January 2021 to April 2021?

A) $21
B) $63
C) $84
D) $101

Step 1: Equate the two equations

$$122 - \frac{1}{4}P = \frac{1}{2}P + 59$$

Step 2: Solve for the variable

$$\frac{1}{2}P + \frac{1}{4}P = 122 - 59 \rightarrow \frac{3}{4}P = 63 \rightarrow P = 63 \times \frac{4}{3} = 84$$

The correct answer choice is **C**.

Example 2:

$$a = 5.3 + 0.82d$$
$$b = 8.9 + 0.67d$$

A street vendor added fried cookies and funnel cake to the menu. In the equations above, a and b represent the sales, in dollars, of fried cookies and funnel cake, respectively, in d days since the addition to the menu. Which of the following is closest to the sales of fried cookies when they were equal to sales of funnel cake?

A) $14
B) $18
C) $23
D) $25

Step 1: Equate the two equations

For the sales of fried cookies to be equal to the sales of funnel cake, the values of a and b must be equal. Equate the two equations to determine the value of d that makes the two equations equal.

$$5.3 + 0.82d = 8.9 + 0.67d$$

Step 2: Solve for the variable

$$0.82d - 0.67d = 8.9 - 5.3$$
$$0.15d = 3.6 \rightarrow d = 24$$

Step 3: Solve the equation

The values of a and b will be the same when $d = 24$. Since the question asks for the sales of fried cookies = a, substitute $d = 24$ in the equation for fried cookies.

$$a = 5.3 + 0.82d \rightarrow a = 5.3 + (0.82 \times 24) = 24.98$$

The correct answer choice is **D**.

Example 3:

A supermarket announced a sale on its freshly baked cherry pies. The weekly cost of making cherry pies is $19.20 plus $1.60 per pie. The selling price of each cherry pie is $4.80. How many whole cherry pies must be sold in a week for the cost of making cherry pies to equal the sales from cherry pies, in dollars?

Step 1: Determine the two equations

Since the question does not give the equation for the weekly cost of making cherry pies or for the weekly sales of cherry pies, create the two equations based on the given information.

Let the number of cherry pies = p.

Let one week cost of making p cherry pies = c. Hence,

$$c = 19.20 + 1.60p$$

Let one-week sales of p cherry pies = s.

$$s = 4.80p$$

Step 2: Equate the two equations

For the weekly sales, in dollars, to be equal to the weekly cost of making, in dollars, the values of c and s must be equal. Equate the two equations to determine the value of p that makes the two equations equal.

$$19.20 + 1.60p = 4.80p$$

Step 3: Solve for the variable

$$19.20 = 4.80p - 1.60p \rightarrow 19.20 = 3.2p \rightarrow p = 6$$

The correct answer is **6**.

Category 21 – Practice Questions

After the two equations are determined, the Desmos graphing calculator can be used to solve the variable in question 4

1 — Desmos

$$D = 48 + \frac{1}{4}p$$

$$S = 150 - \frac{1}{2}p$$

In the equations above, S represents the quantity of a certain microchip produced by a company, and D represents the quantity of that microchip in demand by customers, for the first 8 weeks of 2006. At what price p, in dollars, was the quantity of the microchip produced equal to the quantity of microchip demanded by the customers?

A) $48
B) $95
C) $99
D) $136

2 — Desmos

$$l = 10.50 + 4.50x$$

$$c = 36.50 + 2.50x$$

In the equations above, l and c represent the sales, in dollars, of lemonade and Italian ice, respectively, at a certain market stall during x weeks last summer. What were the sales for Italian ice, in dollars, when equal to the sales for lemonade, in dollars?

A) $5
B) $13
C) $69
D) $70

3 — Desmos

$$s = 35 + 3p$$

$$d = 75 + p$$

In the equations above, s is the quantity of a certain brand of LED bulbs produced by a manufacturing company, and d is the quantity of the LED bulbs ordered by customers. In terms of the product price p, in dollars, at what price is the quantity of the LED bulbs produced the same as the quantity of the LED bulbs ordered by the customers?

A) $20
B) $35
C) $55
D) $75

4

$$S = 19{,}646 + 149W$$

A company that specializes in manufacturing a heart rate monitor watch calculates the quarterly earnings, S, in dollars, for W watches sold during a quarter, using the above equation. The company has estimated that, in the next quarter, the total cost of manufacturing the watches will be $37,750 plus $25 per watch. How many watches, W, must the company sell next quarter for the total earnings, S, in dollars, to equal the total manufacturing costs, in dollars?

A) 98
B) 124
C) 146
D) 158

Digital SAT Math Manual and Workbook

Section 4 – Review Questions

The Desmos graphing calculator can be used to solve the intersection point in questions 12, 13, 14, and 19, and to solve the variable in questions 21 and 23.

1

Last week, Samara walked s miles per day for 4 days, and Chuck walked p miles per day for 6 days. Which of the following equations represents the total number of miles Samara and Chuck walked last week?

A) $10sp$
B) $4s + p$
C) $4p + 6s$
D) $4s + 6p$

2

$$315 = p + 21d$$

An elementary school teacher will read a book to the class over the next several days. At the end of each day, the teacher plans to keep track of the number of pages left to read using the above equation. If p is the number of pages left at the end of each day, and d is the number of days the teacher reads the book, which of the following is the best interpretation of the number 315?

A) The total number of pages in the book the teacher will be reading.
B) The number of days it will take the teacher to read the book.
C) The rate at which the teacher will be reading the book each day.
D) The average number of pages the teacher will read each day.

3

Sara estimates to burn t calories per minute walking on a treadmill and 6 calories per minute running on it. Which of the following equations represents the total calories, C, Sara estimates to burn by walking on the treadmill for 35 minutes and running on the treadmill for 10 minutes?

A) $C = 410t$
B) $C = 35 + 60t$
C) $C = 35t + 60$
D) $C = 35t + 6$

4

$$B = 0.2p$$

The equation above can be used to approximate the increase in Body Mass Index, B, of a 5-foot tall adult weighing p pounds, where $100 \leq p \leq 200$. Which of the following statements agrees with the equation?

A) For each increase of 2 pounds in weight, B increases by approximately 0.2.
B) For each increase of 0.2 pound in weight, B increases by approximately 1.
C) For each increase of 1 pound in weight, B increases by approximately 0.2.
D) For each increase of 1 pound in weight, B increases by approximately 2.

5

A shipping company charges different rates for shipping packages during peak hours and off-peak hours. The company has several locations. The number of packages shipped by a location during the off-peak hours, x, cannot be greater than the number of packages shipped during the peak hours, y, in a given day. Each location is allowed to ship a maximum of 150 packages per day. Which of the following system of inequalities represents the constraints on x and y for each location per day?

A) $x + y \leq 150$
   $x \geq y$

B) $x + y \leq 150$
   $x \leq y$

C) $x + y \geq 150$
   $x \geq y$

D) $x + y \geq 150$
   $x \leq y$

6

Sita works two shifts as a barista at a 24-hour coffee shop. During the morning shift she earns $18 per hour, and during the night shift she earns $34 per hour. Last Friday, Sita worked a total of 10 hours and earned $276. Which of the following systems can determine the number of hours, M, Sita worked during the morning shift, and the number of hours, N, Sita worked during the night shift?

A) $M + N = 10$
   $18M + 34N = 276$

B) $M + N = 2(10)$
   $34N + 18N = 276$

C) $M + N = 2(10)$
   $18M + 34N = 276$

D) $M + N = 10$
   $18M + 34N = 2(276)$

7

A teaching assistant works at an after-school program as an Algebra I tutor for m hours per week and a Spanish tutor for n hours per week. Each week, the teahing assistant is required to teach at least 7 hours of Spanish but no more than 15 hours of Algebra I and Spanish combined. If the teaching assistant charges $50 per hour for teaching Algebra I and $38 per hour for teaching Spanish, and must earn a minimum of $500 weekly, which of the following system of inequalities represents the constraints on m and n?

A) $m + n \leq 7$
   $38m + 50n \geq 500$
   $0 \leq n \leq 7$

B) $m + n \leq 15$
   $38m + 50n \geq 500$
   $7 \leq n \leq 15$

C) $m + n \leq 15$
   $50m + 38n \geq 500$
   $0 \leq n \leq 7$

D) $m + n \leq 15$
   $50m + 38n \geq 500$
   $7 \leq n \leq 15$

8

The cost of daily admission to an amusement park is $40, and each ride at the park costs $2. Which of the following expressions gives the total cost, in dollars, of the admission ticket and n rides for a day?

A) $40 + 2n$

B) $40 + 40n$

C) $42 + n$

D) $42n$

9

$$g(t) = 10 + 0.75t$$

In 2015, Ken planted a 10-foot tall tree in his backyard. The height of the tree, in feet, t years after 2015 can be modeled by the linear function g defined above. Which of the following is the best interpretation of the equation $g(12) = 19$?

A) The number of years the tree will grow in Ken's backyard after 2015.

B) The height of the tree is estimated to be 19 feet in 12 years after 2015.

C) The average increase in the height of the tree each year is estimated to be 19 feet after 2015.

D) The maximum height of the tree is estimated to be 19 feet.

10

Teri filled 3.5 gallons of fuel in her car. If her car consumes 1 gallon of fuel for every 19.5 miles, which of the following inequalities represents the maximum number of miles m Teri can drive her car with 3.5 gallons of fuel?

A) $m \geq 3.5$

B) $m \leq 19.5$

C) $m \geq 19.5$

D) $m \leq 68.25$

11

A tutoring center bought c iPads and d desks for a total of \$1,377. The equation $389c + 72d = 1,377$ represents the situation in context. What is the interpretation of $72d$ in this context?

A) The number of desks bought by the tutoring center.

B) The price, in dollars, of each desk bought by the tutoring center.

C) The total amount, in dollars, the tutoring center spent on buying d desks.

D) The total amount, in dollars, the tutoring center spent on buying iPads and desks.

12

John has 50 coins in his pocket consisting of nickels and dimes. The total value of the coins is \$3.50. How many dimes does John have in his pocket?

A) 7
B) 10
C) 20
D) 30

13

A restaurant sells extra-large burgers on the first day of each month. The cost of making the extra-large burgers for a day is \$41.50 plus \$0.45 for each extra-large burger. The profit from selling the extra-large burgers for a day is \$29.50 plus \$1.95 for each extra-large burger. How many extra-large burgers must be sold on the first day of each month for the cost of making the extra-large burgers, in dollars, to equal the profit from the sales, in dollars?

A) 8
B) 11
C) 20
D) 24

14

Advance tickets for the entrance to a fair were sold at the reduced price of \$9 per ticket. On the day of the fair, the tickets were sold at the regular price of \$29. If a total of \$4,960 was collected from the advance and regular ticket sales, and a total of 240 tickets were sold, how many tickets were sold at the regular price?

A) 100
B) 140
C) 200
D) 230

15

In the current academic year, a certain school has 52 teachers in total. Over the next 3 academic years, the school plans to add at least 4, but no more than 9 teachers per year. If no teacher left the school during the next 3 academic years, which of the following inequalities represents all possible values of the number of teachers, g, at the school at the end of next 3 academic years?

A) $12 < g < 27$
B) $56 \leq g \leq 61$
C) $64 \leq g \leq 79$
D) $64 \leq g \leq 90$

16

$$g(m) = p + 68m$$

In January 2020, the number of trout fish in a certain local pond was estimated to be p. The function shown above estimates the number of trout fish in m months after January 2020. Which of the following is the best interpretation of the number 68 in this context?

A) The total number of trout fish m months after January 2020.

B) The estimated average monthly increase in the number of trout fish before January 2020.

C) The estimated average increase in the number of trout fish per month after January 2020 for m years.

D) The estimated average increase in the number of trout fish each month after January for m months.

17

In 2015-16 school year, 176 students were enrolled at a high school. During the next 5 years, the school increased the enrollment by a constant number, n, to a total of 236 students in 2020-21 school year. If after the 2020-21 school year, the high school continues to increase the enrollment by n each year for t years, which of the following equations can determine the number of students, r, enrolled at the high school in t years, where $1 \leq t \leq 4$?

A) $r = 176 + 5t$

B) $r = 176 + 12t$

C) $r = 236 + 12t$

D) $r = 412 + 12t$

18

Sammy opened a bank account with $700. During the next 12 months, Sammy will make monthly deposits of at least $100 but not more than $150 per month in this bank account. Which of the following inequalities represents all possible amounts, s, in dollars, in the bank account after the 12 monthly deposits, assuming that no withdrawals were made, and no interest was collected?

A) $800 \leq s \leq 950$

B) $800 \leq s \leq 1{,}250$

C) $1{,}200 \leq s \leq 1{,}800$

D) $1{,}900 \leq s \leq 2{,}500$

19

A baker has 104 cupcakes to distribute in 6-pack and 14-pack containers. The baker distributes the cupcakes in a total of 12 containers. If each container is full and all the cupcakes have been evenly distributed, how many cupcakes are in the 14-pack containers?

A) 4

B) 8

C) 56

D) 60

20

$$B = 29.92 - 0.0012a$$

The above equation approximates the barometric pressure B, in inches Hg, exerted by air molecules at an altitude of a feet above the sea level, where $0 \leq a \leq 8{,}000$. At what value of a, in feet, does the barometric pressure decrease by 1 inch Hg?

A) 0.0012

B) 29.92

C) $\frac{1}{0.01}$

D) $\frac{1}{0.0012}$

21

Casey and her friend Lilian subscribe to separate cell phone data plans. Casey pays a monthly fee of $24.99 in addition to $0.08 per call. Lilian pays a monthly fee of $16.99 in addition to $0.28 per call. For how many calls in a month will the two data plans have the same cost, in dollars?

22 — Desmos

A trucking company estimates the daily cost, C, in dollars, of hiring truck drivers using the equation $C = 500 + 55nh$, where n is the number of truck drivers and h is total number of hours n truck drivers work in a day. If on a certain day, the total cost of hiring 3 truck drivers was $3,965, how many total hours did the 3 truck drivers work?

23

A teacher is packing cookies in paper bags for a school party. If the teacher packs 5 cookies per bag, exactly 4 additional bags will be required to pack the remaining cookies. If the teacher packs 10 cookies per bag, exactly 1 bag will not be used. How many cookies is the teacher packing?

Section 5 – Polynomial and Undefined Functions

Category 22 – Standard Form Polynomial Functions

Category 23 – Tables and Graphs of Polynomial Functions

Category 24 – Nested Polynomial Functions

Category 25 – Zeros, Factors, and Factored Form Polynomial Functions

Category 26 – Graph Transformations of Polynomial Functions

Category 27 – Remainders in Polynomial Functions

Category 28 – Undefined Functions

Section 5 – Review Questions

Category 22 – Standard Form Polynomial Functions

Key Points

- A standard form polynomial function contains terms in the form ax^n, where n is a positive integer. For example, $f(x) = ax^3 + 24$, or $f(x) = ax^4 + bx^2 + x + 3$, or $f(x) = ax + 2$, where a and b are constants.

  (Note that polynomial functions containing 1 as the highest value of n are known as linear functions and are covered in Section 1, and polynomial functions containing 2 as the highest value of n are known as quadratic functions and are covered in Section 6).

- $f(x)$ is the y-value of a polynomial function for an input value of x. For example, if $x = 2$ in the function $f(x) = 3x^4 + 4x^2 + x + 3$, then $y = f(2) = 3(2)^4 + 4(2)^2 + (2) + 3$.
- The input value of x can be represented by any letter. For example, $f(a), f(b)$, or $f(t)$.
- A function can be given any name. For example, $g(x), h(t)$, or $f(a)$, where x, t, and a are the inputs, respectively.
- A function can be evaluated for a single value or multiple values of x. For example, $f(a) + f(b)$ or $\frac{f(a)}{f(b)}$, where a and b are two different input values of x for the function f.

How to Solve

In the given equation, plug in the given input value of x to determine the corresponding value of y. For example, if the question asks for $f(2)$, then plug in 2 as the value of x in the given equation, and if the question asks for $f(2x + 3)$, then plug in $2x + 3$ as the value of x in the given equation.

Remember $y = f(x)$. For example, $f(-2) = 8$ means that when $x = -2$, the value of y for the function f is 8.

*Several questions in this category can be solved using the Desmos graphing calculator.

*Example 1:

The function f is defined by $f(x) = x^3 - 5x$. What is the value of $4f(3) - f(4)$?

A) 4
B) 9
C) 12
D) 44

Step 1: Plug in the given value of x in the function

To get the value of $f(3)$, plug in $x = 3$.
$$f(3) = 3^3 - 5(3) = 27 - 15 \rightarrow f(3) = 12$$
To get the value of $f(4)$, plug in $x = 4$.
$$f(4) = 4^3 - 5(4) = 64 - 20 \rightarrow f(4) = 44$$

Step 2: Solve for $4f(3) - f(4)$
$$4f(3) - f(4) = 4(12) - 44 = 48 - 44 = 4$$

The correct answer choice is **A**.

*Desmos Graphing Calculator Solution

Type the definition of function f. In the next row, type what must be solved. In this example, $4f(3) - f(4)$ is to be solved. Typing this will display its value to the right in the same row. See below.

The value of $4f(3) - f(4)$ is displayed as $= 4$.

Desmos graphing calculator will also display the graph (not shown in the figure below). However, it is irrelevant to solving this question.

*Example 2:

The function g is defined by $g(x) = 2x^3 + 9x - 47$, and the function h is defined by $h(x) = 2x^3 - 21$. For what value of a does $g(a) - h(a) = 1$?

Step 1: Solve for a

The input value can be any letter. Substitute the definition of the functions and equate to 1. $g(x) - h(x) = 1$ can be written as $g(a) - h(a) = 1$

$$g(a) - h(a) = 1 \rightarrow (2a^3 + 9x - 47) - (2a^3 - 21) = 1 \rightarrow 2a^3 + 9x - 47 - 2a^3 + 21 = 1 \rightarrow$$
$$9a - 26 = 1 \rightarrow 9a = 27 \rightarrow a = 3$$

Hence, $a = 3$.

The correct answer is **3**.

*Desmos Graphing Calculator Solution

Type the definition of $g(x)$ and $h(x)$ in the equation $g(a) - h(a) = 1$ and read the value of x where the graph of the equation passes through the x-axis. See the vertical line in the graph below.

$x = 3$. Hence, $a = 3$.

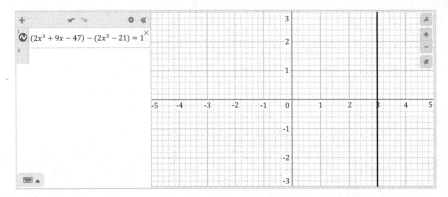

Digital SAT Math Manual and Workbook

Category 22 – Practice Questions

After the equations in the system are determined, the Desmos graphing calculator can be used to solve the variable in question 5.

1 — Desmos

The function f is defined by $f(x) = x^4 - 3x^2 - 4$. What is the value of $f(-2) - f(1)?$

A) -4
B) -2
C) 0
D) 6

2 — Desmos

$$f(x) = \frac{3x - 7}{2}$$

The function f is defined as shown above. Which of the following expressions represents $f(2x + 5)?$

A) $x - 6$
B) $3x - 1$
C) $3x + 4$
D) $6x + 8$

3 — Desmos

$$f(x) = 4x^4 - 57$$

The function f is defined as shown above, and $3f(b) = 21$. What is the positive value of $b?$

A) 0
B) 2
C) 4
D) 7

4 — Desmos

The function f is defined by $f(x) = x^5 + 4x^4 + x$ for all values of x. The function g is defined by $g(x) = 4x^3 - 17x^2 - 74$ for all values of x. What is the product of $f(-3)$ and $g(5)?$

A) -15
B) -2
C) 78
D) 79

5

$$g(x) = \frac{mx^2 + n}{2}$$

The function g shown above is true for all values of x, and m and n are constants. If $g(10) = 300$, and $g(20) = 1{,}500$, what is the value of $m?$

A) 1
B) 8
C) 15
D) 24

6 — Desmos

$$g(x) = 3x^4 - 2x - 4$$
$$f(x) = -3x^4 + 5x - 5$$

The functions g and f are defined above. For what value of t does $g(t) + f(t) = 0?$

A) -5
B) -3
C) 1
D) 3

Digital SAT Math Manual and Workbook

Category 23 – Tables and Graphs of Polynomial Functions

Key Points
- A polynomial function may be represented in a table or as a graph.
- A table contains two columns. For a function f, the x column contains the input values of x, and the $f(x)$ column contains the corresponding output values, where $y = f(x)$.
- On the graph of a function f, $f(x)$ is the y-value corresponding to a given value of x on the x-axis.

How to Solve

Remember that $y = f(x)$ on the graph of the function f. For example, $f(3) = 8$ means that when $x = 3$ on the graph, the value of y is 8.

Example 1:

x	$f(x)$
2	3
3	4
4	6

For the function f, the above table shows three values of x and their corresponding values of $f(x)$, where $y = f(x)$.

Question 1
What is the value of $f(3)$?

Step 1: Read the value of $f(x)$ from the table

Since $x = 3$, look for 3 in the x column and read the corresponding value from the $f(x)$ column.

$$f(3) = 4$$

The correct answer is **4**.

Question 2
For what value of x does $f(x) = 3$?

Step 1: Read the value of x from the table

Since $f(x) = 3$, look for 3 in the $f(x)$ column and read the corresponding value from the x column.

$$x = 2$$

The correct answer is **2**.

Example 2:

x	f(x)
2	3
3	4
5	8

For the function f, three values of x and their corresponding values of $f(x)$ are shown in the table above, where $y = f(x)$. If $2f(x) = f(x + 2)$ for all values of x, what is the value of $f(4)$?

Step 1: Read the value of $f(x)$ from the table

The table does not contain $x = 4$. Hence, determine a value of x that can give $f(x + 2) = f(4)$ and exists in the table. If $x = 2$, then

$$2f(x) = f(x + 2) \rightarrow 2f(2) = f(2 + 2) \rightarrow 2f(2) = f(4)$$

The value of $f(2)$ can be read from the table.

$$f(2) = 3$$

Hence,

$$2f(2) = f(4) \rightarrow 2 \times 3 = f(4) \rightarrow 6 = f(4)$$

The correct answer is **6**.

Example 3:

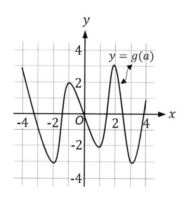

The complete graph of the function g, where $y = g(a)$, is shown above in the xy-plane. How many values of a does $g(a) = g(-1)$?

A) 1
B) 2
C) 4
D) 5

Step 1: Read the value of y from the graph for the given value of x

The question asks for the number of x-values where $y = g(-1)$. The first step is to determine the y value for $x = -1$. Hence, read the y-value from the graph where $x = -1$.

$$y = 2$$

Step 2: Count the number of x-values from the graph for the y-value from Step 1

For ease, draw a line across the graph at $y = 2$ and count the number of points of intersection on the line. See the figure on the right. There are four values of x where $y = 2$. In other words, four values of x define $y = 2$.
The correct answer choice is **C**.

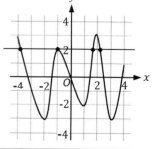

Category 23 – Practice Questions

1

x	$g(x)$
2	5
4	-2
12	-4

For the function g, three values of x and their corresponding values of $g(x)$ are shown in the table above. If $2g(x) = g(3x)$ for all values of x, which of the following is the value of $g(6)$?

A) 3
B) 5
C) 6
D) 10

2

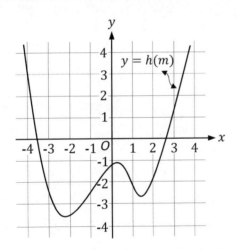

In the xy-plane, the complete graph of the function h is shown above, and $y = h(m)$. If $h(m) = c$ has 4 solutions and c is a constant, what is one possible value of c?

A) -3
B) -2
C) 0
D) 1

3

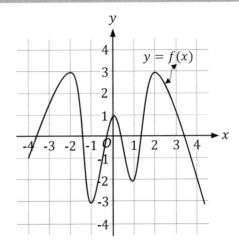

In the xy-plane, the graph of the function f is shown above, where $y = f(x)$. Which of the following satisfies $f(x) = 3$?

A) $f(-2)$ and $f(2)$
B) $f(-2)$ and $f(3)$
C) $f(-3)$
D) $f(3)$

4

x	3	1	0
$f(x)$	4	2	-1

In the table above, three values of x and their corresponding values of $f(x)$ values are given. If $3f(x) = 12$, what is the value of x?

5

x	$f(x)$
1	-3
2	1
3	2
4	4

The table above shows selected values of x and their corresponding $f(x)$ values of the function f. What is the value of $\dfrac{f(2)-f(1)}{f(4)}$?

Digital SAT Math Manual and Workbook

Category 24 – Nested Polynomial Functions

Key Points
- A polynomial function may be nested in another function.
  - For example, in $g(f(2))$, the function f is nested within the function g. The output value of the nested function f becomes the input value of the function g. For example, if $f(2) = 5$, then $g(f(2)) = g(5)$.
- A polynomial function may contain another function in its definition.
  - For example, in $g(x) = 5 + 2f(x)$, the function g contains the function f in its definition. The input value of x will be the input value of x in all the functions. For example, if $x = 6$, then $g(6) = 5 + 2f(6)$.

How to Solve
Remember that the output value of the nested function must be determined first.

*Several questions in this category can be solved using the Desmos graphing calculator.

*Example 1:
The function f is defined by $f(x) = x^2 + 2x$, and the function g is defined by $g(x) = 5 + 2f(x)$. What is the value of $g(3)$?

Step 1: Plug in the given value of x in the function f
$$f(3) = 3^2 + 2(3) = 9 + 6 \rightarrow f(3) = 15$$

Step 2: Plug in the given value of x in the function g
$$g(3) = 5 + 2(15) = 5 + 30 \rightarrow g(3) = 35$$

The correct answer is **35**.

*Desmos Graphing Calculator Solution
Type the definition of function f. In the next row, type the definition of function g. In the next row, type what must be solved. In this example, $g(3)$ is to be solved. Typing this will display its value to the right in the same row. See below.

The value of $g(3)$ is displayed as $= 35$.

Desmos graphing calculator will also display the graph (not shown in the figure below). However, it is irrelevant to solving this question.

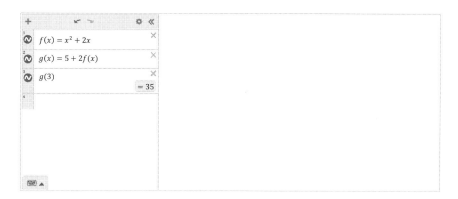

Digital SAT Math Manual and Workbook

Example 2:

x	-6	-1	3	4
$f(x)$	12	6	-1	-6
$g(x)$	6	4	0	-6

The table above shows some values of x and their corresponding values of $f(x)$ and $g(x)$. What is the value of $f(g(4))$?

A) -6
B) -1
C) 6
D) 12

Step 1: Read the value of $g(x)$ for the nested function

Look for 4 in the x column and read the corresponding value from the $g(x)$ column.
$$g(4) = -6$$

Step 2: Read the value of $f(x)$ for the outside function

Since $g(4) = -6$, the outside function is
$$f(g(4)) = f(-6)$$
Look for -6 in the x column and read the corresponding value from the $f(x)$ column.
$$f(-6) = 12$$

The correct answer choice is **D**.

Category 24 – Practice Questions

1

x	$f(x)$	$g(x)$
-2	0	-3
-1	-3	7
0	3	5
3	0	4
7	4	2

The above table shows some values of x and their corresponding values of $f(x)$ and $g(x)$. For what value of k does $g(f(3)) + f(g(-1)) + k = 1$, where k is a constant?

A) -8
B) -5
C) 1
D) 6

2

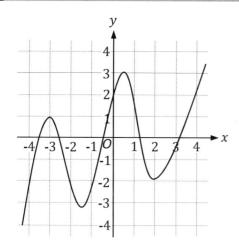

The graph of the function h in the xy-plane is shown above, where $y = h(x)$. The function g is defined by $g(x) = 2x^4 + 3$. What is the value of $g(h(-3)) - 2$?

A) -2
B) 1
C) 3
D) 5

3 Desmos

The function g is defined by $g(x) = x^2 + 4$, and the function h is defined by $h(x) = c - g(2)$. For what value of c does $h(x) = -5$?

A) 0
B) 3
C) 8
D) 9

4 Desmos

The function g is defined by $f(x) = x^2 - x$, and the function f is defined by $g(x) = x^3 - 20$. What is the value of $f(g(3))$?

A) 6
B) 14
C) 27
D) 42

5 Desmos

If the function f is defined by $f(x) = 4x - 19$, and the function g is defined by $g(x) = 3f(x - 1) - 3$, what is the value of $g(7)$?

A) 2
B) 5
C) 12
D) 15

6 Desmos

The function f satisfies $f(3) = 5$. The function g is defined by $g(x) = \dfrac{2x^3 - 98}{19}$. What is the value of $g(f(3))$?

Digital SAT Math Manual and Workbook

Category 25 – Zeros, Factors, and Factored Form Polynomial Functions

Key Points
- The zeros of a polynomial function are the values of x where the graph of the polynomial function intersects the x-axis. They are also known as the roots, solutions, and x-intercepts.
  - If n is a zero of a function, where n is a real number, then the factor is $(x - n)$ when the graph intersects the positive x-axis, and $(x + n)$ when the graph intersects the negative x-axis.

  When the graph touches the x-axis at n and curves back without crossing through the x-axis, then there will be two identical factors for n at that point.
- If the graph intersects the origin $(0, 0)$, the zero is 0, and the corresponding factor is x or a multiple of x.
- See the graph of function f below as an example. The graph has 3 distinct zeros at $x = -2, 1$ and 3. The corresponding factors are $(x + 2), (x - 1)$, and $(x - 3)^2$. Since the graph curves back at 3, $(x - 3)^2$ are two identical factors but one distinct x-intercept. The factored form equation is $f(x) = (x + 2)(x - 1)(x - 3)^2$.

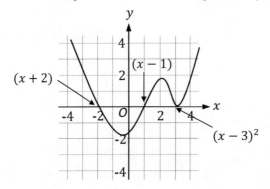

How to Solve
* The Desmos graphing calculator can be used to determine the y-intercept and zeros. However, from a factored form polynomial it is just as easy to determine the zeros.

Example 1:

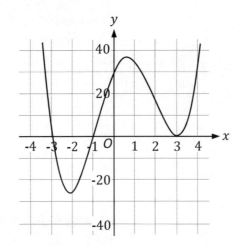

In the xy-plane, the graph of a polynomial function g is given above. Which of the following defines the function g?

A) $g(x) = (x + 3)(x + 1)(x - 3)$
B) $g(x) = (x + 3)(x - 1)(x - 3)$
C) $g(x) = (x + 3)(x + 1)(x - 3)^2$
D) $g(x) = (x - 1)(x - 3)^2$

Step 1: Determine the points on the x-axis where the graph intersects the x-axis

The graph intersects the x-axis at -1 and -3. The corresponding factors are $(x + 1)$ and $(x + 3)$, respectively.

Step 2: Determine the points on the x-axis where the graph touches the x-axis and curves back

The graph touches the x-axis at 3 and curves back. The corresponding factor is $(x - 3)^2$.

Step 3: Select the answer choice with matching factors

The factors are $(x + 3)(x + 1)(x - 3)^2$.

The correct answer choice is **C**.

Example 2:

$$5x(x + 3)(x - 3)^2(x - 1)^2$$

The factors of a polynomial $f(x)$ are shown above. How many distinct zeros does $f(x)$ have?

Step 1: Determine the zeros

For $(x + 3)$, the zero is -3.

For $(x - 3)^2$, the distinct zero is 3.

For $(x - 1)^2$, the distinct zero is 1.

For $5x$, the zero is 0.

The four distinct zeros are $-3, 0, 1,$ and 3.

The correct answer is **4**.

*Type the polynomial in the Desmos graphing calculator and count the distinct zeros. Above may be quicker.

Example 3:

x	$h(x)$
-1	0
0	-3
2	2
3	0

In the above table, selected values of x and their corresponding values of $h(x)$ are given for the function h, where $y = h(x)$. What x-intercepts of the function h are given in the table?

A) $\{-3\}$
B) $\{-1, 2\}$
C) $\{-1, 3\}$
D) $\{0, 3\}$

Step 1: Determine the values of x where $y = 0$

At the x-intercept, $y = h(x) = 0$. In the table, look for x-values where $h(x) = 0$.

$$x = -1 \text{ and } 3$$

The correct answer choice is **C**.

Category 25 – Practice Questions

1

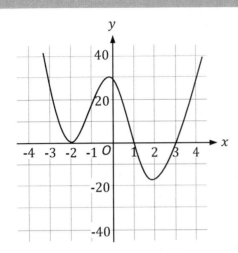

In the xy-plane, the graph of the function f, where $y = f(x)$, is shown above. Which of the following defines the function f?

A) $f(x) = (x + 3)(x + 1)(x - 2)$
B) $f(x) = (x + 2)(x - 3)(x + 1)$
C) $f(x) = (x - 1)(x - 3)(x + 2)^2$
D) $f(x) = (x + 3)(x - 2)^2(x + 1)^2$

2

x	$f(x)$
-2	0
0	-8
4	-2
8	0
0	16

In the above table, selected values of x and their corresponding values of $y = f(x)$ are given for the function f. What are the given zeros of function f?

A) $\{-8, 16\}$
B) $\{-8, 8\}$
C) $\{-2, 4\}$
D) $\{-2, 8\}$

3 Desmos

$$x(x - 1)(x - 3)(x + 2)^2$$

The factors of a polynomial $p(x)$ are shown above. Which of the following are the distinct zeros of $p(x)$?

A) $\{-2, 1, 3\}$
B) $\{-2, 0, 1, 3\}$
C) $\{-2, 1, 2, 3\}$
D) $\{0, 1, 2, 3\}$

4 Desmos

$$p(x) = (x - 4)(x^2 - 4)$$

A polynomial function p is shown above. How many distinct zeros does the function p have?

A) 1
B) 2
C) 3
D) 5

5

x	$h(x)$
10	0
4	3
2	0
0	-8
5	0
0	-1

In the above table, all the values of a polynomial $h(x)$ are given, where $y = h(x)$. What is the product of the zeros of $h(x)$?

Category 26 – Graph Transformations of Polynomial Functions

Key Points

- A horizontal (left or right) translation of a polynomial graph shifts the graph along the x-axis. A vertical (up or down) translation of a polynomial graph shifts the graph along the y-axis.
    - A horizonal translation of the graph of $f(x)$ by c units to the right can be written as $f(x-c)$ and c units to the left can be written as $f(x+c)$.
    - A vertical translation of the graph of $f(x)$ by c units up can be written as $f(x)+c$ and c units down can be written as $f(x)-c$.
    - See examples below for the translation of the graph of $f(x) = (x-1)(x+1)(x+4)$ by c units.
        - c units right: $f(x-c) = (x-1-c)(x+1-c)(x+4-c)$.
        - c units left: $f(x+c) = (x-1+c)(x+1+c)(x+4+c)$.
        - c units up: $f(x)+c = (x-1)(x+1)(x+4)+c$.
        - c units down: $f(x)-c = (x-1)(x+1)(x+4)-c$.

How to Solve

* The Desmos graphing calculator can also be used to determine the y-intercept and zeros of a translated graph.

Example 1:

The graph of $y = f(x)$ is defined by $f(x) = (x-6)(x-2.5)(x+5.5)$. The graph of $y = g(x)$ is a result of translation of the graph of the function f right 3.5 units in the xy-plane. Which equation defines function g?

A) $g(x) = (x-9.5)(x-6)(x+2)$
B) $g(x) = (x-2.5)(x+1)(x+3)$
C) $g(x) = (x-4.5)(x-5.5)(x+2)$
D) $g(x) = (x+2)(x+1)(x+8)$

Step 1: Determine the translation

Subtract 3.5 units from each value of x.

$$g(x) = f(x-3.5) = (x-3.5-6)(x-3.5-2.5)(x-3.5+5.5) =$$
$$(x-9.5)(x-6)(x+2)$$

The correct answer choice is **A**.

*Desmos Graphing Calculator Solution

In Desmos, there is no need to subtract 3.5 from x-values. The function $g(x)$ can be written as $g(x) = f(x-3.5)$. Type the definition of function f. In the next row, type $g(x) = f(x-3.5)$. Read the zeros of the function g and match to the factors given in the answer choices. See below a partial graph of $g(x)$. Graph of $f(x)$ is not shown. The zeros are -2, 6, and 9.5. The corresponding factors are $(x+2)$, $(x-6)$, and $(x-9.5)$, respectively.

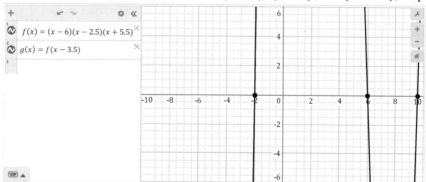

Digital SAT Math Manual and Workbook

Category 26 – Practice Questions

1 — Desmos

$$f(x) = (x+2)(x-1)(x-4)$$

The function f is defined above. Which table of values represents $y = f(x+2)$?

A)

x	y
-2	0
-1	-10
2	-8

B)

x	y
-2	0
1	10
2	8

C)

x	y
-4	0
-2	8
1	-10

D)

x	y
-4	0
2	8
3	10

2 — Desmos

$$f(x) = (2x-3)(x+7)(x+8)^2$$

The function f is defined above. In the xy-plane, the graph of $y = g(x)$ is a result of translating the graph of $y = f(x)$ right 7 units. Which of the following defines function g?

A) $g(x) = x(2x+4)(x+1)^2$

B) $g(x) = x(2x-17)(x+1)^2$

C) $g(x) = (2x-7)(x+14)(x-7)^2$

D) $g(x) = (2x+4)(x+14)(x+15)^2$

3 — Desmos

The function g is defined by $g(x) = (x-5)(x-1)(x+8)$. The graph of $y = f(x)$ is a result of translating the graph of $y = g(x)$ down 12 units in the xy-plane. What is the value of $f(0)$?

Category 27 – Remainders in Polynomial Functions

Key Points

- **Remainder Theorem**: When a polynomial is divided by a linear expression $x - n$, where n is a real number, the remainder can be determined by substituting $x = n$ in the polynomial. For example, for a polynomial function $p(x) = ax^3 + bx + c$, the remainder is $p(n) = an^3 + bn + c$.
- **Factor Theorem**: When a polynomial is divided by a linear expression $x - n$, where n is a real number, and the remainder obtained by substituting $x = n$ in the polynomial is 0, then n is a zero and $x - n$ is a factor of the polynomial. For example, for a polynomial function $p(x) = ax^3 + bx + c$, if $p(n) = an^2 + bn + c = 0$, then $x - n$ is a factor of $p(x)$.

How to Solve

Remember that when a polynomial is divided by $x - n$, then $x = n$, and when a polynomial is divided by $x + n$, then $x = -n$.

*Several questions on remainder theorem can be solved using the Desmos graphing calculator.

*Example 1:

$$f(x) = 5x^2 + 15x + 11$$

What is the reminder when the above polynomial $f(x)$ is divided by $x + 2$?

A) −2
B) 1
C) 2
D) 5

Step 1: Plug in the value of x in the equation

Since the polynomial is divided by $x + 2$, $x = -2$. Plug in $x = -2$ to determine the remainder.

$$f(-2) = (5 \times (-2)^2) + (15 \times (-2)) + 11 = (5 \times 4) + (-30) + 11 = 20 - 30 + 11 = 1$$

The correct answer choice is **B**.

*Desmos Graphing Calculator Solution

Type the definition of the function f. In the next row, type what must be solved. In this example, $f(-2) = $ remainder is to be solved. Typing this will display its value to the right in the same row. See below.

The value of $f(-2)$ is displayed as $= 1$. Hence, the remainder is 1.

Desmos graphing calculator will also display the graph (not shown in the figure below). However, it is irrelevant to solving this question.

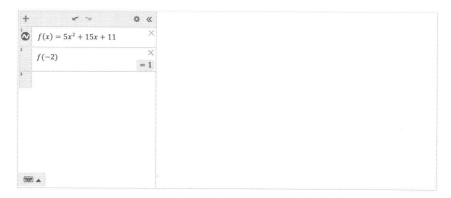

Example 2:

What is the value of B in the equation $\frac{2x^3 - 7x + 8}{x-1} = 2x - 1 + \frac{B}{x-1}$, where B is a constant?

Step 1: Plug in the value of x in the equation

The equation can be read as: when $2x^3 - 7x + 8$ is divided by $x - 1$, the quotient is $2x - 1$ and remainder is B.

Plug in $x = 1$ in the expression $2x^3 - 7x + 8$ to determine the remainder B.

$$B = 2(1)^3 - 7(1) + 8 = 2 - 7 + 8 = 3$$

The correct answer is **3**.

Desmos Graphing Calculator Solution

Type the polynomial equation $2x^3 - 7x + 8$ as a polynomial function $p(x) = 2x^3 - 7x + 8$. In the next row, type what must be solved. In this example, $p(1) = $ remainder $= B$ is to be solved. Typing this will display its value to the right in the same row. See below.

The value of $p(1)$ is displayed as $= 3$. Hence, the remainder $= B$ is 3.

Desmos graphing calculator will also display the graph (not shown in the figure below). However, it is irrelevant to solving this question.

Example 3:

$$p(x) = x^3 + x^2 - ax + 6$$

In the above polynomial $p(x)$, what is the value of a, where a is a constant and $x - 2$ is a factor of $p(x)$?

Step 1: Plug in the value of x in the equation and set the equation to 0

Since $x - 2$ is a factor of the polynomial, the reminder for $x = 2$ is 0.

$$p(2) = 2^3 + 2^2 - 2a + 6 = 0 \rightarrow$$
$$8 + 4 - 2a + 6 = 0 \rightarrow 18 - 2a = 0 \rightarrow 2a = 18 \rightarrow a = 9$$

The correct answer is **9**.

* This question can be solved using the slider feature of the Desmos graphing calculator. This requires careful manipulation. Students proficient with this feature can try it out.

Category 27 – Practice Questions

1 — Desmos

$$p(x) = 3x^3 - 3x^2 - cx + 2$$

One of the factors of the polynomial $p(x)$ shown above is $x - 2$. What is the value of the constant c?

A) 2
B) 7
C) 8
D) 15

2 — Desmos

$$\frac{2x^2 + 9x + 5}{x + 4} = 2x + 1 + \frac{A}{x + 4}$$

In the above equation, what is the value of the constant A?

A) -4
B) -2
C) 1
D) 4

3 — Desmos

When the polynomial $p(x)$ is divided by $(x - 1)$, the remainder is 0. Which of the following could define function p?

A) $p(x) = -2x^2 - 3x + 5$
B) $p(x) = -x^2 - x + 1$
C) $p(x) = x^2 + x - 1$
D) $p(x) = 2x^2 + x - 1$

4

For a polynomial $p(x)$, if $p\left(-\frac{1}{2}\right) = 0$, which of the following must be true?

A) $x - 1$ is a factor of $p(x)$
B) $x + 2$ is a factor of $p(x)$
C) $2x - 1$ is a factor of $p(x)$
D) $2x + 1$ is a factor of $p(x)$

5 — Desmos

Which of the following is a factor of the polynomial $p(x) = 3x^3 - x^2 - 6x + 2$?

A) $x - 1$
B) $3x - 1$
C) $2x + 1$
D) $2x + 3$

6

For a polynomial $p(x)$, if $p(-5) = 4$, which of the following must be true?

A) $x = -4$ is a zero of $p(x)$
B) $x = 4$ is a zero of $p(x)$
C) $x - 5$ is a factor of $p(x)$
D) $x + 5$ is not a factor of $p(x)$

7 — Desmos

$$f(x) = 3x^3 + 8x^2 + 11$$

What is the reminder when the function defined above is divided by $(x + 3)$?

Category 28 – Undefined Functions

Key Points
- A function or a numeric expression is undefined when the denominator equals 0.

How to Solve

Set the expression in the denominator equal to 0 and solve.

*All questions in this category can be solved using the Desmos graphing calculator. Type the expression from the denominator in the Desmos graphing calculator. Set the expression equal to 0, and determine the value(s) of the variable.

Example 1:

$$\frac{5x^2 - x}{2(4x - 8)}$$

For what value of x is the above expression undefined?

A) 1
B) 2
C) 3
D) 8

Step 1: Set the denominator to 0

$$2(4x - 8) = 0$$

Step 2: Solve

$$4x - 8 = 0 \rightarrow 4x = 8 \rightarrow x = 2$$

The correct answer choice is **B**.

Example 2:

$$f(x) = \frac{6}{x^2 - 6x + 9}$$

For what value of x is the above function f undefined?

A) −3
B) −2
C) 0
D) 3

Step 1: Set the denominator to 0

$$x^2 - 6x + 9 = 0$$

Step 2: Solve

Factor.

$$(x - 3)(x - 3) = 0 \rightarrow x = 3$$

The correct answer choice is **D**.

Category 28 – Practice Questions

1 Desmos

$$\frac{5x^3 + 11x}{6x + 2x + 16}$$

For what value of x is the above expression undefined?

A) -2
B) 0
C) 2
D) 5

2 Desmos

For what value of x is the expression $\frac{2x+4x+9}{3x-12}$ undefined?

A) 1
B) 2
C) 4
D) 6

3 Desmos

$$f(x) = \frac{8x + 8}{(x^2 - 11x + 27) + (x - 2)}$$

The function f shown above is undefined. What is value of x?

A) -2
B) 0
C) 3
D) 5

4 Desmos

$$\frac{(x-4)^2}{(x+4)^2 - (16x+1)}$$

For what values of x is the above expression undefined?

I. -4
II. 3
III. 5

A) I only
B) II only
C) I and II only
D) II and III only

Digital SAT Math Manual and Workbook

Section 5 – Review Questions

1

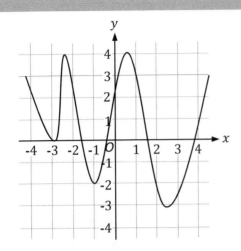

The complete graph of the function t in the xy-plane is shown above, where $y = t(x)$. If $g(m) = t(-1)$, how many distinct values of m define $y = g(m)$?

A) 3
B) 4
C) 5
D) 6

2 — Desmos

$$g(x) = (x-1)(2x-3)(3x+2)$$

The function g is defined above. Which of the following is NOT an x-intercept on the graph of the function g in the xy-plane?

I. 1
II. $\frac{2}{3}$
III. $\frac{3}{2}$

A) I only
B) II only
C) III only
D) I and III only

3

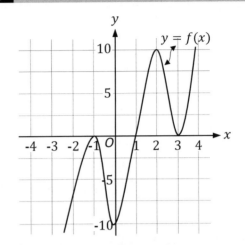

In the xy-plane, which of the following could define the graph of the polynomial $f(x)$ shown above?

A) $f(x) = (x-1)(x-3)^2(x+1)^2$
B) $f(x) = (x-1)(x+1)^2(x+3)^2$
C) $f(x) = (x+1)(x-3)^2(x-1)^2$
D) $f(x) = (x+1)(x+3)^2(x-1)^2$

4

$$y = 2x(x-k)^2(x+k)^2$$

How many distinct zeros does the graph of the above equation have in the xy-plane, where k is a constant?

A) 1
B) 2
C) 3
D) 5

5 — Desmos

$$g(x) = 3x - 6$$

In the xy-plane, the graph of the function g is defined by the equation above. Which of the following is an x-intercept of the graph, where $y = g(x)$?

A) $(-3, g(-3))$
B) $(0, g(0))$
C) $(2, g(0))$
D) $(2, g(2))$

6 — Desmos

The function f is defined by $f(x) = 3x - 10$, and the function g is defined by $g(x) = 2f(x + 2) - 5$. What is the value of $g(8)$?

A) 15
B) 23
C) 35
D) 40

7 — Desmos

$$g(x) = (x - 3)(x - 8)(x + 1)$$

The function g is defined above. In the xy-plane, the graph of the function f is a result of translating the graph of the function g left 3 units. The graph of $y = f(x)$ has x-intercepts at $(a, 0)$, $(b, 0)$, and $(c, 0)$, where a, b, and c are constants. What is the value of $a + b + c$?

A) -21
B) -3
C) 1
D) 3

8 — Desmos

The function f is defined by $f(x) = \dfrac{17.8x^2 + b}{3}$. A function g satisfies $g(b) = 10$. For what value of b does $f(g(b)) = 600$, where b is a constant?

9

For the function f, if $2f(x) = f(x + 2)$ for all values of x and $f(5) = 8$, what is the value of $f(3)$?

10 — Desmos

The function f is defined by the equation $f(x) = x^4 - 21$, What is the value of $f(-3)$?

11

For a polynomial $p(x)$, $p\left(-\dfrac{2}{3}\right) = 0$. Which of the following must be a factor of $p(x)$?

A) $x - 3$
B) $x + 2$
C) $3x - 2$
D) $3x + 2$

12

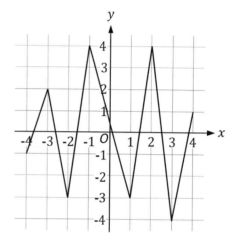

In the xy-plane, the graph of the function h is shown above, where $y = h(x)$. If $h(t) = h(2)$, which of the following could be a value of t?

A) -1
B) 0
C) 1
D) 3

13 — Desmos

$$p(x) = 5x^3 + 8x^2 - 3x + 2$$

Which of the following could be a zero of the above polynomial function p?

A) -3
B) -2
C) 1
D) 5

Digital SAT Math Manual and Workbook

14 Desmos

$$f(x) = 2x(x-8)(x+9)^2$$

The function f is defined above. What is the sum of all possible values of x for $f(5-c) = 0$, where c is a constant?

A) 5
B) 11
C) 16
D) 30

15

x	-6	-3	0	2
f	-4	-2	-1	0

The table above shows selected (x, y) values on the graph of the function f. Which of the following is a factor of $f(x)$?

A) $x - 1$
B) $x - 2$
C) $x + 1$
D) $x + 2$

16

x	$f(x)$	$g(x)$
-2	9	-1
0	6	2
1	2	5
4	1	-2
5	-3	4

The table above shows selected values of x and their corresponding values of $y = f(x)$ and $y = g(x)$. If $f(g(4)) - g(f(4)) = k$, what is the value of the constant k?

A) 4
B) 5
C) 9
D) 14

17 Desmos

$$p(x) = x^3 - 7x + 3$$

What is the remainder when the polynomial $p(x)$ shown above is divided by $x - 3$?

A) -2
B) -1
C) 0
D) 9

18 Desmos

$$\frac{3x^2 + 2x + 5}{(x^2 - x - 9) + 3(x - 2)}$$

For what value(s) of x is the above expression undefined?

A) -3
B) 2
C) -5 and 3
D) -2 and 9

19 Desmos

$$g(x) = (0.2x + 1)(x - 4)$$

For the function g defined above, what is the value of $g(24)$?

20 Desmos

The function h is defined by $h(x) = ax^2 + ax + 4$, where a is a constant. If $h(2) = 10$, what is the value of $h(3)$?

21 Desmos

The function f is defined by $f(x) = 9x - 1$, and the function h is defined by $h(x) = 5x + 2$. For what value of x does $f(x) - h(x) = 9$?

Section 6 – Quadratic Equations and Parabola

Category 29 – Quadratic Equations and Factors
Category 30 – Quadratic Equations and Number of Roots
Category 31 – Sum and Product of Quadratic Roots
Category 32 – Standard Form Equation of a Parabola
Category 33 – Vertex Form Equation of a Parabola
Category 34 – Factored Form Equation of a Parabola
Category 35 – Equivalent Equations of a Parabola
Category 36 – Parabola Intersections and System of Equations
Category 37 – Graph Transformations of a Parabola
Category 38 – Equivalent Quadratic Expressions
Section 6 – Review Questions

Category 29 – Quadratic Equations and Factors

Key Points

- The standard form of a quadratic equation is $y = ax^2 + bx + c$, where a, b, and c are constants. a and b are also known as coefficients of x^2 and x, respectively. The highest power of x in a quadratic equation is 2.
  - The roots of a quadratic equation in the standard form are the values of x when $y = 0$.
  - On a graph, roots are the value of x where the graph intersects the x-axis. At this point, $y = 0$.
  - The roots are also known as the solutions, zeros, and x-intercepts.
  - A quadratic equation written in the form $ax^2 + bx + c = 0$ can be factored to solve for the roots. For example, the factors of the equation $x^2 - 3x - 10 = 0$ are $(x + 1)$ and $(x - 4)$, and the corresponding roots are -1 and 4, respectively,
  - When $a = 1$, the value of c is the product of the two roots of the quadratic equation.
- The roots of a quadratic equation can also be determined using the quadratic formula $\frac{-b \pm \sqrt{b^2 - 4ac}}{2a}$.
- Equations in the form $ax^{2(n)} + bx^{(n)} + c = 0$, where n is a positive number, can be solved as quadratic equations. For example, $x^6 - 7x^3 - 8 = 0$ can be rewritten as $x^{2(3)} - 7x^{(3)} - 8 = 0 \rightarrow x^2 - 7x - 8 = 0$ and factored. Each x^3 unit is represented as x in the quadratic equivalent. Hence, each value of x obtained by factoring $x^2 - 7x - 8 = 0$ is for x^3. The solutions to the given equation are their cube root value.

How to Solve

Use the quadratic formula when factoring is not straightforward or when the answer choices include a square root. Factoring is quicker when $a = 1$ and there are factors of c that add up to the value of b.

Rearrange the quadratic equation before factoring, if needed. For example, $2x^2 - 6x = -4 \rightarrow 2x^2 - 6x + 4 = 0$.

A common multiple in a quadratic equation can be removed to simplify the equation before factoring. For example, $2x^2 - 6x + 4 = 0 \rightarrow 2(x^2 - 3x + 2) = 0 \rightarrow x^2 - 3x + 2 = 0$.

*Several questions in this category can be solved using the Desmos graphing calculator. Rearranging or simplifying an equation is not required. When answer choices are given as fractions or square roots, type them in Desmos, one at a time, to convert to a decimal and match.

*Example 1:
What is the positive solution to the equation $x^2 - 3x - 10 = 0$?

Step 1: Determine the factors

$a = 1, b = -3, c = -10$.

-5 and 2 multiply to -10 (value of c) and add to -3 (value of b). Hence, the two factors of the equation are $(x + 2)$ and $(x - 5)$.

$$(x + 2)(x - 5) = 0$$

Step 2: Determine the roots

Each factor equates to 0.

$$(x + 2) = 0 \rightarrow x = -2$$
$$(x - 5) = 0 \rightarrow x = 5$$

The two roots are -2 and 5. The question asks for a positive solution. The positive root is 5.

The correct answer is **5**.

*Desmos Graphing Calculator Solution

Type the equation and read the values of x where the graph intersects the x-axis. See below. $x = -2$ and 5.

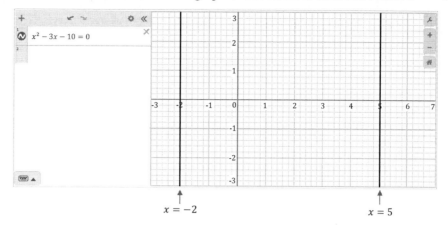

*Example 2:

Which of the following are the roots of the equation $5x^2 - 5x - 1 = 0$?

A) $\dfrac{5 \pm \sqrt{4}}{5}$

B) $\dfrac{5 \pm 5\sqrt{5}}{10}$

C) $\dfrac{5 \pm 3\sqrt{5}}{10}$

D) $\dfrac{5 \pm \sqrt{5}}{10}$

Step 1: Determine the roots using the quadratic formula

$a = 5, b = -5, c = -1$.

$$\dfrac{-(-5) \pm \sqrt{(-5)^2 - (4 \times 5 \times -1)}}{2 \times 5} \to \dfrac{5 \pm \sqrt{25 + 20}}{10} \to \dfrac{5 \pm \sqrt{45}}{10}$$

Since none of the answer choices have $\sqrt{45}$, simplify it further. Look for a factor of 45 that is a perfect square.

$$\dfrac{5 \pm \sqrt{5 \times 9}}{10} \to \dfrac{5 \pm (\sqrt{5} \times \sqrt{9})}{10} \to \dfrac{5 \pm 3\sqrt{5}}{10}$$

The correct answer choice is **C**.

*Type the equation and read the values of x where the graph intersects the x-axis. Since the Desmos graphing calculator displays values as decimals, type each square root answer choice in Desmos to convert to decimal and match.

*Example 3:

What is one possible solution to the equation $x^6 - 28x^3 + 27 = 0$?

Step 1: Determine the factors

Let $n = x^3$. The equation can be rewritten as $n^2 - 28n + 27 = 0$.

$a = 1, b = -28, c = 27$.

-1 and -27 multiply to 27 (value of c) and add to -28 (value of b). Hence, the factors are $(n - 1)$ and $(n - 27)$.

Step 2: Determine the roots

Substitute $n = x^3$ in each factor and equate to 0.

$$(x^3 - 1) = 0 \to x^3 = 1 \to x^3 = 1^3 \to x = 1$$
$$(x^3 - 27) = 0 \to x^3 = 27 \to x^3 = 3^3 \to x = 3$$

Hence, the two solutions are 1 and 3. Either could be entered as the correct answer.

The correct answer is **1** or **3**.

*Type the equation and read the values of x where the graph intersects the x-axis. Enter either value as correct answer.

Category 29 – Practice Questions

1 — Desmos

$$2x^2 + 6x - 80 = 0$$

Which of the following is a solution to the above equation?

A) -8
B) -5
C) 2
D) 3

2 — Desmos

$$x^2 - 7x + 12 = 0$$

What are the roots of the above equation?

A) $\{-3, 4\}$
B) $\{3, 4\}$
C) $\{2, 7\}$
D) $\{3, 8\}$

3 — Desmos

$$3x(x + 4) + 1 = 2x(x + 5) + 6$$

Which of the following is a solution to the equation above?

A) $-2 - \sqrt{6}$
B) $-2 - \sqrt{24}$
C) $-1 - \sqrt{2}$
D) $-1 - \sqrt{6}$

4 — Desmos

$$x^2 - 21 = 175$$

What is a solution to the above equation?

A) -14
B) -7
C) 4
D) 9

5 — Desmos

$$x^6 - 7x^3 - 8 = 0$$

Which of the following is a solution to the given equation?

A) 1
B) 2
C) 8
D) 21

6 — Desmos

$$2x^2 - 5x - 12 = 0$$

Which of the following are the factors of the given equation?

A) $(x - 2)(x + 2)$
B) $(x - 2)(x + 5)$
C) $(x - 4)(2x + 3)$
D) $(x + 4)(2x - 3)$

Digital SAT Math Manual and Workbook

Category 30 – Quadratic Equations and Number of Roots

Key Points
- A quadratic equation may have one, two, or no real solutions.
- From a quadratic equation in the form $ax^2 + bx + c = 0$, where a, b, and c are constants, the solutions (same as roots, zeros, and x-intercepts) can be determined using the quadratic formula $\frac{-b \pm \sqrt{b^2 - 4ac}}{2a}$.
- The expression $b^2 - 4ac$ of the quadratic formula is known as the discriminant.
  - $b^2 - 4ac > 0$ indicates two distinct real solutions for the quadratic equation.
  - $b^2 - 4ac = 0$ indicates one distinct real solution for the quadratic equation. (This happens when both the roots are the same.)
  - $b^2 - 4ac < 0$ indicates no real solution for the quadratic equation. (This happens when the values of the roots are negative square root. Negative square roots are not real numbers.)

How to Solve
*Several questions in this category can be solved using the Desmos graphing calculator. Type the equation and count the number of points where the corresponding graph intersects the x-axis.

Example 1:
$$5x^2 - 12x + 9 = 0$$
How many distinct real solutions does the given equation have?

A) Zero
B) Exactly one
C) Exactly two
D) Infinitely many

Step 1: Determine the number of solutions using the discriminant
$a = 5, b = -12, c = 9$.
Plug in the values in the discriminant.
$$b^2 - 4ac = (-12)^2 - (4 \times 5 \times 9) = 144 - 180 = -36$$
Since the discriminant < 0, the equation has no real solution.
The correct answer choice is **A**.

Example 2:
The equation $4x^2 - 12x + k = 0$ has one distinct real solution, where k is a constant. What is the value of k?

Step 1: Set the discriminant equal to 0
$a = 4$. $b = -12$. $c = k$.
Since the quadratic function has one solution, the discriminant equals 0.
Plug in the values in the discriminant and set it equal to 0.
$$b^2 - 4ac = 0 \rightarrow (-12)^2 - (4 \times 4 \times k) = 0 \rightarrow 144 - 16k = 0 \rightarrow 16k = 144 \rightarrow k = 9$$
The correct answer is **9**.

Category 30 – Practice Questions

Students comfortable with the slider feature can solve questions 3 and 4 using the Desmos graphing calculator

1 Desmos

$$3x^2 + 4x + 7 = 0$$

How many distinct real solutions does the above equation have?

A) Zero
B) Exactly one
C) Exactly two
D) Infinitely many

2

$$ax^2 + 6x + c = 0$$

The equation above has exactly one solution, and a and c are constants. Which of the following is the product of a and c?

A) -6
B) 1
C) 6
D) 9

3

$$ax^2 - 8x + 8 = 0$$

The equation above has exactly one solution. What is the value of a, where a is a constant?

4

$$4x^2 - 4x - k = 0$$

In the equation above, k is a constant. If the equation has no real solution, which of the following could be a possible value of k?

A) -2
B) -1
C) 0
D) 2

5 Desmos

$$7x^2 - 10x + 4 = 0$$

Which of the following must be true for the quadratic equation shown above?

A) The equation has exactly two real solutions.
B) The equation has exactly one real solution.
C) The equation has no real solution.
D) The equation has infinitely many solutions.

6 Desmos

Which quadratic equation has exactly one solution?

A) $3x^2 - 6x - 1 = 0$
B) $3x^2 - 6x + 16 = 0$
C) $9x^2 - 6x + 1 = 0$
D) $9x^2 + 6x + 15 = 0$

Digital SAT Math Manual and Workbook

Category 31 – Sum and Product of Quadratic Roots

Key Points
- From a quadratic equation in the form $ax^2 + bx + c = 0$, the sum and product of the roots (zeros, solutions, or x-intercepts) can be determined as follows:
  - The sum of the roots $= -\dfrac{b}{a}$.
  - The product of the roots $= \dfrac{c}{a}$.

How to Solve
If a question asks for the sum or product of the roots of a quadratic equation/function in the standard form, using the above formulas is the easiest approach. There is no need to solve roots by factoring.

*Questions in this category that ask for sum or product can be solved using the Desmos graphing calculator. Type the equation and read the solutions. Determine their sum/product, as needed. Using the above formulas may be quicker.

Example 1:
In the quadratic equation $4x^2 + 8x + 3 = 0$, what is the product of the roots?

Step 1: Use the product formula
$a = 4, c = 3$.

$$\frac{c}{a} = \frac{3}{4} = 0.75$$

The correct answer is $\dfrac{3}{4}$ or $\mathbf{0.75}$.

Example 2:
$$2x^2 + 9x + k = 0$$

The above equation has two distinct roots. If one of the roots is -5, which of the following is the other root, where k is a constant?

A) $\dfrac{1}{2}$

B) $\dfrac{3}{2}$

C) 2

D) 5

Step 1: Use the sum formula
$a = 2, b = 9$.

$$\text{sum of roots} = -\frac{b}{a} = -\frac{9}{2}$$

Step 2: Determine the second root
It is given that one of the roots $= -5$. Let the second root $= x$. Hence, sum of roots $= -5 + x$.
Equate this with the sum of roots from Step 1.

$$-5 + x = -\frac{9}{2} \quad \rightarrow \quad x = -\frac{9}{2} + 5 = \frac{1}{2}$$

The correct answer choice is **A**.

Category 31 – Practice Questions
Students comfortable with the slider feature can solve questions 2, 3, and 4 using the Desmos graphing calculator

1 — Desmos

$$2n^2 + 3n - 20 = 0$$

What is the product of all the values of n that satisfy the above equation?

A) -20
B) -10
C) 2
D) 3

2

$$2x^2 - 7x + k = 0$$

The above equation has two distinct roots. If one of the roots is 2, which of the following is the other root, where k is a constant?

A) $\frac{3}{2}$
B) $\frac{5}{2}$
C) $\frac{7}{2}$
D) 3

3

$$2x^2 - bx - 12 = 0$$

The two distinct roots of the given quadratic equation are m and n. Which of the following can be the possible values of m and n, where b is a constant?

A) $\{-2, -12\}$
B) $\{-2, -6\}$
C) $\{-1, 6\}$
D) $\{1, 6\}$

4

$$2x^2 - kx + 9 = 0$$

The above quadratic function has two distinct roots. One of the roots is 3. Which of the following is the other root, where k is a constant?

A) -3
B) -1
C) $\frac{3}{2}$
D) $\frac{3}{5}$

5 — Desmos

$$3x^2 + 13x + 5 = 0$$

In the above quadratic equation, if m is the product of the zeros and n is the sum of the zeros, what is $m - n$?

A) $\frac{3}{5}$
B) $\frac{5}{3}$
C) 4
D) 6

6 — Desmos

What is the sum of the solutions of the equation $3x^2 - 15x - 42 = 0$?

Digital SAT Math Manual and Workbook

Category 32 – Standard Form Equation of a Parabola

Key Points

- In the xy-plane, a quadratic function graphs a parabola (Fig. 1, Fig. 2, and Fig. 3).
- The standard form of a quadratic function is $f(x) = ax^2 + bx + c$, where a, b, and c are constants.
  - $f(x)$ is the value of y for a particular value of x on the graph of a parabola.
  - The constant c represents the y-coordinate of the y-intercept of the parabola.
- A parabola is shaped as an arc. It can open upward or downward.
  - If the value of a is positive, the parabola opens upward (Fig. 1).
  - If the value of a is negative, the parabola opens downward (Fig. 2).
  - The width of a parabola is determined by the value of a in an inverse relationship. The width increases when the value of a decreases and vice versa.
- The tip of a parabola is known as the vertex.
  - In a parabola opening downward, the y-coordinate of the vertex is the maximum value of the parabola.
  - In a parabola opening upward, the y-coordinate of the vertex is the minimum value of the parabola.
  - A straight vertical line passing through the vertex is known as the axis of symmetry. The axis of symmetry divides the parabola symmetrically into two equal halves.
  - From a standard form equation, the x-coordinate of the vertex can be determined as $-\frac{b}{2a}$.
- Two points on a parabola that have the same y-value are equidistant from the axis of symmetry. See points A and B in Fig. 2 below. The have the same y-value. The midpoint of their x-values is the x-coordinate of the vertex.
- A parabola may intersect the x-axis at zero, exactly one, or exactly two points. The point(s) where the parabola intersects the x-axis are known as the x-intercept(s) (same as root(s), solution(s), and zeros). See figures below.
  - When a parabola intersects the x-axis at two points, there are two x-intercepts and, hence, two real solutions (Fig. 1 and Fig. 2 below).
    The x-coordinate of the vertex is the midpoint of the two x-intercepts. Midpoint formula is $\frac{x_2+x_1}{2}$, where x_1 and x_2 are the two x-intercepts.
  - When a parabola touches the x-axis and curves back without crossing through the x-axis, there is one distinct x-intercept and, hence, one real solution (Fig. 3, top parabola).
  - When a parabola does not cross or touch the x-axis, there are no x-intercepts, hence, no real solutions. (Fig. 3, bottom parabola).

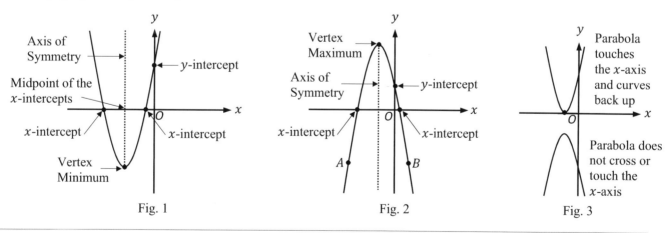

Fig. 1   Fig. 2   Fig. 3

How to Solve

*Several questions in this category can be solved using the Desmos graphing calculator.

Remember the following for questions regarding a ball or a similar object thrown in the air.
- When a ball is thrown up in the air from the ground (Fig. 1) or launched from a platform (Fig. 2), the movement of the ball in the air and back to the ground is a parabola. The time is along the x-axis, and the height is along the y-axis. This is the y-intercept of the parabola.
- When a ball is launched from the ground, the y-intercept is 0 (Fig. 1). When a ball is launched from a platform, the y-intercept is the height of the platform (Fig. 2).
- The maximum height of the ball in the air is the y-coordinate of the vertex.
- The time taken by the ball to reach the maximum height in the air is the x-coordinate of the vertex.
- The total time taken by the ball to reach the ground is the non-zero positive x-intercept.
- The time taken by the ball to reach a specific height can be determined by plugging in the given height as the value of y in the given equation and solving for x.

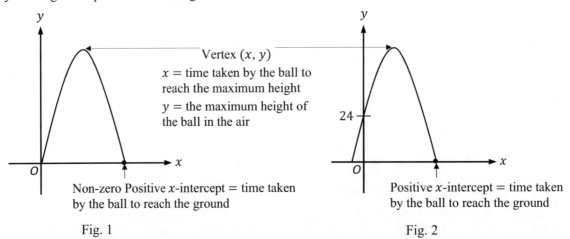

Fig. 1

Fig. 2

Example 1:

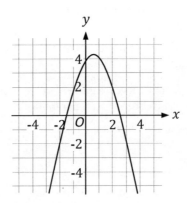

In the xy-plane, which of the following could be an equation of the above graph?

A) $y = -2x^2 + 3x + 2$
B) $y = -x^2 + x + 4$
C) $y = x^2 + 5x - 2$
D) $y = 2x^2 + 3x + 4$

Step 1: Determine if the parabola opens upward or downward
Since the parabola opens downward, a is negative. This eliminates answer choices C and D.

Step 2: Determine the y-intercept
The graph shows that the y-intercept is 4. This eliminates answer choice A.
The correct answer choice is **B**.

*Example 2:

$$y = 6x^2 + 12x + 4$$

In the xy-plane, the graph of the above equation is a parabola. Which of the following are the (x, y) coordinates of the vertex of the parabola?

A) $(-1, -2)$
B) $(-1, 2)$
C) $(2, 2)$
D) $(2, 4)$

Step 1: Determine the x-coordinate of the vertex

$a = 6, b = 12$.

$$-\frac{b}{2a} = -\frac{12}{2 \times 6} = -1$$

Hence, $x = -1$.
This eliminates answer choices C and D.

Step 2: Determine the y-coordinate of the vertex

Plug in $x = -1$ in the equation to get the value of y.

$$6(-1)^2 + 12(-1) + 4 = 6(1) + (-12) + 4 = 6 - 12 + 4 = -2$$

Hence, $y = -2$.
The correct answer choice is **A**.

*Desmos Graphing Calculator Solution

Type the equation and read the x- and y-coordinates of the vertex. See below.
x-coordinate $= -1$ and y-coordinate $= -2$. Hence, $(x, y) = (-1, -2)$.

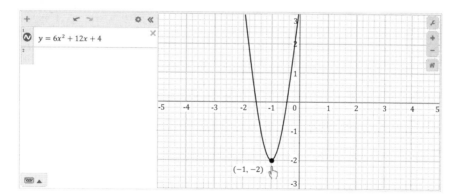

Example 3:

In the xy-plane, the graph of $y = f(x)$ is a parabola opening upwards and passing through the points $(-5, -33)$ and $(25, -33)$. For what value of x does the function f reaches its minimum?

Step 1: Determine the x-coordinate of the vertex

Since both the given points have the same y-value, they are equidistant from the midpoint of the parabola. The x-value of the midpoint is the x-coordinate of the vertex (the minimum/maximum x-value of a function). Hence,

$$\text{midpoint of } x = \frac{25 - 5}{2} = \frac{20}{2} = 10$$

The correct answer is **10**.

Digital SAT Math Manual and Workbook

Example 4:
$$h(t) = -16t^2 + 32t$$

The function h given above models the height of a ball, in feet, t seconds after it is thrown in the air from the ground. What is the maximum height, in feet, of the ball in the air, where $y = h(t)$?

Step 1: Determine the x-coordinate of the vertex

$a = -16, b = 32$.

$$-\frac{b}{2a} = -\frac{32}{2 \times (-16)} = -\frac{32}{-32} = 1$$

Step 2: Determine the y-coordinate of the vertex

Plug in $x = 1$ in the equation to get the value of y.

$$(-16(1 \times 1)) + (32 \times 1) = -16 + 32 = 16$$

The correct answer is **16**.

Desmos Graphing Calculator Solution

Type the equation and read the y-coordinate of the vertex. See below. The graph below is moved up to view the coordinates of the vertex.

y-coordinate $= 16$.

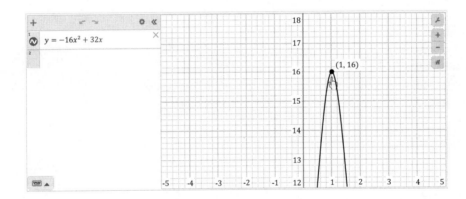

Category 32 – Practice Questions

1 — Desmos

A projectile is launched from a platform. The equation $h = -16t^2 + 81t + 9$ models the height h, in meters, of the projectile from the ground t seconds after launch. Which of the following is the height of the platform, in meters?

A) 2
B) 8
C) 9
D) 16

2

In the xy-plane, the graph of a parabola intersects the x-axis at -5 and 11. Which of the following is the x-coordinate of the vertex?

A) 3
B) 5
C) 6
D) 8

3 — Desmos

$$f(x) = x^2 - 8x + 17$$

The equation shown above graphs a parabola in the xy-plane. Which of the following (x, y) pair is the minimum value of the function f?

A) $(-1, 4)$
B) $(4, 1)$
C) $(4, 4)$
D) $(8, 17)$

4 — Desmos

$$y = -x^2 - 2x + 3$$

Which of the following is the graph of the above equation, in the xy-plane?

A)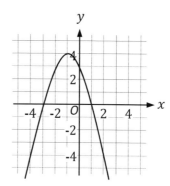

B)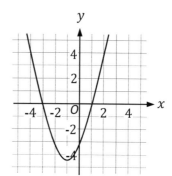

C)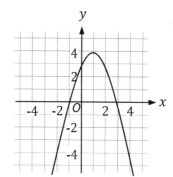

D)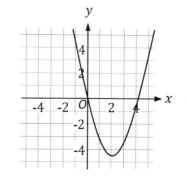

Digital SAT Math Manual and Workbook

5

$$h(t) = -16t^2 + 48t$$

The height of a ball, in feet, t seconds after it is thrown in the air from the ground is modeled by the above function h. According to the model, which of the following is the maximum height of the ball, in feet, in the air?

A) 16
B) 26
C) 32
D) 36

6

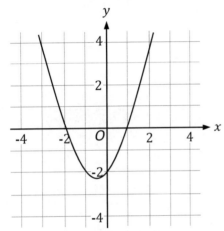

Which of the following could be an equation of the above graph, in the xy-plane?

A) $y = -x^2 + 4x + 2$
B) $y = -x^2 + x - 2$
C) $y = x^2 + x - 2$
D) $y = x^2 + 4x + 2$

7

$$h(t) = -16t^2 + 80t + 96$$

When an object is thrown in the air from 96-inch high platform, the height of the object in the air after t seconds can be determined by the function h shown above. After how many seconds does the object hit the ground?

8

$$f(x) = -\frac{1}{2}x^2 + 40x - 60$$

A shoe manufacturing company opened a new retail store in a certain shopping mall. The parabola graphed by the above equation models the company's opening day earnings, y, in dollars, as a function of the shoe price, x, in dollars, where $y = f(x)$. On the opening day, the maximum earnings of the company, in dollars, were for what shoe price, in dollars?

9

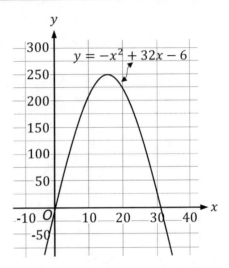

The daily profit, y, in dollars, of a bakery selling cakes for x dollars, can be modeled by the graph of the above parabola in the xy-plane. If the maximum daily profit of the bakery, in dollars, is p, what is the value of p based on the above model?

Category 33 – Vertex Form Equation of a Parabola

Key Points
- The vertex form of a quadratic function is $f(x) = a(x - h)^2 + k$, where $y = f(x)$, and the constants h and k are the x- and y-coordinates of the vertex, respectively.
    - Since h is the x-coordinate of the vertex, it is the midpoint of the two x-intercepts of a parabola.

How to Solve

The x- and y-coordinates of the vertex can be directly read from the vertex form equation as the values of (h, k). Remember that the value of h has the opposite sign than in $(x - h)^2$. For example, in $f(x) = a(x - 2)^2 + k$, $h = 2$, and in $f(x) = a(x + 2)^2 + k$, $h = -2$.

The y-intercept of the parabola can be determined by plugging in 0 for x in the given equation.

The value of a can be determined by plugging in any point from the graph in the given equation.

*Several questions in this category can be solved using the Desmos graphing calculator.

Example 1:

$$y = c(x + 2)^2 + 1$$

The equation above graphs a parabola passing through the point $(-1, 3)$ in the xy-plane, where $y = f(x)$. What is the value of c, where c is a constant?

A) -2
B) -1
C) 2
D) 3

Step 1: Plug in the given point

Plug in the given point $(-1, 3)$ in the equation and solve for c. (Note that a is represented as c in this example.)

$$3 = c(-1 + 2)^2 + 1 \rightarrow 3 = c(1)^2 + 1 \rightarrow 3 = c + 1 \rightarrow c = 2$$

The correct answer choice is **C**.

Example 2:

$$g(x) = -\frac{1}{4}(x - 8)^2 + 20$$

In the xy-plane, the graph of a parabola is defined by the function g given above, where $y = g(x)$. What is the y-coordinate of the y-intercept of the parabola?

Step 1: Determine the y-intercept

Plug in $x = 0$ in the equation and solve for y.

$$y = -\frac{1}{4}(0 - 8)^2 + 20 = -\frac{1}{4}(64) + 20 = -16 + 20 = 4$$

The correct answer is **4**.

*Type the equation in the Desmos graphing calculator and read the value of y at the y-intercept.

Example 3:

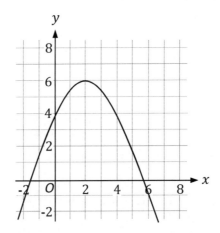

In the xy-plane, the above graph of the quadratic function P models the growth y, in thousands, of a certain species of insects for x days of exposure to a certain chemical compound.

Question 1

Which of the following could define P?

A) $P = -\frac{1}{2}(x - 2)^2 + 6$

B) $P = -\frac{1}{2}(x + 2)^2 + 6$

C) $P = \frac{1}{2}(x - 2)^2 + 6$

D) $P = \frac{1}{2}(x + 2)^2 + 4$

Step 1: Determine if the parabola opens upward or downward

Since the parabola opens downward, a is negative. This eliminates answer choices C and D.

Step 2: Determine the vertex from the graph

The vertex is at $(2, 6)$. Hence, $(x - h) = (x - 2)$ and $k = 6$. This eliminates answer choice B.

The correct answer choice is **A**.

Question 2

What is the maximum growth, in thousands, of the insects modeled by the function P?

Step 1: Determine the y-coordinate of the vertex from the graph

The growth is represented on the y-axis. Hence, the maximum growth is the y-coordinate of the vertex = 6.

The correct answer is **6**.

Category 33 – Practice Questions

Students comfortable with the slider feature can solve question 7 using the Desmos graphing calculator

1

$$h(x) = -a(x-s)^2 - t$$

The graph of the above function h is a parabola in the xy-plane, where $y = h(x)$, and a, s, and t are constants. Which of the following is true about the graph of the function h, where the maximum values of s and t appears as constants or coefficients?

A) The vertex is $(-s, -t)$, and the graph opens downward.

B) The vertex is $(s, -t)$, and the graph opens downward.

C) The vertex is $(-s, -t)$, and the graph opens upward.

D) The vertex is $(s, -t)$, and the graph opens upward.

2

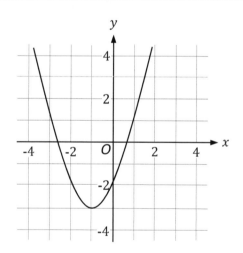

In the xy-plane, the graph of the above parabola is defined by $f(x) = a(x+b)^2 - 3$. What is the value of b, where a and b are constants?

A) -2
B) -1
C) 1
D) 2

3

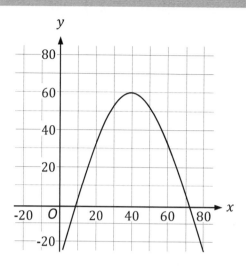

A travel agency in a certain metropolitan city sells city sightseeing tour packages. In the xy-plane, the above graph of the quadratic function T models the number of tour packages, y, the agency sells daily as a function of tour package price, x, in dollars. Which of the following could define function T?

A) $T(x) = -\frac{1}{16}(x-40)^2 + 60$

B) $T(x) = -\frac{1}{16}(x-60)^2 + 40$

C) $T(x) = -\frac{1}{16}(x+40)^2 + 60$

D) $T(x) = -\frac{1}{16}(x+60)^2 + 40$

4   Desmos

The graph of the function f, defined by $f(x) = (x-2)^2 - 4$, intersects the x-axis at points 0 and b, where b is a constant. What is the value of b?

Digital SAT Math Manual and Workbook

5

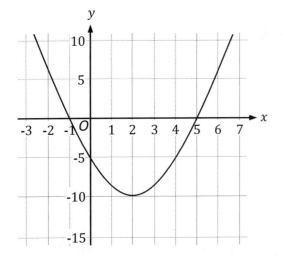

The graph of a parabola, in the xy-plane, is shown above. In which of the following (x, y) pairs, the minimum values of x and y appears as constants or coefficients?

A) $(-10, 2)$
B) $(0, -5)$
C) $(2, -5)$
D) $(2, -10)$

6   Desmos

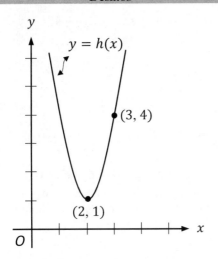

In the xy-plane, the graph of the function h is the parabola shown above. Which of the following could define function h, where $y = h(x)$?

A) $h(x) = (x - 2)^2 + 1$
B) $h(x) = 2(x - 2)^2 + 1$
C) $h(x) = 3(x - 2)^2 + 1$
D) $h(x) = (x + 2)^2 + 1$

7

In the xy-plane, the graph of function f is a parabola with vertex (h, k), where h and k are constants and $y = f(x)$. If $f(-5) = f(11)$, what is the value of h?

A) 3
B) 5
C) 6
D) 10

8

$$f(x) = k(x - 3)^2 - 6$$

In the xy-plane, the above function f graphs a parabola passing through the origin, where $y = f(x)$. What is the value of k, where k is a constant?

A) $\frac{2}{3}$
B) $\frac{5}{6}$
C) 2
D) 6

9   Desmos

$$p(x) = -(x - 4)^2 + 22$$

A retail store sells various brands of perfume. In the xy-plane, the parabola graphed by the function p defined above, models the quarterly profit, $p(x)$, of the retail store, in thousands of dollars, for the top selling perfume brand as a function of percent discount, x, offered on that brand. Based on the model, if q is the quarterly profit, in thousands of dollars, when no discount is offered, what is the value of q, where $y = p(x)$?

Category 34 – Factored Form Equation of a Parabola

Key Points

- The factored form of a quadratic function is $f(x) = a(x - r)(x - s)$, where $y = f(x)$, and the constants r and s are the x-intercepts of the parabola.
  - When a parabola does not intersect the x-axis, the quadratic function cannot be written in the factored form.
- The x-coordinate of the vertex is the midpoint of the two x-intercepts. It can be determined as $\frac{x_2+x_1}{2}$, where x_1 and x_2 are the two x-intercepts.

How to Solve

The x-coordinate of the vertex can be determined using the midpoint formula. The y-coordinate of the vertex can be determined by plugging the value of the x-coordinate of the vertex in the equation.

The y-intercept of the parabola can be determined by plugging in 0 for x in the given equation.

The value of a can be determined by plugging in any point from the graph in the given equation.

*Several questions in this category can be solved using the Desmos graphing calculator.

*Example 1:

$$f(x) = (x - 6)(x + 2)$$

The function f defined above graphs a parabola in the xy-plane, where $y = f(x)$. What are the (x, y) coordinates of the parabola vertex?

A) $(2, -2)$
B) $(2, -16)$
C) $(6, -2)$
D) $(16, -2)$

Step 1: Determine the x-coordinate of the vertex

The two x-intercepts from the equation are 6 and -2. Hence, the x-coordinate of the vertex is

$$\frac{6 + (-2)}{2} = \frac{4}{2} = 2$$

This eliminates answer choices C and D.

Step 2: Determine the y-coordinate of the vertex

Plug in $x = 2$ in the given equation to get the value of y.

$$y = (2 - 6)(2 + 2) = (-4)(4) = -16$$

The correct answer choice is **B**.

*Desmos Graphing Calculator Solution

Type the equation and read the coordinates of the vertex. See below.
$(x, y) = (2, -16)$.

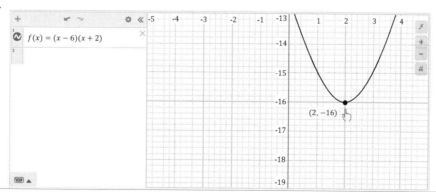

Digital SAT Math Manual and Workbook

Category 34 – Practice Questions

Students comfortable with the slider feature can solve question 4 using the Desmos graphing calculator

1 — Desmos

$$t(x) = -4(x-1)(x+1)$$

In the xy-plane, the graph of the function t defined above is a parabola. For which of the following values of (x, y) does the function $t(x)$ reach its maximum?

A) $(-4, 0)$
B) $(0, -4)$
C) $(0, 4)$
D) $(4, 4)$

2

$$g(x) = (x+15)(x-45)$$

For the function g defined above, which of the following is the distance between the two x-intercepts of $y = g(x)$ in the xy-plane?

A) 15
B) 20
C) 30
D) 60

3 — Desmos

$$f(x) = -3(x-5)(x-7)$$

The quadratic function f defined above models a company's annual profit, y, in millions of dollars, as a function of the product price, x, in dollars, where $y = f(x)$. Which of the following is the maximum annual profit of the company, in millions of dollars, based on the model?

A) 3
B) 5
C) 12
D) 35

4

In the xy-plane, the vertex of a parabola is $(-2, -16)$. The graph of the parabola is defined by $f(x) = (x+n)(x+6)$, where n is a constant and $y = f(x)$. Which is the value of n, where n is a real number?

A) -6
B) -2
C) 2
D) 8

5

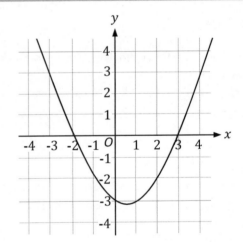

In the xy-plane, the graph of a parabola is shown above. If the equation of the parabola is written in the form $f(x) = k(x+m)(x+n)$, where $k, m,$ and n are constants, what is the value of k?

A) -2
B) -3
C) $\frac{1}{2}$
D) $\frac{2}{3}$

Digital SAT Math Manual and Workbook

Category 35 – Equivalent Equations of a Parabola

Key Points
- Equivalent forms of a quadratic function graph the same parabola. The equivalent equations are interchangeable. For example, the vertex form of the quadratic function $f(x) = (x - 3)^2 - 11$, and the standard form of the quadratic function $f(x) = x^2 - 6x - 2$ are equivalent. See below.

$$f(x) = (x - 3)^2 - 11 = (x - 3)(x - 3) - 11 = x^2 - 6x + 9 - 11 = x^2 - 6x - 2$$

  Similarly, the standard form $f(x) = x^2 + 2x - 24$ and factored form $f(x) = (x - 4)(x + 6)$ represent the same parabola.
- The value of a is same in the equivalent forms of a quadratic function.

How to Solve

It is helpful to remember that the easiest approach to match a given standard form to a vertex form or a factored form in the answer choices is to determine the x-coordinate of the vertex from the given standard form using $-\frac{b}{2a}$. Match this value of x to the midpoint of the two factors in a factored form and value of h in a vertex form.

*Several questions in this category can be solved using the Desmos graphing calculator. Type the given equation. In the next row, enter the equation from each answer choice, one at a time, and determine which equation from the answer choice graphs the same parabola.

Example 1:
$$f(x) = 2x^2 + 4x - 1$$

In the xy-plane, the graph of the above function f is a parabola, where $y = f(x)$. Which of the following is an equivalent equation where the minimum values of x and y appear as constants or coefficients?

A) $f(x) = (x + 1)^2 - 3$
B) $f(x) = 2(x - 2)^2 - 3$
C) $f(x) = 2(x + 1)^2 - 4$
D) $f(x) = 2(x + 1)^2 - 3$

Step 1: Determine the x-coordinate of the vertex

$a = 2, b = 4$.

$$-\frac{b}{2a} = -\frac{4}{(2 \times 2)} = -1$$

Since $x = -1$, $(x - h) = (x - (-1)) = (x + 1)$. This eliminates answer choice B.

Since $a = 2$ in the standard form equation, the equivalent vertex form equation will also have $a = 2$. This eliminates answer choice A.

(Note that after the process of elimination, the value of y may be apparent or solved using the mental math.)

Step 2: Determine the y-coordinate of the vertex

Plug in $x = -1$ in the equation to get the value of y.

$$y = 2(-1)^2 + (4 \times -1) - 1 = 2 - 4 - 1 = -3$$

This eliminates answer choice C which has the y-coordinate of the vertex $= -4$.

The correct answer choice is **D**.

* Type the given equation. This will graph the corresponding parabola. In the next row, type the equation from each answer choice, one at a time, and match the resulting parabola with the parabola of the given equation.

Category 35 – Practice Questions
Students comfortable with the slider feature can solve question 6 using the Desmos graphing calculator

1 — Desmos

$$f(x) = x^2 + 6x + 13$$

In the xy-plane, the parabola of the function f is defined by the above equation, where $y = f(x)$. Which of the following is an equivalent form of the function f where the minimum values of x and y appear as constants?

A) $f(x) = (x - 3)^2 - 4$
B) $f(x) = (x - 4)^2 + 7$
C) $f(x) = (x + 3)^2 + 4$
D) $f(x) = (x + 3)^2 + 13$

2 — Desmos

$$y = 0.5x^2 + 4x + 1$$

The graph of the above equation is a parabola in the xy-plane. Which of the following equivalent equations includes the x- and y-coordinates of the vertex as constants or coefficients?

A) $y = 0.5(x - 4)^2 + 1$
B) $y = 0.5(x + 4)^2 - 7$
C) $y = (x + 2)^2 + 12$
D) $y = 2(x + 4)^2 + 1$

3 — Desmos

$$y = 1.25x^2 + 7.5x + 1$$

Which of the following equivalent forms of the above equation includes the minimum values of x and y as constants or coefficients?

A) $y = 0.5(x - 3)^2 + 1$
B) $y = 1.25(x - 3)^2 + 8.75$
C) $y = 1.25(x + 3)^2 - 6.5$
D) $y = 1.25(x + 3)^2 - 10.25$

4

$$g(x) = -2(x + 2)^2 + 1$$

In the xy-plane, the graph of the above function g is a parabola. If the equation of the function g is written in the form $g(x) = ax^2 + bx + c$ where a, b, and c are constants and $y = g(x)$, which of the following equations could represent the function g?

A) $g(x) = -ax^2 - bx - 7$
B) $g(x) = -ax^2 + bx + 1$
C) $g(x) = -ax^2 - bx + 1$
D) $g(x) = ax^2 + bx - 7$

5 — Desmos

The function f is defined by $f(x) = -(x - 7)(x + 2)$, where $y = f(x)$. In which of the following equivalent equations do the minimum values of x and y appear as constants or coefficients?

A) $f(x) = -(x - 2)^2 - 2.5$
B) $f(x) = -(x - 2.5)^2 - 14$
C) $f(x) = -(x - 2.5)^2 + 20.25$
D) $f(x) = (x - 2.5)^2 - 20$

6

The expression $x^2 - 24x - 112$ can be rewritten as $(x + 2r)(x - 2s)$, where r and s are constants. What is the value of $s - r$?

Digital SAT Math Manual and Workbook

Category 36 – Parabola Intersections and Systems of Equations

Key Points
- The graphs of a vertical parabola and a line may intersect at zero, one or two points.
  - A vertical line intersects the parabola at one point (Fig. 1).
  - A horizontal line may intersect the parabola at one or two distinct points (Fig. 2 and Fig. 3).

  A horizontal line that touches the parabola at the vertex without passing through it is a line tangent to the vertex (Fig. 2). The y-value of the linear equation and y-coordinate of the vertex of the parabola are the same at this point. For example, if the equation of the horizontal line is $y = 8$, then the y-coordinate of the parabola $= 8$.
  - A slanting line may intersect the parabola at one or two distinct points (Fig. 4 and Fig. 5). A slanting line is tangent to the parabola when it touches the parabola at one point without passing through it (Fig. 4).
- The graphs of two vertical parabolas may intersect at exactly one or two points.
  - When two vertical parabolas intersect at one point, they intersect at the vertex (Fig. 6).
- The equations of an intersecting parabola and a line, or the equations of two intersecting parabolas, comprise a system of equations. The number of solutions and intersection point(s) (x, y) of the system can be determined by equating the two equations to form one quadratic equation in the form $ax^2 + bx + c = 0$.
  - The number of solutions to the system can be determined by evaluating the discriminant $b^2 - 4ac$.
    - $b^2 - 4ac > 0$ indicates two distinct real solutions.
    - $b^2 - 4ac = 0$ indicates one distinct real solution.
    - $b^2 - 4ac < 0$ indicates no real solution.
  - The point(s) of intersection can be determined by solving the quadratic equation for x and y.

Fig. 1

Fig. 2

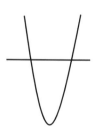
Fig. 3

Fig. 4

Fig. 5

Fig. 6

How to Solve

The equations in a system must be set to y before they can be equated. For example, $y + 2x = 5x^2 - 1$ must be converted to $y = 5x^2 - 2x - 1$ and $-2y = 4x - 1$ must be converted to $y = -2x + \frac{1}{2}$.

*Several questions in this category can be solved using the Desmos graphing calculator. The conversion mentioned above is not required when using Desmos.

*Example 1:

$$y - 5 = 2x^2 + 7x$$
$$-4x + y = 9$$

How many real solutions does the above system of equations have?

A) Zero
B) Exactly one
C) Exactly two
D) Infinitely many

Step 1: Equate the two equations

Convert the equations to the correct form before equating.

$$-4x + y = 9 \rightarrow y = 4x + 9$$
$$y - 5 = 2x^2 + 7x \rightarrow y = 2x^2 + 7x + 5$$

Equate and create one quadratic equation by moving all terms to one side.

$$4x + 9 = 2x^2 + 7x + 5$$
$$2x^2 + 7x + 5 - 4x - 9 = 0 \rightarrow 2x^2 + 3x - 4 = 0$$

Step 2: Set up the discriminant

$a = 2, b = 3, c = -4$.

$$b^2 - 4ac = 3^2 - (4 \times 2 \times -4) = 9 + 32 = 41$$

Since the discriminant > 0, the system has two real solutions.

The correct answer choice is **C**.

*Desmos Graphing Calculator Solution

Type each equation in a separate row and determine the number of intersection points of the two graphs. See below. Zoom in or out, if needed, to view the intersection points.

The two graphs intersect at two points.

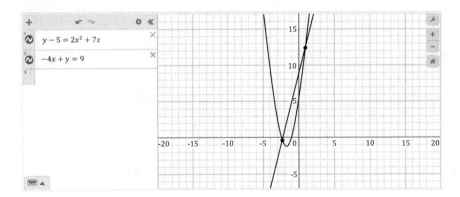

Example 2:

In the xy-plane, the graph of a parabola defined by $y = x^2 + 7x + 7$ intersects the graph of a line defined by $y = 2x + 3$ at exactly two points. Which of the following (x, y) are the solutions to the system?

A) $\{(-1, -4), (-1, 1)\}$
B) $\{(-1, -4), (-1, -5)\}$
C) $\{(-4, -4), (-1, 1)\}$
D) $\{(-4, -5), (-1, 1)\}$

Step 1: Equate the two equations

$$x^2 + 7x + 7 = 2x + 3$$

Create one quadratic equation by moving all terms to one side.

$$x^2 + 7x + 7 - 2x - 3 = 0 \rightarrow x^2 + 5x + 4 = 0$$

Step 2: Determine the values of x

$$x^2 + 5x + 4 = 0 \rightarrow (x + 4)(x + 1) = 0 \rightarrow x = -4 \text{ and } x = -1$$

The two values of x are -4 and -1. This eliminates answer choices A and B where both values of $x = -1$.

Step 3: Determine the corresponding values of y

Plug in the values of x in either equation. Plug it in the linear equation as it is easier to solve.

For $x = -4$:

$$y = (2 \times -4) + 3 = -8 + 3 = -5$$

This eliminates answer choice C since neither of the points in the answer choice have $y = -5$.

The correct answer choice is **D**.

Note that if the above elimination was not possible, then proceed with solving for the second value of x.

Desmos Graphing Calculator Solution

Type each equation in a separate row and read the intersection points of the two graphs. See below. Zoom in or out, if needed, to view the intersection points.

The two graphs intersect at points $(-4, -5)$ and $(-1, 1)$.

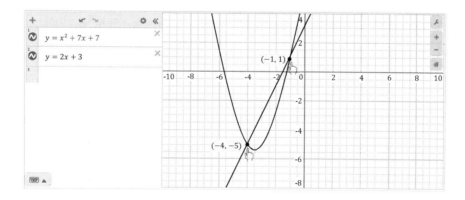

Digital SAT Math Manual and Workbook

Category 36 – Practice Questions

Students comfortable with the slider feature can solve questions 3, 4 and 6 using the Desmos graphing calculator

1 — Desmos

$$y = 96$$
$$y = 2x^2 - 2$$

The graphs of the equations given above intersect at the point (x, y) in the xy-plane. What is a possible value of x?

A) -7
B) -2
C) 4
D) 49

2 — Desmos

In the xy-plane, the graph of the equation $y + 4x = 2x^2 + 1$ intersects with the graph of the equation $y = (x-1)(x-2)$ at how many points?

A) None
B) Exactly one
C) Exactly two
D) Infinitely many

3

In the xy-plane, the graph of a line defined by $2y = 4x + 8$ intersects with the graph of a parabola defined by $y = -ax^2 - 4x - 5$ at exactly one point. What is the value of a, where a is a constant?

A) 1
B) 2
C) 4
D) 8

4

In the xy-plane, the parabola defined by an equation in the form $y = -(x - m)^2 + n$, where m and n are constants, intersects the line defined by $y = 9$ at exactly one point. What is the value of n?

5 — Desmos

The graphs of $y = x^2 - 7x + 12$ and $x = y + 4$, in the xy-plane, intersect at a point (s, t). What is the value of s?

6

In the xy-plane, the graph of line l defined by $y - kx = 1$ intersects the graph of the parabola defined by $y = x^2 - kx + 10$ at exactly one point, where k is a constant. If line l has a positive slope, what is the slope of line l?

Digital SAT Math Manual and Workbook

Category 37 – Graph Transformations of a Parabola

Key Points

- A horizontal (left or right) translation is the shift of a parabola along the x-axis. A vertical (up or down) translation is the shift of a parabola along the y-axis.
  - A horizonal translation of the graph of $f(x)$ by n units to the right can be written as $f(x-n)$, and n units to the left can be written as $f(x+n)$.
  - A vertical translation of the graph of $f(x)$ by n units up can be written as $f(x)+n$, and n units down can be written as $f(x)-n$.
  - In the vertex form $f(x) = a(x-h)^2 + k$, the horizontal translation is the change in the value of h, and the vertical translation is the change in the value of k.
  - In the standard form $f(x) = ax^2 + bx + c$, the horizontal translation is the change in the values of all the x terms, and the vertical translation is the change in the value of c.
  - In the factored form $f(x) = a(x-r)(x-s)$, the horizontal translation of a parabola is the change in the values of the x-intercepts r and s, and the vertical translation is addition or subtraction of the translated units to the equation.
- A reflection flips a parabola across the x-axis or y-axis.
  - The reflection of a parabola across the x-axis does not change the x-values, but all the y-values change to the opposite negative/positive operator. A reflection of the graph of $f(x)$ over the x-axis can be written as $-f(x)$.
  - The reflection of a parabola across the y-axis does not change the y-values, but all the x-values change to the opposite negative/positive operator. A reflection of the graph of $f(x)$ over the x-axis can be written as $f(-x)$.

How to Solve

See translation examples below.
- Vertex form $f(x) = (x-2)^2 + 2$:
  - 1 unit right: $f(x-1) = (x-2-1)^2 + 2 = (x-3)^2 + 2$.
  - 1 unit left: $f(x+1) = (x-2+1)^2 + 2 = (x-1)^2 + 2$.
  - 1 unit up: $f(x) + 1 = (x-2)^2 + 2 + 1 = (x-2)^2 + 3$.
  - 1 unit down: $f(x) - 1 = (x-2)^2 + 2 - 1 = (x-2)^2 + 1$.
- Standard form $f(x) = x^2 - 4x + 6$:
  - 1 unit right: $f(x-1) = (x-1)^2 - 4(x-1) + 6 = x^2 - 6x + 11$.
  - 1 unit left: $f(x+1) = (x+1)^2 - 4(x+1) + 6 = x^2 - 2x + 3$.
  - 1 unit up: $f(x) + 1 = x^2 - 4x + 6 + 1 = x^2 - 4x + 7$.
  - 1 unit down: $f(x) - 1 = x^2 - 4x + 6 - 1 = x^2 - 4x + 5$.
- Factored form $f(x) = (x-2)(x+7)$:
  - 1 unit right: $f(x-1) = (x-2-1)(x+7-1) = (x-3)(x+6)$.
  - 1 unit left: $f(x+1) = (x-2+1)(x+7+1) = (x-1)(x+8)$..
  - 1 unit up: $f(x) + 1 = (x-2)(x+7) + 1$.
  - 1 unit down: $f(x) - 1 = (x-2)(x+7) - 1$.

Example 1:
$$f(x) = x^2 - 4x + 3$$
The function f shown above graphs a parabola in the xy-plane. If $g(x) = f(x-2)$, what is the value of $g(0)$, where $y = g(x)$?

Step 1: Determine the function $g(x)$
$$g(x) = f(x-2) = (x-2)^2 - 4(x-2) + 3$$

Step 2: Determine $g(0)$

$g(0)$ is the y-coordinate of the y-intercept. Since $x = 0$ at the y-intercept, plug in 0 as the value of x and determine y.
$$y = g(0) = (0-2)^2 - 4(0-2) + 3 = 4 + 8 + 3 = 15$$

The correct answer is **15**.

*This question can be solved using the Desmos graphing calculator by typing the definition of the function f in the first row, $g(x) = f(x-2)$ in the second row, and $g(0)$ in the third row. The value of $g(0)$ will be displayed to the right of the row as $= 15$.

Example 2:

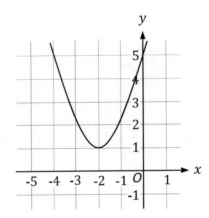

The equation of the graph of the above parabola in the xy-plane can be written in the form $y = a(x-h)^2 + k$, where the minimum values of h and k appear as constants or coefficients. Which of the following could be an equation of the above parabola translated 3 units left and 4 units up?

A) $y = (x-5)^2 + 1$
B) $y = (x-1)^2 + 1$
C) $y = (x+1)^2 + 5$
D) $y = (x+5)^2 + 5$

Step 1: Determine the translation

Since the equation is in the vertex form, the transformed vertex can be directly read from the given graph as shown in the figure on the right.

The vertex of the transformed graph is $(-5, 5)$. Hence, the equation of the transformed graph is
$$y = (x+5)^2 + 5$$
The correct answer choice is **D**.

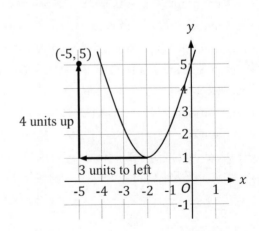

Category 37 – Practice Questions

1 — Desmos

In the xy-plane, if the graph of the parabola defined by the equation $y = 2(x+3)^2 - 1$ is reflected across the y-axis, which of the following is the equation of the reflected graph?

A) $y = -2(x+3)^2 - 1$
B) $y = -2(-x+3)^2 - 1$
C) $y = 2(x-3)^2 + 1$
D) $y = 2(-x+3)^2 - 1$

2 — Desmos

The function f is defined by $f(x) = 2x^2 - 7$. The function g is defined by $g(x) = f(x) - 5$. Which table gives three values of x and their corresponding values of $g(x)$?

A)

x	-3	-1	2
$g(x)$	11	-5	1

B)

x	-2	-1	3
$g(x)$	-4	-10	6

C)

x	-3	1	2
$g(x)$	11	-10	1

D)

x	-2	-1	1
$g(x)$	-4	-10	6

3 — Desmos

In the xy-plane, if the graph defined by the equation $y = 2(x-3)^2 - 8$ is translated left 11 units, which of the following is an equation of the translated graph?

A) $y = 2(x-14)^2 - 8$
B) $y = 2(x+8)^2 - 8$
C) $y = 2(x+3)^2 + 11$
D) $y = 2(x+14)^2 + 3$

4 — Desmos

In the xy-plane, the equation $y = x^2 + 4$ graphs a parabola. If the parabola is translated and the equation of the translated parabola is $y = (x-4)^2$, which of the following statements is true about the translation of the parabola?

A) Right 4 units and down 4 units.
B) Right 4 units and up 4 units.
C) Left 4 units and down 4 units.
D) Left 4 units and up 4 units.

5 — Desmos

The function f is defined by $f(x) = 2x^2 - 8x + 7$. The function g is defined by $g(x) = f(x+7)$. What is the value of $g(0)$, where $y = g(x)$?

6 — Desmos

$$g(x) = -\frac{1}{2}(x-5)(x-7)$$

The function g is defined above, where $y = g(x)$. The graph of the function f is a result of the translation of the graph of the function g up 24 units in the xy-plane. What is the value of $y = f(1)$?

Category 38 – Equivalent Quadratic Expressions

Key Points
- Two expressions are equivalent when the coefficients and constants in both expressions are the same.
- An equation has infinite solutions when the expression on one side of the equation is equal to the expression on the other side of the equation. For example, in the equation $4x^2 + 8x + k = 2mx^2 + 8x + 5$, the values of the coefficient m and constant k are not known. The expressions on both sides of the equation will be equivalent when $m = 2$ and $k = 5$, and the equation will have infinite solutions.

How to Solve

Remember that if an equation has a variable on one side only, then the coefficient of that variable on the other side must be 0. For example, in the equation $4x^2 + 5 = 4x^2 + kx + 5$, $k = 0$ since the left-side expression does not have the variable x. See below. Same applies to constants.

$$4x^2 + 5 = 4x^2 + (0)x + 5 \rightarrow 4x^2 + 5 = 4x^2 + 0 + 5 \rightarrow 4x^2 + 5 = 4x^2 + 5$$

When there are multiple terms of x or x^2 on one side of an equation, factor them. See example below, where a and b are constants.

$$3ax^2 + 4x^2 + 5bx + x + 1 = 10x^2 + 6x + 1 \rightarrow (3a + 4)x^2 + (5b + 1)x + 1 = 10x^2 + 6x + 1$$

The expressions on both sides of the equation must be in the standard form before evaluating the coefficients and constants. See example below.

$$x(2x + 5) + 1 = kx^2 + 5x + 1 \rightarrow 2x^2 + 5x + 1 = kx^2 + 5x + 1$$

Example 1:

$$(ax + 2)(bx + 2) = 5x^2 + 4x + 4$$

The equation above is true for all values of x. What is the value of $a + b$, where a and b are constants?

Step 1: Equate the corresponding coefficients and constants of both sides

"True for all values of x" implies the equation has infinitely many solutions. Hence, the expression on one side of the equation must be equal to the expression on the other side of the equation.

FOIL the left-side expression.

$$abx^2 + 2ax + 2bx + 4 = 5x^2 + 4x + 4$$

Factor all terms of x.

$$abx^2 + (2a + 2b)x + 4 = 5x^2 + 4x + 4$$

Equate the coefficients of the x terms.

$$(2a + 2b) = 4$$

Note that $2a + 2b$ can be factored as $2(a + b)$. Subsequently, dividing both sides of $(2a + 2b) = 4$ by 2 will give the value of $a + b$.

$$2(a + b) = 4$$
$$a + b = 2$$

The correct answer is **2**.

Example 2:

The equation $(mx + 1)(nx + 3) = 3x^2 + kx + 3$ is true for all values of x. What are the two possible values of k, where m and n are positive integers?

A) $\{1, 3\}$
B) $\{3, 4\}$
C) $\{4, 6\}$
D) $\{6, 10\}$

Step 1: Equate the coefficients and constants of both sides

For the equation to have infinitely many solutions, expressions on both sides of the equation must be equal.

FOIL the left-side expression.

$$mnx^2 + 3mx + nx + 3 = 3x^2 + kx + 3$$

Factor all terms of x.

$$mnx^2 + (3m + n)x + 3 = 3x^2 + kx + 3$$

Equate the coefficients of x^2 and x.

$$mn = 3$$
$$3m + n = k$$

Step 2: Determine the value of k

The values of m and n must be determined before the value of k can be solved for.

Determine the values of m and n: Since $mn = 3$, m and n are factors of 3. Since m and n are greater than 0, the only two factors of 3 can be 1 and 3. However, it is not known which factor is m and which factor is n. Hence, the possible values of m and n are

$$m = 1 \text{ and } n = 3 \text{ or } m = 3 \text{ and } n = 1$$

Determine the values of k: Plug in the above two combinations of m- and n-values in the equation $3m + n = k$.

For $m = 1$ and $n = 3$: $k = 3m + n = (3 \times 1) + 3 = 6$.

For $m = 3$ and $n = 1$: $k = 3m + n = (3 \times 3) + 1 = 10$.

The two possible values of k are 6 and 10.

The correct answer choice is **D**.

Category 38 – Practice Questions

1

The expressions $(x + 3)(ax + c)$ and $6x^2 + bx + 9$ are equivalent. What is the value of b, where a, b, and c are constants?

A) 0
B) 3
C) 15
D) 21

2

$$7(x^2 + 0.04c) - x^2$$

If the expression $0.2ax^2 + 0.28c$ is equivalent to the above expression, what is the value of a, where a and c are constants?

A) 6
B) 14
C) 30
D) 38

3

$$x^2 + kx^2 + c = 4cx^2 - 0.25$$

The equation above is true for all values of x, where c and k are constants and $c \neq k$. What is the value of k?

A) −2
B) −1
C) 0
D) 4

4

$$(3ax + 4)(bx + c) = 6x^2 + 4x$$

The equation above has infinitely many solutions, and a, b, and c are constants. Which of the following must be true about the values of a, b, and c?

A) $a = 1, b = 2, c = 0$
B) $a = 2, b = 1, c = 0$
C) $a = 2, b = 2, c = 2$
D) $a = 2, b = 1, c = 4$

5

$$0.6ax^2 + 4cx + 5 = 5.4x^2 + 5$$

For what value of c does the given equation have infinitely many solutions when $a = 9$?

A) 0
B) 4
C) 6
D) 9

6

$$(2x + 3)(2x + 1) = 4x^2 + 8x + c - 2$$

For what value of c does the above equation have infinitely many solutions, where c is a constant?

Section 6 – Review Questions

Students comfortable with the slider feature can solve questions 12, 15, and 23 using the Desmos graphing calculator

1

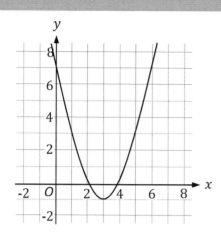

In the xy-plane, if the equation of the above parabola is written in the form $y = ax^2 + bx + c$, where a, b, and c are constants, which of the following could be the value of c?

A) -1
B) 4
C) 7
D) 8

2 Desmos

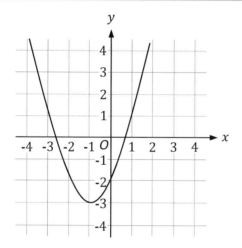

Which of the following equations represents the translation of the above graph left 2 units and up 4 units, where the minimum values of x and y appear as constants or coefficients?

A) $y = (x + 1)^2 - 3$
B) $y = (x + 1)^2 - 1$
C) $y = (x + 2)^2 + 1$
D) $y = (x + 3)^2 + 1$

3 Desmos

In the xy-plane, the graph of the function f is defined by $f(x) = (x - 1)^2 + 2$, and the graph of the function g is defined by $f(x) = (x + 2)^2 - 1$. When $g(x)$ is compared to $f(x)$ which of the following is true about the vertex of the two graphs?

A) The vertex of $g(x)$ is 1 unit right and 2 units above the vertex of $f(x)$.
B) The vertex of $g(x)$ is 1 unit left and 2 units below the vertex of $f(x)$.
C) The vertex of $g(x)$ is 3 units right and 3 units below the vertex of $f(x)$.
D) The vertex of $g(x)$ is 3 units left and 3 units below the vertex of $f(x)$.

4 Desmos

A parabola intersects the x-axis at two points, and the axis of symmetry is at $x = 2$. Which of the following could be the equation of the parabola?

A) $y = (x - 2)(x - 2)$
B) $y = (x - 1)(x + 5)$
C) $y = (x + 1)(x - 5)$
D) $y = (x + 2)(x + 2)$

5 Desmos

The graph of $y = h(x)$ in the xy-plane has a minimum value of -12. Which of the following could define function h?

A) $h(x) = -5(x - 2)^2 - 12$
B) $h(x) = -12(x - 1)^2 - 5$
C) $h(x) = 12(x - 12)^2 - 5$
D) $h(x) = 5(x - 1)^2 - 12$

Digital SAT Math Manual and Workbook

6 — Desmos

In the xy-plane, the graphs of $x - y = -4$ and $y = x^2 - 5x + 4$ intersect at exactly two points. Which of the following (x, y) points lies on graphs of both the given equations, where $x > 0$?

A) $(0, -4)$
B) $(6, 4)$
C) $(6, 10)$
D) $(8, 10)$

7 — Desmos

$$4x(x + 1) - 2 = 3x(x + 3) - 5$$

Which of the following is a solution to the given equation?

A) $2.5 - \frac{\sqrt{13}}{2}$
B) $2.5 - \frac{\sqrt{3}}{2}$
C) $1.5 + \frac{\sqrt{5}}{2}$
D) $1 + \frac{\sqrt{13}}{2}$

8 — Desmos

$$f(x) = 2x^2 - 7x + 3$$

What is one possible x-intercept of the function f shown above?

9

$$2x^2 + kx + 10 = 0$$

If $(x + 5)$ is a factor of the quadratic equation above, what is the value of the constant k?

10 — Desmos

In the xy-plane, the points $(2, 0)$ and $(k, 0)$ lie on the graph of the equation $y = x^2 - 10x + 16$, where k is a constant. What is the value of k?

11 — Desmos

$$y = x^2 - 8x + 13$$

The graph of the equation above is a parabola in the xy-plane. Which of the following equivalent equations includes the minimum values of x and y as constants or coefficients?

A) $y = (x - 4)^2 - 3$
B) $y = (x - 3)^2 + 2$
C) $y = (x - 4)^2 + 7$
D) $y = (x + 3) + 2$

12

The function g is defined by $g(x) = ax^2 + bx + c$, where a, b, and c are constants. The graph of $y = g(x)$ in the xy-plane passes through the points $(5, 0)$ and $(-17, 0)$. If $a < -2$, which of the following could be the value of $a - b$?

A) -11
B) -22
C) 22
D) 44

13

$$g(x) = (-k - x)(x - 12)$$

The function g is defined above, where k is a constant. In the xy-plane, the graph $y = g(x)$ intersects the x-axis at exactly two points with midpoint at 3.5. What is the value of $g(10)$?

14

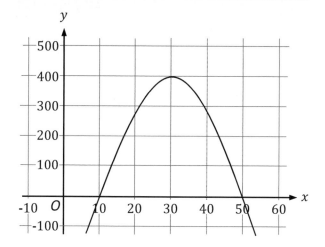

In the xy-plane, the above parabola predicts the weekly profit y, in thousands of dollars, of a furniture store based on the weekly advertising cost x, in hundreds of dollars. Which of the following is the maximum weekly profit, in thousands of dollars, predicted by the parabola?

A) 30
B) 50
C) 200
D) 400

15

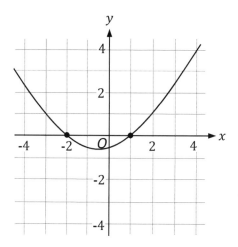

The graph of $y = \frac{1}{4}x^2 + bx + c$ is shown above, where b and c are constants. What is the value of $a - b - c$?

16

$$f(x) = (x-1)(x-7)$$

The function f defined above graphs a parabola in the xy-plane. What are the (x, y) coordinates of the vertex of the parabola defined by $y = f(x + 16)$?

A) $(-12, -9)$
B) $(-12, -6)$
C) $(4, -9)$
D) $(12, 9)$

17

The parabola defined by the function h in the xy-plane opens upward and intersects the x-axis at exactly two points. If $h(-5) = h(19)$, for what value of x does the function h reach its minimum, where $y = h(x)$?

A) 5
B) 7
C) 12
D) 24

18

The equation $(ax + 3)(bx + 4) = 10x^2 + kx + 12$ is true for all values of x. What are the two possible values of k when $a + b = 7$, where a and b are positive integers?

A) $\{2, 26\}$
B) $\{12, 26\}$
C) $\{23, 23\}$
D) $\{23, 26\}$

19 — Desmos

$$x + y = -a$$
$$x = y - 2x^2 + 2$$

The above system of equations has exactly one solution (x, y), where a is a constant. What is the value of x?

A) $-\dfrac{1}{4}$

B) $-\dfrac{1}{2}$

C) $\dfrac{5}{2}$

D) 4

20 — Desmos

$$3(3x^2 + 2) = (7x + 3)x$$

How many distinct real solutions does the above equation have?

A) Zero
B) Exactly one
C) Exactly two
D) Infinitely many

21 — Desmos

$$x - 31x^{\frac{1}{2}} + 108 = 0$$

Which of the following is a solution to the given equation?

A) 4
B) 27
C) 108
D) 729

22 — Desmos

$$f(x) = -2(x + 1)(x - 9)$$

The graph of the above function f is a parabola, in the xy-plane. Which of the following equivalent equations includes the x- and y-coordinates of the vertex as constants or coefficients?

A) $f(x) = -2(x - 8)^2 + 11$
B) $f(x) = -2(x - 4)^2 + 11$
C) $f(x) = -2(x - 4)^2 + 50$
D) $f(x) = 2(x - 8)^2 + 18$

23

$$ax^2 - 8x + 8 = 0$$

The equation above has exactly one solution. What is the value of a, where a is a constant?

24 — Desmos

$$h(t) = -16t^2 + 48t + 64$$

When a projectile is launched in the air from a 64-feet-high platform, the height of the ball in the air, in feet, after t seconds can be modeled by the above equation. According to the model, how many seconds after launch the ball reaches the ground?

25 — Desmos

$$\dfrac{1}{54}x^2 - \left(2 - \dfrac{k}{18}\right)x - 45 = 0$$

The above equation has exactly two solutions, where k is a constant. The sum of the solutions is -3. What is the value of k?

Section 7 – Absolute Value

Category 39 – Absolute Value and Linear Equations
Category 40 – Absolute Value and Linear Inequalities
Category 41 – Absolute Value and Functions
Section 7 – Review Questions

Category 39 – Absolute Value and Linear Equations

Key Points
- The absolute value of a real number is denoted within two bars and is always a non-negative number. For example, the value of $|x|$ (absolute value of x) and $|-x|$ (absolute value of $-x$) is x.
- The above is also true for absolute value expressions. For example, in the equation $|2x + 5| = 7$, the value of $2x + 5$ could be -7 or 7, as the absolute value of -7 and 7 is 7. Hence, an expression within the absolute value bars is solved by removing the bars and giving the equation two values, one positive and one negative.
- Since the absolute value is always non-negative, an absolute value expression cannot equate to a negative number.
- Solving absolute value equations may result in a solution that does not solve an equation, known as an extraneous solution.

How to Solve
The absolute value expression must be on one side of the equation. For example, $|2x + 5| + 5 = 7 \rightarrow |2x + 5| = 2$.

If the absolute value expression equates to an expression, then the negative value applies to the entire expression. For example, the solutions of $|2x + 5| = 7 - x$, can be determined as $2x + 5 = (7 - x)$ and $2x + 5 = -(7 - x)$.

*Several questions in this category can be solved by directly typing the given equation in the Desmos graphing calculator. The steps in the above examples are unnecessary when using Desmos.
Note that the Desmos graphing calculator does not graph extraneous solutions, hence, no need to check for them.

*Example 1:
a and b are the two solutions to the equation $|2x - 1| = 7$. What is the value of a, where $a > b$?

Step 1: Solve for the positive value
$$2x - 1 = 7 \rightarrow 2x = 7 + 1 = 8 \rightarrow x = 4$$

Step 2: Solve for the negative value
$$2x - 1 = -7 \rightarrow 2x = -7 + 1 = -6 \rightarrow x = -3$$

Step 3: Determine a
The two solutions are 4 and -3. Plug in each solution in the equation to check for an extraneous solution.
$|2x - 1| = 7 \rightarrow |2(4) - 1| = 7 \rightarrow |8 - 1| = 7 \rightarrow 7 = 7$.
$|2x - 1| = 7 \rightarrow |2(-3) - 1| = 7 \rightarrow |-6 - 1| = 7 \rightarrow |-7| = 7 \rightarrow 7 = 7$.
Hence, 4 and -3 are not extraneous solutions. Since 4 is greater than -3, $a = 4$.
The correct answer is **4**.

*Desmos Graphing Calculator Solution
Type the equation and read the value(s) of x where the line(s) pass through the x-axis. These are the solutions. See the vertical lines in the graph below. The two values of x are -3 and 4. Since $4 > -3$, $a = 4$.

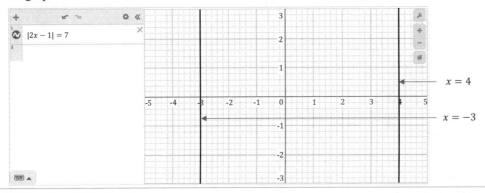

Digital SAT Math Manual and Workbook

*Example 2:

If $|2x - 3| + 1 = 8$ and $|y + 2| = 5$, what is one possible value of $|x + y|$?

Equation $|2x - 3| + 1 = 8$

Step 1: Solve for the positive value

Before solving move the integer not within absolute value sign to the right-side of the equation.
$$|2x - 3| = 8 - 1 \rightarrow |2x - 3| = 7 \rightarrow$$
$$2x - 3 = 7 \rightarrow 2x = 10 \rightarrow x = 5$$

Since the question asks for one solution, there no need to determine the other value of x. In this example, the second value of x is shown below.

Step 2: Solve for the negative value

$$2x - 3 = -7 \rightarrow 2x = -7 + 3 \rightarrow 2x = -4 \rightarrow x = -2$$

Equation $|y + 2| = 5$

Step 1: Solve for the positive value

$$y + 2 = 5 \rightarrow y = 5 - 2 \rightarrow y = 3$$

There is no need to determine the other value of y. In this example, the second value of y is shown below.

Step 2: Solve for the negative value

$$y + 2 = -5 \rightarrow y = -5 - 2 = -7$$

Step 3: Solve for $|x + y|$ (Note that in this example there are no extraneous solutions.)

The possible combinations can be

For $x = 5$ and $y = 3$: $|5 + 3| = |8| = 8$

For $x = 5$ and $y = -7$: $|5 - 7| = |-2| = 2$

For $x = -2$ and $y = 3$: $|-2 + 3| = |1| = 1$

For $x = -2$ and $y = -7$: $|-2 - 7| = |-9| = 9$

Hence, the possible values of $|x + y|$ are **1, 2, 8, and 9**. Any of them can be entered as the correct answer.

*Desmos Graphing Calculator Solution

Type the equation $|2x - 3| + 1 = 8$ and read the values of x where the graph of the equation passes through the x-axis. See the vertical lines in the graph below.

Type the equation $|y + 2| = 5$ in the next row and read the values of y where the graph of the equation passes through the y-axis. See the horizontal lines in the graph below.

$x = -2$ and 5. $y = -7$ and 3.

Determine $|x + y|$ using either value of x and y, as shown above in Step 3.

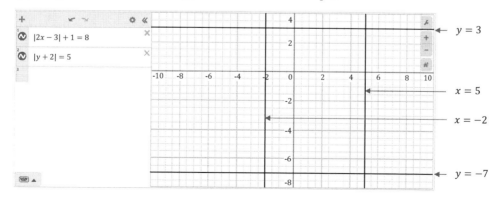

Digital SAT Math Manual and Workbook

Category 39 – Practice Questions

1 — Desmos

$$|x - 4| + 8 = 6$$

How many values of x satisfy the above equation?

A) 0
B) 2
C) 4
D) 6

2 — Desmos

$$|2x - 7| - 2 = 13$$

In the above equation, a and b are the two values of x and $a > b$. What is the absolute value of b?

A) -4
B) 4
C) 11
D) 15

3 — Desmos

$$|2x + 5| - 1 = 6$$

If s and t are the two possible solutions of the above equation and $s = 1$, what is the value of $|t|$?

4 — Desmos

The equation $|x - 4| + 3 = 6$ has two solutions. What is the sum of the two solutions?

5 — Desmos

What is one possible value of x in the equation $|3x - 6| + x = 2x$?

A) 1.5
B) 2.0
C) 3.5
D) 4.0

6 — Desmos

The two solutions of the equation $|2x + 5| = 7$ are m and n. What is the value of $|m + n|$?

7 — Desmos

If $|x + 3| = 1$ and $|2y - 3| = 5$, what is one possible value of $|xy|$?

8 — Desmos

If $|4x - 3| + 2 = 7$ and $y = -2$, what is one possible value of $|xy|$, where $x > 0$?

9 — Desmos

If $|x + 5| = 3$ and $|y + 2| = 3$, what is one possible value of $|x + y|$, where $y > 0$?

Digital SAT Math Manual and Workbook

Category 40 – Absolute Value and Linear Inequalities

Key Points
- Absolute value inequalities fall into two types: less than ($<$ and $\leq$) and greater than ($>$ and $\geq$). An example of less than is $|x| < a$, and an example of greater than is $|x| > a$, where a is a non-negative number.
  - For $|x| < a$, the solution set is any number between $-a$ and a. For example, if $a = 3$, then the solution set of $|x| < 3$ is $-3 < x < 3$. The solution is any number between -3 and 3, but excluding -3 and 3.

    For $|x| \leq 3$, the solution set is $-3 \leq x \leq 3$. It includes -3 and 3.
  - For $|x| > a$, the solution set is $x > a$ and $x < -a$. For example, if $a = 3$, then the solution set is $x > 3$ and $x < -3$. The solution is any number greater than 3 and less than -3.

    For $|x| \geq 3$, the solution set is $x \geq 3$ and $x \leq -3$.
  - The above rules also apply to expressions. For example, the solution set of $|2x + 1| < 3$ is $-3 < 2x + 1 < 3$, and the solution set of $|2x + 1| > 3$ is $2x + 1 > 3$ and $2x + 1 < -3$.
- An absolute value inequality can be created for a range of numbers using the following formula, where x is the variable for the range of numbers and a and b are the smallest and largest values of x, respectively.

  $|x -$ midpoint of a and $b\ | <$ distance of a or b from the midpoint
  - For example, if the smallest value of x is 10 and largest value of x is 40, then the midpoint of 10 and 40 is 25 and both 10 and 40 are at distance of 15 from the midpoint. The equation is $|x - 25| < 15$.

How to Solve
See below examples for further explanation on how the solution set of absolute value inequalities is determined.
- $|x| < 3$ represents any number from 0 to less than 3. The three integers that satisfy this condition are 0, 1, and 2. Since the absolute value of -1 is 1 and of -2 is 2, these two numbers also satisfy the condition. Hence, the solution set is the distance from 0 in both directions. The solution set to the inequality $|x| < 3$ are five integers, $-2, -1, 0, 1,$ and 2. See the darker area on the number line below. The solution set is $-3 < x < 3$.

- $|x| > 3$ represents any number greater than 3. However, the absolute values of all the numbers less than -3 is also greater than 3. For example, the absolute value of -4 is 4, the absolute value of -5 is 5, and so on. See the two darker areas on the number line below. For this reason, the solution set is $x > 3$ and $x < -3$.

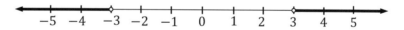

*Several questions in this category can be solved using the Desmos graphing calculator.

Example 1:

An urgent care clinic determined that between 50 to 80 patients come to the clinic on any given day. Which of the following inequalities can determine all the possible number of patients, p, that may come to the clinic on any given day?

A) $|p - 50| < 80$
B) $|p - 80| < 50$
C) $|p - 65| < 15$
D) $|p - 65| = 30$

Step 1: Determine the midpoint of the two numbers

$$\frac{50 + 80}{2} = \frac{130}{2} = 65$$

This eliminates answer choices A and B.

Step 2: Determine the distance of the two numbers from the midpoint

Since 65 is the midpoint of 50 and 80, both the numbers are at a distance of 15 from the midpoint. This eliminates answer choice D.

The correct answer choice is **C**.

*Example 2:

How many integer values of x satisfy $|2x + 3| < 5$?

Step 1: Determine the solution set

Since the absolute value has a less than inequality symbol, the solution set is

$$-5 < 2x + 3 < 5$$

Isolate x by subtracting 3 from both sides and then dividing both sides by 2.

$$-5 - 3 < 2x + 3 - 3 < 5 - 3 \rightarrow -8 < 2x < 2 \rightarrow$$

$$-\frac{8}{2} < \frac{2x}{2} < \frac{2}{2} \rightarrow -4 < x < 1$$

Since x is greater than -4 and less 1, the integer values of x can be $-3, -2, -1$, and 0. Hence, there are 4 possible integer values of x.

The correct answer is **4**.

*Desmos Graphing Calculator Solution

Type the inequality and the read the integer values of x that are within the solution set. The solution set is the shaded region on the graph. See below.

The integers within the solution set are $-3, -2, -1$, and 0.

Note that -4 and 1 on the dotted lines are not within the solution set.

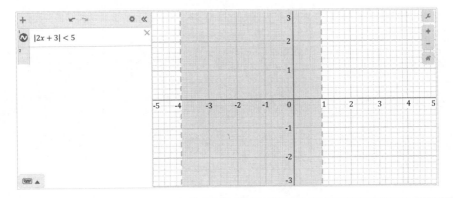

Digital SAT Math Manual and Workbook

Example 3:

$$|2x - 3| > 9$$

Which of the following can NOT be a possible solution to the above inequality?

A) $x = 8$
B) $x = |-4|$
C) $x = |-7|$
D) $x < -6$

Step 1: Determine the solution set

Since the absolute value has a greater than inequality symbol, the solution sets is

$$2x - 3 > 9 \text{ and } 2x - 3 < -9$$

For $2x - 3 > 9$, isolate x.

$$2x > 9 + 3 \;\to\; 2x > 12 \;\to\; \frac{2x}{2} > \frac{12}{2} \;\to\; x > 6$$

For $2x - 3 < -9$, isolate x.

$$2x < -9 + 3 \;\to\; 2x < -6 \;\to\; \frac{2x}{2} < \frac{-6}{2} \;\to\; x < -3$$

Since x is less than -3 or greater than 6, the integers $-3, -2, -1, 0, 1, 2, 3, 4, 5, 6$ cannot be the values of x. Evaluate each answer choice. Answer choice B cannot be a value of x since $|-4| = 4$ is not in the solution set. The correct answer choice is **B**.

Desmos Graphing Calculator Solution

Type the inequality and evaluate each answer choice if it is within the solution set visible as the shaded regions on the graph. See below.

$x = 8$ is within the solution set.

$x = |-4| = 4$ is not within the solution set. Note that $x = -4$ is within the solution set but the absolute value of $-4 = 4$ is not.

$x = |-7| = 7$ is within the solution set.

$x < -6$ is within the solution set.

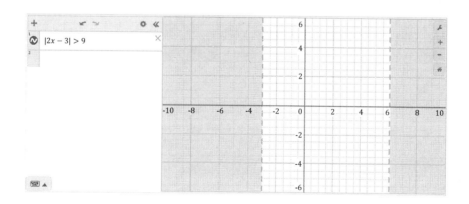

Digital SAT Math Manual and Workbook

Category 40 – Practice Questions

1 — Desmos

$|x + 3| < 2$

How many integer values of x satisfy the above inequality?

A) 0
B) 2
C) 3
D) 5

2

Giraffes are the tallest land animal in the world. When a baby giraffe is born, it can weigh between 100 and 150 pounds. Which of the following inequalities can determine all the possible weights, w, in pounds, of a newborn baby giraffe?

A) $|w - 125| < 25$
B) $|w - 125| < 50$
C) $|w - 150| < 25$
D) $|w - 150| < 50$

3 — Desmos

If $|a| > 4$, which of the following are true?

I. $a > 4$
II. $a < -4$
III. $-4 < a < 4$

A) I only
B) III only
C) I and II only
D) I and III only

4 — Desmos

$|r - 79{,}000| \leq 34{,}000$

Each year, a health care research company mails out surveys to all the residents of a certain that are above the age of 50. The above inequality estimates the number of residents who will complete the survey in any year. Based on the inequality, which of the following could be the maximum number of residents, r, estimated to complete the survey in a year?

A) 24,000
B) 41,000
C) 45,000
D) 113,000

5 — Desmos

Which of the following can give all the values of x that satisfy $|x - 1| < 4$?

A) $|x| < 3$
B) $-3 < x < 5$
C) $-4 < x < 4$
D) $-1 < x < 4$

6 — Desmos

$|2x + 3| > 5$

Which of the following could be the solutions to the above inequality?

I. $|-3|$
II. -2
III. 6

A) II only
B) III only
C) I and II only
D) I and III only

Category 41 – Absolute Value and Functions

Key Points

- The absolute value of a function is always positive. For example, if $f(x) = -2$, then $|f(x)| = |-2| = 2$.
- On the absolute value graph of a function, all the negative y-values are converted to positive y-values.
- Fig. 1 below shows the graph of a linear function $f(x) = x$. Fig. 2 shows the corresponding absolute value graph where the negative y-values (dashed line) are converted to positive values. This gives the absolute value graph a V-shape. The vertex of the graph is at the tip of V.

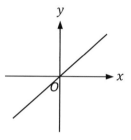   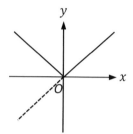

Fig. 1 $f(x) = x$ Fig. 2 $f(x) = |x|$

- The linear equation for an absolute value graph is $y = a|x - h| + k$, where h is the x-coordinate of the vertex and k is the y-coordinate of the vertex. In the above example, since the vertex is at origin, both h and k are 0. a determines the width of the V.
- If the above linear graph of $f(x) = x$ is shifted horizontally (right or left) or vertically (up or down), the vertex of the absolute value graph will shift accordingly.
  - In the equation $y = a|x - h| + k$, a negative h indicates a right shift by h units, and a positive h indicates a left shift by h units. A negative k indicates downward shift by k units, and a positive k indicates an upward shift by k units.
  - For example, if the graph of $f(x) = x$ is moved right 2 units and down 1 unit, the equation of the absolute value graph is $f(x) = |x - 2| - 1$, and the graph will form a V at the vertex $(2, -1)$.
- The absolute value graph of a non-linear function is not a V-shape. V is a characteristic of a linear absolute value graph with the equation in the form $y = a|x - h| + k$.
- Fig. 3 below shows the graph of a non-linear polynomial function. Fig. 4 shows the corresponding absolute value graph. All the negative values of y (dashed lines) are converted to positive values.

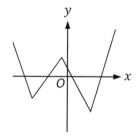   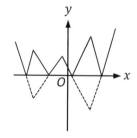

Fig. 3   Fig. 4

How to Solve

* Some of the questions in this category can be solved using the Desmos graphing calculator.

A given graph can be matched to the equations in the answer choices. Type each equation from the answer choices, one at a time, and match the corresponding graph with the given graph.

A given equation can be matched to the graphs in the answer choices. Type the equation and match the corresponding graph with the graphs in the answer choices.

Example 1:

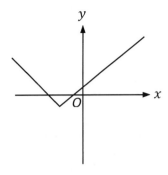

Which of the following could be the equation of the above graph, in the xy-plane?

A) $y = |x| - 1$
B) $y = |x - 2|$
C) $y = |x - 2| + 2$
D) $y = |x + 1| - 1$

Step 1: Determine the shift in the graph

The vertex of the graph is below 0 and to the left. Hence, the y-coordinate of the vertex must be negative, and the x-coordinate of the vertex must be positive.

This eliminates answers choices A, B, and C. In the correct answer choice D, $x + 1$ is 1 unit shift left, and the y-coordinate is negative.

The correct answer choice is **D**.

*Desmos Graphing Calculator Solution

Enter the equation from each answer choice, one at a time, and determine which equation graphs the given graph. Above shown approach may be quicker.

Example 2:

x	-2	0	1	7
$f(x)$	2	1	-5	-2

In the table above, four values of x and their corresponding values of $f(x)$ are given. What is the value of $|f(7) - f(0)|$?

A) -3
B) -1
C) 3
D) 7

Step 1: Read the value of $f(x)$ from the table

To get the value of $f(7)$, look for $x = 7$ in the x column and read the corresponding value from the $f(x)$ column.
$$f(7) = -2$$
To get the value of $f(0)$, look for $x = 0$ in the x column and read the corresponding value from the $f(x)$ column.
$$f(0) = 1$$

Step 2: Solve for $|f(7) - f(0)|$

$$|f(7) - f(0)| = |-2 - 1| = |-3| = 3$$

The correct answer choice is **C**.

Category 41 – Practice Questions

1 Desmos

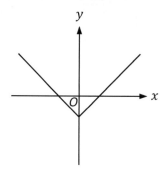

Which of the following could be the equation of the above graph, in the xy-plane?

A) $y = |x| - 2$
B) $y = |x| + 1$
C) $y = |x + 1|$
D) $y = |x + 1| - 1$

2 Desmos

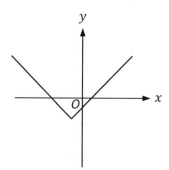

Which of the following could be the equation of the above graph, in the xy-plane, where $y = f(x)$?

A) $f(x) = |x - 1|$
B) $f(x) = |x - 1| - 2$
C) $f(x) = |x + 1| - 2$
D) $f(x) = |x + 1| + 3$

3 Desmos

In the xy-plane, which of the following could be the graph of $g(x) = |x - 1| + 1$, where $y = g(x)$?

A)
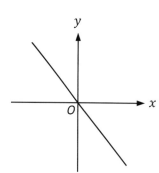

B)
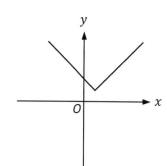

C)
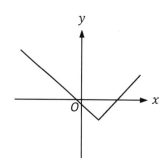

D)
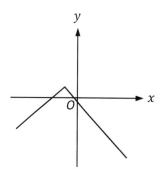

Digital SAT Math Manual and Workbook   169

4

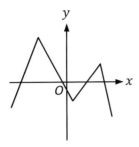

In the xy-plane, the graph of the function g is shown above. Which of the following could be the graph of $y = |g(x)|$?

A)

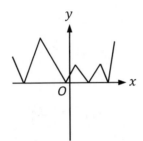

B)

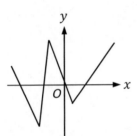

C)

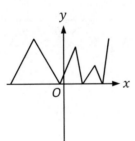

D)

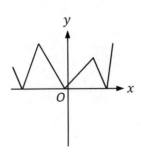

5

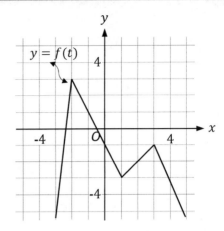

The complete graph of the function f, where $y = f(t)$, is shown above in the xy-plane. For which of the following values of t is $f(t) = |f(t)|$?

A) −4
B) −2
C) 3
D) 4

6

x	4	−2	1	3
$f(x)$	2	0	−2	−1

In the table above, four values of x and their corresponding values of $f(x)$ are given. What is the absolute value of $(2f(1) - f(3))$?

A) −3
B) −2
C) 3
D) 6

7   Desmos

The function g is defined by $g(x) = 3x - 10$, and for the function f, $f(-2) = -10$. Which of the following is the value of $|f(-2) + g(5)|$?

A) −5
B) −2
C) 2
D) 5

Digital SAT Math Manual and Workbook

Section 7 – Review Questions

1 Desmos

$|x - 3| > 5$

Which of the following could be the solution to the above inequality?

A) $x = |-1|$
B) $x = |-3|$
C) $x = -5$
D) $x = 6$

2 Desmos

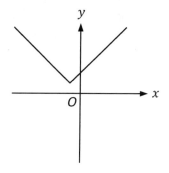

Which of the following could be the equation of the above graph, in the xy-plane?

A) $y = |x - 1| + 1$
B) $y = |x - 2| - 2$
C) $y = |x + 2| - 1$
D) $y = |x + 1| + 1$

3 Desmos

$|6 - x| = 4$

The above equation has two solutions, s and t. If $s = 10$, what is the value of t?

4

The height of trees in a certain wildlife conservation is between 40 and 70 feet. Which of the following inequalities can determine all the possible heights, h, in feet, of a tree in the wildlife conservation?

A) $|h - 55| < 15$
B) $|h - 70| < 30$
C) $|h - 55| < 30$
D) $|h - 40| < 70$

5

A spotted female deer can weigh between 25 to 45 kilograms. Which of the following inequalities gives all the possible weights, w, in kilograms, of a spotted female deer?

A) $|w - 25| < 45$
B) $|w - 35| < 10$
C) $|w - 45| < 25$
D) $|w + 35| < 65$

6 Desmos

$|2x - 1| < 3$

Which of the following can give all the values of x that satisfy the given inequality?

A) $|x| < 2$
B) $-3 < x < 3$
C) $-2 < x < 4$
D) $-1 < x < 2$

Digital SAT Math Manual and Workbook

7

In the xy-plane, which of the following could be the equation of the above graph?

A) $y = |x - 1|$
B) $y = |x + 1| - 1$
C) $y = 2|x - 1| - 2$
D) $y = 2|x + 1| + 1$

8

The complete graph of the function f is shown above in the xy-plane. Which of the following is the sum of the absolute values of x that satisfy $y = f(3)$?

A) -3
B) 1
C) 4
D) 7

9

$$|l - 38| \leq 16$$

The above inequality estimates the length, in inches, of garden snakes in a wooded area of a certain state park. Based on the inequality, which of the following could be the length, l, in inches, of the smallest garden snake in the wooded area of the state park?

A) 16
B) 22
C) 38
D) 54

10

The function g defined by $g(x) = x^2 - 2x - 11$ is true for all values of x. Which of the following is the absolute value of $(g(3) - g(5))$?

A) 2
B) 4
C) 12
D) 16

11

$$|2x + 7| + 1 = 4$$

The two solutions of the given equation are a and b. What is the value of $|a + b|$?

12

For $|2x + 1| = 3$ and $|2y + 3| = 7$, what is one possible value of $x + y$, where $y > x > 0$?

Section 8 – Ratios, Proportions, and Rates

Category 42 – Ratios and Proportions
Category 43 – Rates
Section 8 – Review Questions

Category 42 – Ratios and Proportions

Key Points

- A ratio is a comparison of two numbers.
    - A ratio may compare the parts of two or more numbers within a total. For example, if there are a total of 5 oatmeal and sugar cookies, of which 2 are oatmeal and 3 are sugar, then the ratio of the number of oatmeal cookies to the number of sugar cookies is $2:3$.
    - A ratio may compare a part to the total. From the above example, the ratio of the number of oatmeal cookies to the total number of cookies is $2:5$, and the ratio of the number of sugar cookies to the total number of cookies is $3:5$.
    - A ratio can also be written as a fraction. The fraction of oatmeal cookies is $\frac{2}{5}$, and the fraction of sugar cookies is $\frac{3}{5}$.
- A proportion equates equal ratios. If one number of the ratio increases, then the other numbers increase proportionally. For example, if the number of oatmeal and sugar cookies (from the above example) were proportionally increased three times, then the ratio would be $(2:3) \times 3 = 6:9$. As a fraction, the proportion can be written as $\frac{2}{3} = \frac{6}{9}$.

How to Solve

The numerator and denominator of each fraction in a proportion must represent the same thing. For example, in the below proportions all the numerators represent oatmeal cookies, and all the denominators represent total cookies.

$$\frac{\text{oatmeal cookies}}{\text{total cookies}} = \frac{2}{5} = \frac{4}{10} = \frac{6}{15} = \frac{8}{20}$$

In the above example, the ratios are $2:5 = 4:10 = 6:15 = 8:20$. The lowest ratio is $2:5$. Any ratio in a proportion can be simplified to the lowest ratio. Look for common multiples. For example, both the numbers in the ratio $6:15$ can be divided by 3, resulting in

$$\frac{6}{3} : \frac{15}{3} = 2:5$$

Note that the ratios in the answer choices are usually given as the lowest ratio.

Example 1:

In a certain school, the total number of students on the wrestling and karate teams is 60. If there are 24 students on the wrestling team, what is the ratio of the number of students on the wrestling team to the number of students on the karate team?

A) $2:3$

B) $2:5$

C) $3:2$

D) $8:15$

Step 1: Determine the ratio

Number of students on wrestling team $= 24$.

Number of students on karate team $=$ total students on both teams $-$ number of students on wrestling team.

$$60 - 24 = 36$$

students on wrestling team:students on karate team $= 24:36 = 2:3$

The correct answer choice is **A**.

Digital SAT Math Manual and Workbook

Example 2:

Hyperion dwarf is a 379.7 feet tall redwood tree discovered in 2006. What is the equivalent height of Hyperion dwarf tree in meters, rounded to the nearest tenth? (1 meter = 3.28084 feet)

A) 88
B) 92.4
C) 115.7
D) 155.8

Step 1: Set up a proportion

Let the height of the tree in meters $= x$.

It is given that 1 meter = 3.28084 feet. Set up a proportion for feet and meters as follows.

$$\frac{\text{feet}}{\text{meters}} = \frac{3.28084}{1} = \frac{379.7}{x}$$

Step 2: Solve

Cross multiply.

$$3.28084x = 379.7 \quad \rightarrow \quad x = 115.73 = 115.7$$

The correct answer choice is **C**.

Example 3:

A farmer sells apples and oranges at a local market during the summer. Last week, the ratio of oranges sold to apples sold, in pounds, was 4: 7. If 112 pounds of apples were sold last week, how many pounds of oranges were sold last week?

Step 1: Set up a proportion

Let the pounds of oranges sold $= x$.

Set up a proportion for pounds of oranges sold and pounds of apples sold as follows.

$$\frac{\text{pounds of oranges sold}}{\text{pounds of apples sold}} = \frac{4}{7} = \frac{x}{112}$$

Step 2: Solve

Cross multiply.

$$7 \times x = 4 \times 112 \quad \rightarrow \quad 7x = 448 \quad \rightarrow \quad x = 64$$

The correct answer is **64**.

Example 4:

An architect created a scaling system for a building. Every 10 feet represents 0.2 centimeters on the scale. If the architect draws the height of a building as 9 centimeters on the scaling system, what is the height of the building in feet?

Step 1: Set up a proportion

Let the height in feet $= x$.

Set up a proportion for feet and centimeters as follows.

$$\frac{\text{feet}}{\text{centimeters}} = \frac{10}{0.2} = \frac{x}{9}$$

Step 2: Solve

Cross multiply.

$$0.2 \times x = 9 \times 10 \quad \rightarrow \quad 0.2x = 90 \quad \rightarrow \quad x = 450$$

The correct answer is **450**.

Category 42 – Practice Questions

1

An elementary school offers music and drama classes to all students enrolled in the school. A student must select either a music class or a drama class in a given school year. In the current school year, 120 students selected drama, and the ratio of the number of students in the music class to the number of students in the drama class is $2:5$. How many students are enrolled in the school in the current school year?

A) 48
B) 120
C) 142
D) 168

2

Kara is mixing ingredients to bake 4 trays of muffins and 7 trays of cookies. She requires $5\frac{1}{2}$ cups of butter in total. If the same amount of butter is required for each tray of muffins and cookies, how many cups of butter are required for 4 trays of muffins?

A) $\frac{4}{7}$
B) $\frac{11}{8}$
C) 2
D) 11

3

A certain hotel has guest rooms on 10 floors, and each floor has the same number of guest rooms, x. Each housekeeper cleans 18 guest rooms per day. Which equation represents the total number of housekeepers, K, needed per day to clean all the guest rooms on any 3 floors of the hotel?

A) $K = \frac{x}{18}$
B) $K = \frac{x}{9}$
C) $K = \frac{x}{6}$
D) $K = 54x$

4

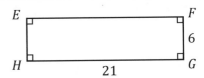

In the above figure, the ratio of GH to FG is 21 to 6. If the length of FG is increased by 5 units, by how many units must the length of GH change to maintain the ratio?

A) It must decrease by 5 units.
B) It must increase by 5 units.
C) It must decrease by 17.5 units.
D) It must increase by 17.5 units.

5

	Company X	Company Y	Total
Product A	807	1,005	1,812
Product B	408	800	1,208
Total	1,215	1,805	3,020

Company X and Company Y both sell Product A and Product B. The table above shows the number of Product A and Product B sold at each company in May 2019. Of the total number of Product A and Product B sold at Company X and Company Y, which of the following is closest to the fraction of Product A sold at Company X and Company Y in May 2019?

A) $\frac{1}{3}$
B) $\frac{1}{2}$
C) $\frac{3}{5}$
D) $\frac{5}{7}$

6

The ratio $a:5:12$ is equivalent to the ratio $3:b:24$. What is the value of $2(a+b)$?

A) 3
B) 10
C) 11
D) 23

7

One box of 50 mini muffins contains bran and corn muffins in the ratio of $2:3$, respectively. How many more corn muffins are in the box than bran muffins?

A) 10
B) 12
C) 20
D) 30

8

Aiko bought 48 ounces of regular sugar cookies and 48 ounces of low sugar cookies. The regular sugar cookies come in packets of 12 ounces and each packet contains 8 cookies. The low sugar cookies come in packets of 8 ounces and each packet contains 12 cookies. If L is the number of low sugar cookies in 48 ounces and R is the number of regular sugar cookies in 48 ounces, what is $L - R$?

A) 4
B) 40
C) 48
D) 64

9

Laura mixes $\frac{1}{4}$ cup of protein mix A with $\frac{3}{4}$ cup of protein mix B. Protein mix A contains 28 grams of protein per cup, and protein mix B contains 20 grams of protein per cup. How many grams of protein are in one cup of the protein mix Laura created?

A) 7
B) 12
C) 22
D) 48

10

On a map, the distance between two airports in a certain city is 7.5 inches. If 0.5 inch on the map corresponds to an actual distance of 14 miles, how many miles apart are the two airports?

11

A healthy baby elephant can weigh approximately 200 pounds at birth. What is the approximate weight of a healthy baby elephant at birth in kilograms, rounded to the nearest tenth? (1 kilogram = 2.20462 pounds)

12

A customer bought 12 bottles of water for $16.80. How much did the customer pay for each bottle of water, in dollars? (ignore the dollar sign).

Digital SAT Math Manual and Workbook

Category 43 – Rates

Key Points
- A rate is a ratio of two units of measurement. For example, 35 miles per hour has two units of measurements; miles and hours. The ratio can be written as 35 miles:1 hour or $\frac{35 \text{ miles}}{1 \text{ hour}}$. Similarly, 35 miles per gallon is 35 miles:1 gallon or $\frac{35 \text{ miles}}{1 \text{ gallon}}$.
- When two rates are compared, both units in the two rates must be compared, respectively. For example, when comparing the speed of a car in miles per hour to the speed in kilometers per second, miles must be compared to kilometers and per hour to per second.

How to Solve
Questions on rates can be solved using conversion factors or by setting up a proportion.

Conversion factors are a quicker method when working with several units of measurements.
- It is important to determine what the starting and ending units should be in the conversion process.
- When working with time units, a shortcut approach is to convert all time units to the smallest time unit before solving (see Alternative 1 in Example 1 below).

In this book, most questions on rates are solved using conversion factors. However, some of the questions may be quickly solved with simpler calculations. For example, if a car is traveling at a speed of 40 miles per hour, then in 15 minutes (one-fourth of an hour) the car will travel one-fourth the distance = 10 miles.

Example 1:
If a bus is driving at an average speed of 36 kilometers per hour, what is the equivalent speed in feet per second, rounded to the nearest tenth? (1 kilometer = 3,280 feet)

A) 10.5 feet per second
B) 32.8 feet per second
C) 36.0 feet per second
D) 60.0 feet per second

Step 1: Use conversion factors

Conversion factors should be set up such that the units cancel from left to right. The question is asking to convert kilometers per hour to feet per second. Hence, the starting units should be kilometers per hour and the ending units should be feet per second.

Converting hour to seconds requires two conversion factors, minutes per hour and seconds per minute.

$$\frac{36 \text{ kilometers}}{1 \text{ hour}} \times \frac{1 \text{ hour}}{60 \text{ minutes}} \times \frac{1 \text{ minute}}{60 \text{ seconds}} \times \frac{3,280 \text{ feet}}{1 \text{ kilometer}}$$

Cancel units from left to right.

$$\frac{36 \text{ kilometers}}{1 \text{ hour}} \times \frac{1 \text{ hour}}{60 \text{ minutes}} \times \frac{1 \text{ minute}}{60 \text{ seconds}} \times \frac{3,280 \text{ feet}}{1 \text{ kilometer}} = \frac{36 \times 3,280 \text{ feet}}{60 \times 60 \text{ seconds}} = \frac{32.8 \text{ feet}}{\text{seconds}} = 32.8 \text{ feet per second}$$

In the first conversion factor, the ratio is written as 36 kilometers:1 hour. Hence, hour is in the denominator.

The second conversion factor converts hours to minutes. Since the hours in the first and second conversion factors must cancel out, hours must be in the numerator of the second conversion factor. Hence, the ratio can be written as 1 hour:60 minutes (hours in the numerator). Writing it as 60 minutes:1 hour is incorrect as the hours will not cancel.

Similarly, in the third conversion factor the ratio must be written as 1 minute:60 seconds (minute in the numerator) so the minutes of the second and third conversion factors can cancel.

The correct answer choice is **B**.

Digital SAT Math Manual and Workbook

Alternative 1: Having one time unit during the conversion process can save time and avoid confusion with conversion factors. Since 1 hour = 3,600 seconds, replace 1 hour with 3,600 seconds.

$$\frac{36 \text{ kilometers}}{3,600 \text{ seconds}} \times \frac{3,280 \text{ feet}}{1 \text{ kilometer}} = \frac{36 \times 3,280 \text{ feet}}{3,600 \text{ seconds}} = 32.8 \text{ feet per second}$$

Alternative 2: See the solution below using proportion.

Start by converting kilometers per hour to feet per hour. Set up a proportion for kilometers and feet.

Let the unknown feet = x.

$$\frac{\text{kilometers}}{\text{feet}} \rightarrow \frac{36}{x} = \frac{1}{3,280}$$

$$x = 36 \times 3,280 \text{ feet per hour}$$

To convert feet per hour to feet per second divide by 3,600.

$$\frac{36 \times 3,280}{3,600} = 32.8 \text{ feet per second}$$

Example 2:

Taxi A and Taxi B pick up passengers from the same taxi stand and leave at the same time in opposite directions on a straight path. Taxi A is going at the average speed of 40 miles per hour. Taxi B is going at the average speed of 30 miles per hour. How many miles apart the taxis will be in 15 minutes?

Step 1: Use the conversion factors

Since the taxis are traveling in opposite directions, the distance between them is the sum of the distance traveled by each taxi in 15 minutes. Since miles traveled in 15 minutes must be determined, the starting unit should be 15 minutes and ending unit should be miles.

Taxi A: 40 miles per hour = 40 miles in 60 minutes.

$$15 \text{ minutes} \times \frac{40 \text{ miles}}{60 \text{ minutes}} = \frac{15 \times 40 \text{ miles}}{60} = 10 \text{ miles}$$

Taxi B: 30 miles per hour = 30 miles in 60 minutes.

$$15 \text{ minutes} \times \frac{30 \text{ miles}}{60 \text{ minutes}} = \frac{15 \times 30 \text{ miles}}{60} = 7.5 \text{ miles}$$

The distance between taxi A and taxi B = 10 + 7.5 = 17.5 miles.

The correct answer is **17.5**.

Example 3:

Preena drove 44 miles from her home to a shopping mall. The fuel consumption of Preena's car is 28 miles per gallon, and the cost of fuel is $2.89 per gallon. What is the cost, in dollars, of the fuel consumed during Preena's drive from her home to the shopping mall, rounded to the nearest hundred?

A) $0.50
B) $2.01
C) $3.52
D) $4.54

Step 1: Use the conversion factors

Since the dollar cost of 44 miles must be determined, the starting unit should be 44 miles and ending unit should be dollars. (This is an example of when using conversion factors is the quickest approach to solve a question.)

$$44 \text{ miles} \times \frac{1 \text{ gallon}}{28 \text{ miles}} \times \frac{2.89 \text{ dollars}}{1 \text{ gallon}} = \frac{44 \times 2.89 \text{ dollars}}{28} = 4.54 \text{ dollars}$$

The correct answer is **D**.

Category 43 – Practice Questions

1

A car driving at an average speed of 30 miles per hour will travel how many miles in 10 minutes?

A) 3
B) 5
C) 10
D) 30

2

A wheel is rolling at an average speed of x inches per minute. Which of the following equations represents the time, in seconds, it will take for the wheel to roll y inches, where x and y are constants?

A) xy
B) $60xy$
C) $\dfrac{12x}{y}$
D) $\dfrac{60y}{x}$

3

Sam drove at an average speed of 45 miles per hour for a total of 140 minutes. How many miles did Sam drive?

4

Casper drove his truck on a certain highway for 2 hours at an average speed of 50 miles per hour. If the fuel consumption of Casper's truck on the highway is 20 miles per gallon, and the cost of fuel is $3 per gallon, which of the following is the cost of the fuel consumed during the 2 hour drive on the highway, assuming Casper did not stop during the 2 hours?

A) $3
B) $12
C) $15
D) $20

5

Water flows from a tank at the rate of 768 ounces per minute. Which of the following is equivalent to the rate of water flow in gallons per second?
(1 gallon = 128 ounces)

A) 0.1 gallon per second
B) 0.5 gallon per second
C) 1.1 gallons per second
D) 6 gallons per second

6

Jolie and Charlie started bicycling from the same point in a straight line in opposite directions for 40 minutes. Jodie rode the bicycle at an average speed of 10 miles per hour. Charlie rode the bicycle at an average speed of 18 miles per hour. After 15 minutes from the start, Jolie and Charlie were approximately how many miles apart?

A) 2
B) 3
C) 5
D) 7

Digital SAT Math Manual and Workbook

7

Jerry took a non-stop flight from New York to London. The total flight distance was 3,459 miles. The plane flew for 4 hours at an average speed of 526 miles per hour and for the remaining x minutes at an average speed of 420 miles per hour. Ignoring the air resistance, which of the following is closest to the value of x?

A) 3
B) 27
C) 102
D) 194

8

Two birds take off from a tree at the same time in a straight line and same direction. If bird A is flying at an average speed of 18 miles per hour, and bird B is flying at an average speed of 24 miles per hour, how far behind, in miles, is bird A from bird B in 10 minutes?

A) 1.0
B) 1.5
C) 3.1
D) 4.5

9

A water tank pumps out sprays of water around a farmland at the rate of 36 gallons per hour. How many ounces of water is pumped out per second? (1 gallon = 128 ounces)

A) 0.01
B) 0.92
C) 1.28
D) 3.60

10

Rosario drove from her home to a shopping mall for 45 minutes. For the first 15 minutes, she drove at an average speed of 60 miles per hour. For the remaining 30 minutes, she drove at an average speed of 40 miles per hour. How many miles did Rosario drive from her home to the shopping mall?

A) 30
B) 35
C) 55
D) 90

11

A train traveling at an average speed of 180 kilometers per hour travels how many meters in 1 second? (1 kilometer = 1,000 meters)

12

If Maria rides her bicycle at an average speed of 20 miles per hour, how many minutes will it take her to ride 4 miles?

13

John drives 100 miles on each working day. The fuel consumption of his car is 30 miles per gallon. In 4 working days, how many liters of fuel is consumed by John's car, rounded to the nearest tenth? (1 gallon = 3.8 liters)

Section 8 – Review Questions

1

If Samantha rides her bike at an average speed of 30 kilometers per hour, how many minutes will it take her to ride 10 kilometers?

A) 10
B) 20
C) 55
D) 60

2

Sara reads p pages in m minutes. Which of the following expressions could represent the number of pages Sara reads in 3 hours in terms of p and m?

A) $3pm$
B) $180pm$
C) $\dfrac{3p}{m}$
D) $\dfrac{180p}{m}$

3

A bald eagle can achieve a flying speed of 30 miles per hour using powerful wingbeats, and up to 100 miles per hour when diving straight down to catch a prey. If a bald eagle dives straight down at the speed of 60 miles per hour to catch a prey 0.2 miles away, how many seconds will it take the eagle to catch the prey?

A) 4
B) 5
C) 12
D) 30

4

A mixture contains 20 grams of salt in 500 milliliters of water. If a second mixture is created in the same proportion, which of the following could be the ratios of salt to water in the second mixture?

I. $1:25$
II. $3:50$
III. $5:125$

A) II only
B) III only
C) I and III only
D) II and III only

5

A meteorologist report showed that in a certain city in 2019, the ratio of the total annual rainfall, in inches, to the rainfall in the month of March, in inches, was 12.4 to 3.1. If r is the total inches of annual rainfall in 2019, which of the following expressions represents the rainfall in March 2019, in inches, in terms of r?

A) $\dfrac{r}{4}$
B) $\dfrac{12}{r}$
C) $3.1r$
D) 12.4

Digital SAT Math Manual and Workbook

6

A train is traveling at an average speed of 120 miles per hour. What is the equivalent average speed of the train in feet per second?
(1 mile is 5,280 feet)

A) 44 feet per second
B) 52 feet per second
C) 120 feet per second
D) 176 feet per second

7

A painter takes 8 hours to paint 140 square feet of an area. For every 100 square feet of an area, the painter earns $250. How many hours will it take the painter to earn $1,400?

A) 20
B) 32
C) 44
D) 100

8

A study revealed that in 15 minutes a pilot whale can dive up to a depth of 3,280 feet to catch a squid. What is the approximate equivalent depth, in miles?
(1 mile = 5,280 feet)

A) 0.6
B) 1.1
C) 1.6
D) 16.2

9

Plane A and Plane B are flying from California to Sydney. Plane A flies at an average speed of 600 miles per hour, and Plane B flies at an average speed of 500 miles per hour. If the two planes continue to fly at the above speeds for the next 30 minutes, how many more miles would Plane A fly than Plane B, ignoring the wind speed?

10

A hiker follows a map of a hiking trail. Each mile on the map is scaled to 0.2 centimeters. If the hiking trail is 30 miles, how many centimeters represent it on the map?

11

Names of roads and highways	Distance in centimeter
State Road 27	$\frac{1}{8}$
Highway 2	$1\frac{1}{4}$
Highway 17	$\frac{1}{4}$
State Road 4	$\frac{3}{4}$

Bentley is planning a road trip in a car, and using a map that represents 24 miles as $\frac{1}{2}$ centimeter to determine the distance he will be driving on various roads and highways. The above table summarizes the distance on the map in centimeters. If Bentley estimates that the fuel consumption of the car on State Road 27 and State Road 4 will be 28 miles per gallon, how many gallons of fuel will be consumed driving on both these roads?

Section 9 – Percentages

Category 44 – Percentages of a Number and Percent Increase/Decrease
Category 45 – The Original Number before a Percent Increase/Decrease
Category 46 – A Number Percent of Another Number
Category 47 – Percent Change
Section 9 – Review Questions

Category 44 – Percentages of a Number and Percent Increase/Decrease

Key Points

- Percent (%) refers to parts of a number per 100. For example, 32 parts per 100 is 32%. It can also be written as $\frac{32}{100}$ or 0.32. Similarly, 260 parts per 100 is 260% or $\frac{260}{100}$ or 2.6.
- A percent decrease refers to a decrease in parts of a number per 100. For example, a 20% decrease of number n is $100 - 20 = 80\% n$ or $\frac{80}{100} n$ or $0.8n$.
- A percent increase refers to an increase in parts of a number per 100. For example, a 20% increase of number n is $100 + 20 = 120\% n$ or $\frac{120}{100} n$ or $1.2n$. Similarly, 250% increase of number n is $100 + 250 = 350\% n$ or $3.5n$.
- Multiple increases and decreases can be multiplied together. For example, a 20% increase (1.2) of a number n, followed by a 10% increase (1.1) and then followed by a 25% decrease (0.75) is $(1.2 \times 1.1 \times 0.75)n = 0.99n$.
  - The order of multiplication does not matter. $(0.75 \times 1.2 \times 1.1 \times n)$, or $(1.1 \times 0.75 \times 1.2 \times n)$, or $(n \times 1.2 \times 0.75 \times 1.1)$ will give the same answer.

How to Solve

The quickest approach to determining the percent of a number or the percent increase/decrease of a number is to convert the percent to a decimal and multiply it by the given number. For example,

- 10% of $50 = 0.1 \times 50 = 5$.
- 10% increase of $50 = 1.1 \times 50 = 55$.
- 10% decrease of $50 = 0.9 \times 50 = 45$.

Remember that incremental percent increases and decreases are multiplied not added. For example, a 10% increase followed by a 20% increase is not $10\% + 2\% = 30\%$ increase.

The distinction between the percent of a number and percent increase of a number is important to remember, especially when the percent increase is greater than 100. For example, 300% of 50 is $3 \times 50 = 150$, whereas a 300% increase of 50 is $(1 + 3) \times 50 = 4 \times 50 = 200$.

*Percent of a number can be determined using the Desmos graphing calculator.

*Example 1:

What is 6% of 150% of 80% of 50?

Step 1: Convert percent to decimal

$$80\% = 0.8$$
$$150\% = 1.5$$
$$6\% = 0.06$$

Step 2: Determine the final value

Multiply all decimals and the given number.

$$0.8 \times 1.5 \times 0.06 \times 50 = 3.6$$

The correct answer is **3.6**.

*In the Desmos graphing calculator, type each percent, one at a time, followed by 50, in a row in the Expression List. This will result in 80% of 150% of 6% of 50. Note that as each percent is typed, "of" will automatically appear after that. Hence, typing "of" is not required. The answer will be displayed to the right in the same row as = 3.6.

Example 2:

In 2015, 80 students were enrolled in a music club at a certain high school. In 2016, the number of students enrolled in the music class increased by 10%. In 2017, 25% fewer students enrolled in the music club than in 2016. How many students were enrolled in the music class in 2017?

A) 52

B) 66

C) 88

D) 108

Step 1: Convert percent to decimal

$$10 \text{ percent increase in } 2016 = 1 + 0.1 = 1.1$$
$$25 \text{ percent fewer in } 2017 = 25 \text{ percent decrease in } 2017 = 1 - 0.25 = 0.75$$

Step 2: Determine the final value

$$1.1 \times 0.75 \times 80 = 66$$

The correct answer choice is **B**.

Example 3:

A garden center has discounted the original price of each rose bush by 14% for the entire month of June. Each Sunday during June, an additional 23% discount is offered on the already discounted price. If the original price of a rose bush is $39.99 and no sales tax is collected, which of the following expressions represents the discounted price of a rose bush, in dollars, on a Sunday in June?

A) $(39.99)(0.14)(0.23)$

B) $(39.99)(0.86)(0.23)$

C) $(39.99)(0.86)(0.77)$

D) $(39.99)(1.14)(1.23)$

Step 1: Convert percent to decimal

$$14 \text{ percent discount} = 14 \text{ percent decrease in price} = 1 - 0.14 = 0.86$$
$$23 \text{ percent discount} = 23 \text{ percent decrease in price} = 1 - 0.23 = 0.77$$

Step 2: Determine the final value

Original price = $39.99.

Total percent discount = $(0.86)(0.77)$.

$$\text{final price} = (39.99)(0.86)(0.77)$$

The correct answer choice is **C**.

Category 44 – Practice Questions

1

The value of a number k is decreased by 25% and then increased by 6%. Which of the following expressions represents the final value of k?

A) $(0.75)(1.06)(k)$
B) $(0.81)(1.06)(k)$
C) $(1.25)(0.4)(k)$
D) $(1.25)(1.6)(k)$

2

If 72 is decreased by 25% and then increased by 150%, which of the following is closest to the result?

A) 54
B) 81
C) 90
D) 135

3

Every week, John analyzes his stock portfolio on Friday night. Last week, the starting balance of the portfolio on Monday was s dollars. The portfolio increased by 55% on Tuesday, decreased by 13% on Wednesday, increased by 117% on Thursday, and remained unchanged on Monday and Friday. Which of the following expressions represents the ending balance of John's stock portfolio last week on Friday night?

A) $(1.55)(0.87)(1.17)(s)$
B) $(1.55)(0.87)(2.17)(s)$
C) $(1.55)(1.13)(0.83)(s)$
D) $(4.59)(s)$

4

A library uses a computer system to check-in and check-out books. The librarian monitors the inventory of books each morning before opening the library and each evening after closing the library. Last Monday, the library had a total of 1,040 books in its inventory before the opening time. After the closing time, 20% of books from the inventory were checked out and 125 books were returned. Which of the following was the number of books in the library last Monday after closing?

A) 333
B) 832
C) 957
D) 1,248

5

An electronic store is offering a 35% discount on the television that Jenny wants to buy. She has a coupon for 12% discount that can be applied to the already discounted price of the television. If p dollars is the price of the television without any discount, which of the following expressions represents the total amount, in dollars, Jenny will pay after both the discounts are applied and 8% sales tax is added to the final price?

A) $(0.65)(0.88)(1.08)(p)$
B) $(0.65)(1.12)(1.8)(p)$
C) $(1.35)(0.88)(0.92)(p)$
D) $(1.35)(1.12)(1.08)(p)$

6

Jane has a collection of 125 music CDs. She is planning on giving 20% of the collection to her brother and 35% to her cousin. How many CDs will Jane have left after she gives them to her brother and cousin?

A) 56
B) 65
C) 70
D) 110

7 — Desmos

What is 200% of 30% of 25% of 60?

A) 9
B) 54
C) 68
D) 150

8

In the current school year, 200 students are enrolled in chemistry courses at a certain high school. The school administration has projected an increase of 10% enrollment in chemistry courses each year for the next 2 academic years. Which of the following is the total number of students projected to be enrolled in the chemistry courses in 2 academic years from the current year?

A) 210
B) 220
C) 240
D) 242

9

In 2015, an independent research company projected that by 2020 the number of residents in a remote island will increase by 160%. In 2020, there were 3,680 residents on the remote island. How many additional residents were projected by 2020?

A) 1,000
B) 2,208
C) 5,888
D) 9,568

10

In 2019, Rita received 6% more bonus than the estimated bonus of d dollars. How much bonus did Rita receive in 2019 in terms of d?

A) $1.06d$
B) $1.6d$
C) $d + 1.06$
D) $d + 6$

11

Tom took three history tests during the first semester of school. On the first test, he scored an 80. On the second test, he scored 20% less than the first test, and on the third test, he scored 25% more than the second test. What was the score of Tom's third history test?

Digital SAT Math Manual and Workbook

Category 45 – The Original Number before a Percent Increase/Decrease

Key Points
- When a number is modified by a percent increase or decrease, the original number (before the increase or decrease) can be determined as follows, where the end number is the number after percent increase/decrease.

$$\text{original number} = \frac{\text{end number}}{1 \pm \text{percent increase or decrease, as decimal}}$$

- If the original number was decreased by a certain percent, then the denominator is $1 - \text{percent decrease}$. For example, the denominator for a 30% decrease is $1 - 0.3 = 0.7$.
- If the original number was increased by a certain percent, then the denominator is $1 + \text{percent increase}$. For example, the denominator for a 30% increase is $1 + 0.3 = 1.3$.
- Multiple increases and decreases can be multiplied. For example, if the original number was decreased by 30% and then increased by 20%, the denominator is (0.7×1.2).

How to Solve
If a question gives a dollar cost with sales tax, remember to include it in the denominator as a percent increase.

Example 1:
Tina bought a shirt at a 15% discount. The price of the discounted shirt after an addition of 6% sales tax was $18.02.

Question 1
If the original price of the shirt before the sales tax and discount was a dollars, which of the following expressions represents the value of a?

A) $\dfrac{18.02}{(0.85)(0.6)}$

B) $\dfrac{18.02}{(0.85)(1.06)}$

C) $(0.85)(0.94)18.02$

D) $(0.85)(1.6)18.02$

Step 1: Convert percent to decimal
$$\text{discount} = 15\% \text{ decrease} = 1 - 0.15 = 0.85$$
$$\text{sales tax} = 6\% \text{ increase} = 1 + 0.06 = 1.06$$

Step 2: Determine the original value
End price = $18.02. Total increase/decrease = $(0.85)(1.06)$.
$$\text{original price} = \frac{18.02}{(0.85)(1.06)}$$

The correct answer choice is **B**.

Question 2
What was the original price of the shirt, in dollars, excluding the sales tax?

Proceed from Step 2 of Question 1 and solve the equation for the original price.
$$\frac{18.02}{0.85 \times 1.06} = 20$$

The correct answer is **20**.

Category 45 – Practice Questions

1

The number n when decreased by 20% and then increased by 5% is 42. Which of the following expressions represents the number n?

A) $\dfrac{42}{(0.8)(1.05)}$

B) $\dfrac{42}{(1.2)(1.05)}$

C) $(0.8)(1.05)42$

D) $(0.8)(0.95)42$

2

A retail company closed 27% of its worldwide stores between January 2018 and December 2022. At the end of December 2022, the company had 584 stores open. How many open stores did the retail company have worldwide before the closing began in January 2018?

A) 426
B) 700
C) 742
D) 800

3

Yulana bought a shirt at a 40% discount. The total price of the shirt after the discount and inclusion of 6% sales tax was $15.90. What was the original price of the shirt before the discount was applied and sales tax was included?

A) $6
B) $10
C) $25
D) $28

4

When the number p is increased by 20% and then decreased by 10%, the value is 378. What is number p?

A) 302
B) 350
C) 378
D) 416

5

A bookstore has discounted the original price of all the books by 30%. Sam's library membership card gives him a 5% discount over the discounted price. If Sam paid $5.32 for a book and no sales tax was collected, what was the original price of the book?

A) $3
B) $5
C) $8
D) $10

6

A manufacturing company's profit for 2018 was 10.5 million dollars. This was 25% higher than the profit of 2017, in millions of dollars. The profit of 2017, in millions of dollars, was 20% higher than the profit of 2016. Which of the following is closest to the company's profit in 2016, in millions of dollars?

A) 7
B) 8
C) 10
D) 19

Category 46 – A Number Percent of Another Number

Key Points
- If x and y are two numbers, then x is what percent of y (also worded as what percent of y is x) can be determined as follows.

$$\frac{x}{y} \times 100$$

How to Solve
Translate the question as 'x is what percent of y' and solve.

Example 1:
In 1980, approximately 3 million geese migrated to the central part of United States during winter. In 2015, the number of geese that migrated increased to approximately 15 million. The geese migration in 1980 was what percent of the geese migration in 2015?

A) 12%
B) 20%
C) 33%
D) 50%

Step 1: Translate question into 'x is what percent of y'

Geese migration in 1980 = 3. Geese migration in 2015 = 15.

The question is asking "geese migration in 1980 was what percent of geese migration in 2015". This is same as "3 is what percent of 15". Hence, the numerator = 3 and denominator = 15.

$$\frac{3}{15} \times 100 = 20\%$$

The correct answer choice is **B**.

Example 2:
In 1980, approximately 3 million geese migrated to the central part of United States during winter. In 2015, the geese migration increased by 400%. In 1980, the geese migration was what percent of the geese migration in 2015?

A) 12%
B) 20%
C) 40%
D) 140%

Step 1: Determine the number of geese in 2015

The number of geese in 2015 must be determined before solving.

$$400\% \text{ percent increase} = 1 + 4 = 5$$
$$\text{number of geese } 3 \times 5 = 15$$

Step 2: Translate question into 'x is what percent of y'

Follow Step 1 of Example 1.

The correct answer choice is **B**.

Digital SAT Math Manual and Workbook

Category 46 – Practice Questions

1

What percent of 30 is 12?

A) 35%
B) 40%
C) 60%
D) 75%

2

An office manager is shopping for a new table for the office lobby. The original price of the table the office manager wants to buy is $250. Store A is selling the table for the discounted price of $215, whereas Store B is selling the same table for the discounted price of $200. What is the difference in the discount, in percent, of the table at Store A and Store B?

A) 6%
B) 9%
C) 15%
D) 35%

3

If a number p is increased by 25%, what percent is p of the increased number, where $p = 72$?

A) 25%
B) 75%
C) 77%
D) 80%

4

Jeremy bought a computer for $1,200 from Store A. No sales tax was collected. At Store B, the same computer was advertised for $1,180 and an additional 10% in-store discount. If a is the price of the computer, in dollars, at store B after the 10% in-store discount on the advertised price, what percent of $1,200 is a?

A) 85.5%
B) 88.5%
C) 90.0%
D) 98.5%

5

Chris went to a local fair with his friends and bought a ride pass for $40. For each ride, $3.20 is deducted from the value of the ride pass. What percent of the initial value of the ride pass is each ride?

A) 3.2%
B) 4.5%
C) 7%
D) 8%

6

Neena bought a pair of shoes for $43.20 inclusive of an 8% sales tax. When she returned the shoes after 3 months, she was refunded $36, which included the full refund of 8% sales tax. The return price is what percent of the original price, excluding any sales tax?

A) 21%
B) 80%
C) 82%
D) 84%

Digital SAT Math Manual and Workbook

Category 47 – Percent Change

Key Points
- Percent change is the percent by which a number is changed (increased or decreased).
  - The number before the change is referred to as the "old value", and the number after the change is referred to as the "new value".
  - When the new value is higher than the old value, the percentage change is an increase and is positive. When the new value is lower than the old value, the percentage change is a decrease and is negative.
- The formula for percent change is

$$\text{percent change} = \frac{\text{new value} - \text{old value}}{\text{old value}} \times 100$$

How to Solve
When the percent change is negative, ignore the negative sign. It simply means that the percent change is a decrease.

Example 1:
Last year, Natalie saved $6,340. This year she plans to save $5,200. Which of the following is closest to the percent change in Natalie's savings from last year to this year?

A) 18%
B) 25%
C) 76%
D) 81%

Step 1: Determine old value and new value
Old value is the amount Natalie saved last year = $6,340.
New value is the amount Natalie plans to save this year = $5,200.

Step 2: Determine the percent change

$$\frac{5{,}200 - 6{,}340}{6{,}340} \times 100 = \frac{-1{,}140}{6{,}340} \times 100 = -17.98\%$$

The percent change is negative, indicating a decrease of 17.98%. Answer choice A is closest.
The correct answer choice is **A**.

Category 47 – Practice Questions

1

In 2015, a car dealership reported a profit of 1.2 million dollars. In 2017, the profit increased to 1.6 million dollars. Which of the following is the percent change in profit, rounded to the nearest tenth?

A) 25.0%
B) 33.3%
C) 65.5%
D) 80.5%

2

The original price of a scarf is $20. The final price after the discount is $8, excluding sales tax. What is the percent change in the price of the scarf after the discount?

A) 35%
B) 40%
C) 60%
D) 80%

3

An online retailer has reduced the sale price of a certain computer from $3,200 to $2,300. The original and reduced prices are inclusive of a $200 warranty that is not affected by the price reduction. What is the percent change in the price of the computer, rounded to the nearest whole number?

A) 28%
B) 30%
C) 41%
D) 60%

4

Month	Number of students
January	80
February	88
March	110
April	120
May	132

A certain school offers a monthly meal plan to all students at the school. The table above shows the number of students enrolled in the meal plan each month for a five-month period in 2020. Based on the table, during which two months was the percent change in the number of students the greatest?

A) From January to February
B) From February to March
C) From March to April
D) From April to May

5

The value of a certain home increased from $342,000 to $410,400 in a three-year period. What was the percent change in the value of the home in the three-year period?

A) 20%
B) 25%
C) 80%
D) 120%

Section 9 – Review Questions

1

Makenna got a $75 gift card to a clothing store on her birthday. If Makenna bought a shirt for $9 and a jacket for $17.25 using the gift card, the remaining balance on the gift card is what percent of the starting value of the gift card?

A) 35%
B) 55%
C) 65%
D) 80%

2

Last year, a company gave its employees 12 paid vacation days in a year. This year, the company announced that the employees will get 14 paid vacation days in a year. By what percent did the number of vacation days change from last year to this year?

A) Decreased by 11.66%
B) Decreased by 20%
C) Increased by 11.66%
D) Increased by 16.66%

3

Juana paid d dollars for a hat after 15% discount and addition of 8% sales tax. In terms of d, which of the following expressions represents the price of the hat before the 15% discount and excluding the 8% sales tax?

A) $\dfrac{d}{(0.85)(1.08)}$
B) $\dfrac{d}{(1.15)(1.08)}$
C) $(0.85)(0.92)d$
D) $(1.15)(0.92)d$

4

An environmental research company is studying the population of two species of birds, Bird A and Bird B, in a certain forest. In 2019, the populations of Bird A and Bird B were the same. From 2016 to 2019, the population of Bird A increased by 5%, and the population of Bird B increased by 20%. If the population of Bird A in 2016 was 6,000, what was the population of Bird B in 2016?

A) 4,800
B) 5,250
C) 6,300
D) 7,200

5

If the beginning value of a number is $2k$ and ending value is $0.6k$, what is the percent change in the value of the number, where k is a constant?

A) 30%
B) 60%
C) 70%
D) 140%

6

The population of a certain species of fish decreased by 6% from 1999 to 2004. From 2005 to 2009, the population of fish increased by 19%, and from 2010 to 2015, the population of fish increased by 22%. If s was the population of fish in 1999, which of the following expressions represents the population of fish in 2015?

A) $(0.94)(0.81)(0.78)(s)$
B) $(0.94)(1.19)(1.22)(s)$
C) $(0.94)(1.41)(s)$
D) $(1.35)(s)$

7

Of all the members currently enrolled in a certain fitness club, 140 members participated in a yoga class or a karate class. If 40% of all the members enrolled in the fitness club participated in a yoga class or a karate class, and each member participated in one class, how many total members are currently enrolled in the fitness club?

A) 52
B) 140
C) 210
D) 350

8

Jim went to an amusement arcade with his friends. At the arcade, he bought a cashless card worth $20 to play his favorite game. If Jim played 36 rounds of his favorite game and for every 3 rounds of games played $0.50 was deducted from the cashless card, the dollar amount remaining on the cashless card is what percent of the starting amount of $20?

A) 30%
B) 40%
C) 60%
D) 70%

9   Desmos

What is 14% of 1,050?

A) 14
B) 105
C) 147
D) 250

10   Desmos

Out of the 275 trees planted at an orchard, 48% were pear trees. How many pear trees were planted?

11

A supermarket chain closed 20% of its stores between 2015 and 2018. In 2018, 112 stores were open. How many stores were open in 2015?

12

A number n when decreased by 10% is equal to x. A number p when increased by 20% is equal to x. If number n is 40, what is number p?

13

Last Friday, Kamla rented a concert hall for a dance performance. Her total earnings from the performance were x dollars. If she had $784 left after paying 20% in miscellaneous costs, what is x?

14

The students at a certain high school are given the option to join an annual cooking club. In the current academic year, 40% of the students joined the cooking club. If the number of students who joined the club is 96 less than the number of students who did not join the club, how many students attend the high school in the current academic year?

Digital SAT Math Manual and Workbook

Section 10 – Exponents and Exponential Functions

Category 48 – Exponents

Category 49 – Linear Versus Exponential Growth and Decay

Category 50 – Exponential Growth and Decay

Category 51 – Graphs of Exponential Growth and Decay Functions

Section 10 – Review Questions

Category 48 – Exponents

Key Points

- When a number is multiplied by itself several times, such as $3 \times 3 \times 3 \times 3$, the number is called the base and number of times the base is multiplied by itself is called the exponent. Since 3 is multiplied by itself 4 times, 3 is the base and 4 is the exponent. It can be written as 3^4. The same applies for an expression. For example, $3abk \times 3abk \times 3abk \times 3abk \times 3abk$ can be written as $(3abk)^5$, where $3abk$ is the base and 5 is the exponent.
- When a number or an expression has a negative sign that is not within the parentheses, then the negative sign is not part of the base. When the negative sign is within the parentheses, then it is part of the base. For example, $-a^3$ is $-(a \times a \times a)$ and $(-a)^3$ is $(-a \times -a \times -a)$.
- The following are the exponent rules:
  - $x^0 = 1$
  - $x^a \times x^b = x^{a+b}$
  - $\frac{x^a}{x^b} = x^{a-b}$
  - $(x^a)^b = x^{ab}$
  - $(xy)^a = x^a y^a$
  - $\left(\frac{x}{y}\right)^a = \frac{x^a}{y^a}$
  - $x^{-a} = \frac{1}{x^a}$
- When a number or an expression is within a root (square root, cube root, and so on), the root can be removed and replaced with a fractional exponent. The value of the root is the denominator of the fraction. The entire expression within the root must be to the power of the fractional exponent. For example,
  - $\sqrt{x} = x^{\frac{1}{2}}$
  - $\sqrt[3]{x^3} = (x^3)^{\frac{1}{3}} = x^{\frac{3}{3}} = x$
  - $\sqrt[4]{x^5} = (x^5)^{\frac{1}{4}} = x^{\frac{5}{4}}$
  - $\sqrt[6]{xy} = (xy)^{\frac{1}{6}}$
  - $\sqrt[4]{x^3 y^3} = \sqrt[4]{(xy)^3} = ((xy)^3)^{\frac{1}{4}} = (xy)^{\frac{3}{4}}$
  - $\sqrt[3]{3y^3} = (3y^3)^{\frac{1}{3}} = 3^{\frac{1}{3}} \times y^{\frac{3}{3}} = 3^{\frac{1}{3}} y$
- When the bases of two numbers or expressions are the same, the exponents can be equated. For example, if $y^a = y^b$, then $a = b$.

How to Solve

A question may require equating two exponents that do not have the same base, but the bases are multiples of the same number. For example, in the equation $8^2 = 2^x$, since the bases are different the value of x cannot be determined by equating the exponents. When 8^2 is rewritten as $(2^3)^2$, the equation is $2^6 = 2^x$. Now since the bases are the same, the exponents can be equated. Hence, $x = 6$. In such questions, being able to recognize multiples can be helpful. See a few examples of multiples below.

- $4 = 2^2, 8 = 2^3, 16 = 4^2 = 2^4, 32 = 2^5, 64 = 8^2 = 4^3 = 2^6$.
- $9 = 3^2, 27 = 3^3, 81 = 9^2 = 3^4$.
- $25 = 5^2, 125 = 5^3$.

Example 1:

Which expression is equivalent to $\frac{m^4 n^5}{m^2 n^2} \times n^{-2}$, where m and n are positive?

A) $m^6 n^5$

B) $m^2 n$

C) $\frac{m^4 n^3}{m^{-2} n^{-2}}$

D) $\frac{m^{-2} n^{-1}}{m^2 n^2}$

Step 1: Simplify by applying rules

Apply the $\frac{x^a}{x^b} = x^{a-b}$ rule to m and n and simplify.

$$(m^{4-2} n^{5-2}) \times n^{-2} \rightarrow m^2 n^3 \times n^{-2}$$

Apply the $x^a \times x^b = x^{a+b}$ rule to n.

$$m^2 n^{3-2} \rightarrow m^2 n$$

The correct answer choice is **B**.

Example 2:

Which expression is equivalent to $\frac{\sqrt[3]{x^4}}{\sqrt[4]{x^5}}$, where $x > 0$?

A) $x^{\frac{3}{4}}$

B) $x^{\frac{4}{5}}$

C) $x^{\frac{3}{5}}$

D) $x^{\frac{1}{12}}$

Step 1: Simplify by applying rules

Replace roots with fractional exponents.

$$\frac{x^{\frac{4}{3}}}{x^{\frac{5}{4}}}$$

Apply the $\frac{x^a}{x^b} = x^{a-b}$ rule and simplify the fractional exponent.

$$x^{\frac{4}{3} - \frac{5}{4}} \rightarrow x^{\frac{16-15}{12}} \rightarrow x^{\frac{1}{12}}$$

The correct answer choice is **D**.

Example 3:

What is the value of m in the equation $\sqrt{16t^4} = (2t)^{m-1}$, where m is a positive number?

Step 1: Simplify by applying rules

In the left expression, replace root with fractional exponent and write 16 as 2^4. This will result in the same bases on both sides of the equation.

$$(16t^4)^{\frac{1}{2}} = (2t)^{m-1} \rightarrow (2^4 t^4)^{\frac{1}{2}} = (2t)^{m-1} \rightarrow (2t)^{4 \times \frac{1}{2}} = (2t)^{m-1} \rightarrow (2t)^2 = (2t)^{m-1}$$

Since the base $(2t)$ is the same on both sides, the exponents can be equated.

$$m - 1 = 2 \rightarrow m = 3$$

The correct answer is **3**.

Category 48 – Practice Questions

1

Which of the following is equivalent to $3^2 \times 27^4$?

A) 3
B) 51
C) 3^{14}
D) 27^6

2

In the equation $y = 259(a)^x$, a is greater than 1. What is the value of y when $x = 0$?

A) 0
B) 259
C) $259a$
D) $\dfrac{259}{a}$

3

In the equation $(9^3)^{n+1} = (81)^3 \times 3^{3n}$, what is the value of n?

A) 2
B) 3
C) 6
D) 8

4

If $4^{3a-1} = 2^{3+a} \times 32^b$, which of the following could represent the value of b in terms of a?

A) a
B) $a - 1$
C) $a - b$
D) $ab + 1$

5

Which of the following expressions is equivalent to $(16x^5y^3)^{\frac{1}{2}}$, where x and y are positive numbers?

A) $4\sqrt{x^4y^2}$
B) $4x^5y^3\sqrt{x^5y^3}$
C) $4\sqrt{x^5y}$
D) $4x^2y\sqrt{xy}$

6

Which expression is equivalent to $(3y)^{\frac{3}{a}}$, where $y > 0$?

A) $\sqrt[a]{3y^3}$
B) $\sqrt[3]{27y^a}$
C) $\sqrt[a]{27y^3}$
D) $ay^{\frac{3}{2}}$

7

$$\dfrac{\sqrt{5a^4}}{\sqrt[4]{5a^3}}$$

In the above expression a is a positive number. If the expression is equivalent to k, which of the following expressions can represent k?

A) $a^{\frac{4}{3}}$
B) $5a^7$
C) $\sqrt[4]{5a^5}$
D) $\sqrt[5]{5a^3}$

Digital SAT Math Manual and Workbook

8

Which of the following expressions is equivalent to $(27a^9)^{\frac{1}{3}}$ for all the positive values of a?

A) $a^{\frac{5}{2}}$
B) $3a^3$
C) $\sqrt[3]{3a^6}$
D) $\sqrt[2]{27a^9}$

9

If $9^{4a} = \sqrt[5]{3^4}$, what is the value of a?

A) $\frac{1}{10}$
B) $\frac{1}{5}$
C) $\frac{5}{4}$
D) 4

10

Which of the following is equivalent to $\sqrt{r} \sqrt[3]{r}$, where $r > 0$?

A) $r^{\frac{5}{6}}$
B) r^4
C) $2r^{\frac{1}{3}}$
D) r

11

In the equation $2^a y^4 = 80$ and $2^b y^4 = 5$, what is the value of $a - b$, where $y > 0$?

A) -2
B) 0
C) 2
D) 4

12

$$\left(\frac{x^5 y^{-2}}{x^{-2} y^3}\right) x^{-6} y^6$$

Which of the following expressions is equivalent to the above expression, where x and y are positive numbers?

A) xy
B) $x^{-5} y$
C) $\frac{x^3 y}{x^{-2}}$
D) $\frac{x^3 y^4}{x^2 y^2}$

13

If $\sqrt[3]{64m^3} = 20$, what is the value of m, where $m > 0$?

14

$$\frac{\sqrt{s^3 s^5}}{\sqrt[5]{s^2}} = s^{\frac{x}{y}}$$

What is the value of $\frac{x}{y}$ in the above expression for all positive values of s?

15

If $a^2 = 10$ and $b^5 = 50$, what is the value of $(a^6)(b^{-5})$?

Category 49 – Linear Versus Exponential Growth and Decay

Key Points
- A linear increase or decrease occurs at a constant rate. Exponential growth starts slowly followed by a rapid increase. Exponential decay starts with a rapid decrease followed by a slower decrease. See examples below.
  - If the number 400 is increased by 2 each day, then the increase each day is the same. On the first day of increase, the number will be 402, 404 the day after, 406 the day after, 408 the day after, and so on. This is a linear increase (or increasing linearly). If the number 400 is doubled each day, then the increase each day is significantly greater. On the first day of increase, the number will be 800, 1,600 the day after, 3,200 the day after, 6,400 the day after, and so on. This is exponential growth (increase).
  - If the number 400 is decreased by 2 each day, then the decrease each day is the same. On the first day of decrease, the number will be 398, 396 the day after, 394 the day after, 392 the day after, and so on. This is a linear decrease (or decreasing linearly). If the number 400 is decreased by half each day, then the decrease each day is significantly smaller. On the first day of decrease the number will be 200, 100 the day after, 50 the day after, 25 the day after, and so on. This is exponential decay (decrease).
- The graph of linear increase and linear decrease is a straight line (Fig. 1 and Fig. 2, respectively). The graph of exponential growth rises slowly from left to right followed by a sharp curve upward (Fig. 3). The graph of exponential decay drops sharply from left to right as a curve followed by a slower decrease (Fig. 4).

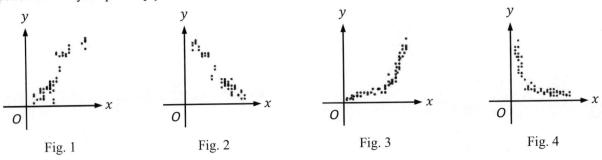

Fig. 1   Fig. 2   Fig. 3   Fig. 4

How to Solve
Words/phrases like "double", "half", "x percent more than the preceding year" refer to an exponential growth/decay.

Example 1:
In which of the following tables is the relation between the values of m and their corresponding n values non-linear?

A)

m	3	5	7	9
n	4.5	5.9	7.3	8.7

B)

m	0.5	1	1.5	2
n	3	9	27	81

C)

m	6	4.5	3	1.5
n	21	15	9	3

D)

m	1	2	3	4
n	0	2	4	6

Step 1: Determine the relationship between the two variables

In tables A, C, and D, the values of m and n both change at a constant rate. This corresponds to a linear relationship. In table B, the value of n increases 3 times for every 0.5 increase in the value of m. This is an exponential increase. Alternatively, determine the slope between 2 sets of points in each table. If the slope is the same, then the relationship is linear (see Section 1 for further details on lines and slope).

The correct answer choice is **B**.

Digital SAT Math Manual and Workbook

Category 49 – Practice Questions

1

In which of the following tables is the relation between the values of x and their corresponding y values non-linear?

A)

x	0.3	0.6	0.9	1.2
y	2	4	6	8

B)

x	1	3	5	7
y	2	8	32	128

C)

x	20	40	60	80
y	13	9	5	1

D)

x	3	6	9	12
y	4.5	6	7.5	9

2

A colony of bacteria doubles every 30 minutes. Which of the following most accurately describes the relationship between time and bacterial growth?

A) Decreasing linear
B) Increasing linear
C) Exponential decay
D) Exponential growth

3

The results of a survey conducted in 2002 in a city in the United States showed that the population of the city is expected to decrease by 1,600 each year. Which of the following describes the relationship between the time in years and expected population of the city?

A) Decreasing linear
B) Increasing linear
C) Exponential decay
D) Exponential growth

4

The population of a certain city is projected to grow exponentially each year for 10 years starting from 2019. Which of the following could describe how the population of the city changes each year?

A) Each year, the population of the city is 10 times more than the previous year.
B) Each year, the population of the city is 2.5% more than the previous year.
C) Each year, the population of the city is 2,000 less than the previous year.
D) Each year, the population of the city is 4% less than the previous year.

5

Team A and Team B are competing in a 2 hour boat race. Every 20 minutes, Team A is ahead of Team B by one-fourth the distance than the preceding 20 minutes. Which of the following best describes the relationship between time in minutes and distance of Team A in relation to Team B?

A) Decreasing linear
B) Increasing linear
C) Exponential decay
D) Exponential growth

Category 50 – Exponential Growth and Decay

Key Points
- The formula for exponential growth or decay is $y = a(b)^x$. The components of the equation are:
  - a is the initial number and is greater than 0.
  - b is the rate of change in the value of a.
  - x is the number of time intervals when the change occurs.
  - y is the accumulated total after x time intervals.
- The rate of change in exponential growth and decay can be calculated as follows:
  - In exponential growth, $b = 1 + r$, where r is the percent growth rate as decimal. For example, if the growth rate is 20%, then $b = 1 + 0.2 = 1.2$. The value of b will always be greater than 1.
  - In exponential decay, $b = 1 - r$, where r is the percent decay rate as decimal. For example, if the decay rate is 20%, then $b = 1 - 0.2 = 0.8$. The value of b will always be less than 1 but greater than 0.
- The exponential growth or decay function is $f(x) = a(b)^x$, where $f(x)$ is the y value for an input value of x.
- When an interest rate is compounded on a monetary amount (for example, 6% interest compounded every 3 months on the dollar amount in a savings account), the growth of the monetary amount over time is exponential.
  - The formula for compound interest is $A = P\left(1 + \frac{r}{n}\right)^{nt}$. The components of the equation are:
    - P is the principal amount (the initial amount).
    - r is the compounded percent interest rate, as decimal.
    - t is the number of years.
    - n is the number of times the interest is compounded per year.
    - A is the amount accumulated after t years.
  - When the interest rate is compounded annually, then $n = 1$. The formula is simplified to $A = P(1 + r)^t$.

How to Solve
It is important to interpret the time interval correctly. For example, if an increase occurs twice per year, then the time interval is $2t$ per year in t years. If an increase occurs once every 2 years, then the time interval is $\frac{1}{2}t$, same as $\frac{t}{2}$, per year in t years. Time interval could be t years, m months, w weeks, s seconds, and so on.

Example 1:
From 1960 to 1990, the population of an endangered species of insects decreased exponentially every 3 years by 7%. If the population of the endangered species of insects was 1,980 in 1960, which of the following equations can determine the decrease, D, in the population of the endangered species of insects 15 years after 1960?

A) $D = 1,980 \, (0.7)^3$
B) $D = 1,980 \, (0.93)^{3t}$
C) $D = 1,980 \, (0.93)^5$
D) $D = 1,980 \, (1.07)^t$

Step 1: Determine the components of the exponential equation
Since the question states 'species decreased exponentially every 3 years by 7%', the question is on exponential decay.
$a = 1,980$. $r = 7\% = 0.07$. $b = 1 - r = 1 - 0.07 = 0.93$. $y = D$.

Time interval = every 3 years. In 15 years, the decrease will occur $\frac{15}{3} = 5$ times. Hence, $x = 5$.

$$y = a(b)^x \rightarrow D = 1,980 \, (0.93)^5$$

The correct answer choice is **C**.

Example 2:

Kara started a new job in 2010 at an annual salary of $90,000. Each year, her salary increased by 2% than the preceding year.

Question 1

Which of the following equations models Kara's salary S, in dollars, t years after 2010?

A) $S = 90,000(0.92)^t$
B) $S = 90,000(1.2)^t$
C) $S = 90,000(1 + 8)^t$
D) $S = 90,000(1.02)^t$

Step 1: Determine the components of the exponential equation

Since each year the salary increased by 2% than the preceding year, the question is on exponential growth.
$a = 90,000$. $r = 2\% = 0.02$. $b = 1 + r = 1.02$. $y = S$. Since time interval = once per year, in one year the increase will occur one time. Hence, in t years the increase will occur t times.

$$y = a(b)^x \rightarrow S = 90,000(1.02)^t$$

The correct answer choice is **D**.

Question 2

By how much, in dollars, did Kara's salary increase in 3 years after 2010?

A) $5,400
B) $5,508
C) $8,000
D) $9,600

Continue from Step 1 of Question 1 to determine the total salary in 3 years. Substitute $t = 3$, in $90,000(1.02)^t$.

$$90,000(1.02)^3 = 90,000(1.02)(1.02)(1.02) = 95,508.72 = \$95,508$$

Salary increase in 3 years = $95,508 - 90,000 = \$5,508$.
The correct answer choice is **B**.

Example 3:

Janice deposited $2,000 dollars in a savings account at an annual interest rate of 6% compounded monthly. Which of the following equations models the accumulated amount A, in dollars, after 4 years, assuming no deposits or withdrawals were made after the initial deposit?

A) $A = 2,000(1.6)^t$
B) $A = 2,000(1.06)^4$
C) $A = 2,000(1.06)^{4t}$
D) $A = 2,000(1.005)^{48}$

Step 1: Determine the components of the compound interest rate equation

Since the interest is compounded monthly, use the complete compound interest rate formula.
$P = 2,000$. $r = 6\% = 0.06$. $t = 4$ years. $n = 12$ (since the interest is compounded each month and there are 12 months in a year).
Plug in the values in the formula.

$$A = P\left(1 + \frac{r}{n}\right)^{nt} \rightarrow A = 2,000\left(1 + \frac{0.06}{12}\right)^{12 \times 4} \rightarrow A = 2,000(1 + 0.005)^{48} \rightarrow A = 2,000(1.005)^{48}$$

The correct answer choice is **D**.

Note that if the savings account was compounded annually, then $n = 1$ and $A = P(1 + r)^t \rightarrow A = 2,000(1.06)^4$.

Category 50 – Practice Questions

1

$$P(t) = 3.2(1.06)^t$$

The function P above estimates the population, in millions, of a certain city t years after 1990. Which of the following is the best interpretation of the number 3.2 in this context?

A) The estimated population, in millions, of the city after 1990.

B) The estimated population, in millions, of the city t years after 1990.

C) The estimated population, in millions, of the city in 1990.

D) The estimated population, in millions, of the city in 3.2 years.

2

A radioactive material with a mass of 150 grams decays exponentially at the rate of 1% every 4 months. Which of the following equations represents the mass of the material, D, in grams, in m months?

A) $D = 150(0.1)^m$

B) $D = 150(0.9)^{4m}$

C) $D = 150(0.99)^m$

D) $D = 150(0.99)^{\frac{m}{4}}$

3

$$P = 550(1.16)^{\frac{t}{2}}$$

The equation above models the number of products P sold by an online retail company in t years after 2020. Which of the following is the most appropriate interpretation about the value of P after 2020?

A) Each year after 2020, the value of P increases by 1.16%.

B) Each year after 2020, the value of P increases by 16%.

C) Every 2 years after 2020, the value of P increases by 1.16%.

D) Every 2 years after 2020, the value of P increases by 16%.

4

A scientist is testing the effect of a chemical on the growth of 200,000 bacterial colonies. If the treatment with the chemical compound results in a 50% reduction of bacterial colonies every 10 minutes, how many bacterial colonies remain after 30 minutes of treatment?

A) 25,000

B) 50,000

C) 70,000

D) 75,000

5

$$G(n) = 2{,}300(1.26)^{\frac{n}{3}}$$

The function G defined above estimates the number of wasps in a certain wooded area in n years. If the equation is rewritten as $G(n) = 2{,}300\left(1 + \frac{k}{100}\right)^n$, where k is a constant, which of the following is closest to the value of k?

A) 6

B) 8

C) 12

D) 17

6

$$R = 1080(c)^t$$

The equation above models the revenue of a manufacturing company t years after 2019. The model forecasts the revenue to increase 9% each year than the preceding year, where $1 \leq t \leq 5$. Which of the following is the value of c?

A) 0.94

B) 1.00

C) 1.09

D) 1.94

7

Sam deposited $2,000 in a bank account earning 8% interest compounded quarterly. Which of the following equations represents the accumulated amount A, in dollars, at the end of 3 years, assuming no deposits or withdrawals were made after the initial deposit of $2,000? (3 months = 1 quarter).

A) $A = 2,000(0.97)^3$
B) $A = 2,000(1.02)^{12}$
C) $A = 2,000(1.03)^{12}$
D) $A = 2,000(1.3)^3$

8

$$M = 400(2)^m$$
$$Q = 2,100(3)^q$$

A manufacturing company has created two models to predict the sales, in thousands of dollars, of a new product to be launched soon. The two models are shown above. M is sales per month for m months after the product launch. Q is sales per quarter for q quarters after the product launch. How many more sales, in thousands of dollars, are predicted by model M than by model Q, 6 months after the product launch? (3 months = 1 quarter)

A) 6,700
B) 9,050
C) 18,900
D) 25,600

9

A team of scientists concluded that since 1900 the number of trees in a certain forest doubled every 29 years. If a is the approximate number of trees in 1900, which of the following equations most appropriately models the number of trees n in t years after 1900?

A) $n = a(1.2)^{29t}$
B) $n = a(2)^{\frac{t}{a}}$
C) $n = a(2)^{\frac{t}{29}}$
D) $n = 29(2)^t$

10

The function $f(m) = 12(1.23)^m$ estimates the price, in dollars, of coffee beans over a period of six consecutive months after May 2020. If m represents the number of months after May 2020, which of the following is the best interpretation of "$f(3)$ is approximately equal to 22" in this context?

A) The approximate price of coffee beans is estimated to be $22 three months after May 2020.
B) The approximate price of coffee beans is estimated to be $22 three years after May 2020.
C) The approximate price of coffee beans is estimated to be thrice of $22 after May 2020.
D) The approximate price of coffee beans will increase by $22 three months after May 2020.

11

Jenny and Sara invested d dollars at the same time. Jenny's investment earned 6% interest rate compounded semi-annually. Sara's investment earned 5% interest rate compounded annually. If X is Jenny's accumulated investment, in dollars, after 4 years, and Y is Sara's accumulated investment, in dollars, after 4 years, which of the following expressions represents $X - Y$, assuming no deposits or withdrawals were made during 4 years?

A) $d(1.01)^4$
B) $d(1.11)^{4t}$
C) $d(1.06)^4 - d(1.05)^4$
D) $d(1.03)^8 - d(1.05)^4$

12

In 2015, Kavita opened a new bank account and deposited d dollars at the interest rate of 10% compounded annually. At the end of 3 years, Kavita had $1,331 in her bank account. What is the value of d, in dollars, assuming no deposits or withdrawals were made in 3 years?

A) $931
B) $988
C) $1,000
D) $1,210

Category 51 – Graphs of Exponential Growth and Decay Functions

Key Points
- In the xy-plane, the graph of an exponential growth or decay function is defined by $f(x) = a(b)^x$. When $a = 1$, the function simplifies to $f(x) = (b)^x$. For example, in $f(x) = 4(3)^x$, $a = 4$, and in $f(x) = (3)^x$, $a = 1$.
  - The coordinates of the y-intercept are $(0, a)$, where a is the y-coordinate of the y-intercept.
  - The graph always passes through the points $(0, a)$ and $(1, ab)$. For $a = 1$, these points are $(0, 1)$ and $(1, b)$.
- The graph of $f(x) = a(b)^x$ can be translated vertically or horizontally or reflected across the x-axis or y-axis.
  - The equation of a graph translated up by c units is $f(x) = a(b)^x + c$, and the equation of a graph translated down by c units is $f(x) = a(b)^x - c$. The y-coordinate of the y-intercept $= a$ will translate by the same number of units. For example, if the graph of $y = 4(2)^x$ is translated down by 3 units, then the equation of the translated graph is $y = 4(2)^x - 3$, and the y-intercept of the translated graph is $(0, 4 - 3) = (0, 1)$.
  - The equation of a graph translated to the left by c units is $f(x) = a(b)^{x+c}$, and equation of a graph translated to the right by c units is $f(x) = a(b)^{x-c}$. For example, if the graph of $y = 4(2)^x$ is translated to the left by 2 units, then the equation of the translated graph is $y = 4(2)^{x+2} \rightarrow y = 4(2)^x(2)^2 \rightarrow y = 16(2)^x$.
  - The equation of a graph reflected across the x-axis is $f(x) = -a(b)^x$. The values of x remain the same, but the values of y have the reverse $+/-$ operator. The graph passes through the points $(0, -a)$ and $(1, -ab)$.
  - The equation of a graph reflected across the y-axis is $f(x) = a(b)^{-x}$. The values of y remain the same, but the values of x have the reverse $+/-$ operator. The graph passes through the points $(0, a)$ and $(-1, ab)$.

How to Solve
*Some of the questions in this category can be solved using the Desmos graphing calculator.

Example 1:
Which of the following is the graph of the equation $y = 2(2)^x$?

A) B) C) D)

Step 1: Determine values of a and b from the equation
$a = 2$. $b = 2$.

Step 2: Determine the graph that passes through the points $(0, a)$ and $(1, ab)$
$(0, a) = (0, 2)$ and $(1, ab) = (1, 2 \times 2) = (1, 4)$.
Only the graph in answer choice A passes through the above points.
The correct answer choice is **A**.

***Desmos Graphing Calculator Solution**
Type the given equation and match its graph to the graphs given in the answer choices. It will match answer choice A.

Category 51 – Practice Questions

1 — Desmos

Which of the following is the graph of the equation $y = (3)^x$?

A)
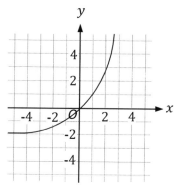

B)
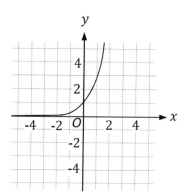

C)
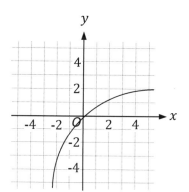

D)
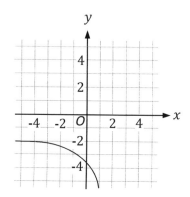

2

$$f(x) = 6(2)^x + \frac{11}{3}$$

The function f is defined above. In the xy-plane, the graph of $y = g(x)$ is a result of translation of the graph of $y = f(x)$ right 3 units. Which of the following defines the function g?

A) $g(x) = 6(5)^x + \frac{11}{3}$

B) $g(x) = 6(2)^{3x} + \frac{11}{3}$

C) $g(x) = \frac{3}{4}(2)^x + \frac{11}{3}$

D) $g(x) = \frac{3}{2}(6)^x + \frac{11}{3}$

3

The graph of the equation $y = f(x)$ in the xy-plane, passes through the points (m, n) and $(m + 1, 4n)$. Which of the following equations could define f?

A) $f(x) = 2(4)^x$

B) $f(x) = 4(2)^x$

C) $f(x) = \frac{1}{4}(1.4)^x$

D) $f(x) = \frac{1}{4}(1)^x$

4

The function f is defined by $f(x) = a(b)^x$, where a and b are constants. In the xy-plane, the graph of $y = f(x) + 11$ has a y-intercept at $(0, 49.5)$. The sum of a and b is 40. What is the value of b?

Section 10 – Review Questions

1

$$P = 12(1.03)^t$$

The equation above models the exponential increase in price, P, in dollars, of one pound of wheat by k percent per year for t years. Which of the following is percent value of k?

A) 3%
B) 5%
C) 6%
D) 12%

2

An environmental scientist studied the population of flies in a certain forest for d days. The scientist found that the population, in hundreds, decreased by 3% every 8 days. If the population of flies at the start of the scientist's study is n, which of the following represents the population, P, of flies, in hundreds, in the forest in d days?

A) $P = n(0.97)^{8t}$
B) $P = n(0.97)^{\frac{d}{8}}$
C) $P = n(0.03)^d$
D) $P = n - (0.03)^d$

3

$$f(t) = a(b)^t$$

Which of the following appropriately describes the relationship between a and t modeled by the exponential function f shown above, where t is a positive integer, b is a constant, and $0 < b < 1$?

A) An increase in the value of a causes an increase in the value of t.
B) An increase in the value of t does not change the value of a.
C) An increase in the value of t causes an increase in the value of a.
D) An increase in the value of t causes a decrease in the value of a.

4

Function f is defined as shown below, where a is a real number greater than 0.

$$f(a) \text{ is equal to 4\% of } a$$

Which of the following describes the function f?

A) Decreasing linear
B) Increasing linear
C) Exponential decay
D) Exponential growth

5

$$\sqrt[4]{x^2 - 1}$$

If $x - 1 = 16$, which of the following is equivalent to the above expression, where $x > 0$?

A) $4(x - 1)$
B) $4(x + 1)$
C) $2(x + 1)^{\frac{1}{4}}$
D) $4(x + 1)^4$

6

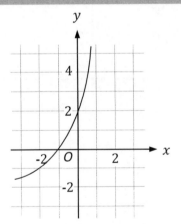

The graph of $y = 4(2)^x - c$ is shown above, where c is a constant. What is the value of c?

A) -1
B) 0
C) 2
D) 4

Digital SAT Math Manual and Workbook

7

$$(x^2)^3(\sqrt[4]{x^3}) = x^a$$

What is the value of a in the above equation, where $x > 0$?

8

$$\frac{\sqrt[3]{x^7}}{\sqrt[3]{x^4}}$$

If the above expression is equivalent to x^{mn} for all positive values of x, what is the value of mn?

9

Tim opened a savings account and deposited d dollars at an interest rate of 10% compounded annually. After 3 years, he had $1,655 more than the original deposit of d dollars in his savings account. Assuming no withdrawals or deposits were made in 3 years, which of the following is the value of d?

A) $1,695
B) $2,164
C) $4,995
D) $5,000

10

Ramona deposited $2,000 dollars in a savings account at an annual rate of 8% compounded quarterly. Which of the following equations models the amount A, in dollars, in Ramona's savings account after t years? (1 quarter = 3 months)

A) $A = 2{,}000(1.0075)^{2t}$
B) $A = 2{,}000(1.08)^{3}$
C) $A = 2{,}000(1.08)^{2t}$
D) $A = 2{,}000(1.02)^{4t}$

11

The function $A(m) = a(0.5)^{\frac{m}{20}}$ models the number of bacterial colonies m minutes after the start of a laboratory experiment, where a is the number of bacterial colonies at the start of the experiment and $A(m)$ is the number of bacterial colonies after m minutes. What is the best interpretation of $(0.5)^{\frac{m}{20}}$?

A) The number of bacterial colonies reduced by 5% every minute.
B) The number of bacterial colonies reduced by half every 20 minutes.
C) The number of bacterial colonies increased by 5% every minute.
D) The number of bacterial colonies increased by 20 every minute.

12

The population of beetles, y, in a certain city decreases exponentially each year, x, for t years. In the xy-plane, which of the following graphs could represent this relationship between x and y?

A)
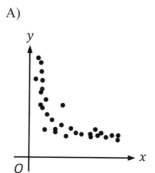

B)
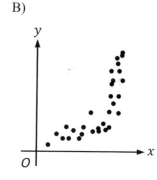

C)
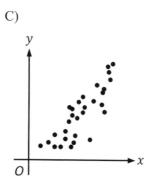

D)
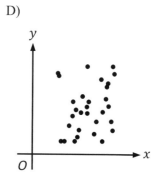

Section 11 –
Manipulate Expressions and Equations

Category 52 – Fractions with Expressions in the Denominator
Category 53 – Rearrange Variables in an Equation
Category 54 – Combine and Factor Like Terms
Category 55 – Expressions with Square Root
Section 11 – Review Questions

Category 52 – Fractions with Expressions in the Denominator

Key Points
- An equation may contain fractions that have expressions in the denominator. The key to solving these equations is to determine the strategy that will simplify or remove the expressions from the denominator.
- The following factors are helpful to remember.
  - $(x + y)(x + y) = x^2 + 2xy + y^2$
  - $(x - y)(x - y) = x^2 - 2xy + y^2$
  - $(x - y)(x + y) = x^2 - y^2$
    - $(x - 1)(x + 1) = x^2 - 1$
    - $(x - 2)(x + 2) = x^2 - 4$
- Solving equations with expressions in the denominator may result in a solution that does not solve an equation, known as an extraneous solution.

How to Solve

If the expressions in the denominators of two or more fractions are the same, then the numerators can be added/subtracted to create one fraction.

If an equation is a mix of fractions and numbers, then move the numbers on one side and fractions on the other side of the equation.

Remember that multiplying and dividing a fraction by the same number or expression does not alter the value of the fraction. For example, $\frac{x}{x+2}$ is same as $\frac{8(x)}{8(x+2)}$ or $\frac{(x+5)(x)}{(x+5)(x+2)}$, and so on.

Example 1:

$$\frac{2(x + 2)}{x + 3} = 3 - \frac{6}{x + 3}$$

In the above equation, what is the value of x?

Step 1: Determine the strategy

Since the denominators of the fractions have the same expression, the numerators can be added to create one fraction that equates to 3.

Step 2: Solve

Move fractions on one side of the equation.

$$\frac{2(x + 2)}{x + 3} + \frac{6}{x + 3} = 3$$

Create one fraction.

$$\frac{2(x + 2) + 6}{x + 3} = 3 \rightarrow \frac{2x + 4 + 6}{x + 3} = 3 \rightarrow \frac{2x + 10}{x + 3} = 3$$

Cross multiply and solve.

$$2x + 10 = 3(x + 3) \rightarrow 2x + 10 = 3x + 9 \rightarrow 3x - 2x = 10 - 9 \rightarrow x = 1$$

Check for extraneous solution. Plug $x = 1$ in the given equation, and check if the two sides of the equation are equal.

$$\frac{2(1 + 2)}{1 + 3} = 3 - \frac{6}{1 + 3} \rightarrow \frac{6}{4} = 3 - \frac{6}{4} \rightarrow \frac{6}{4} = \frac{6}{4}$$

1 is not an extraneous solution.

The correct answer is **1**.

Example 2:

$$\frac{x}{x-3} - \frac{2x+13}{x^2-9}$$

If the given expression is equivalent to 1, what value of x satisfies the expression?

Step 1: Determine the strategy

The two factors of $x^2 - 9$ are $(x + 3)$ and $(x - 3)$. Multiplying the numerator and denominator of the left fraction by $(x + 3)$ will result in the same denominator for the two fractions. The numerators can then be added.

Step 2: Solve (check for extraneous solutions as shown in Example 1)

Multiply the numerator and denominator of the left fraction by $(x + 3)$ and equate the expression to 1.

$$\frac{x(x+3)}{(x-3)(x+3)} - \frac{2x+13}{x^2-9} = 1 \rightarrow \frac{x(x+3)}{x^2-9} - \frac{2x+13}{x^2-9} = 1$$

Create one fraction and solve.

$$\frac{x(x+3) - (2x+13)}{x^2-9} = 1 \rightarrow \frac{x^2+3x-2x-13}{x^2-9} = 1 \rightarrow \frac{x^2+x-13}{x^2-9} = 1 \rightarrow$$

$$x^2 + x - 13 = x^2 - 9 \rightarrow x^2 + x - x^2 = -9 + 13 \rightarrow x = 4$$

The correct answer is **4**.

Example 3:

Which expression is equivalent to $\frac{x}{x-3} - \frac{2x+13}{x^2-9}$, where $x > 0$?

A) $\frac{x-13}{x-3}$

B) $\frac{2x+13}{x^2-3}$

C) $\frac{x^2+x-13}{x^2-9}$

D) $\frac{x^2-x+13}{x^2-9}$

Step 1: Determine the strategy

The two factors of $x^2 - 9$ are $(x + 3)$ and $(x - 3)$. Multiplying the numerator and denominator of the left fraction by $(x + 3)$ will result in the same denominator for the two fractions. The expression can then be simplified.

Step 2: Simplify

$$\frac{x(x+3)}{(x-3)(x+3)} - \frac{2x+13}{x^2-9} = \frac{x(x+3)}{x^2-9} - \frac{2x+13}{x^2-9} = \frac{x(x+3)-(2x+13)}{x^2-9} =$$

$$\frac{x^2+3x-2x-13}{x^2-9} = \frac{x^2+x-13}{x^2-9}$$

The correct answer choice is **C**.

Example 4:

$$\frac{12}{x-y} + \frac{10}{x^2-y^2}$$

What is the value of the above expression if $x - y = 2$ and $x + y = 5$?

Step 1: Determine the strategy

The two factors of $x^2 - y^2$ are $(x - y)$ and $(x + y)$. The values of both the factors are given to solve the equation.

Step 2: Solve

$$\frac{12}{x-y} + \frac{10}{(x-y)(x+y)} = \frac{12}{2} + \frac{10}{(2)(5)} = 6 + \frac{10}{10} = 6 + 1 = 7$$

The correct answer is **7**.

Digital SAT Math Manual and Workbook

Category 52 – Practice Questions

1

$$\frac{3(x+1)}{x-2} - \frac{3x+4}{x-2}$$

The above expression is equivalent to 1. What is the value of x?

A) -1
B) -2
C) 1
D) 2

2

Which of the following expressions is equivalent to $\frac{m-4}{n(n-4)} + \frac{m(n-5)}{mn^2-4mn}$?

A) $\frac{m-9}{n-4n}$

B) $\frac{m+n-9}{n^2-4n}$

C) $\frac{4(m^2+n^2)}{n^2-m}$

D) $\frac{m^2+n^2-1}{mn^2-4mn}$

3

$$\frac{6}{x+5} + \frac{3}{x-2} = \frac{7x+9}{(x+5)(x-2)}$$

In the above equation, what is the value of x?

A) 3
B) 6
C) 9
D) 15

4

$$\frac{3}{x-1} + \frac{k}{x^2-1} = \frac{3x+8}{x^2-1}$$

In the above equation, what is the value of k, where k is a constant?

A) -2
B) -1
C) 2
D) 5

5

$$\frac{3a^2+7ab}{(a+b)} = 9 + \frac{ab-3b^2}{(a+b)}$$

In the above equation, what is the value of $a+b$?

6

$$\frac{2}{x-y} + \frac{5}{x^2-y^2}$$

If $x^2 - y^2 = 3$ and $x + y = 11$, what is the value of the above expression?

7

$$\frac{y^2-9}{y+3} = 5$$

What is the value of y in the above equation?

Digital SAT Math Manual and Workbook

Category 53 – Rearrange Variables in an Equation

Key Points
- The variables in an equation can be rearranged to isolate one variable from the others. For example, in the equation $a + h = yc - t(b + s)$, the variable h can be isolated by removing a from the left-side. This will express the variables a, b, c, s, t, and y in terms of the variable h. Any variable in the equation can be isolated by rearranging the variables.

How to Solve
Determine which variable must be isolated. Most likely, this will be mentioned in the last sentence of the question.

Example 1:

$$S = 5 + \left(\frac{2Mt + Et}{t^2}\right)$$

Raj has created the above equation to determine his running speed, where S is the speed in kilometers per hour, M and E are variables, and t is the time in hours. Which of the following expresses time t, in terms of the speed, M, and E?

A) $t = \sqrt{\frac{2M+E}{S-5}}$

B) $t = \frac{2M+E}{S-5}$

C) $t = \frac{S-5}{2MT+Et}$

D) $t = \frac{2Mt+Et}{S-5}$

Step 1: Rearrange

t must be removed from the denominator and isolated on one side of the equation. This can be achieved using the 4 steps shown below using the properties of equality.

Step 1: Subtract 5 from both sides of the equation to remove it from the right expression.

$$S - 5 = \cancel{5} + \left(\frac{2Mt + Et}{t^2}\right) - \cancel{5} \rightarrow S - 5 = \frac{2Mt + Et}{t^2}$$

Step 2: Factor t in the right expression and cancel it from the numerator and denominator.

$$S - 5 = \frac{t(2M + E)}{t \times t} \rightarrow S - 5 = \frac{\cancel{t}(2M + E)}{\cancel{t} \times t} \rightarrow S - 5 = \frac{(2M + E)}{t}$$

Step 3: Multiply both sides by t to move it to the numerator.

$$t(S - 5) = \frac{(2M + E) \times \cancel{t}}{\cancel{t}} \rightarrow t(S - 5) = (2M + E)$$

Step 4: Divide both sides by $(S - 5)$ to isolate t.

$$\frac{t\cancel{(S-5)}}{\cancel{(S-5)}} = \frac{(2M + E)}{(S - 5)} \rightarrow t = \frac{2M + E}{S - 5}$$

The correct answer choice is **B**.

Category 53 – Practice Questions

1

The law of universal gravitation states that every point mass attracts every other point mass in the universe with a force that is directly proportional to the product of their masses and inversely proportional to the square of the distance between their centers. The formula is written as $F = G\frac{m_1 m_2}{r^2}$, where F is the gravitational force, m_1 and m_2 are the two masses, r is the distance between the center of the two masses, and G is the gravitational constant. Which of the following expresses the distance between the center of the two masses r in terms of the masses of the two objects, the gravitational force, and the gravitational constant?

A) $r = F\frac{m_1 m_2}{G}$

B) $r = \sqrt{G\frac{m_1 m_2}{F}}$

C) $r = G\sqrt{\frac{m_1 m_2}{F}}$

D) $r = F\sqrt{\frac{m_1 m_2}{G}}$

2

$$R = \frac{(8 \times \mu)l}{\pi \times r^4}$$

Pressure of a fluid as it travels through a cylindrical pipe can be calculated by the above formula. R is the airway resistance, μ is the dynamic viscosity, l is the length of the pipe, r is the radius of the pipe, and π is pi. Which of the following gives the dynamic viscosity μ in terms of the length of the pipe, the radius of the pipe, the airway resistance, and pi?

A) $\mu = \frac{R\pi r^4}{8l}$

B) $\mu = \frac{R\pi r^4 - 8l}{l}$

C) $\mu = R\pi r^4 - 8l$

D) $\mu = R\pi r^4 8l$

3

$$A = \frac{a+b}{2}h$$

The above formula is for the area A of a trapezoid in terms of its height h and two parallel bases a and b. Which of the following expresses the height h of the trapezoid in terms of the area and two parallel bases?

A) $h = 2A(a+b)$

B) $h = 2Aab$

C) $h = \frac{A}{2a+2b}$

D) $h = \frac{2A}{a+b}$

4

$$\frac{ut + 2u + 1}{u+1} = 1 + \frac{us - ut^2}{u+1}$$

Which of the following is equivalent to the expression above?

A) $s = \frac{u+t-1}{u}$

B) $s = \frac{t^2+t+1}{u}$

C) $s = t^2 + t + 1$

D) $s = u^2 + t^2 + 1$

5

$$(1+i) = (1+r)(1+\pi)$$

The above formula determines the relationship between real and nominal interest rates during inflation, where i is the nominal interest rate, r is the real interest rate, and π is the inflation rate. Which of the following expresses the inflation rate π in terms of the nominal and real interest rates?

A) $\pi = \frac{1+i}{1+r} - 1$

B) $\pi = \frac{1+i}{1+r} + 1$

C) $\pi = (1+i) - (1+r)$

D) $\pi = (1+i) + (1+r)$

Category 54 – Combine and Factor Like Terms

Key Points
- Like terms have the same variable(s) with the same exponent. For example, $3x^2$ and x^2 are like terms. They have the same variable x and exponent 2. Similarly, x^3y^2 and $4x^3y^2$ are like terms since the variables are the same and have the same exponent. x^3y^2 and $4x^2y^2$ are not like terms since the exponents of the variable x are different.
- Like terms can be added or subtracted. For example, in the expression $2x^2 + xy + x^2 + 5xy$, the like terms $2x^2$ and x^2 can be added to give $3x^2$, and the like terms xy and $5xy$ can be added to give $6xy$.
- Like terms can be factored. For example, in the expression $2x^2 + xy$, like term x can be factored as $x(2x + y)$.

How to Solve
If the expression has parentheses, then simplify before solving. Use the laws of exponents to multiply the variables.

Example 1:
Which of the following is equivalent to $3x(x^2 - x) + 7x^2 - 2x^3$?

A) $-4x^2 - x^3$
B) $4x^2 - x^3$
C) $x + 3x^2 - x^3$
D) $x + x^2 - 2x^3$

Step 1: Simplify the expression within the parentheses and add/subtract like terms

$$3x(x^2 - x) + 7x^2 - 2x^3 \rightarrow (3x \times x^2) - (3x \times x) + 7x^2 - 2x^3 \rightarrow$$
$$3x^3 - 3x^2 + 7x^2 - 2x^3 \rightarrow 4x^2 - x^3$$

The correct answer choice is **B**.

* The Desmos graphing calculator can be used to easily match the given expression to each answer choice when the expression has one variable.

Category 54 – Practice Questions

1 *Desmos*

Which of the following is equivalent to $2(x^2 - 1) + 10x^3 - 2x^2$?

A) $10x^3$
B) $10x^3 - 2$
C) $2x^2 - 10x^3 - 2$
D) $2x^2 + 6x^3 - 1$

2 *Desmos*

Which of the following is equivalent to $4x(x^3 + 3x^2) - 3(x^4 - 2x^3) + x^4$?

A) $2x^3(x + 9)$
B) $2(x^4 + 3x^3)$
C) $2x(x + 9x^3)$
D) $2x^3(x^3 - x^2) - 12x^3$

3

Which of the following is equivalent to $m^2 + 3n^3 - 2mn - m(m - 2)$?

A) $3n^3$
B) $3n^3 + m^2 - 2mn$
C) $3n^3 - m^2 + 2m$
D) $3m^3 - 2mn + 2m$

4

Which of the following is equivalent to the sum of $s^2t - 3t^3$ and $3s^2t + 5t^3 + t$?

A) $-s^2 + t^2$
B) $4s^3 + 2t^3$
C) $t(4s^2 + 2t^2 + 1)$
D) $t(4s^2 + 2t^3 + 1)$

Digital SAT Math Manual and Workbook

Category 55 – Expressions with Square Root

Key Points
- When an equation contains a square root expression, the square root can be removed by squaring both sides of the equation.
- Solving equations with square root expressions may result in a solution that does not solve an equation, known as an extraneous solution. Equations that have 2 solutions are more likely to have an extraneous solution.

How to Solve

Move all the terms not under the square root to one side of the equation. For example,
$$\sqrt{2x+1} - 3 = 2 + x \rightarrow \sqrt{2x+1} = 2 + 3 + x \rightarrow \sqrt{2x+1} = 5 + x$$
The entire expression on each side must be squared. For example,
$$\sqrt{2x+1} = 5\sqrt{x-1} \rightarrow (\sqrt{2x+1})^2 = (5\sqrt{x-1})^2$$
When there are two values of x, plug them in the given equation to check for an extraneous solution. The values must be plugged in the given equation, not in any equation formed during the calculation process.

*Several questions in this category can be solved using the Desmos graphing calculator. The above is not required when using Desmos. Checking for extraneous solutions is also not required as Desmos does not graph them.

*Example 1:
$$\sqrt{9x - 1} = 2\sqrt{x + 6}$$
Which value of x satisfies the equation above?

A) 2
B) 3
C) 5
D) 9

Step 1: Square both sides
$$(\sqrt{9x-1})^2 = (2\sqrt{x+6})^2 \rightarrow 9x - 1 = 4(x + 6)$$

Step 2: Solve
$$9x - 1 = 4x + 24 \rightarrow 5x = 25 \rightarrow x = 5$$

The correct answer choice is **C**.

*Desmos Graphing Calculator Solution

Type the equation and read the value of x where the graph of the equation passes through the x-axis. See the vertical line in the graph below. The value of x is 5.

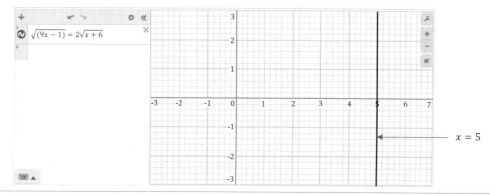

Digital SAT Math Manual and Workbook

*Example 2:

$$\sqrt{12 - 2x} + 2 = x$$

Which of the following are the solutions of x, in the above equation?

A) $\{-4, 2\}$
B) $\{-2, 4\}$
C) -2
D) 4

Step 1: Square both sides

Move 2 to the right-side and square both sides.

$$\sqrt{12 - 2x} = x - 2 \;\rightarrow\; \left(\sqrt{12 - 2x}\right)^2 = (x-2)^2 \;\rightarrow\; 12 - 2x = (x-2)^2$$

Step 2: Solve

FOIL the right-side expression. Then, create a quadratic equation and factor.

$$12 - 2x = x^2 - 4x + 4 \;\rightarrow\; x^2 - 4x + 4 + 2x - 12 = 0 \;\rightarrow$$
$$x^2 - 2x - 8 = 0 \;\rightarrow\; (x - 4)(x + 2) = 0$$

The two solutions of x are -2 and 4.

Step 3: Check for extraneous solution

Plug in $x = -2$ into the given equation.

$$\sqrt{12 - 2x} + 2 = x \;\rightarrow\; \sqrt{12 - 2(-2)} + 2 = -2 \;\rightarrow\; \sqrt{12 + 4} + 2 = -2 \;\rightarrow$$
$$\sqrt{16} + 2 = -2 \;\rightarrow\; 4 + 2 = -2 \;\rightarrow\; 6 = -2$$

When $x = -2$, the two sides of the equation do not have the same value. Hence, -2 is an extraneous solution.

Plug in $x = 4$ into the given equation.

$$\sqrt{12 - 2x} + 2 = x \;\rightarrow\; \sqrt{12 - 2(4)} + 2 = 4 \;\rightarrow\; \sqrt{12 - 8} + 2 = 4 \;\rightarrow$$
$$\sqrt{4} + 2 = 4 \;\rightarrow\; 2 + 2 = 4 \;\rightarrow\; 4 = 4$$

When $x = 4$, the two sides of the equation have the same value. Hence, 4 is not an extraneous solution.

The correct answer choice is **D**.

*Desmos Graphing Calculator Solution

Type the equation and read the value of x where the graph of the equation passes through the x-axis. See the vertical line in the graph below. The value of x is 4.

Note that the graphing calculator does not graph extraneous solutions. In this example, there is one solution, hence, one value of x. The extraneous solution $x = -2$ is not graphed. Zoom out to verify the number of solutions.

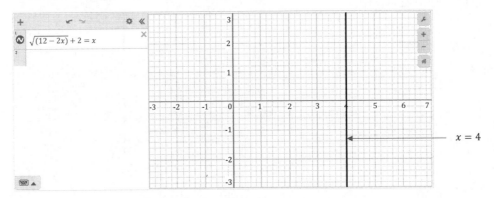

Category 55 – Practice Questions

1 — Desmos

$$\sqrt{x+5} - 2 = 3$$

What value of x satisfies the above equation?

A) 0
B) 7
C) 9
D) 20

2 — Desmos

$$\sqrt{\frac{27}{x}} + 1 = 4$$

Which of the following can be the value of x in the above equation?

A) 2
B) 3
C) 5
D) 9

3 — Desmos

$$\sqrt{x^2 + 5} = 3$$

What value of x satisfies the above equation, where $x > 0$?

A) -1
B) 1
C) 2
D) 4

4 — Desmos

If $\sqrt{5x - 1} = 3\sqrt{x - 1}$, what is the value of x?

5 — Desmos

$$3\sqrt{x+2} - \sqrt{x+26} = 0$$

What is the value of x in the given equation?

6 — Desmos

$$\frac{1}{2}\sqrt{x+5} + 1 = 3$$

In the above equation, what is a value of x?

7 — Desmos

$$\sqrt{7 - 2x} + 2 = x$$

Which of the following are the solutions of the above equation?

I. -1
II. 1
III. 3

A) I only
B) III only
C) I and III only
D) II and III only

8 — Desmos

The function f is defined by $f(x) = 4\sqrt{3x}$ for all values of x. For what value of x does $f(x) = \sqrt{96}$?

A) 1
B) 2
C) 6
D) 12

Section 11 – Review Questions

1

$$\frac{1}{(a-b)(a^2-b^2)}$$

If $a - b = 2$ and $a + b = 3$, what is value of the above expression?

A) $\frac{1}{12}$

B) $\frac{1}{6}$

C) 6

D) 7

2

$$m = \frac{1}{2}am + 4$$

The ideal body weight for a child less than one-year old can be calculated by the above formula, where m is the weight of the child in kilograms and a is the age of the child in months. Which of the following represents the age of a child a in terms of m?

A) $a = 8m$

B) $a = 2 - \frac{8}{m}$

C) $a = m - \frac{4}{m}$

D) $a = 2 + \frac{8}{m}$

3

$$K = \frac{1}{2}(D^2 + H) + D^2$$

In terms of H, which of the following is equivalent to the equation above, where D, H, and K are variables?

A) $2K + D$

B) $K + 2D^2$

C) $K - 3D^2$

D) $2K - 3D^2$

4 Desmos

$$\frac{2y^2 + y}{y - 2} - \frac{y^2 + 5y - 4}{y - 2}$$

If the above expression is equal to 3, which of the following is the value of y?

A) 2

B) 4

C) 5

D) 12

5

$$s = \frac{at^2}{2} + v_o t + s_o$$

The equation above is the second equation of motion for position-time relationship. It applies to a particle moving linearly in a straight line with constant acceleration, where s is the final position, a is the acceleration, t is the time, v_o is the initial linear velocity, and s is the initial position. Which of the following gives the initial linear velocity v_o in terms of the acceleration, the time, the initial position, and the final position?

A) $v_o = \frac{s - s_o}{t} - \frac{at}{2}$

B) $v_o = \frac{s - s_o - at}{2t}$

C) $v_o = s - \frac{at^2 - s_o}{2}$

D) $v_o = s - \frac{at^2}{2} - t + s_o$

6 Desmos

$$\sqrt{2k + 17} = 7$$

What value of k satisfies the above equation?

A) -5

B) -1

C) 11

D) 16

Digital SAT Math Manual and Workbook

7 — Desmos

$$\sqrt{5c^2 - 4} = 2c$$

What values of c satisfy the above equation?

I. -2
II. -1
III. 2

A) II only
B) III only
C) I and II only
D) I and III only

8 — Desmos

$$\frac{2}{\frac{1}{x+2} + \frac{1}{x-2}} = x - 1$$

Which of the following is the value of x in the above equation?

A) 0
B) 1
C) 4
D) 12

9 — Desmos

$$\sqrt{\frac{36}{4x^2}} - 1 = 0$$

Which of the following is one possible value of x in the above equation?

A) 0
B) 3
C) 4
D) 6

10

$$a^2 - b^2 = \frac{2a^2 + 4ab + 2b^2}{a + b}$$

What is the value of $a - b$ in the above equation?

11

Which of the following expressions is equivalent to $4a(a^2 + b) - 2a^2 - ab$?

A) $2a^2 - ab$
B) $2a^2 - 2ab$
C) $2a^3 - 2a^2 + 3ab$
D) $4a^3 - 2a^2 + 3ab$

12

Which of the following expressions is equivalent to $x(2x^2 + y) - 2x(x^2 - y^2)$?

A) $2(x - 2y^2)$
B) $xy(1 + 2y)$
C) $xy^2(2 + x)$
D) x^2y^2

13 — Desmos

$$\frac{x^2 - 9}{2(x - 3)} = 4$$

In the above equation, what is the value of x?

14 — Desmos

$$\frac{1}{3}\sqrt{5x + 6}$$

If the above expression is equal to 2, what is the value of x?

Section 12 – Data Analysis and Interpretation

Category 56 – Probability
Category 57 – Graphs with Line Segments and Curves
Category 58 – Scatter Plots and Lines of Best Fit
Category 59 – Bar Graphs
Category 60 – Histograms and Dot Plots
Category 61 – Mean
Category 62 – Histograms, Dot Plots, and Mean
Category 63 – Median
Category 64 – Histograms, Dot Plots, Bar Graphs, and Median
Category 65 – Box Plots and Median
Category 66 – Mode
Category 67 – Standard Deviation and Range
Category 68 – Compare Mean, Median, Mode, SD, and Range
Category 69 – Interpretation of Sample Data in Studies and Surveys
Section 12 – Review Questions

Category 56 – Probability

Key Points
- Probability is the likelihood of achieving certain or desired outcomes from the total possible outcomes, at random.

$$\text{probability} = \frac{\text{number of certain/desired outcomes}}{\text{number of total possible outcomes}}$$

How to Solve

It is important to identify the numerator and denominator correctly. For example, if a red or a blue color marble is desired from a bag containing marbles of various colors, then the desired outcomes must consider all red marbles and all blue marbles that are in the bag, and the total possible outcomes must consider all the marbles in the bag.

$$\text{probability} = \frac{\text{all red marbles + all blue marbles}}{\text{all marbles}}$$

Similarly, if a red marble is desired out of red, blue, green, and white marbles, then desired outcomes = all red marbles and total outcomes = all red marbles + all blue marbles + all green marbles + all white marbles.

Example 1:
The table below shows the number of freshman, sophomore, junior, and senior class students enrolled in various sports at a certain high school. Each student is enrolled in one sport.

Team	Freshman	Sophomore	Junior	Senior	Total
Baseball	21	25	12	29	87
Football	15	22	15	30	82
Wrestling	7	28	30	2	67
Boxing	5	11	9	7	32
Total	48	86	66	68	268

Question 1
If one of the students is selected at random, what is the probability that the student is on the boxing team?

A) $\frac{7}{52}$

B) $\frac{8}{67}$

C) $\frac{12}{67}$

D) $\frac{11}{268}$

Step 1: Determine the probability

desired outcomes = all students on boxing team.

total possible outcomes = all students.

$$\text{probability} = \frac{\text{all students on boxing team}}{\text{all students}} = \frac{32}{268} = \frac{8}{67}$$

The correct answer choice is **B**.

Digital SAT Math Manual and Workbook

Question 2

Which of the following is closest to the probability that a randomly selected junior or senior student will be on the football or wrestling team?

A) 0.28
B) 0.36
C) 0.39
D) 0.57

Step 1: Determine the probability

Note that the phrase "randomly selected junior or senior student" implies that the selection of a student on the football or wrestling team is from junior or senior students. Hence, including freshmen or sophomores in the total possible outcomes is incorrect. This is important to look out for in Probability questions.

desired outcomes = all juniors on football team, all juniors on wrestling team, all seniors on football team, and seniors on wrestling team.

total possible outcomes = all junior students and all senior students.

$$\text{probability} = \frac{\text{all juniors on football} + \text{all juniors on wrestling} + \text{all seniors on football} + \text{all seniors on wrestling}}{\text{all juniors} + \text{all seniors}}$$

$$\frac{15 + 30 + 30 + 2}{66 + 68} = \frac{77}{134} = 0.57$$

The correct answer choice is **D**.

Example 2:

The table below shows the number of medium and large sized jackets in two colors at a department store. If one jacket is selected at random, the probability of selecting a large red color jacket is $\frac{1}{6}$. What is the value of x?

Color	Jacket size	
	Medium	Large
Black	4	5
Red	11	x

Step 1: Determine the probability

It is given that the probability of selecting a large red jacket from all the jackets is $\frac{1}{6}$. Hence,

desired outcomes = all large red jackets.
total possible outcomes = all jackets.

$$\text{probabiliy} = \frac{\text{all large red jackets}}{\text{all jackets}} = \frac{1}{6}$$

$$\frac{x}{4 + 5 + 11 + x} = \frac{1}{6} \rightarrow \frac{x}{20 + x} = \frac{1}{6}$$

Cross multiply.

$$6x = 20 + x \rightarrow 5x + 20 \rightarrow x = 4$$

The correct answer is **4**.

Category 56 – Practice Questions

1

Color	Electric cars	Gas cars	Total
White	25	151	176
Red	136	152	288
Blue	311	205	516
Total	472	508	980

The above table summarizes the number of electric and gas cars available in three different colors at a car dealership. If a blue car is selected at random, what is the probability that it is electric?

A) $\frac{205}{516}$

B) $\frac{311}{472}$

C) $\frac{311}{516}$

D) $\frac{311}{980}$

2

A defective six-faced die has two faces with the number 5. What is the probability of rolling the number 5 of the defective die?

A) $\frac{1}{6}$

B) $\frac{1}{3}$

C) $\frac{5}{6}$

D) 2

3

Size	Color			Total
	Red	Green	Blue	
Small	18	6	9	33
Medium	8	30	11	49
Large	6	10	2	18
Total	32	46	22	100

The table above shows the distribution of 100 marbles of assorted colors and sizes. If all the large marbles are removed from the bag, what is the closest probability that a marble selected at random is a small green or a small blue marble?

A) $\frac{15}{82}$

B) $\frac{15}{68}$

C) $\frac{68}{100}$

D) $\frac{82}{100}$

4

A library bought a total of 140 novels. $\frac{4}{7}$ were mystery novels, and the remaining were either adventure novels or science fiction novels. If one of the 140 novels is selected at random, the probability of selecting an adventure novel is $\frac{1}{10}$. How many science fiction novels did the library buy?

5

	Team A	Team B	Team C
Coffee Brand A	6	2	5
Coffee Brand B	a	5	6

The above table shows the number of participants on three teams assigned to test two different brands of coffee. If one of the participants is selected at random, the probability that the participant belongs to Team A and is assigned to test Coffee Brand B is $\frac{1}{9}$. What is the value of a?

Category 57 – Graphs with Line Segments and Curves

Key Points
- A graph illustrates the relationship between two variables plotted as data points. One variable is represented on the horizontal axis and other on the vertical axis. Each data point is represented as a dot and corresponds to a value on the horizontal axis and a value on the vertical axis.
- The data points may be connected by straight line segments or by curves.

How to Solve
The value of a data point can be determined by reading the value of that dot on the horizontal and vertical axes. Use best approximation when reading data points not on the graph grid lines.

Example 1:

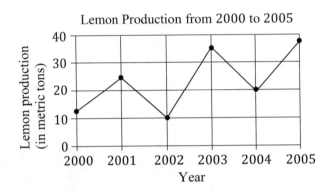

The above graph shows the lemon production, in metric tons, at an orchard in the United States from 2000 to 2005. During which of the following one-year period was the increase in lemon production greatest, in metric tons?

A) 2000 to 2001
B) 2002 to 2003
C) 2003 to 2004
D) 2004 to 2005

Step 1: Read the data points from the graph

Each data point represents the lemon production in a year. It can be seen from the graph that the greatest difference in the increase of lemon production is from 2002 to 2003. If unsure, evaluate each answer choice as shown below.

Answer choice A: In 2000, lemon production = 12. In 2001, lemon production = 24. Difference = 24 − 12 = 12.
Answer choice B: In 2002, lemon production = 10. In 2003, lemon production = 35. Difference = 35 − 10 = 25.
Answer choice C: In 2003, lemon production = 35. In 2004, lemon production = 20. Difference = 20 − 35 = −15.
Answer choice D: In 2004, lemon production = 20. In 2005, lemon production = 38. Difference = 38 − 20 = 18.

The correct answer choice is **B**.

If the question had given a curve graph instead of a line segment graph, it would look as follows.

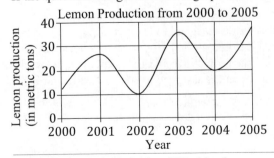

Digital SAT Math Manual and Workbook

Example 2:

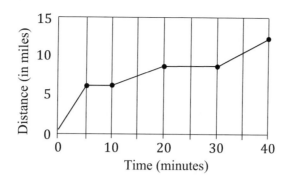

Sonya drove from her home to a park with stops along the way. She made the first stop to pick up food from a restaurant, after which she continued driving. She made the second stop to purchase a book from a bookstore, after which she continued to drive to the park. The graph above shows the number of miles Sonya drove, and the time, in minutes, it took her to reach the park. Based on the graph, for approximately how many minutes did Sonya stop during the drive from her home to the park?

Step 1: Read the data points from the graph

The change in distance with time indicates driving. This will be an upward slanting line on the graph. A horizontal line indicates that the distance did not change with time, hence, no driving. The graph shows that the distance did not change from 5 to 10 minutes and 20 to 30 minutes during the drive from home to the park.

5 to 10 minutes = 5 minutes duration.

20 to 30 minutes = 10 minutes duration.

Total duration = 5 + 10 = 15.

The correct answer is **15**.

Example 3:

Sonya drove from her home to a park with stops along the way. She made the first stop to pick up food from a restaurant, after which she continued driving. She made the second stop to purchase a book from a bookstore, after which she continued to drive to the park. Which of the following graphs represents the situation in context?

A)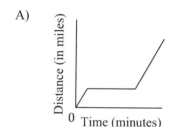

B)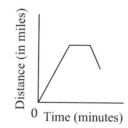

C)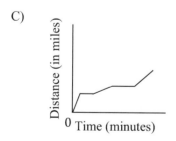

D)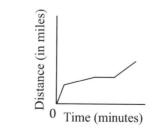

Match the sequence of events in the question to the flow of events on the graphs. Since Sonya made two stops, the graph should have two horizontal lines corresponding to no driving. This eliminates answer choices A, B, and D. The correct answer choice is **C**.

Category 57 – Practice Questions

1

Every Monday, Quinn buys a 50 ml bottle of a protein shake and drinks it over a period of 90 minutes. Last Monday, Quinn finished half the protein shake within 30 minutes of opening the bottle, and the remaining half 30 minutes later over a period of 30 minutes. Which of the following graphs represents the situation in context?

A)
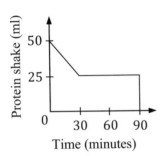

B)
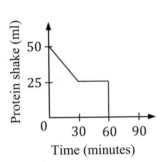

C)
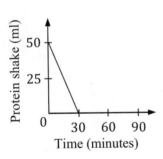

D)
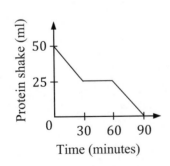

2

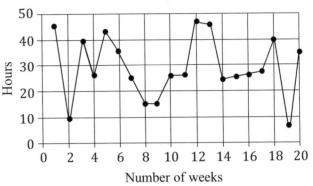

The graph above shows the number of hours Casey watched television each week over a period of 20 weeks. During which two consecutive weeks did Casey watch the least hours of television?

A) Week 1 and week 2
B) Week 7 and week 8
C) Week 8 and week 9
D) Week 18 and week 19

3

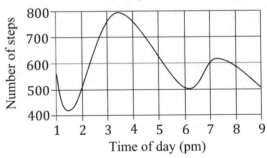

The graph above shows the number of steps Cecilia recorded using a step tracker watch from 1 pm to 9 pm last Sunday. For which of the following one-hour periods is the difference between the number of steps the greatest?

A) From 2 pm to 3 pm
B) From 3 pm to 4 pm
C) From 4 pm to 5 pm
D) From 6 pm to 7 pm

4

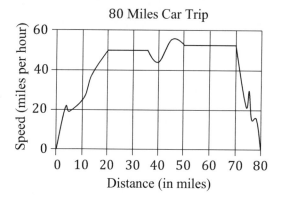

During an 80 miles car trip, Geeta drove at varying speeds, in miles per hour, as shown in the above graph. According to the graph, for approximately how many miles did Geeta maintain a constant speed?

A) 15
B) 20
C) 35
D) 50

5

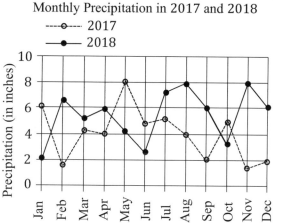

The above line graph shows the monthly precipitation in a city during 2017 and 2018. According to the graph, in which month was the precipitation in 2018 twice that of 2017?

A) May
B) August
C) September
D) December

6

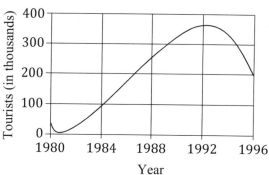

The above graph shows the number of tourists, in thousands, visiting a certain island from 1980 to 1996. During which four-year period was the increase in the number of tourists the greatest?

A) 1980 to 1984
B) 1984 to 1988
C) 1988 to 1992
D) 1992 to 1996

7

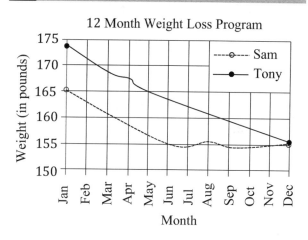

Last year, Tony and Sam enrolled in a 12-month weight loss program from January through December. Their monthly weight, in pounds, from the start to the end of the program is represented by the above line graph. Based on the graph, which of the following statements must be true?

A) At the end of the program, Tony and Sam lost the same amount of weight, in pounds.
B) At the end of the program, Sam lost greater weight than Tony, in pounds.
C) At the end of the program, Tony lost greater weight than Sam, in pounds.
D) At the end of the program, neither Tony nor Sam lost any weight, in pounds.

Digital SAT Math Manual and Workbook

Category 58 – Scatter Plots and Lines of Best Fit

Key Points

- A scatter plot shows the correlation between two variables plotted as data points. One variable is represented on the horizontal axis, and the other variable is represented on the vertical axis. Each data point is represented as a dot and corresponds to a value on the horizontal axis and a value on the vertical axis. See Fig. 1, Fig. 2, and Fig. 3.
    - In a positive correlation, one variable increases as the other variable increases (Fig. 1).
    - In a negative correlation, one variable decreases as the other variable increases (Fig. 2).
    - When the data points are scattered on the graph, there is no correlation between the two variables (Fig. 3).
- A line of best fit on a scatter plot expresses the linear relationship between the data points and can be used to make predictions. It is a straight line drawn through the maximum number of data points on a scatter plot.
    - When the data points are concentrated around the line of best fit, the correlation is high (strong) (Fig. 1).
    - When the data points are spread out around the line of best fit, the correlation is low (weak) (Fig. 2).
    - The actual value of a data point is the value of the dot on the scatter plot. The predicted value of the same data point is the value on the line of best fit. The points that lie on the line of best fit are the points for which the predictions are most accurate. In Fig. 4 below, the prediction is accurate for point B. The predicted value of point A is higher (overestimated), and the predicted value of point C is lower (underestimated).
    - The equation of a line of best fit is the slope-intercept equation, $y = mx + b$. The point where the line of best fit intersects the y-axis (vertical axis) is the y-intercept of the line. At the y-intercept, x (horizontal axis) = 0.

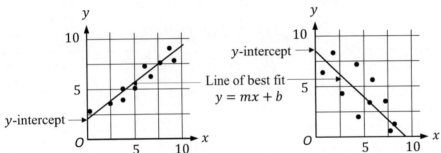

Fig. 1 Positive Correlation   Fig. 2 Negative Correlation   Fig. 3 No Correlation

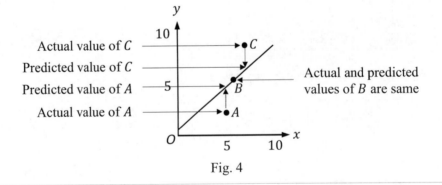

Fig. 4

How to Solve

The slope of the line of best fit can be determined by selecting any two points on the line and using the slope formula shown below, where m is the slope and (x_1, y_1) and (x_2, y_2) are the two points on the line of best fit. It is easiest to select points that are on the grid lines of the graph. (For further information on slope, refer to Section 1 on Lines.)

$$m = \frac{y_2 - y_1}{x_2 - x_1}$$

Remember that the data points below the line are overestimated, and the data points above the line are underestimated.

Digital SAT Math Manual and Workbook

Example 1:

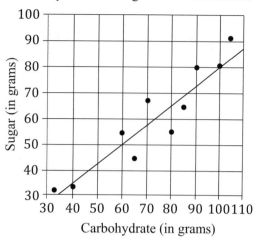

The graph above shows the grams of carbohydrate and sugar in 10 milkshakes. A line of best fit for the data is also shown.

Question 1

Which of the following is the sugar, in grams, predicted by the line of best fit in a milk shake containing 60 grams of carbohydrate?

A) 50
B) 70
C) 81
D) 100

Step 1: Read the data point on the line of best fit

60 grams of carbohydrate (horizontal axis) correspond to 50 grams of sugar (vertical axis).

The correct answer choice is **A**.

Question 2

Which of the following is the approximate difference between the sugar, in grams, predicted by the line of best fit and the actual sugar, in grams, in a milk shake containing 70 grams of carbohydrate?

A) 0
B) 4
C) 5
D) 10

Step 1: Read the data point on the line of best fit

70 grams of carbohydrate (horizontal axis) correspond to approximately 58 grams of sugar (vertical axis).

Step 2: Read the data point on the scatter plot

Look for the dot on the scatter plot that corresponds to 70 grams of carbohydrate (horizontal axis). Read the corresponding grams of sugar (vertical axis). The corresponding amount of sugar is approximately 68 grams.

Step 3: Calculate the difference

$$68 - 58 = 10$$

The correct answer choice is **D**.

The graph is repeated for Questions 3 and 4.

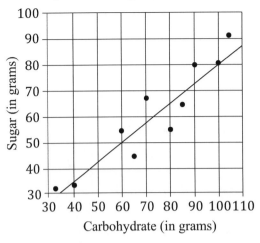
Carbohydrate and Sugar in 10 Milk Shakes

Question 3

Which of the following could be an equation of a line of best fit?

A) $y = \frac{1}{2}x + 10$

B) $y = \frac{1}{2}x - 2$

C) $y = \frac{3}{4}x + 1$

D) $y = \frac{3}{4}x + 30$

Step 1: Determine the slope of the line of best fit

The slope is determined below using the points (60, 50) and (100, 80) on the line of best fit.

$$m = \frac{y_2 - y_1}{x_2 - x_1} = \frac{80 - 50}{100 - 60} = \frac{30}{40} = \frac{3}{4}$$

This eliminates answer choices A and B. From the graph, it is seen that the y-intercept is less than 30. This eliminates answer choice D.

The correct answer choice is **C**.

Question 4

Based on the line of best fit, which of the following best interprets the relationship between the amount of sugar and amount of carbohydrate, in grams, in the 10 milk shakes?

A) For every 1 gram of sugar, the predicted increase in carbohydrate is approximately 1.3 grams.

B) For every 1 gram of carbohydrate, the predicted increase in sugar is approximately 1.4 grams.

C) For every 1 gram of carbohydrate, the predicted increase in sugar is 5 grams.

D) For every 1 gram of sugar, there is no change in carbohydrate.

Step 1: Determine the slope of the line of best fit

The relationship between sugar and carbohydrate is defined by the slope of the line of best fit. See question 3 above for calculation of the slope.

$$\text{slope} = \frac{\text{rise (change in } y)}{\text{run (change in } x)} = \frac{3}{4} = \frac{3 \text{ grams of sugar}}{4 \text{ grams of carbohydrate}} = \frac{1 \text{ gram of sugar}}{1.33 \text{ grams of carbohydrate}}$$

Since the slope is positive, for every 1 gram of sugar, carbohydrate increases approximately by 1.3 grams.

The correct answer choice is **A**.

Category 58 – Practice Questions

1

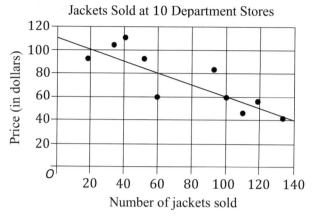

Jackets Sold at 10 Department Stores

The scatter plot above shows the prices of jackets, in dollars, and the number of jackets sold per month at 10 department stores. A line of best fit is also shown. Which of the following could be an equation of the line of best fit?

A) $y = -0.5x + 112$

B) $y = -0.5x + 20$

C) $y = 0.5x + 110$

D) $y = 2x + 115$

2

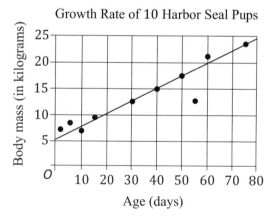

Growth Rate of 10 Harbor Seal Pups

The above scatter plot shows the body mass, in kilograms, of 10 harbor seal pups from ages 1 to 80 days. A line of best fit is also given. Based on the graph, which of the following best estimates the increase in body mass, in kilograms, for every 20 days increase in age?

A) 2

B) 5

C) 8

D) 10

3

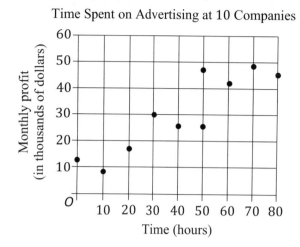

Time Spent on Advertising at 10 Companies

The above scatter plot shows the monthly profit, in thousands of dollars, of 10 companies and number of hours the companies spent on advertising each month. Which of the following is the best interpretation of the y-intercept of a line of best fit?

A) The predicted monthly profit of a company in thousands of dollars when unlimited time is spent on advertising each month.

B) The predicted monthly profit of a company in thousands of dollars when 10 hours are spent on advertising each month.

C) The predicted monthly profit of a company in thousands of dollars when 80 hours are spent on advertising each month.

D) The predicted monthly profit of a company in thousands of dollars when no time is spent on advertising each month.

4

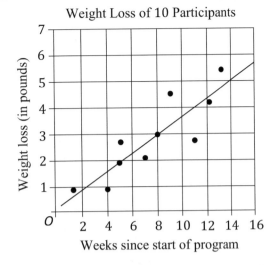

The above scatter plot shows the weight loss, in pounds, of 10 participants in a weight loss program and the number of weeks since start of the program. Which of the following best interprets the relationship between the weeks in the program and weight loss of the participants, in pounds?

A) For every 1 week in the program, the predicted weight loss is 0.33 pounds.

B) For every 1 week in the program, the predicted weight loss is 2 pounds.

C) For every 1 week in the program, the predicted weight loss is 3.33 pounds.

D) For every 1 week in the program, there is no predicted weight loss.

5

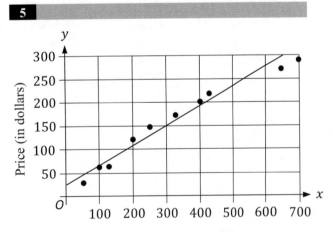

The scatter plot above shows the relationship between variables x and y for 10 data points. What is an equation of a line of best fit?

A) $y = -0.5x - 5$

B) $y = -0.4x + 25$

C) $y = 0.4x + 28$

D) $y = 2x - 25$

6

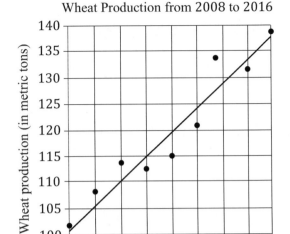

The scatter plot above shows the amount of wheat production, in millions of metric tons, in a certain country from 2008 to 2016. A line of best fit for the data is also shown. What is the approximate amount of wheat production, in millions of metric tons, predicted by the line of best fit in 2012?

A) 110

B) 115

C) 120

D) 128

7

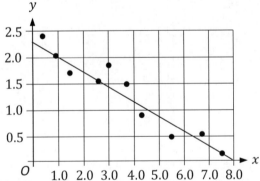

The scatter plot above shows the relationship between variables x and y for 10 data points. A line of best fit for the data is shown. How many points are underestimated by the line of best fit?

Category 59 – Bar Graphs

Key Points
- A bar graph shows data grouped into categories. For example, book genre, year, color, height, etc. The data is represented as rectangular bars that can be horizontal or vertical. The height or the length of a bar determines the number of data points in a category.
- A bar graph may contain sub-groups within each category. For example, if the category is department, then each department may have sub-groups for expense type. Sub-groups may be displayed side by side as bars within each category or may be stacked on each other as a column.

How to Solve
Determine the number of data points in each category or sub-group by reading the height of a vertical bar or the length of a horizontal bar. The correct answer may sometimes be apparent by looking at the graph.

Example 1:

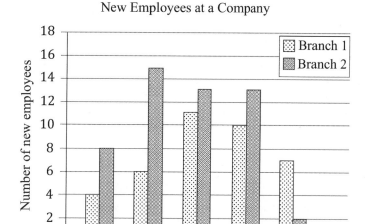

The above graph shows the number of new employees hired at Branch 1 and Branch 2 of a company from January to May. During which of the following months was the greatest number of new employees hired at Branch 1 and Branch 2 combined?

A) January
B) February
C) April
D) May

Step 1: Read the height of each bar

This is an example of sub-groups displayed side by side. The category is month, and the sub-group is branch.
The graph shows that January and May have relatively shorter bars indicating fewer new employees. Hence, answer choices A and D can be eliminated. Determine the total number of new employees for the remaining answer choices.

February: In Branch 1, the number of new employees = 6. In Branch 2, the number of new employees = 15.
$$6 + 15 = 21$$
April: In Branch 1, the number of new employees = 10. In Branch 2, the number of new employees = 13.
$$10 + 13 = 23$$
The correct answer choice is **C**.

Digital SAT Math Manual and Workbook

Example 2:

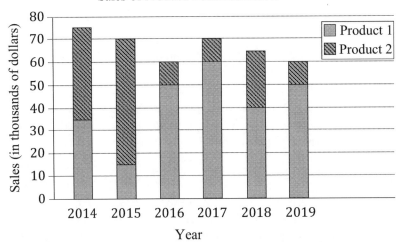

The above bar graph shows the sales, in thousands of dollars, of Product 1 and Product 2 at a certain company from 2014 to 2019. Based on the graph, Product 1 sales, in thousands of dollars, are what fraction of the total sales of Product 1 and Product 2 combined, in thousands of dollars, from 2014 to 2019?

A) $\frac{3}{8}$

B) $\frac{5}{8}$

C) $\frac{3}{5}$

D) $\frac{2}{3}$

Step 1: Read the height of each bar

This is an example of a stacked bar graph. The category is year. The two sub-groups are Product 1 and Product 2. The Product 2 bar is stacked on the Product 1 bar. The height of each sub-group bar must be read from the bottom of each bar.

Product 1: Read the vertical axis from the bottom of the bar to the top of the bar. Since Product 1 is the lower bar, it starts from 0.

2014 = 35. 2015 = 15. 2016 = 50. 2017 = 60. 2018 = 40. 2019 = 50.

$$35 + 15 + 50 + 60 + 40 + 50 = 250$$

Product 2: Read the vertical axis from the bottom of the Product 2 bar to the top of the Product 2 bar. The height of this bar is the difference between the two numbers. (Remember that the top bar does not start from 0.)

2014 bar is from 35 to 75. The difference is $75 - 35 = 40$.

2015 bar is from 15 to 70. The difference is $70 - 15 = 55$.

2016 bar is from 50 to 60. The difference is $60 - 50 = 10$.

2017 bar is from 60 to 70. The difference is $70 - 60 = 10$.

2018 bar is from 40 to 65. The difference is $65 - 40 = 25$.

2019 bar is from 50 to 60. The difference is $60 - 50 = 10$.

$$40 + 55 + 10 + 10 + 25 + 10 = 150$$

Step 2: Determine the fraction

$$\frac{\text{Product 1 sales}}{\text{Product 1 sales} + \text{Product 2 sales}} = \frac{250}{250 + 150} = \frac{250}{400} = \frac{5}{8}$$

The correct answer choice is **B**.

Category 59 – Practice Questions

1

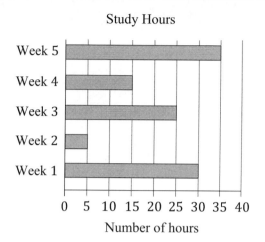

The number of hours Payton studied each week for 5 consecutive weeks is represented in the above bar graph. Based on the data in the graph, during which of the following periods did the number of hours change by the greatest?

A) From week 1 to week 2
B) From week 2 to week 3
C) From week 3 to week 4
D) From week 4 to week 5

2

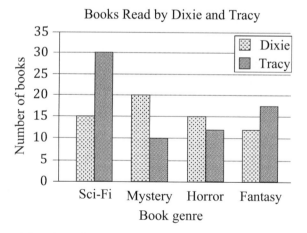

The above bar graph shows the number of books Dixie and Tracy read by genre during the last 6 months. For which book genre, did Dixie read double the number of books than Tracy?

A) Sci-Fi
B) Mystery
C) Horror
D) Fantasy

3

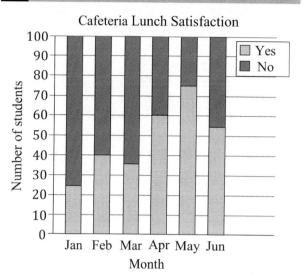

A high school surveyed 100 students each month from January to June to determine if the students were satisfied with the lunch offered at the school cafeteria. The above graph summarizes the responses of the 100 students for each month as "Yes" or "No". Based on the graph, what percent of students responded "No" in May?

A) 25%
B) 45%
C) 50%
D) 75%

4

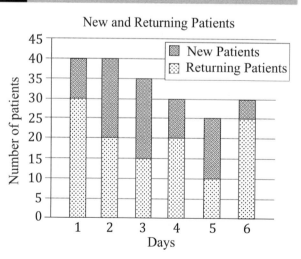

The above graph shows the daily number of new and returning patients who visited a certain medical center during a 6-day period. How many new patients visited the medical center over the course of these days?

Category 60 – Histograms and Dot Plots

Key Points
- A histogram shows the distribution of data points in defined groups.
  - The number of data points (also known as frequency) in each group are represented by a rectangular bar.
  - The groups in a histogram are generally along the horizontal axis and may be comprised of a single numeric value or a range of numeric values.
  - For example, if a histogram summarizes the distribution of the number of fruit servings eaten by 50 people in a month, then the groups on the horizontal axis represent the number of fruit servings, and the height of each bar in a group (read on the vertical axis) represents the number of people in that group. Each bar may represent a single serving, such as, the first bar represents 1 serving, the second bar represents 2 servings, and so on, or as a range of numbers, such as, the first bar represents 0 to 5 servings, the second bar represents 6 to 10 servings, and so on.
- A dot plot shows the distribution of relatively small data sets. Data points are represented as dots. The groups are represented on the horizontal axis. The number of dots on each group represents the number of data points in that group.
- The data distribution in a histogram and dot plot is continuous (a main difference from bar graphs). In the above example, if the first bar represents 1 serving and second bar represents 2 servings, then the third bar must represent 3 servings. The third bar cannot represent 4 servings or 10 servings. Similarly, if the first bar represents 0 to 5 servings and second bar represents 6 to 10 servings, then the third bar must represent 11 to 15 servings.

How to Solve
In a histogram, determine the frequency in each group by reading the height of a vertical bar or the length of a horizontal bar.

In a dot plot, count the number of dots in each group.

Example 1:

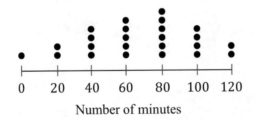

Number of minutes

The above dot plot shows the distribution of the number of minutes 24 students spend on daily homework. Based on the data in the dot plot, how many students spend 80 or more minutes on daily homework?

Step 1: Count the number of dots in each group

Each dot represents one student. The question asks for the number of students who spend 80 or more minutes on homework. Count the number of dots for 80, 100, and 120 minutes.

For 80 minutes, there are 6 dots = 6 students.

For 100 minutes, there are 4 dots = 4 students.

For 120 minutes, there are 2 dots = 2 students.

Step 2: Determine the total

$$6 + 4 + 2 = 12$$

The correct answer is **12**.

Example 2:

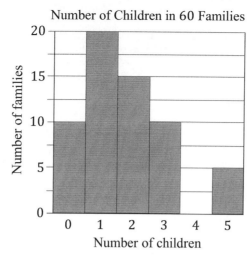

The above histogram shows the distribution of the number of children in 60 families.

Question 1

If a is the number of families with 3 or more children and b is the total number of families, what is $a:b$?

A) $1:4$
B) $1:3$
C) $2:3$
D) $3:4$

Step 1: Read the height of each bar

Determine the number of families with 3, 4, and 5 children and add them. The number of families is the height of the vertical bar and can be read from the vertical axis.

For the bar corresponding to 3 children, there are 10 families.

For the bar corresponding to 4 children, there are 0 families.

For the bar corresponding to 5 children, there are 5 families.

$$10 + 0 + 5 = 15$$

Step 2: Determine $a:b$:

$$a:b = \text{families with 3 or more children:total number of families} = 15:60 = 1:4$$

The correct answer choice is **A**.

Question 2

Based on the data in the histogram above, what is the total number of children in 60 families?

A) 80
B) 105
C) 115
D) 120

Step 1: Determine the total

The total number of children is the sum of children in all the 60 families. Multiply the number of children in each bar with the corresponding number of families (height of the vertical bar) and add the numbers.

$$(0 \times 10) + (1 \times 20) + (2 \times 15) + (3 \times 10) + (4 \times 0) + (5 \times 5) = 0 + 20 + 30 + 30 + 0 + 25 = 105$$

The correct answer choice is **B**.

Category 60 – Practice Questions

1

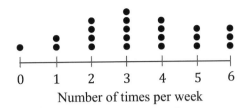

Dinner Per Week of 22 Families

Number of times per week

The above dot plot shows the distribution of the number of times 22 families go out for dinner during a week. Based on the data in the data plot, how many families go out for dinner 3 to 4 times per week?

A) 9
B) 10
C) 15
D) 22

2

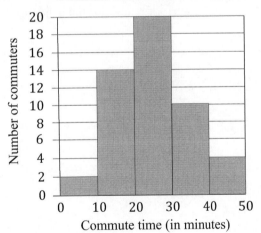

Commute Time of 50 Commuters

The histogram above summarizes the distribution of the commute time, in minutes, of 50 commuters from home to work. The first bar represents a commute time of less than 10 minutes, the second bar represents a commute time of at least 10 minutes, but less than 20 minutes, and so on. How many commuters have a commute time of 20 minutes or greater, but less than 40 minutes?

A) 10
B) 14
C) 30
D) 34

3

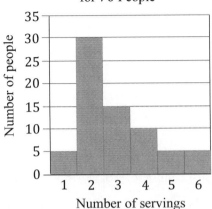

Daily Servings of Vegetables for 70 People

70 people at a nutrition center were asked how many servings of vegetables they eat per day. The histogram above summarizes the distribution of the number of servings for the 70 people. Based on the histogram, what percent of people ate at least 3 daily servings of vegetables?

A) 30%
B) 50%
C) 75%
D) 90%

4

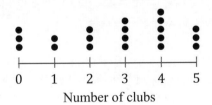

20 Students Enrolled in Clubs at School

Number of clubs

The above dot plot shows the distribution of the number of clubs 20 students are enrolled in at a certain middle school. Based on the data in the dot plot, the largest number of students are enrolled in how many clubs?

Digital SAT Math Manual and Workbook

Category 61 – Mean

Key Points
- The average (arithmetic mean) is the sum of numbers in a data set divided by the total count of numbers in the data set.

$$\text{mean} = \frac{\text{sum of numbers}}{\text{total count of numbers}}$$

How to Solve

When the mean of a set of numbers is given, the sum of the numbers can be determined as (mean × count of numbers). For example, if 7.5 is the mean of a set of 4 numbers, then the sum of the numbers is $4 \times 7.5 = 30$.

When grouped numbers are given, the sum of numbers in each group must be determined before calculating the mean. For example, if 7 students are 150 inches tall and 3 students are 165 inches tall, then the total height of $7 + 3 = 10$ students is $(7 \times 150) + (3 \times 165)$. Dividing this total by 10 will give the mean height of the 10 students.

*The mean of a list of numbers can be determined using the Desmos graphing calculator.

Example 1:
A team scored 12, 10, 8, 6, and 9 points in 5 games.

*Question 1

What is the mean score of the team in 5 games?

Step 1: Determine the mean

Total count of numbers = 5.

5 numbers are 12, 10, 8, 6, 9.

$$\frac{12 + 10 + 8 + 6 + 9}{5} = \frac{45}{5} = 9$$

The correct answer is **9**.

*In the Desmos graphing calculator, type "mean (12, 10, 8, 6, and 9)" in a row in the Expression List. The answer will be displayed to the right in the same row as = 9.

Question 2.

If the team wants a mean score of 10 by the end of the 6th game, how many points are needed in the 6th game?

Step 1: Set up the mean

Total count of numbers after 6th game = 6.

Let the score of 6th game = x.

The 6 numbers are 12, 10, 8, 6, 9, x.

Since the mean of the 6 numbers should be 10, set up the mean and equate it to 10.

$$\frac{12 + 10 + 8 + 6 + 9 + x}{6} = 10 \rightarrow \frac{45 + x}{6} = 10$$

Cross multiply.

$$45 + x = 10 \times 6 \rightarrow x = 60 - 45 = 15$$

The correct answer is **15**.

Digital SAT Math Manual and Workbook

Example 2:

Weight (pounds)	Number of packets
1	10
2	4
3	4
5	2

The table above shows the number of almond packets Karina bought and their weight in pounds. What is the mean weight, in pounds, of all the almond packets Karina bought?

Step 1: Determine the sum of numbers

Total number of packets is $10 + 4 + 4 + 2 = 20$. Hence, the total count of numbers is 20.

The total weight of the 20 packages must be added and then divided by 20.

The total weight of 10 packets that weigh 1 pound each is $10 \times 1 = 10$.

The total weight of 4 packets that weigh 2 pounds each is $4 \times 2 = 8$.

The total weight of 4 packets that weigh 3 pounds each is $4 \times 3 = 12$.

The total weight of 2 packets that weigh 5 pounds each is $2 \times 5 = 10$.

Step 2: Determine the mean

$$\frac{10 + 8 + 12 + 10}{20} = 2$$

The correct answer is **2**.

Example 3:

The average weight, in pounds, of 12 students in class A is 115 pounds. The average weight, in pounds, of 18 students in class B is 110 pounds. What is the average weight of all the students in class A and class B?

Step 1: Determine the sum of numbers

Total number of students in both the classes $= 12 + 18 = 30$. Hence, the total count of numbers is 30.

The total weight of the 30 students must be added and then divided by 30.

The total weight of 12 students in class A is $12 \times 115 = 1,380$.

The total weight of 18 students in class B is $18 \times 110 = 1,980$.

Step 2: Determine the mean

$$\frac{1,380 + 1,980}{30} = 112$$

The correct answer is **112**.

Category 61 – Practice Questions

1

The average (arithmetic mean) score of Mr. Daniel's class of 40 students is a, and the average score of Mr. Power's class of 20 students is b. In terms of a and b, which of the following represents the average score of all the students in both the classes?

A) $\frac{1}{6}(a + b)$

B) $\frac{1}{3}(2a + b)$

C) $40a + 20b$

D) $30ab$

2

$$50, 120, 230, 80, 220$$

If the number y is added to the above set of 5 numbers, the mean of the set will be 134. What is number y?

3

Gianna took 4 biology tests and scored 85, 88, 87, and 92. Given that all the scores are integers out of 100, and all the tests are equally weighted, what is the minimum score Gianna will need on the fifth biology test for a mean score of at least 90 for all the 5 biology tests?

4

The mean of two numbers is 32. If one of the numbers is three times the other number, what is the value of the lesser number?

5

In a data set of 12 integers, two of the integers are 11 and 15. The mean of the 12 integers is 38. If 11 and 15 are removed from the set, what is the mean of the remaining 10 integers in the data set?

6

Daisy took 7 tests in the first semester of school. The mean score of the 7 tests is 92. If the mean score of the first 5 tests is 96, what is the mean score of the last 2 tests?

7

Weight (pounds)	Number of dumbbells
5	6
10	10
20	4

Rita bought dumbbells of three different weights, in pounds. The table above shows the weights of the dumbbells, in pounds, and the number of dumbbells for each weight Rita bought. What is the mean weight of all the dumbbells, in pounds?

8

A data set consisting of 12 integers is divided into 3 groups, Group A, Group B, and Group C. Each group consists of 4 integers, and none of the integers are repeated in a group. The mean of the integers in Group A is 210, the mean of the integers in Group B is 148, and the mean of the integers in Group C is 74. What is the mean of the data set?

Category 62 – Histograms, Dot Plots, and Mean

Key Points
- The mean of the data in a histogram or a dot plot is the sum of values in all the groups divided by the number of data points.

How to Solve
For each bar in a histogram, multiply the number of data points (frequency) with the value of the group. Sum the numbers for all the bars and divide by the number of data points.

In a dot plot, count the number of dots in each group and multiply the count by the value of the group. Sum the numbers and divide by the number of data points.

Example 1:

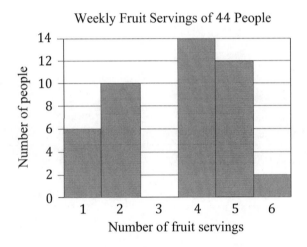

The histogram above shows the distribution of the number of fruit servings 44 people ate in a week. What is the mean number of fruit servings per person?

Step 1: Determine the total

Multiply the height of each bar with the number of fruit servings for that bar. Add all the numbers.

The bar for 1 serving has 6 people. The total servings are $(1 \times 6) = 6$.

The bar for 2 servings has 10 people. The total servings are $(2 \times 10) = 20$.

The bar for 4 servings has 14 people. The total servings are $(4 \times 14) = 56$.

The bar for 5 servings has 12 people. The total servings are $(5 \times 12) = 60$.

The bar for 6 servings has 2 people. The total servings are $(6 \times 2) = 12$.

$$\text{total servings of all 50 people} = 6 + 20 + 56 + 60 + 12 = 154$$

Step 2: Determine the mean

Total servings = 154. Total people = 44.

$$\frac{154}{44} = 3.5$$

The correct answer is **3.5**.

Example 2:

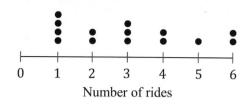

Number of Rides for 14 Kids

The dot plot above shows the number of rides 14 kids rode at a fair. What is the mean number of rides per kid?

A) 1
B) 3
C) 4
D) 7

Step 1: Determine the total

To determine the total number of rides for all the 14 kids, multiply the number of rides with the number of dots on it. Add all the numbers.

$$(1 \times 4) + (2 \times 2) + (3 \times 3) + (4 \times 2) + (5 \times 1) + (6 \times 2) =$$
$$4 + 4 + 9 + 8 + 5 + 12 = 42$$

Step 2: Determine the mean

Total rides = 42. Total kids = 14.

$$\frac{42}{14} = 3$$

The correct answer choice is **B**.

Category 62 – Practice Questions

1

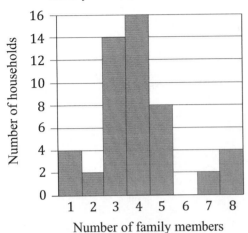

Family Members in 50 Households

The histogram above shows the distribution of the number of family members in a household for 50 households. Based on the data in the histogram, which of the following is the mean number of family members per household?

A) 1
B) 3
C) 4
D) 5

2

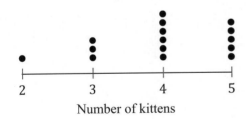

Kittens of 15 Cats

The dot plot above shows the distribution of the number of kittens born to 15 cats. Based on the data in the dot plot, which of the following is the mean number of kittens per cat?

A) 3
B) 4
C) 12
D) 30

3

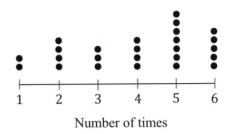

25 School Buses Late to School

The dot plot above shows the number of times 25 school buses were late to school last week. Based on the above dot plot, what is the average number of times a school bus was late to school last week?

4

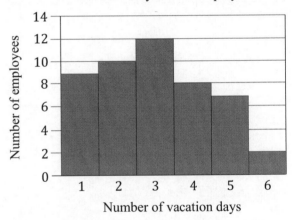

Vacation Days of 48 Employees

The histogram above shows the distribution of the number of vacation days taken by 48 employees at a certain company in January 2015. Based on the histogram, what is the mean number of vacation days taken per employee?

Category 63 – Median

Key Points
- In a data set of sorted numbers, the median is determined based on the count of numbers in the set.
  - If the data set contains an odd count of numbers, then the median is the middle number. For example, in a set of 5 numbers, the 3rd number is the middle number and the median.
  - If the data set contains an even count of numbers, then the median is the average of the two middle numbers. For example, in a set of 6 numbers, the 3rd and 4th numbers are the middle numbers. The median is the average of the 3rd and 4th numbers.
- In a grouped set of data, the group that includes the median number of the data set is the median group. For example, if there are 27 students in a data set, then the median is in the group that includes the 14th student. The median can be any number in the median group.

How to Solve
*The median of a list of numbers can be determined using the Desmos graphing calculator.

Example 1:
$$1, 12, 4, 18, 16, 14, 10, 25, 6, 20$$
What is the median of the above set of numbers?

Step 1: Sort the numbers from least to greatest
1, 4, 6, 10, 12, 14, 16, 18, 20, 25

Step 2: Determine the middle number
Since there are 10 numbers in the set, the median is the average of the two middle numbers (5th and 6th numbers).
$$\frac{12 + 14}{2} = \frac{26}{2} = 13$$
The correct answer is **13**.

*In the Desmos graphing calculator, type "median (1, 12, 4, 18, 16, 14, 10)" in a row in the Expression List. The answer will be displayed to the right in the same row as = 13.

Example 2:

Year	2012	2013	2014	2015	2016
Number of students	163	171	154	165	150

The table above shows the number of students enrolled in an elementary school from 2012 to 2016. Which of the following year contains the median number of students enrolled from 2012 to 2016?

A) 2012
B) 2014
C) 2015
D) 2016

Step 1: Sort the number of students from least to greatest
150, 154, 163, 165, 171

Step 2: Determine the middle number
Since there are 5 numbers in the data set, the median is the 3rd number = 163. The corresponding year is 2012. The correct answer choice is **A**.

*In the Desmos graphing calculator, type median (163, 171, 154, 165, 150) in a row in the Expression List. The answer will be displayed to the right in the same row as = 163. Read the corresponding year.

Example 3:

The table below shows the score range of 21 students in a class, where each score is an integer.

Score range	Number of students
51 - 60	1
61 - 70	4
71 - 80	3
81 - 90	8
91 - 100	5

Question 1

The median score of the students in the class falls into which of the following score range?

A) 51 - 60
B) 61 - 70
C) 81 - 90
D) 91 - 100

Step 1: Determine the median

The questions on grouped data are generally sorted by the group from least to greatest.

The scores in the above table are grouped in increments of 10.

There are 21 students in the class. The median of 21 students from 1 to 21 is 11. Hence, the score range that contains the 11th student is the median score range.

Starting from the top of the table, continue a cumulative count of the number of students till the 11th student is reached. See table below. 11th student is in the 81 - 90 score range.

Score range	Number of students	Cumulative count of students
51 - 60	1	1st student.
61 - 70	4	2nd, 3rd, 4th, and 5th student.
71 - 80	3	6th, 7th, and 8th student.
81 - 90	8	9th, 10th, **11th**, 12th, 13th, 14th, 15th, and 16th student.
91 - 100	5	17th, 18th, 19th, 20th, and 21st student.

The correct answer choice is **C**.

Question 2

Which of the following could be a median score of the class?

A) 69
B) 72
C) 80
D) 90

Continue from Step 1 of Question 1. Any score in the median score range can be the median. Hence, any score between 81 and 90 could be a median score. This eliminates answer choices A, B, and C.

The correct answer choice is **D**.

Category 63 – Practice Questions

1 — Desmos

The table below shows the annual rainfall, in inches, in New York City from 2010 to 2014.

Year	2010	2011	2012	2013	2014
Rainfall (in inches)	49.37	72.81	38.51	46.32	53.79

The median annual rainfall, in inches, in New York City from 2010 to 2014 was in which of the following years?

A) 2010
B) 2011
C) 2012
D) 2014

2

In a small company of 27 total employees, 15 employees receive an annual salary between $40,000 - $60,000, 9 employees receive an annual salary between $61,000 - $75,000, and 3 employees receive an annual salary between $76,000 - $90,000. Which of the following could be a median salary of the 27 employees?

A) $30,000
B) $54,000
C) $68,000
D) $78,000

3 — Desmos

Set 1	12.5	10.1	5.2	17.5	15.3	14.5	13.5
Set 2	49.5	72.8	38.5	47.5	12.5	50.1	48.5

The table above shows two sets of numbers. If the median of Set 1 is A, and the median of Set 2 is B, by how much does B exceed A?

A) 17
B) 20
C) 34
D) 35

4

y, 8, 15, 5, 11

In the above set of 5 integers, y is the median. Which of the following could be the values of y?

I. 8
II. 10
III. 12

A) I only
B) III only
C) I and II only
D) II and III only

5

Number of books	Number of students
1 - 3	11
4 - 6	16
7 - 9	3
10 - 12	18
13 - 15	1

The bookstore at a certain elementary school sells children books throughout the year. Last year, 49 students bought one or more books from the school bookstore. The above table shows the number of books, grouped in increments of 3, and the number of students who bought that many books. Which of the following could be a median number of books bought by the 49 students from the school bookstore, last year?

A) 4
B) 8
C) 11
D) 16

6 — Desmos

8.2, 29.0, 5.1, 24.3, 42.7, 25.7

What is the median of the above set of numbers?

Digital SAT Math Manual and Workbook

Category 64 – Histograms, Dot Plots, Bar Graphs, and Median

Key Points
- In a histogram, the bar that includes the median data point of the data set is the median group. For example, if there are 51 data points, then the median is in the bar that includes the 26th data point. The median can be any number represented in the median bar.
- In a dot plot, the median is in the group that includes the dot corresponding to the median data point.
- In a bar graph, the median is the middle number of the height of the bars, ordered least to greatest. For example, in a bar graph of 5 bars if the heights of the bars starting from left to right are 2, 8, 19, 5, 11, then the median is 8.

How to Solve

In a histogram, continue a cumulative count of data points from left to right (or right to left) till the bar that contains the median data point is reached.

In a dot plot, count the dots from left to right till the dot corresponding to the median data point is reached.

In a bar graph, determining the median is simpler since the data is not continuous. Read the height of each vertical bar or the width of each horizontal bar and order the numbers least to greatest. The middle number is the median.

Example 1:

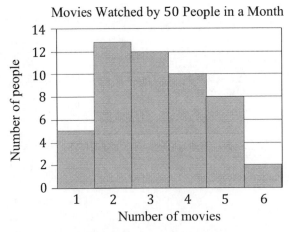

The histogram above shows the distribution of the number of movies 50 people watched in a certain month. Based on the histogram, what is the median number of movies watched by the 50 people in the month?

A) 1
B) 3
C) 6
D) 25

Step 1: Determine the median

Since there are 50 people, the bar that includes the 25th and 26th person contains the median number of movies. Starting from the left bar, continue a cumulative count of the number of people for each bar till the bar containing the 25th to 26th person is reached.

The bar for 1 movie has 5 people. This bar includes 1st to 5th person.

The bar for 2 movies has 13 people. This bar includes 6th to 18th person.

The bar for 3 movies has 12 people. This bar includes 19th to 30th person and, hence, the median data point.

The median number of movies is **3**.

The correct answer choice is **B**.

Note that if the question asked, "how many people watched the median number of movies in a month", then the answer would be 12 since the median bar has 12 people.

Example 2:

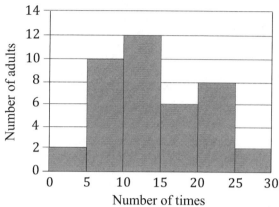
Number of Times 40 Adults Went to Movie Theater in a Year

The above histogram shows the distribution of the number of times 40 adults went to a movie theater in a year. The first bar represents less than 5 times in a year, the second bar represents at least 5 times but less than 10 times in a year, and so on. What is one possible integer value of the median number of times 40 adults went to a movie theater in a year?

Step 1: Determine the median

Since there are 40 adults, the bar that includes the 20th and 21st adult contains the median number of times.

Each bar represents a group of numbers in increments of 5. The question mentions that the value of each bar is from the number at the left boundary to any number till the right boundary but excluding the number at the right boundary. For example, the bar between 10 and 15 can be any number from 10 to less than 15.

Starting from the left bar, continue a cumulative count of the number of adults for each bar till the bar containing the 20th to 21st adults is reached.

The bar between 0 and 5 has 2 adults. This bar includes 1st to 2nd adults.

The bar between 5 and 10 has 10 adults. This bar includes 3rd to 12th adults.

The bar between 10 and 15 has 12 adults. This bar includes 13th to 24th adults and, hence, the median data point. The median can be any integer between 10 and 14.

The correct answer is **10, 11, 12, 13**, or **14**.

Example 3:

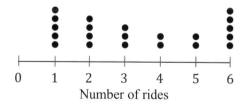
Number of Rides by 21 Kids

The dot plot above shows the number of rides 21 kids rode at a fair. What is the median number of rides?

Step 1: Determine the median

Since there are 21 kids, the group that includes the 11th dot (kid) is the median number of rides.

Count dots from left to right until the 11th dot is reached. 11th dot is on number of rides = 3.

The correct answer is **3**.

Category 64 – Practice Questions

1

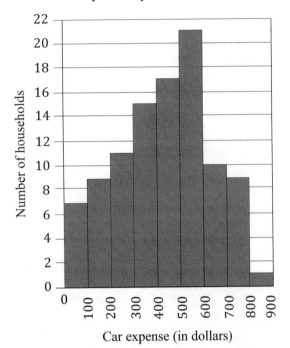

Monthly Car Expense of 100 Households

The histogram above shows the distribution of the monthly car expense, in dollars, of 100 households. The first bar represents less than $100, the second bar represents at least $100, but less than $200, the third bar represents at least $200, but less than $300, and so on. Based on the data in the histogram, which of the following statements are true about the median car expense, in dollars, of the 100 households?

I. The median car expense of the 100 households is between $500 and $600 per month.

II. One possible value of a median car expense of the 100 households is $410.

A) I
B) II
C) Neither I nor II
D) Not enough information is provided.

2

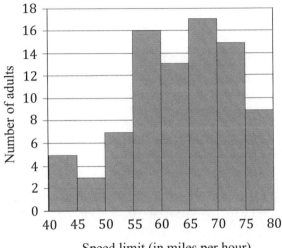

Highway Speed Limit Preference of 85 Adults

85 adults in a certain neighborhood were asked about their preference on the speed limit, in miles per hour, on a highway close to their home. The above graph shows the distribution of the response of the 85 adults. Speed limit was categorized in groups of 5 miles, from 40 miles per hour to 80 miles per hour. The first bar represents at least 40 miles per hour, but less than 45 miles per hour, the second bar represents at least 45 miles per hour, but less than 50 miles per hour, and so on. Based on the data in the graph, which of the following could be a median speed limit, in miles per hour, preferred by the 85 adults?

A) 50
B) 58
C) 62
D) 65

Digital SAT Math Manual and Workbook

3

Weight of 15 Baby Dolphins

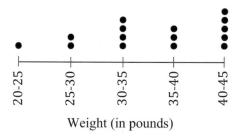

Weight (in pounds)

The above dot plot shows the weight, in pounds, of 15 baby dolphins. Which of the following could be a median weight, in pounds, of the 15 baby dolphins?

A) 30
B) 36
C) 41
D) 42

4

Number of College Degrees for 60 Employees

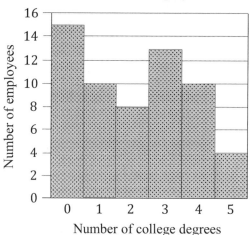

Number of college degrees

The above histogram shows the distribution of the number of college degrees held by 60 employees at a certain company. What is the median number of degrees held by the 60 employees at the company?

5

Student Scores on 21 Quizzes

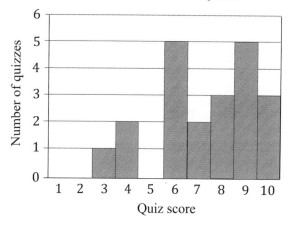

Quiz score

The histogram above shows the quiz scores of 21 students in Ms. Debbie's class. Based on the distribution of the data in the histogram, in how many quizzes taken by the students was the quiz score equal to the median quiz score?

6

Length of 49 Newborn Babies

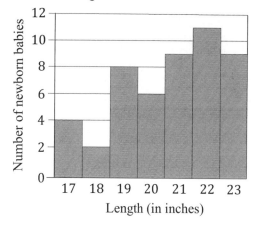

Length (in inches)

The graph above shows the distribution of the length, in inches, of 49 newborn babies. In what number of newborn babies was the length, in inches, equal to the median length, in inches?

Digital SAT Math Manual and Workbook

Category 65 – Box Plots and Median

Key Points
- A box plot (also known as a box and whisker plot) distributes the numbers in a data set from least to greatest into 4 sections. Each section contains approximately 25% of the numbers. See the figure below.

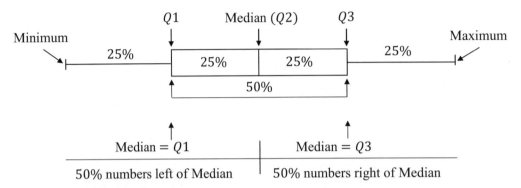

- The middle 50% of the numbers are represented in a box. The median is the middle number of the data set in the box and shown by a vertical line.
- The number at the left end of the box is known as the First Quartile ($Q1$). It is the median of the 50% of the numbers to the left of the median.
- The number at the right end of the box is known as the Third Quartile ($Q3$). It is the median of the 50% of the numbers to the right of the median.
- The minimum is the lowest number in a data set, and the maximum is the highest number in a data set.
- The line between the minimum and $Q1$ and the line between the maximum and $Q3$ is known as the whiskers.
- The distance between the minimum and the maximum is the range of numbers in a data set.
- The box is larger when the middle 50% numbers are spread out farther from each other (see Fig. 1 below). The box is smaller when the middle 50% numbers are closer to each other (see Fig. 2 below).

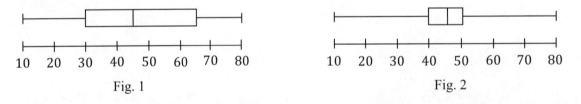

How to Solve

Note that the actual data or the frequency of the data in a data set is not known from a box plot. The numbers that can be read from a boxplot are minimum, $Q1$, median, $Q2$, and maximum.

Since the actual numbers are not known, the mean of the data in a data set cannot be determined from a box plot.

Example 1:

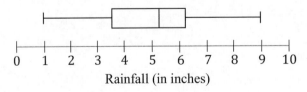

Monthly Rainfall in New York City from 2018 to 2019

Rainfall (in inches)

The above box plot shows the monthly distribution of rainfall, in inches, in New York City from January 2018 to December 2019. Which of the following statements about the data shown in the box plot must be true?

A) The median of the data is 6.2.
B) The mean of the data is 5.2.
C) Approximately 50% of the data is between 3.5 and 6.2.
D) Approximately 50% of the data is between 1 and 9.

Step 1: Compare the answer choices with the data in the box plot

The box plot shows that the median is around 5.2. This eliminates answer choice A.

The mean cannot be determined from a box plot. This eliminates answer choice B.

The box plot shows that the data in the box (about 50% data) is approximately between 3.5 and 6.2. This eliminates answer choice D.

The correct answer choice is **C**.

Example 2:

Rides	1	2	3	4	5	6	7	8	9	10
Number of adults	5	22	11	11	8	5	0	14	2	1

The table above shows the distribution of the number of rides 79 adults rode at an amusement park? Which of the following box plots is the closest representation of the data in the table?

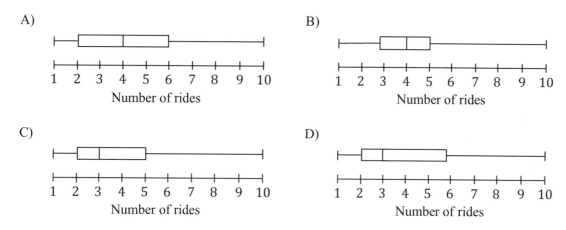

Step 1: Determine the median

Since there are 79 adults, the median is the number of rides for the 40th adult. Staring from the left of the table continue a cumulative count of the number of adults till the 40th adult is reached. The 40th adult took 4 rides. Hence, median = 4. This eliminates answer choices C and D that have median = 3.

Step 2: Determine $Q1$

Since the answer choices with the correct median have different $Q1$ and $Q3$, one of these numbers must be determined for further elimination. Start with $Q1$.

Since there are 79 adults, each side of the median has half the data = 39. Hence, the 50% left-side of the median has 39 adults. The median = $Q1$ is in the number of rides for the 20th adult.

Starting from the left of the table continue a cumulative count of the number of adults till the 20th adult is reached. The 20th adult is in the number of rides = 2. Hence, median = $Q1$ = 2. This eliminates answer choice B that has $Q1$ = 3.

The correct answer choice is **A**.

Note that to determine $Q3$, the easiest approach is to continue a cumulative count of numbers from Right to Left till the median number is reached. In the above example, from right to left continue a cumulative count of the number of adults till the 20th adult is reached. This is in number of rides = 6.

Category 65 – Practice Questions

1

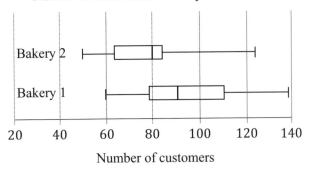

Number of Customers Per Day at 2 Bakeries

The above box plot shows the distribution of the number of customers at two separate bakeries, each day for a certain month. How does the median number of customers, a, at Bakery 1, compare to the median number of customers, b, at Bakery 2?

A) $a = b$
B) $a > b$
C) $a < b$
D) Insufficient information.

2

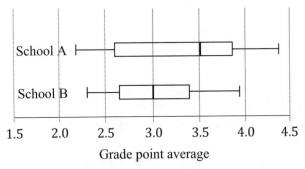

Grade Point Average of Seniors

The above box plot shows the distribution of the grade point averages of 184 seniors at School A and of 168 seniors at School B. By approximately how much does the median grade point average of seniors at School A exceed the median grade point average of seniors at School B?

A) 0.5
B) 1.5
C) 3.0
D) 3.5

3

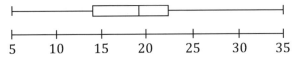

Head Mass of 32 Adult Giraffes

The above box plot shows the distribution of the head mass, in kg, of 32 adult giraffes. Which of the following is the best estimate of the median head mass, in kg, of the 32 adult giraffes?

A) 8
B) 15
C) 19
D) 21

4

Rating	1	2	3	4	5	6	7	8	9	10
Number of responses	9	50	27	41	23	10	9	9	11	3

A random survey of 192 commuters was conducted at a certain train station to rate the satisfaction of the train service at the station on a scale of 1 to 10. The above table shows the number of responses for each rating. Which of the following box plots could represent the distribution of the ratings?

A)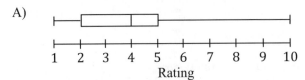

B)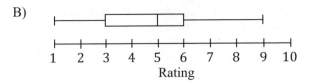

C)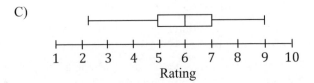

D)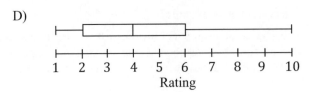

Digital SAT Math Manual and Workbook

258

Category 66 – Mode

Key Points
- The mode is the number that occurs most often in a data set. If a data set does not contain repeated numbers, then there is no mode in the data set.

How to Solve

Remember to sort the numbers in a data set, if not already sorted.

Example 1:

$$1, 6, 4, 10, 16, 4, 10, 25, 4, 20$$

What is the mode in the above set of numbers?

Step 1: Sort the numbers least to greatest

1, 4, 4, 4, 6, 10, 10, 16, 20, 25

Step 2: Determine the most often occurring number

1, 16, 20, and 25 occur once.

10 occurs 2 times.

4 occurs 3 times.

The correct answer is **4**.

Category 66 – Practice Questions

1

10.1, 10.2, 15.1, 15.3, 10.2, 10.6, 15.4, 15.3, 10.2

What is the mode in the above set of numbers?

2

Year	Snowfall (feet)
2010	21.1
2011	21.2
2012	15.2
2013	9.5
2014	10.7
2015	9.4
2016	21.2
2017	15.1

The above table shows the average annual snowfall, in feet, for a certain city from 2010 to 2019. Based on the table, what is the mode of the data?

Category 67 – Standard Deviation and Range

Key Points
- The standard deviation is the spread of numbers in a data set from the mean.
  - When the numbers in a set are closer to the mean, the standard deviation is low.
  - When the numbers in a set are farther from the mean, the standard deviation is high.
- The range is the difference between the lowest and highest number in a data set.

How to Solve
When comparing the standard deviations of two sets of data, the comparative spread of the numbers is usually evident by looking at the numbers in the data sets. Calculating the mean is not required.

Example 1:

| Set A | 40.1 | 60.8 | 52.5 | 82.5 | 11.2 | 90.8 |
| Set B | 52.3 | 55.8 | 32.7 | 65.9 | 62.4 | 45.6 |

Question 1
The table above shows two sets of data. Which of the following statements is true about the ranges of the two sets?
A) The range of Set A is equal to the range of Set B.
B) The range of Set A is greater than the range of Set B.
C) The range of Set B is greater than the range of Set A.
D) The range of Set A and Set B cannot be compared.

Step 1: Compare the range

Set A: The lowest number is 11.2, and the highest number is 90.8. The range is $90.8 - 11.2 = 79.6$.

Set B: The lowest number is 32.7, and the highest number is 65.9. The range is $65.9 - 32.7 = 33.2$.

The range of Set A is greater than the range of Set B.

The correct answer choice is **B**.

Question 2
The table above shows two sets of data. Which of the following statements is true about the standard deviations of the two sets?
A) The standard deviation of Set A is equal to the standard deviation of Set B.
B) The standard deviation of Set A is lower than the standard deviation of Set B.
C) The standard deviation of Set A is greater than the standard deviation of Set B.
D) The standard deviation of Set A and Set B cannot be compared.

Step 1: Compare the standard deviation

It can be seen from the data that the numbers in Set A are spread out farther than the numbers in Set B.

In Set A, the numbers are spread between 11.2 and 90.8.

In Set B, the numbers are spread between 32.7 and 65.9. This spread is lower than the spread in Set A.

Hence, Set A has a greater standard deviation than Set B.

The correct answer choice is **C**.

Category 67 – Practice Questions

1

| Group A | 915 | 810 | 816 | 825 | 790 | 744 |
| Group B | 495 | 546 | 490 | 369 | 100 | 101 |

The table above shows two groups of data. Which of the following statements is true about the ranges of the two groups?

A) The range of Group A is equal to the range of Group B.

B) The range of Group A is less than the range of Group B.

C) The range of Group A is greater than the range of Group B.

D) The range of Group A and Group B cannot be determined.

2

12, 18, 31, 20, 6, 10, 23, 16

If a number x is added to the above set of numbers and is given the value of 52, how will the standard deviation of the set change?

A) The standard deviation of the set will be unchanged.

B) The standard deviation of the set will decrease.

C) The standard deviation of the set will increase.

D) The standard deviation of the set cannot be compared.

3

45, 60, 65, 75, 85, 90

Data set A consists of 6 integers shown above. The mean of data set A is 70. Which of the following integers when added to data set A decreases the standard deviation of the data set?

A) 40
B) 50
C) 72
D) 92

4

The table below shows the number of students participating in Lacrosse and Soccer at a certain high school from 2010 to 2018.

| | Number of students ||
Year	Lacrosse	Soccer
2010	12	47
2011	55	52
2012	43	41
2013	4	55
2014	0	46
2015	4	58
2016	18	51
2017	9	48
2018	4	50

Based on the information given in the table above, which of the following statements is true about the standard deviation of the number of students enrolled in the two teams from 2010 to 2018?

A) The standard deviation of the number of students participating in Soccer is less than the standard deviation of the number of students participating in Lacrosse.

B) The standard deviation of the number of students participating in Soccer is higher than the standard deviation of the number of students participating in Lacrosse.

C) The standard deviation of the number of students participating in Soccer is the same as the standard deviation of the number of students participating in Lacrosse.

D) The standard deviation shows that too many students participated in Soccer.

5

850, 2145, 979, 978, 848, 1727, 851

If 159 is subtracted from the lowest number of the above data set, by how much will the range of the data set change?

Digital SAT Math Manual and Workbook

Category 68 – Compare Mean, Median, Mode, SD, and Range

Key Points
- Adding a constant number to or subtracting a constant number from each number in a data set will change the mean, the median, and the mode. The range and the standard deviation will not change.
- Adding a number to or removing a number from a data set will change the mean. The other measures may or may not change depending on which number is removed.
- Multiplying or dividing each number in a data set by a constant number will change the mean, the median, the mode, the range, and the standard deviation by the same scale. For example, if each number in a data set is multiplied by 3, then each measure will triple.

How to Solve

Note: SD in the category heading is referring to standard deviation.

Evaluate each measure given in the answer choices.

Example 1:

Set A	5	18	24	26	35	40
Set B	23	23	24	25	26	27

The above table shows two groups of numbers. Which of the following is a true statement when comparing Set A and Set B?

A) The means are the same, and the medians are the same.
B) The means are the same, and the standard deviations are the same.
C) The means are the same, and the standard deviations are different.
D) The medians are the same, and the standard deviations are different.

Step 1: Evaluate each measure

Mean:

Mean of Set A is

$$\frac{5 + 18 + 24 + 26 + 35 + 40}{6} = \frac{148}{6} = 24.66$$

Mean of Set B is

$$\frac{23 + 23 + 24 + 25 + 26 + 27}{6} = \frac{148}{6} = 24.66$$

The means of the two data sets are the same.

Median:

The median of Set A is the average of 24 and $26 = 25$.

The median of Set B is the average of 24 and $25 = 24.5$.

The medians are different. This eliminates answer choices A and D.

Standard deviation: In Set A, the numbers are spread from 5 to 40. In Set B, the numbers are spread from 23 to 27. Hence, the numbers in Set A have a greater standard deviation. This eliminates answer choice B.

The correct answer choice is **C**.

Digital SAT Math Manual and Workbook

Example 2:

$$38, 51, 12, 9, 38, 56, 78$$

Question 1

If 3 is subtracted from each number in the above data set, which of the following statements is true about the mean, median, and range of the modified set?

A) The mean will increase by 3.
B) The median will decrease by 3.
C) The range will decrease by 3.
D) All of them will remain unchanged.

Step 1: Evaluate each measure

The given data set ordered from least to greatest is 9, 12, 38, 38, 51, 56, 78.

After subtracting 3 from each number, the modified data set will be 6, 9, 35, 35, 48, 53, 75.

Mean: Subtracting each number by 3 will reduce the mean. This eliminates answer choices A and D.

Median: The middle number 38 will decrease by 3. Answer choice B is correct.

Note that the range will be unaffected since the least and greatest numbers will be reduced by 3, resulting in the same difference.

The correct answer choice is **B**.

Question 2

If 56 is removed from the above data set, which of the following measures will NOT change?

A) The mean, and the median.
B) The mean, and the range.
C) The median, and the range.
D) All of them will change.

Step 1: Evaluate each measure

The original data set ordered from least to greatest is 9, 12, 38, 38, 51, 56, 78.

After removing 56, the modified data set will be 9, 12, 38, 38, 51, 78.

Mean: Removing 56 from the data set will change the mean. This eliminates answer choices A and B.

Median: In the original data set, the median = 38. After removing 56, the median remains the same.

Range: The range will be unaffected since neither the least number nor the greatest number is being removed.

Hence, the median and range will not change. This eliminates answer choice D.

The correct answer choice is **C**.

Category 68 – Practice Questions

1

3, 95, 52, 204, 16, 152, 101

If 5 is added to each number of the above data set, which of the following measures will remain unchanged?

A) Mean
B) Median
C) Range
D) All of them will remain unchanged.

2

Day of week	Rainfall (inches)
Sunday	0.2
Monday	1.1
Tuesday	0
Wednesday	2.5
Thursday	0.2
Friday	4.8
Saturday	0

The table above shows a report produced by a meteorologist for the rainfall, in inches, in a certain city last week. The meteorologist realized that incorrect rainfall was reported for Friday. The correct rainfall was 0.8 inches. The mean, the median, the standard deviation, and the range were recalculated with the corrected rainfall measurements. Which of the following were unaffected after the correction?

A) Mean
B) Median
C) Range
D) Standard deviation

3

A biologist bought 21 plants of varying heights to study the effect of sunlight on the growth of plants. The shortest plant in the study is 14 inches tall. The biologist decides to buy another plant of height 4 inches to include in the study. If the mean, the median, the mode, and the range of the height of the plants are compared before and after including the 4-inch plant in the study, which of the following values must increase by 10?

A) Mean
B) Median
C) Mode
D) Range

4

Distribution of 200 Numbers

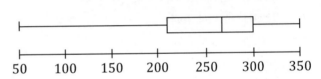

The above box plot shows the distribution of a set of 200 numbers between 50 and 350. If a new set of numbers is created by removing the numbers between 50 and 125, which of the following measurements must change when comparing the original set of numbers with the new set of numbers?

I. Median
II. Range
III. Standard deviation

A) I only
B) III only
C) II and III only
D) I, II, and III

Digital SAT Math Manual and Workbook

5

Employee name	2019 bonus (dollars)
Josie	7,500
Tammy	7,800
Kamal	6,500
Joe	8,100
Aniyah	18,000

The table above shows the 2019 bonuses, in dollars, of 5 employees at a small company. If the 2020 bonus (not shown) of each employee in the above table is 10% greater than the 2019 bonus, which of the following is a true statement when comparing 2019 and 2020 bonuses, in dollars, of the 5 employees?

A) The means and the medians are the same.
B) The means are the same, and the medians are different.
C) The means are different, and the medians are different.
D) The means and the medians cannot be compared.

6

Group A	15	24	26	18	35	32
Group B	27	26	25	23	26	23

The above table shows two groups of numbers. Which of the following is true when comparing the mean, the median, and the range of Group A and Group B?

A) The means are the same, the medians are the same, and the ranges are the same.
B) The means are the same, the medians are the same, and the ranges are different.
C) The means are the same, the medians are different, and the ranges are different.
D) The means are different, the medians are different, and the ranges are different.

7

Scores in 20 Games

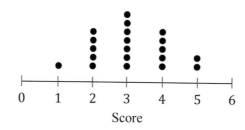

The above dot plot shows the distribution of scores for 20 games played by a team. If the team scores 6 points in each of the next 5 games, which of the following measures will change when the mean, the median, and the range of the scores are recalculated after these 5 games?

I. Mean
II. Median
III. Range

A) I only
B) III only
C) I and II only
D) I and III only

Category 69 – Interpretation of Sample Data in Studies and Surveys

Key Points

- Studies and surveys are conducted using a random sample from the sample population.
  - For example, if a survey is to be conducted on the satisfaction of train service at a certain train station, then it is not practical to survey every single person coming in and out of that train station. A random sample of appropriate size will be surveyed such that the results reflect the true average of the sample population. This process is known as random sampling. In this example, the sample population is all the people coming in and out of that train station.
- If the sample is not random, or is small, or deviates from the sample population, then the study or the survey is flawed.
  - In the above example, if a survey is conducted on the first 50 people at the train station from 9 am to 11 am on Monday and Friday each week, then the sample is not random. It will not represent the true average of the sample population. Similarly, if random people at a coffee shop outside the train station are also included in the survey, then the sample no longer represents the correct sample population.
- A margin of error is the variability by which the results obtained from a random sample are expected to differ from that of the sample population. It is the positive and negative deviation from the results.
  - In the above example, if 62% of the people surveyed in a random sample were satisfied with a margin of error of 4%, then it is plausible that between $62\% - 4\% = 58\%$ and $62\% + 4\% = 66\%$ of the people at that train station will respond similarly.
  - Increasing the random sample size can reduce the margin of error.
- A confidence level is how often the results obtained from a random sample will deviate from another random sample from the same population for the same study or survey.
  - For example, 95% confidence level of a team conducting a survey indicates that the team is confident that if the survey is repeated, as many times, the same results will be obtained 95% of the time and will reflect the true average of the sample population.
- Generalization is applying the results obtained from a random sample to the sample population.
  - The largest population the results can be generalized to is the sample population. In the above example of the train station, the largest population the survey can be generalized to is all the people at that train station. It would be incorrect to generalize the results to people at any other train station.
- An association (or correlation) is the relationship between variables in a study. Note that association is different from cause-and-effect relationship where change in one variable directly causes the change in the other variable.
  - For example, a random sample of people with chronic headaches is randomly divided into two groups. One group is asked to spend at least 4 hours in a park each week reading a book. The other group is asked not to make any change to the regular activities. After six months, both the groups are surveyed. The results show that the group who spent at least 4 hours in a park each week reading a book reported improvement in headaches. This shows an association between improvement in headaches and reading books in the park but not necessarily a cause-and-effect relationship. (If the people with headaches took pain medication specifically to reduce headaches, then it is a cause-and-effect-relationship.)
  - To generalize the results of an association, the samples must be randomly divided into groups.

How to Solve

Use the process of elimination based on the above key points.

Example 1:

A hospital wants to conduct a survey to determine if the admitted patients are satisfied by the meal choices offered to them. Which of the following sampling methods is most appropriate to estimate the satisfaction of the admitted patients on the meal choices offered at the hospital?

A) Selecting 300 random family members of the patients admitted at the hospital and surveying them.

B) Selecting 800 random patients from 10 hospitals in the city and surveying them.

C) Selecting 250 random patients admitted at the hospital and surveying them.

D) Selecting 350 patients admitted at the hospital every Monday and Tuesday mornings and surveying them.

Step 1: Process of elimination

The correct sample should be a random sample of patients admitted at the hospital. This is answer choice C.

Answer choices A and B are incorrect since the samples do not represent the correct sample population. Answer choice D is incorrect since the sample is not random.

The correct answer choice is **C**.

Example 2:

The Board of Education in a certain city interviewed a random sample of 800 residents from the most populated area of the city. Each randomly selected resident was asked whether they are in support of two new elementary schools in the city. Based on the results of these interviews, the Board of Education concluded that 70% residents of the city are in support of two new elementary schools in the city. Which of the following most accurately describes why the Board of Education's conclusion is flawed?

A) The survey should have been conducted on random residents with small children.

B) The residents surveyed did not represent a random sample of the residents in the city.

C) The residents surveyed did not include families that are planning on relocating to the city.

D) Letters should have been sent out to all the residents of the city before reaching a conclusion.

Step 1: Process of elimination

Limiting the sample to one area of the city does not represent a random sample of the residents in the city. The correct sample should be a random sample from all the residents in the city. Answer choice B correctly states that the sample did not represent a random sample of the residents in the city.

Answer choice A is incorrect since the sample is being restricted to residents with small children. Answer choice C does not represent the correct sample population. Answer D is not relevant to the question.

The correct answer choice is **B**.

Example 3:

250 employees at a company were selected at random and asked if they were in support of redesigning the office space. The results of the survey showed that 73% of the employees were in support of the redesign, with a margin of error of 4.5%. Which of the following is the most appropriate interpretation of the survey results?

A) At least 73% of the employees were in support of the redesign of the office space.

B) At most 73% of the employees were in support of the redesign of the office space.

C) It is plausible that between 73% and 77.5% employees were in support of the redesign of the office space.

D) It is plausible that between 68.5% and 77.5% employees were in support of the redesign of the office space.

Step 1: Process of elimination

The 4.5% margin of error indicates that likely between $73\% - 4.5\% = 68.5\%$ and $73\% + 4.5\% = 77.5\%$ of the employees at the company were in support of the redesign of the office space. This matches answer choice D.

Answer choices A and B are incorrect since they are limiting the results to at least or at the most 73% of the employees, respectively. Answer choice C is incorrect since it does not have the correct margin of error.

The correct answer choice is **D**.

Category 69 – Practice Questions

1

A school district wants to assess whether the teachers within all the district schools are satisfied with their salaries. The school district has put together a scoring system that allows the teachers to score their salary satisfaction. The scoring system has a scale of 1 to 10, where 1 is the lowest satisfaction and 10 is the highest satisfaction. Which of the following sampling methods is most appropriate to estimate the salary satisfaction of the teachers in all district schools?

A) Selecting one of the schools in the district at random and asking all the teachers in that school to score salary satisfaction.

B) Selecting 25 teachers at random from each school in the district and asking them to score salary satisfaction.

C) Selecting 50 teachers at random from the school that has the highest number of teachers and asking them to score salary satisfaction.

D) Selecting 100 teachers who are available and asking them to score salary satisfaction.

2

A wild life reasearch company conducted a study on a random sample of 85 male African elephants to determine the average size of their tusks. The company concluded with a 95% confidence level that the average length of their tusk is 5.8 to 6.3 feet. Based on the confidence level, which of the following is the most appropriate conclusion?

A) 95% of all the elephants have tusk length between 5.8 to 6.3 feet.

B) 95% of all male African elephants have tusk length between 5.8 to 6.3 feet.

C) It is probable that the true average length of the tusk of a male African elephant is between 5.8 to 6.3 feet.

D) It is probable that the true average length of the tusk of an African elephant is between 5.8 to 6.3 feet.

3

A random sample of 140 students at a certain high school were asked how much time they spend on homework each day. Based on the responses, the estimated time was 80 minutes, with an associated margin of error of 15 minutes. Which of the following best summarizes the conclusion from the data?

A) The students like to complete homework.

B) The students spend at least 80 minutes per day on homework.

C) It is plausible that the students spend less than 65 minutes each day on homework.

D) It is plausible that the students spend between 65 and 95 minutes each day on homework.

4

A scientist studied the effect of an organic fertilizer on 44 randomly selected miniature hybrid tea roses from a certain geographic region. The scientist concluded that the fertilizer promoted growth in 40 of the 44 miniature hybrid tea roses. What is the largest group the results of the above study can be applied to?

A) 44 miniature hybrid tea roses in the study.

B) All roses in the geographic region.

C) All miniature hybrid tea roses in the geographic region.

D) All hybrid tea roses.

Section 12 – Review Questions

1

The mean of x and 11 is a, and the mean of $3x$ and 5 is b. Which of the following is the mean of a and b in terms of x?

A) $x + 4$
B) $2x + 1$
C) $2x + 8$
D) $4x + 16$

2

The apple production at a certain orchard has decreased at a constant rate each year over an 8-year period. In the xy-plane, if the x-axis represents year, and the y-axis represents apple production, which of the following scatter plots could represent the apple production over the 8-year period?

A)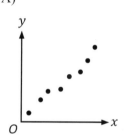

B)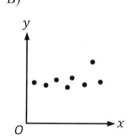

C)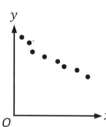

D)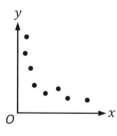

3

A skating ring charges a flat fee of $25 per month inclusive of 20 free visits and $2 for each additional visit during a month. Which of the following graphs could represent the number of visits in terms of the monthly cost?

A)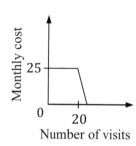

B)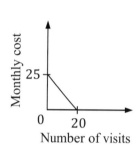

C)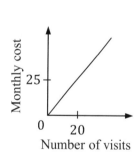

D)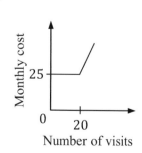

Digital SAT Math Manual and Workbook

4

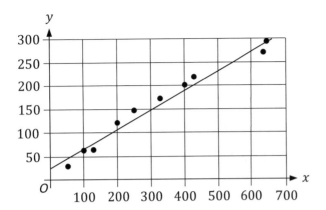

The scatter plot above shows the relationship between variables x and y for data set P. A line of best fit is shown. Data set Q is created by dividing the x-coordinate of each data point from data set P by 20. Which of the following could be an equation of a line of best fit for data set Q?

A) $y = \frac{5}{2}x - 1.42$

B) $y = \frac{2}{5}x + 26.5$

C) $y = 2.5x + 1.42$

D) $y = 8.2x + 27.3$

5

The table below gives the transportation method of 600 commuters in municipalities A, B, and C, in a certain city.

Municipality	Transportation mode			
	Bus	Car	Train	Total
A	106	28	48	182
B	55	103	78	236
C	18	89	75	182
Total	179	220	201	600

If one of these commuters is selected at random, what is the probability of selecting a commuter from municipality A or C whose transportation mode is "Car" or "Train"?

A) 0.25

B) 0.40

C) 0.66

D) 0.75

6

If one integer between 1 and 100 inclusive is selected at random, what is the probability that the integer is a multiple of 11 and an even number?

A) $\frac{1}{25}$

B) $\frac{11}{100}$

C) $\frac{11}{50}$

D) $\frac{9}{100}$

7

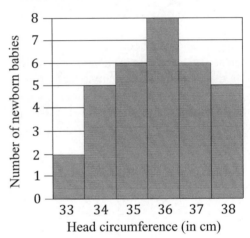

The histogram above summarizes the distribution of the head circumference, in cm, of 32 newborn babies. Which of the following could be the mean of the data shown in the histogram?

A) 34.7

B) 35.8

C) 36.5

D) 37.0

8

An environmental company wants to conduct a survey to determine the chemicals in the water of six lakes in the 200 mile vicinity of a manufacturing plant. Which of the following sampling methods is most appropriate to provide accurate results?

A) Selecting 210 random water samples from one of the lakes within the 200 mile vicinity of the manufacturing plant.

B) Selecting 100 random water samples from two of the lakes within the 200 mile vicinity of the manufacturing plant.

C) Selecting 50 random water samples from each of the six lakes within the 200 mile vicinity of the manufacturing plant.

D) Selecting 200 random water samples from six lakes around the country.

9

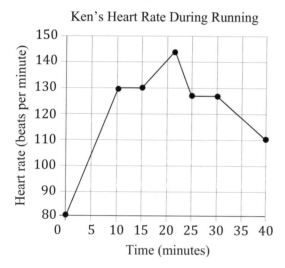

Ken's Heart Rate During Running

The above graph shows Ken's heart rate during a 40-minute run. Based on the graph, which of the following statements can NOT be true?

A) Ken's heart rate increased rapidly during the first 10 minutes of running.

B) Ken's heart rate was constant for 15 minutes during the 40 minute run.

C) Ken's heart rate stayed over 130 for approximately 9 minutes.

D) Ken's heart rate decreased constantly during the last 10 minutes of running.

10

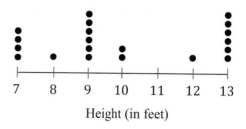

Height of 20 Elephants

Height (in feet)

The dot plot above shows the height, in feet, of 20 elephants. Which of the following is true about the mean and median of the data?

A) Mean = 9 and Median = 9

B) Mean = 9 and Median = 10

C) Mean = 10 and Median = 9

D) Mean = 10 and Median = 13

11

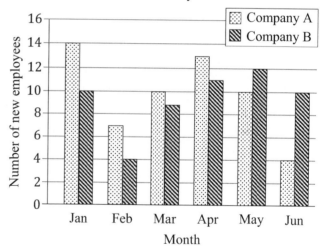

Number of New Employees Hired at 2 Companies from January to June

The above bar graph shows the number of new employees hired at two companies, Company A and Company B, from January to June 2020. Based on the graph, how many more employees were hired at Company A than at Company B from January to June 2020?

A) 2

B) 4

C) 9

D) 11

12

5, 10, 5, 3, 8, 11, 3, 121, 5, 23, 7, 10

What is the mode of the above set of numbers?

A) 3
B) 5
C) 10
D) 11

13

3, 121, x, y, z

In the above set of numbers, 3 is the minimum number and 121 is the maximum number. If the mean, the median, the mode, and the range are calculated for any integer values of x, y, and z, which of the following measures must NOT change?

A) Mean
B) Median
C) Mode
D) Range

14

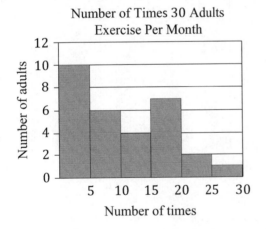

The histogram above summarizes the distribution of the number of times 30 adults exercise per month. The first bar represents less than 5 times per month, the second bar represents at least 5 times but less than 10 times per month, and so on. Which of the following could be the mean and median of the above graph?

A) Mean = 7 and Median = 8
B) Mean = 9 and Median = 10
C) Mean = 9 and Median = 8
D) Mean = 12 and Median = 12

15

A company of 1,550 employees offers complimentary coffee at the company cafeteria. The head of the sales department at the company was interested in determining if the employees in her department liked the complimentary coffee. She selected 175 random employees from her department and asked them about their liking. Based on the responses, she concluded that 44% of the 175 employees liked the coffee. What is the largest group to which the above conclusion can be generalized?

A) 175 employees at the company who were asked about their liking of the complimentary brand of coffee.
B) 44% of the employees at the company.
C) All the employees at the company.
D) All employees in the sales department at the company.

16

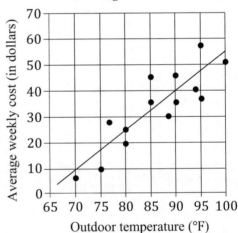

The above scatter plot shows the average weekly air conditioning cost, in dollars, for 14 households at varying outdoor temperatures, in °F. According to the line of best fit, which of the following is closest to the predicted increase in the average weekly air conditioning cost, in dollars, for every 1°F increase in temperature?

A) $1.50
B) $3.00
C) $4.10
D) $8.24

17

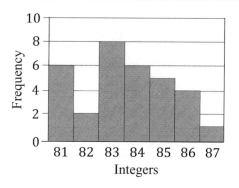

The above histogram shows the frequency distribution of 32 integers in data set A. Data set B is created by subtracting 24 from each integer in data set A. Which of the following correctly compares the medians and ranges of data set A and data set B?

A) The medians and the ranges are the same.
B) The medians are the same, and the ranges are different.
C) The medians are different, and the ranges are the same.
D) The medians and the ranges are different.

18

A total of 150 participants at an event are divided in three teams, Team A, Team B, and Team C. The probability of randomly selecting one participant from Team A is 0.24, and the probability of randomly selecting one participant from Team B is 0.44. How many participants are in Team C?

19

The mean of 7 numbers in a data set is 92. If the lowest number is removed, the mean of the remaining 6 numbers is 94. What is the lowest number in the data set?

20 — Desmos

126, 90, 41, 135, 44, 87, 127, 139

What is the median of the above set of numbers?

21

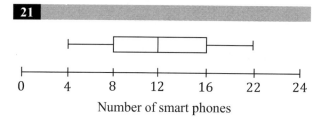

The box plot above shows the distribution of the number of smart phones delivered weekly to a retail store during the first 10 weeks of 2017. What was the maximum number of smart phones delivered to the retail store in a week?

22

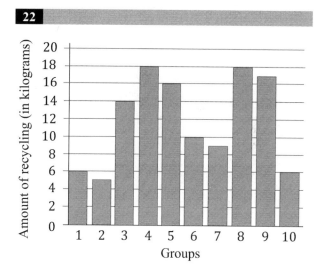

The above bar graph shows the amount of recycling, in kilograms, collected by 10 different groups. What is the median amount of recycling, in kilograms, collected by the 10 groups?

Section 13 – Geometry

Category 70 – Area and Angles of a Circle
Category 71 – Circumference and Arc of a Circle
Category 72 – Equation of a Circle
Category 73 – Parallel and Intersecting Lines
Category 74 – Polygons
Category 75 – Angles, Sides, and Area of a Triangle
Category 76 – Similar Triangles
Category 77 – Squares and Cubes
Category 78 – Rectangles and Right Rectangular Prisms
Category 79 – Trapezoids and Parallelograms
Category 80 – Volume of Cylinders, Spheres, Cones, Pyramids, Prisms
Category 81 – Mass, Volume, and Density Relationship
Category 82 – Combined Geometric Figures
Category 83 – Geometric Figures in the xy-plane
Category 84 – Geometric Figures and Percent
Category 85 – Ratio of Linear Side Length to Area or Volume
Section 13 – Review Questions

Category 70 – Area and Angles of a Circle

Key Points

- A radius of a circle is a straight-line segment from the center of the circle to a point on the circle. In the figure below, AO and CO are two radii of a circle.
- A diameter of a circle is a straight-line segment from one point on the circumference of the circle to another point on the circumference of the circle that passes through the center of the circle.
- The length of the diameter is twice the length of the radius of a circle.
- A chord in a circle is a straight-line segment from one point on the circumference of the circle to another point on the circumference of the circle that does not pass through the center of the circle. See the figure below for chords AB and BC. A perpendicular line from the center of the circle to a chord divides the chord into two equal halves.
- An angle formed between two radii of a circle is known as a central angle. See angle AOC in the figure below.
- An angle formed between two chords originating from the same point on a circle is known as an inscribed angle. See angle ABC in the figure below. An inscribed angle is half the measure of its corresponding central angle.
- The measure of an angle may be given in radians or degrees. One radian is equal to 180°.
    - An angle in radians can be converted to degrees by multiplying with $\frac{180}{\pi}$.
    - An angle in degrees can be converted to radians by multiplying with $\frac{\pi}{180}$.
- The area of a circle is πr^2, where r is the radius of the circle and π is approximately 3.14.
- The area enclosed between two radii is known as a sector. See the figure below for a sector enclosed by AO and CO.
    - When the central angle is given in radians, the area of a sector can be determined as $\frac{1}{2}r^2\theta$, where r is the radius of the circle and θ is the central angle in radians.
    - When the central angle is given in degrees, the area of a sector can be determined as $\frac{\theta}{360} \times \pi r^2$, where r is the radius of the circle and θ is the central angle in degrees.
    - The proportion relationship between the area of a sector and area of the circle is
    $$\frac{\text{area of a sector}}{\text{area of the circle}} = \frac{\text{degree measure of central angle}}{360°}$$
- When a circle is divided into two equal halves, each half is known as a semicircle. The area of each semicircle is half the area of the circle.

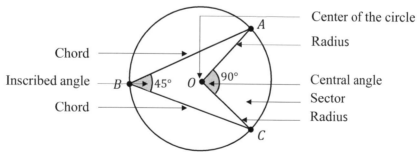

How to Solve

If the area of a circle is given, then the radius can be determined by equating it to πr^2. Note that the square root of r^2 will have two values: a positive value and a negative value. Since the radius is always positive, the negative value can be ignored. For example, if the area of a circle is 9π, then the radius can be determined as follows.
$$\pi r^2 = 9\pi \rightarrow r^2 = 9 \rightarrow r = \pm 3 \rightarrow r = 3$$
Note that a line segment name may be designated with a line on the top of the name. For example, line segment AB is written as $\overline{AB}$.

Example 1:

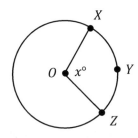

Note: Figure not drawn to scale.

Point O is the center of the circle shown above, and the central angle x is $108°$.

Question 1

The area of the sector formed by angle x is what fraction of the area of the circle?

A) $\frac{1}{3}$

B) $\frac{2}{5}$

C) $\frac{3}{10}$

D) $\frac{5}{12}$

Step 1: Set up a proportion

Central angle $x = 108°$.

$$\frac{\text{area of a sector}}{\text{area of the circle}} = \frac{\text{degree measure of central angle}}{360°} = \frac{108°}{360°} = \frac{3}{10}$$

The correct answer choice is **C**.

Question 2

The area of the circle is 25π. What is the area of the sector formed by the central angle x?

A) 5π

B) 7.5π

C) $\frac{\pi}{2.5}$

D) $\frac{2\pi}{3}$

Step 1: Set up a proportion

Central angle $x = 108°$.

Area of the circle $= 25\pi$.

$$\frac{\text{area of a sector}}{\text{area of the circle}} = \frac{\text{degree measure of central angle}}{360°} \rightarrow \frac{\text{area of a sector}}{25\pi} = \frac{108°}{360°}$$

$$\text{area of a sector} = \frac{108° \times 25\pi}{360°} = 7.5\pi$$

The correct answer choice is **B**.

Digital SAT Math Manual and Workbook

Example 2:

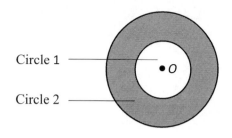

Note: Figure not drawn to scale.

The figure above shows 2 circles with center O. The radius of circle 1 is 1 inch. Circle 2 is outside of Circle 1 and has a radius of 2 inches. What is the area of the shaded region, in square inches?

A) π
B) 3π
C) $\frac{2\pi}{3}$
D) $\frac{3\pi}{2}$

Step 1: Determine the area of the circles

Circle 1 is smaller and covers a portion of the larger Circle 2. Both the circles have the same center O. The shaded area is the area of Circle 2 minus the area of Circle 1.

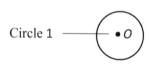 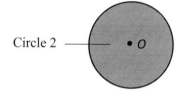 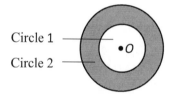

Area of Circle 1: $r = 1$.

$$\pi \times 1 \times 1 = \pi$$

Area of Circle 2: $r = 2$.

$$\pi \times 2 \times 2 = 4\pi$$

Step 2: Determine the area of the shaded region

$$4\pi - \pi = 3\pi$$

The correct answer choice is **B**.

Category 70 – Practice Questions

1

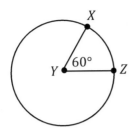

Note: Figure not drawn to scale.

Point Y is the center of the circle shown above. What is the measure of the angle XYZ, in radians?

A) $\frac{\pi}{3}$

B) $\frac{\pi}{2}$

C) π

D) 2π

2

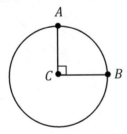

Note: Figure not drawn to scale.

The area of the above circle with center C is 12π. Which of the following is the area enclosed by the right angle ACB?

A) π

B) 3π

C) $\frac{\pi}{12}$

D) $\frac{\pi}{3}$

3

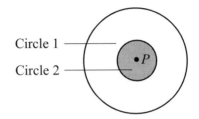

The above figure shows two circles, each drawn from the center P. Circle 2 is drawn within circle 1. Circle 1 has a radius of 5 centimeters and Circle 2 has a radius of 2 centimeters. Which of the following is the closest ratio of the area, in square centimeters, of Circle 1 to the area, in square centimeters, of Circle 2?

A) $2:3$

B) $2:5$

C) $2.5:5$

D) $6.3:1$

4

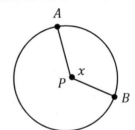

Note: Figure not drawn to scale.

Point P is the center of the circle shown above and angle x is $\frac{2\pi}{3}$ radians. The area of the sector formed by angle x is what fraction of the area of the circle?

A) $\frac{1}{2}$

B) $\frac{1}{3}$

C) $\frac{2}{5}$

D) $\frac{3}{8}$

Digital SAT Math Manual and Workbook

5

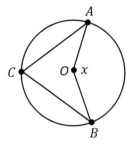

Note: Figure not drawn to scale.

In the figure above, chords AC and BC intersect the circle with center O at point C and $x = 150°$. What is angle ACB in radians?

A) π
B) 5π
C) $\frac{\pi}{12}$
D) $\frac{5\pi}{12}$

6

Note: Figure not drawn to scale.

The above figure shows 3 identical circles tangent to each other. The radius of each circle is 3 inches. The total area of the 3 circles and shaded region is 88 square inches. Which of the following is closest to the area of the shaded region, in square inches?

A) 0.64
B) 2.09
C) 3.22
D) 12.50

7

Which of the following is closest to the area of a circle with a diameter of 5, rounded to the nearest tenth?

A) 19.6
B) 22.5
C) 35.4
D) 78.5

8

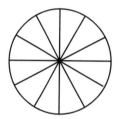

Note: Figure not drawn to scale.

The above figure shows a circle divided into 12 equal sectors. The diameter of the circle is 12. What is the area of each sector?

A) π
B) 3π
C) 5π
D) 12π

9

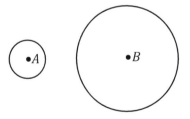

Note: Figure not drawn to scale.

The area of circle B is four times the area of circle A. If the area of circle A is 4π, what is the radius of circle B?

Category 71 – Circumference and Arc of a Circle

Key Points

- The circumference of a circle is $2\pi r$, where r is the radius of the circle and π is approximately 3.14.
- In degrees, the circumference of a full circle is 360°.
- An arc is the portion of the circumference enclosed between the endpoints of two chords or radii on the circumference. In the figure below, arc ABC is enclosed between the endpoints of radii AO and CO and between the endpoints of chords AP and CP.
  - An arc less than a semicircle is known as a minor arc. An arc greater than a semicircle is known as a major arc.
  - The degree measure of an arc is equal to the degree measure of its central angle and twice the degree measure of its inscribed angle. See the figure below.
  - When the central angle is given in radians, the length of an arc can be determined as $s = r\theta$, where s is the length of the arc, r is the radius of the circle, and θ is the central angle in radians.
  - When the central angle is given in degrees, the length of an arc can be determined as $s = 2\pi r \times \frac{\theta}{360}$, where s is the length of the arc, r is the radius of the circle, and θ is the central angle in degrees.
- The proportion relationship between an arc length and the circumference is
$$\frac{\text{arc length}}{\text{circumference}} = \frac{\text{degree measure of central angle}}{360°}$$

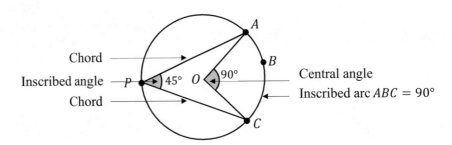

How to Solve

When the circumference of the circle is given and the central angle is in degrees, using the proportion relationship is the easiest method to determine the length of an arc.

Note that an arc name may be designated with an arc on the top of the name. For example, arc ABC can be written as $\overarc{ABC}$.

Example 1:

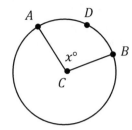

Segments AC and BC are the radii of the circle shown above. Arc ADB has a length of 3π and $\overline{AC} = 5$. What is the degree measure of x?

Step 1: Determine the central angle in degrees

$s = 3\pi$. $r = 5$.

$$s = \frac{\theta}{360} \times 2\pi r \rightarrow 3\pi = \frac{\theta}{360} \times 2\pi \times 5 \rightarrow 3 = \frac{10\theta}{360} \rightarrow 3 = \frac{\theta}{36} \rightarrow \theta = 108°$$

The correct answer is **108**.

Example 2:

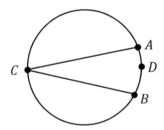

The inscribed angle ACB in the figure above is $\frac{\pi}{6}$ radians. The circumference of the circle is 24 centimeters. What is the length of $\widehat{ADB}$, in centimeters?

A) 3
B) 4
C) 6
D) 10

Step 1: Determine the central angle in degrees
Since the proportion relationship is set up in degrees, convert the inscribed angle to degrees. See the figure below.

$$\text{inscribed angle} = \frac{\pi}{6} \times \frac{180}{\pi} = 30°$$

The central angle in degrees is

$$30° \times 2 = 60°$$

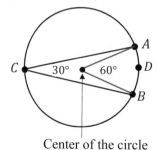

Step 2: Determine the length of arc $\widehat{ADB}$
Circumference = 24.
Central angle = 60°.

$$\frac{\text{arc length}}{\text{circumference}} = \frac{\text{degree measure of central angle}}{360°} \rightarrow \frac{\text{Arc Length}}{24} = \frac{60°}{360°} \rightarrow$$

$$\text{Arc Length} = \frac{60° \times 24}{360°} = 4$$

The correct answer choice is **B**.

Digital SAT Math Manual and Workbook

Category 71 – Practice Questions

1

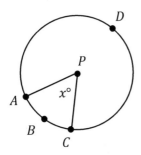

Note: Figure not drawn to scale.

In the circle shown above, P is the center, $x = 60$, and the arc $ABC = 3\pi$. What is the length of arc ADC?

A) 6π
B) 15π
C) $\dfrac{12\pi}{5}$
D) $\dfrac{15\pi}{6}$

2

A circle with radius 2 has a minor arc equal to $\dfrac{2\pi}{5}$ radians. What fraction of the circumference of the circle is the minor arc?

A) $\dfrac{1}{10}$
B) $\dfrac{2}{5}$
C) $\dfrac{1}{2}$
D) $\dfrac{3}{8}$

3

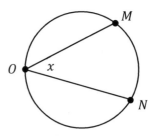

Note: Figure not drawn to scale.

In the figure above, angle x is $\dfrac{\pi}{4}$, and the circumference of the circle is 32 inches. What is the length of the minor arc MN, in inches?

4

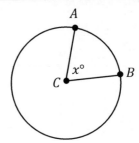

Note: Figure not drawn to scale.

The center of the above circle is C, the radius is 12, and $\widehat{AB}$ is 5π. What is the value of x?

5

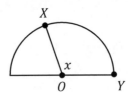

Note: Figure not drawn to scale.

In the above figure, segments OX and OY are the radii of the semicircle, angle x is $\dfrac{2\pi}{3}$, and $\widehat{XY}$ is 2π. What is the length of $\overline{OX}$?

Digital SAT Math Manual and Workbook

Category 72 – Equation of a Circle

Key Points
- The equation of a circle in the standard form is written as $(x - h)^2 + (y - k)^2 = r^2$.
  - r is the radius of the circle.
  - (h, k) are the coordinates of the center of the circle.
  - (x, y) are the coordinates of any point on the circumference of the circle.
- The equation of a circle in the general form is written as $x^2 + y^2 + Ax + By + C = 0$, where A, B, and C are constants. A and B are also known as coefficients of x and y, respectively.
  - The radius and center of a circle cannot be determined from the general form equation. It can be converted to the standard form by completing the square method.
- The center of the circle is the midpoint of the diameter. When two ends of a diameter are given, the center of the circle can be determined using the midpoint formula.
  - If (x_1, y_1) and (x_2, y_2) are the two end points of the diameter, then the x-coordinate of the center is $\frac{x_1+x_2}{2}$, and the y-coordinate of the center is $\frac{y_1+y_2}{2}$.
- If the distance of a point from the center of a circle is less than the radius, then the point lies inside the circle. If the distance of a point from the center of a circle is greater than the radius, then the point is outside the circle.
- Horizontal (left or right) and vertical (up or down) translations of a circle do not change the radius of the circle. A horizontal translation is the shift of the x-coordinate of the center. A vertical translation is the shift of the y-coordinate of the center. See below for a shift by c units of a circle defined by $(x - h)^2 + (y - k)^2 = r^2$.
  - c units right: $(x - h - c)^2 + (y - k)^2 = r^2$. The x-coordinate is $h + c$.
  - c units left: $(x - h + c)^2 + (y - k)^2 = r^2$. The x-coordinate is $h - c$.
  - c units up: $(x - h)^2 + (y - k - c)^2 = r^2$. The y-coordinate is $k + c$.
  - c units down: $(x - h)^2 + (y - k + c)^2 = r^2$. The y-coordinate is $k - c$.

How to Solve

The center and radius of a circle can be directly read from the standard form equation. Note that if the equation of a circle is $(x)^2 + (y - k)^2 = r^2$, then the x-coordinate of the center is 0. Similarly, if the equation is $(x - h)^2 + (y)^2 = r^2$, then the y-coordinate of the center is 0.

In the general form equation, if the coefficients of x^2 and y^2 are greater than 1, then divide the entire equation by the value of the coefficients. For example, divide the equation $3x^2 - 12x + 3y^2 + 42y - 33 = 0$ by 3.

*Coordinates of the center and radius of a circle can be determined from a general form equation using the Desmos graphing calculator. Converting the general form equation to the standard form equation is not required.

Example 1:
The center of a circle in the xy-plane is $(0, 7)$, and the radius is 4. Which of the following is an equation of the circle?
A) $(x)^2 + (y - 7)^2 = 4$
B) $(x)^2 + (y - 7)^2 = 16$
C) $(x - 7)^2 + (y + 7)^2 = 4$
D) $(x - 7)^2 + (y + 7)^2 = 16$

Step 1: Determine the equation

Since the center is $(0, 7)$, the corresponding factors are $(x)^2$ and $(y - 7)^2$. This eliminates answer choices C and D.
Since $r = 4$, $r^2 = 16$. This eliminates answer choice A.
The correct answer choice is **B**.

Example 2:

The points $(3, -2)$ and $(-5, 4)$ are the endpoints of a diameter of a circle in the xy-plane. Which of the following is an equation of the circle?

A) $(x - 1)^2 + (y + 1)^2 = 5$
B) $(x + 1)^2 + (y - 1)^2 = 5$
C) $(x + 1)^2 + (y - 1)^2 = 25$
D) $(x + 1)^2 + (y + 1)^2 = 25$

Step 1: Determine the coordinates of the center

Plug in the diameter endpoints in the midpoint formula.

$$x = \frac{-5 + 3}{2} = \frac{-2}{2} = -1$$

$$y = \frac{4 + (-2)}{2} = \frac{4 - 2}{2} = \frac{2}{2} = 1$$

Hence, the coordinates of the center are $(-1, 1)$. The corresponding the factors are $(x + 1)^2$ and $(y - 1)^2$. The equation can be written as $(x + 1)^2 + (y - 1)^2 = r^2$. This eliminates answer choices A and D.

Step 2: Determine the radius

Plug in either of the two given points in the above equation. Point $(3, -2)$ is plugged in below.

$$(3 + 1)^2 + (-2 - 1)^2 = r^2 \rightarrow$$
$$r^2 = 4^2 + (-3)^2 = 16 + 9 = 25$$

The correct answer choice is **C**.

*Example 3:

In the xy-plane, the graph of $3x^2 + 12x + 3y^2 - 42y - 33 = 0$ is a circle. What is the radius of the circle?

Step 1: Determine the factors for the complete squares of x and y

The quickest approach to determine the factors is to divide the coefficients of x and y by 2. It is important to remember that the number obtained after diving by 2 is the factor (the signs do not get reversed).

Before proceeding, move 33 to the right-side and divide the entire equation by 3.

$$\frac{3x^2 + 12x + 3y^2 - 42y = 33}{3} \rightarrow x^2 + 4x + y^2 - 14y = 11$$

Factor for x: Coefficient of $x = 4$.

$$\frac{4}{2} = 2$$

Hence, the complete square for x is $(x + 2)^2$.

Factor for y: Coefficient of $y = -14$.

$$\frac{-14}{2} = -7$$

Hence, the complete square for y is $(y - 7)^2$.

Step 2: Complete the equation

Left side: Replace $x^2 + 4x + y^2 - 14y$ with $(x + 2)^2 + (y - 7)^2$.

Right side: Square both the factors obtained from Step 1 and add them to the right-side of the equation.

$$(x + 2)^2 + (y - 7)^2 = 11 + (2)^2 + (-7)^2 \rightarrow$$
$$(x + 2)^2 + (y - 7)^2 = 11 + 4 + 49 \rightarrow$$
$$(x + 2)^2 + (y - 7)^2 = 64$$

Since $r^2 = 64$, $r = 8$.

The correct answer is **8**.

Digital SAT Math Manual and Workbook

*Desmos Graphing Calculator Solution

Type the equation. The corresponding circle will be graphed. Determine the length of the diameter from the graph. The length of the radius is half the length of the diameter.

The Desmos graphing calculator marks two opposite vertical points on the circumference of a circle with gray dots. The vertical distance between these points passes through the center and, hence, is the length of the diameter of the circle. The vertical distance can be determined as the distance between the y-coordinates of these points.

Click on the equation of the circle to highlight the dots and read the coordinates of these points. See the graph below. The points are $(-2, 15)$ and $(-2, -1)$, and the y-coordinates are 15 and -1, respectively. The distance between 15 and -1 is 16 (remember the number line). Hence, the diameter is 16, and the radius is 8.

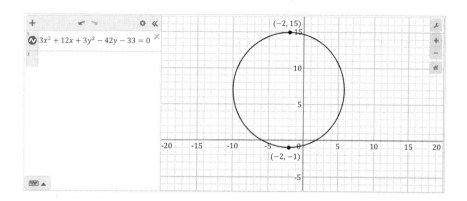

See below on how to determine the center of the circle or the standard form equation from a general form equation, in case there is a question on this. (Use the above method to determine the radius.)

Determine the x-coordinate of center:

The x-coordinate of the center is the x-value of the two opposite vertical points $= -2$.

Determine the y-coordinate of center:

The y-coordinate of the center is the midpoint of the y-coordinates of the two opposite vertical points $(-2, 15)$ and $(-2, -1)$. These coordinates are 15 and -1.

Midpoint $= \dfrac{15+(-1)}{2} = \dfrac{15-1}{2} = \dfrac{14}{2} = 7.$

Determine the equation: Plug in the coordinates of the center and radius in the standard form equation, as below.

$$(x - h)^2 + (y - k)^2 = r^2 \rightarrow$$
$$(x - (-2))^2 + (y - (7))^2 = 8^2 \rightarrow$$
$$(x + 2)^2 + (y - 7)^2 = 64$$

Digital SAT Math Manual and Workbook

Category 72 – Practice Questions

1

The center of a circle in the xy-plane is $(-7, 0)$ and the radius is 6. Which of the following is the equation of the circle?

A) $(x - 7)^2 + y^2 = 6$
B) $(x + 7)^2 + y^2 = 6$
C) $(x - 7)^2 + y^2 = 36$
D) $(x + 7)^2 + y^2 = 36$

2

In the xy-plane, points $(-1, -6)$ and $(1, -2)$ are the endpoints of a diameter of a circle. Which of the following represents the equation of the above circle?

A) $x^2 + (y + 4)^2 = 5$
B) $x^2 + (y + 4)^2 = 25$
C) $(x + 1)^2 + (y - 2)^2 = 5$
D) $(x + 4)^2 + (y + 2)^2 = 25$

3

In the xy-plane, point $(-2, -4)$ is the center of a circle. If the endpoint of a radius on the circle is $(0.5, -2)$, which of the following is the equation of the circle?

A) $(x - 2)^2 + (y - 4)^2 = 5.5$
B) $(x + 2)^2 + (y + 4)^2 = 5.5$
C) $(x - 2)^2 + (y - 4)^2 = 10.25$
D) $(x + 2)^2 + (y + 4)^2 = 10.25$

4 — Desmos

The equation of a circle in the xy-plane is $(x - 2)^2 + (y + 3)^2 = 36$. Which of the following points lies in the interior of the circle?

I. $(-2, 0)$
II. $(-5, 1)$
III. $(3, 3)$

A) I only
B) I and III only
C) II and III only
D) I, II, and III

5

The equation $(x - 2)^2 + (y)^2 = 64$ represents circle P. Circle Q is created by translating circle P up 3 units in the xy-plane. Which of the following represents the equation of circle Q?

A) $(x + 3)^2 + (y)^2 = 64$
B) $(x + 1)^2 + (y - 3)^2 = 64$
C) $(x - 2)^2 + (y - 3)^2 = 64$
D) $(x - 2)^2 + (y + 3)^2 = 64$

6 — Desmos

$$2x^2 - 32x + 2y^2 + 12y - 16 = 0$$

The equation of the circle in the xy-plane is given above. What is the x-coordinate of the center of the circle?

7 — Desmos

The graph of $x^2 - x + y^2 + 13y = \dfrac{77}{2}$ in the xy-plane is a circle. What is the length of the diameter of the circle?

Category 73 – Parallel and Intersecting Lines

Key Points

- At any point on a straight line, the sum of angles is 180°. For example, in Fig. 1 below, ∠1 + ∠2 + ∠3 = 180°.
- Two angles that add up to 180° are known as supplementary angles.
- Two angles that add up to 90° are known as complementary angles.
- Two intersecting lines form four angles. The opposite angles are called vertical angles and are congruent. For example, in Fig. 2 below, lines c and p are intersecting lines. ∠1 = ∠4 and ∠2 = ∠3.
- When a straight line cuts across two parallel lines, several types of angles are formed. In Fig. 2, parallel lines c and d are intersected by line p. The types of angles and their position identified by numbers are shown in the figure.
  - Corresponding angles are congruent. ∠1 = ∠5, ∠2 = ∠6, ∠3 = ∠7, and ∠4 = ∠8.
  - Alternate interior angles are congruent. ∠4 = ∠5 and ∠3 = ∠6.
  - Alternate exterior angles are congruent. ∠1 = ∠8 and ∠2 = ∠7.
  - Same-side interior angles are supplementary angles. ∠3 + ∠5 = 180° and ∠4 + ∠6 = 180°.
  - Same-side exterior angles are supplementary angles. ∠1 + ∠7 = 180° and ∠2 + ∠8 = 180°.
- When two or more parallel lines are intersected by two or more non-parallel lines, the ratio of any two segments on one non-parallel line is equal to the ratio of the corresponding segments on the other non-parallel line. In Fig. 3 below, lines l, m, and n are parallel lines and lines p and q are non-parallel lines. $\frac{AC}{AE} = \frac{BD}{BF}$ and $\frac{CE}{AE} = \frac{DF}{BF}$.

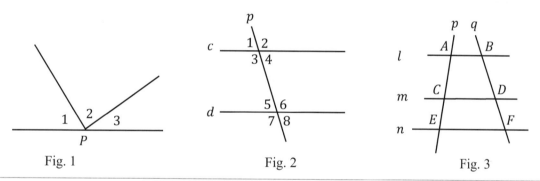

Fig. 1   Fig. 2   Fig. 3

How to Solve

Remember the different types of angles and identify them appropriately in a question.

Example 1:

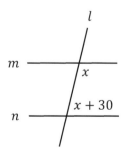

In the figure above, lines m and n are parallel. What is the value of x in degree measure?

Step 1: Identify the types of angles

Since lines m and n are parallel lines, angles x and $x + 30$ are the same-side interior supplementary angles.

$$(x) + (x + 30) = 180 \rightarrow 2x = 150 \rightarrow x = 75$$

The correct answer is **75**.

Example 2:

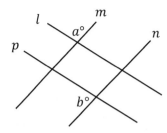

In the above figure, lines l and p are parallel, and lines m and n are parallel. If the measure of angle a is 80°, what is the degree measure of angle b?

Step 1: Identify the types of angles
See the figure below for explanation.

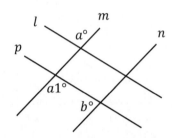

Since lines l and p are parallel lines, a and $a1$ are alternate exterior angles.
$$a = a1 = 80$$
Since lines m and n are parallel lines, $a1$ and b are same-side interior supplementary angles.
$$a1 + b = 180 \rightarrow 80 + b = 180 \rightarrow b = 100$$

The correct answer is **100**.

Example 3:

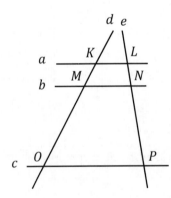

In the figure above, lines d and e intersect parallel lines a, b, and c. Points K and L are on line a, points M and N are on line b, and points O and P are on line c. If $KM = 3$, $KO = 16$, and $LN = 2.2$, what is the length of $\overline{LP}$, rounded to the nearest tenth?

Step 1: Set up segment proportion and solve
$KM = 3$. $KO = 16$. $LN = 2.2$.
The length of LP can be calculated by setting up the following proportion.
$$\frac{KO}{KM} = \frac{LP}{LN} \rightarrow \frac{16}{3} = \frac{LP}{2.2} \rightarrow$$
$$3 \times LP = 16 \times 2.2 \rightarrow$$
$$LP = 11.73$$

The correct answer is **11.7**.

Category 73 – Practice Questions

1

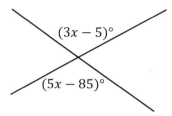

Note: Figure not drawn to scale.

The figure above shows two intersecting lines. What is the value of x?

A) 10
B) 30
C) 40
D) 75

2

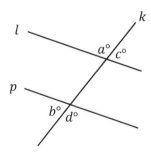

In the figure above, line k intersects parallel lines l and p. For angles a, b, c, and d, which of the following must be true?

I. $a + b = 180$
II. $a + c = 180$
III. $b + c = 180$

A) I only
B) I and II only
C) I and III only
D) I, II, and III

3

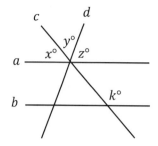

Note: Figure not drawn to scale.

In the figure above, lines c and d intersect parallel lines a and b. Lines c and d intersect line a at the same point. Which of the following must be true about angles k, x, y, and z?

A) $k = y + z$
B) $k = x + y$
C) $k = y - z$
D) $k = x - z$

4

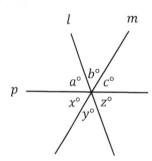

Note: Figure not drawn to scale.

Lines l, m, and p intersect at one point. If $a + b = 120°$, which of the following must be true?

I. $a + y = 120$
II. $b + z = 120$
III. $c + x = 120$

A) I and II only
B) I and III only
C) II and III only
D) I, II, and III

5

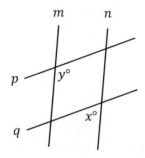

In the figure above, point C lies on $\overline{AB}$. If $38 < y < 42$, what is one possible integer value of x?

6

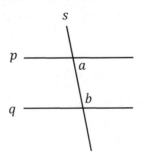

Note: Figure not drawn to scale.

In the figure above, lines m and n and lines p and q are parallel lines. If $y° = x° + 50°$, what is the degree measure of x?

7

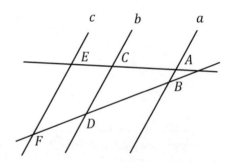

Note: Figure not drawn to scale.

Line s intersects two parallel lines, p and q, as shown in the above figure. If $a° = 3x + 6$ and $b° = 4x - 1$, what is the value of x?

8

Note: Figure not drawn to scale.

In the above figure, l, m, and n are parallel lines. Points A and B are on line l, points C and D are on line m, and points E and F are on line n. If $AE = 8.1$, $BD = 4$, and $DF = 5$, which of the following ranges contain the lengths of $\overline{CE}$?

A) 4.2 to 4.4

B) 4.4 to 4.6

C) 4.6 to 4.8

D) 4.8 to 5.1

9

Note: Figure not drawn to scale.

In the above figure, a, b, and c are parallel lines. Points A and B are on line a, points C and D are on line b, and points E and F are on line c. What is the length of $\overline{DF}$ when $AC = 10$, $CE = 6$, and $BD = 15$?

Digital SAT Math Manual and Workbook

Category 74 – Polygons

Key Points

- A polygon is a geometric shape enclosed by straight line segments. In Fig. 1 below, $ABCDEF$ is a 6 sided polygon.
- Each corner of a polygon is known as a vertex. The number of vertices is equal to the number of sides in a polygon.
- A polygon that has all equal side lengths and equal angle measures is known as a regular polygon. For example, an equilateral triangle or a square.
- A polygon that does not have all the same side lengths and angle measures is known as an irregular polygon.
- The perimeter of a polygon is the sum of the length of all sides.
  - For a regular polygon, the sum is the length of a side × the number of sides (since all the sides are of equal length).
- The sum of the degree measures of the interior angles of any polygon is $180(n-2)$, where n is the number of sides. For example, in Fig. 2 below m, n, o, p, q, and r are the interior angles of a 6 sided polygon. The total degree measure of these angles is $180(6-2) = 720°$.
- The average degree measure of an interior angle of a polygon with n sides is $\frac{180(n-2)}{n}$. For example, in the figure below, the average degree measure of the interior angles is $\frac{720°}{6} = 120°$.
- The sum of the degree measures of the exterior angles of any polygon is always $360°$. In Fig. 2 below, a, b, c, d, e, and f are exterior angles (shown by extended lines) of a 6-sided polygon, and their sum is $360°$.
  - The average degree measure of any exterior angle of a polygon with n sides is $\frac{360}{n}$.

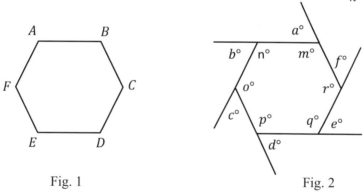

Fig. 1　　　　　　　　　　Fig. 2

How to Solve

Remember that in a regular polygon, the average degree measure of the interior or exterior angles is equal to each individual angle. This is not true for an irregular polygon since each angle is not the same.

Note that quadrilateral is a term used for polygons with 4 sides. For example, a rectangle, a trapezoid, a parallelogram. The sum of the interior angles of a quadrilateral is $360°$.

Example 1:

The sum of the degree measures of the interior angles of a regular polygon with n sides is $540°$. What is the value of n?

Step 1: Determine the number of sides

Sum of the degree measure of interior angles = 540. Hence,

$$180(n-2) = 540 \rightarrow 180n - 360 = 540 \rightarrow 180n = 900 \rightarrow n = 5$$

The correct answer is **5**.

Example 2:

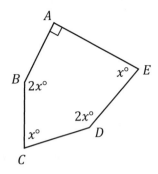

In the figure above, $ABCDE$ is a polygon with 5 sides. What is the value of $2x$?

A) 75
B) 90
C) 125
D) 150

Step 1: Determine the sum of the interior angles

This is an example of an irregular polygon.

$n = 5$. Hence, the sum of the degree measure of all interior angles is
$$180(5 - 2) = 180 \times 3 = 540$$

Step 2: Determine the interior angles

Sum of angles $= 540°$.
$$\angle A + \angle B + \angle C + \angle D + \angle E = 90 + 2x + x + 2x + x = 540 \rightarrow$$
$$90 + 6x = 540 \rightarrow 6x = 450 \rightarrow 2x = 150$$

The correct answer choice is **D**.

Category 74 – Practice Questions

1

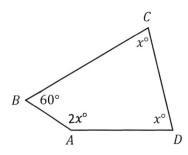

Note: Figure not drawn to scale.

In the figure above, ABCD is a quadrilateral. What is the value of x?

A) 60
B) 75
C) 120
D) 150

2

The average measure of each exterior angle of a regular polygon is 30°. What is the average degree measure of an interior angle of the polygon?

A) 30
B) 100
C) 150
D) 180

3

What is the average degree measure of an exterior angle of a regular polygon with 10 sides?

A) 10
B) 36
C) 360
D) 540

4

The sum of the degree measures of the interior angles of a regular polygon with n sides is 900°. What is the value of n?

5

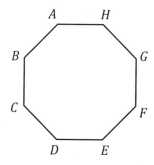

The regular polygon shown above has 8 sides. The length of line segment $\overline{AB}$ is 5 inches. What is the perimeter of the polygon, in inches?

6

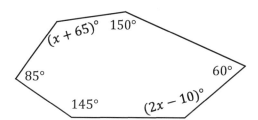

Note: Figure not drawn to scale.

In the polygon above, what is the value of x?

Digital SAT Math Manual and Workbook

Category 75 – Angles, Sides, and Area of a Triangle

Key Points

- A triangle has three sides, three angles, and three vertices (corners).
  - The sum of the degree measures of the three angles is 180°.
  - The sum of the lengths of any two sides of a triangle is greater than the length of the third side. For example, if x, y, and z are the three sides of a triangle, then $x + y > z$, $x + z > y$, and $y + z > x$.
- An exterior angle is formed when any side of a triangle is extended. It is equal to the sum of the two non-adjacent angles. In Fig. 1 below, c is the exterior angle, and a and b are the two non-adjacent angles. $c° = a° + b°$.
- An equilateral triangle has three equal sides and three equal angles. Since the sum of the three angles of a triangle is 180°, each angle of an equilateral triangle is 60°. A perpendicular line segment from any corner to the opposite side (also known as the perpendicular bisector) divides the equilateral triangle into two equal 30°-60°-90° triangles (Fig. 2 below).
- An isosceles triangle has two sides of equal length. The angles opposite to these sides are equal (Fig. 3 below).
- A right triangle has one 90° angle, also known as the right angle. The other two angles are acute angles (an acute measures less than 90°), and their sum is 90° (Fig. 4, Fig. 5, and Fig. 6 below).
  - The side opposite to the right angle is known as the hypotenuse and is the longest side. The other two sides are known as the legs and meet at the 90° angle (Fig. 4 below).
  - In an isosceles right triangle, the measure of each acute angle is 45° (Fig. 5 below). It is also known as a 45°-45°-90° triangle.
  - The right triangles with degree measure of 45°-45°-90° and 30°-60°-90° have known side length relationship.
    - In Fig. 5 below, a is the side opposite to 45° angles and $a\sqrt{2}$ is the side opposite to 90° angle. The ratio of the side lengths in relation to the opposite angles is 45°:45°:90° → $a: a: a\sqrt{2}$.
    - In Fig. 6 below, a is the side opposite to 30° angle, $a\sqrt{3}$ is the side opposite to 60°, and $2a$ is the side opposite to 90° angle. The ratio of the side lengths in relation to the opposite angles is 30°:60°:90° → $a: a\sqrt{3}: 2a$.
  - If the lengths of any two sides of a right triangle are known, the length of the third side can be calculated using the Pythagorean Theorem. Pythagorean Theorem is written as $a^2 + b^2 = c^2$, where c is the hypotenuse and a and b are the two legs of the right triangle.
  - When the lengths of all three sides of a right triangle are integers, their lengths are collectively known as Pythagorean triples. Common Pythagorean triples are 3: 4: 5, 5: 12: 13, and 8: 15: 17 or any of their multiples. The largest ratio corresponds to the hypotenuse, and the smallest ratio corresponds to the smallest side.
- The area of any triangle can be determined as $\frac{1}{2}bh$, where b is the length of the base and h is the height.
- The area of an equilateral triangle can also be determined as $\frac{\sqrt{3}}{4}a^2$, where a is the length of each side.

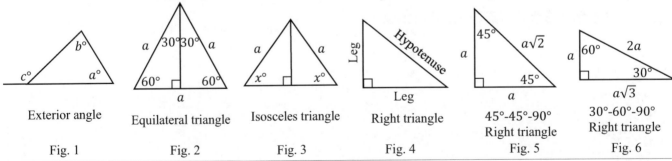

| Exterior angle | Equilateral triangle | Isosceles triangle | Right triangle | 45°-45°-90° Right triangle | 30°-60°-90° Right triangle |
| Fig. 1 | Fig. 2 | Fig. 3 | Fig. 4 | Fig. 5 | Fig. 6 |

How to Solve

In a right triangle, if a question gives the lengths of two sides as integers, check for Pythagorean triples before using the Pythagorean Theorem to determine the length of the third side.

Digital SAT Math Manual and Workbook

Example 1:

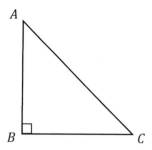

In right triangle ABC shown above, $AB = BC$ and $AC = 6\sqrt{2}$. What is the area of the triangle?

A) 12
B) 18
C) 25
D) 26

Step 1: Determine the base and height

The base BC and height AB are not given. Determine them as shown below.

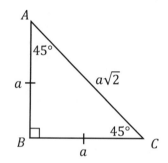

Since $AB = BC$ and angle $ABC = 90°$, triangle ABC is a right isosceles $45°$-$45°$-$90°$ triangle with side relationship seen in the left figure.

$$AB : BC : AC = a : a : a\sqrt{2}$$

It is given that $AC = 6\sqrt{2}$. Hence,

$$AC = 6\sqrt{2} = a\sqrt{2} \rightarrow a = 6$$
$$AB = BC = a = 6$$

Step 2: Determine the area

Base $= BC = 6$. Height $= AB = 6$.

$$\frac{1}{2}bh = \frac{1}{2} \times 6 \times 6 = 18$$

The correct answer choice is **B**.

Example 2:

The perimeter of equilateral triangle XYZ is 24 inches. What is the area of the triangle, in square inches?

A) 8
B) 12
C) $8\sqrt{3}$
D) $16\sqrt{3}$

Step 1: Determine the length of the sides

Since the three sides of an equilateral triangle are equal, divide the perimeter by 3 to get the length of each side.

$$\frac{24}{3} = 8$$

Step 2: Determine the area

$$\frac{\sqrt{3}}{4}a^2 = \frac{\sqrt{3}}{4} \times 8 \times 8 = 16\sqrt{3}$$

The correct answer choice is **D**.

Digital SAT Math Manual and Workbook

Example 3:

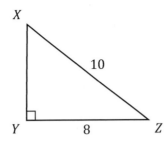

In right triangle XYZ shown above, $YZ = 8$ and $XZ = 10$. What is the area of triangle XYZ?

Step 1: Determine the length of XY

The base of the triangle $YZ = 8$. The height XY is not given.

The ratio of the sides $YZ:XZ$ is $8:10$. This is the ratio of the Pythagorean triple $6:8:10$.

Since YZ and XZ correspond to the ratio components 8 and 10, respectively, the third side XY must correspond to the ratio component 6. Hence,

$$XY:YZ:XZ = XY:8:10 = 6:8:10$$
$$XY = 6$$

Step 2: Determine the area

Base = $YZ = 8$. Height = $XY = 6$.

$$\frac{1}{2}bh = \frac{1}{2} \times 8 \times 6 = 24$$

The correct answer is **24**.

Example 4:

In a triangle DEF, the lengths of $\overline{DE}$ and $\overline{EF}$ are 2 and 7, respectively. Which of the following could be a possible length of the third side $\overline{DF}$?

A) 3

B) 4

C) 6

D) 9

Step 1: Compare the lengths of the sides

The sum of the lengths of two sides is greater than the third side. Drawing a figure may help visualize. See the figure below.

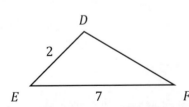

The three combinations for lengths are

$$2 + 7 > DF \rightarrow 9 > DF$$
$$2 + DF > 7 \rightarrow DF > 5$$
$$DF + 7 > 2 \rightarrow DF > -5$$

Since a line cannot have a negative length, $DF > -5$ can be ignored. The remaining two combinations are $9 > DF$ and $DF > 5$. This can be written as $9 > DF > 5$. Hence, DF can have three values: 6, 7, or 8.

The correct answer choice is **C**.

Category 75 – Practice Questions

1

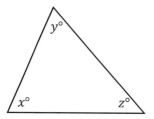

In the figure above, x, y, and z are the three angles of a triangle. Which of the following expresses x in terms of y and z?

A) $x = \frac{y+z}{180}$

B) $x = \frac{y-z}{180}$

C) $x = 180 - y - z$

D) $x = 180 - y + z$

2

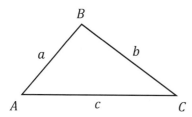

Note: Figure not drawn to scale.

In the figure above, a, b, and c are the lengths of the sides of triangle ABC. If $a = 2$ and $b = 5$, which of the following is NOT true about all the possible lengths of c?

I. $5 > c > 1$

II. $7 > c > 3$

III. $c = 8$

A) I only

B) I and III only

C) II and III only

D) I, II, and III

3

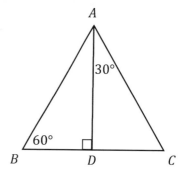

Note: Figure not drawn to scale.

In the figure above, $AD = 2\sqrt{3}$ and bisects $\overline{BC}$ at point D. What is the length of $\overline{AC}$?

4

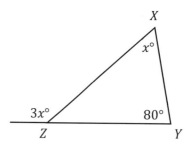

Note: Figure not drawn to scale.

In the figure above, what is the value of $3x$?

5

In a triangle with sides a, b, and c, $a = 3$ and $b = 7$. If $c > 7$, what is one possible integer value of c?

6

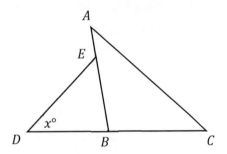

Note: Figure not drawn to scale.

Which of the following is the perimeter of right triangle ABC shown above?

A) $2\sqrt{2} + 10$

B) $4\sqrt{5} + 4$

C) $6\sqrt{5} + 10$

D) 21

7

In the figure above, $AB = BC$, $BD = BE$, and angle $BAC = 40°$. Which of the following is the value of x?

A) 30

B) 40

C) 48

D) 50

8

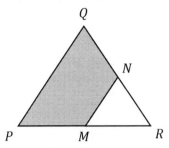

In the figure above, triangle PQR is an equilateral triangle with each side measuring 4 centimeters. M is the midpoint of $\overline{PR}$ and N is the midpoint of $\overline{QR}$. If $MN = 2$ centimeters, what is the area of the shaded region in the figure, in square centimeters?

A) $2\sqrt{5}$

B) $3\sqrt{3}$

C) $4\sqrt{2}$

D) 4

9

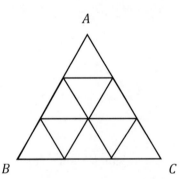

Keisha is creating designs for her art project. She puts together 9 small congruent equilateral triangles adjacent to each other to form one large equilateral triangle ABC shown in the above figure. The area of each small congruent equilateral triangle is $\sqrt{3}$ square inches. Which of the following is the perimeter, in inches, of the equilateral triangle ABC?

A) 6

B) 18

C) $18\sqrt{3}$

D) $27\sqrt{3}$

10

Triangle ABC is an isosceles triangle with $AB = AC$ and angle $B = 50°$. What is the value of angle A in radians?

A) $\dfrac{4\pi}{9}$

B) $\dfrac{\pi}{3}$

C) $\dfrac{3\pi}{2}$

D) 2π

11

The side lengths of right triangle XYZ are $\sqrt{3}$ inches, $4\sqrt{3}$ inches, and $\sqrt{51}$ inches. What is the area of the triangle, in square inches?

A) $2.5\sqrt{3}$

B) $5\sqrt{3}$

C) 6

D) 12

12

In triangle XYZ, angle Y is right angle. If $XY = 9\sqrt{92}$ inches and $XZ = 15\sqrt{92}$ inches. What is the length of YZ, in inches?

A) $6\sqrt{92}$

B) $12\sqrt{92}$

C) $24\sqrt{92}$

D) $\sqrt{135}$

13

In triangle MNO, the measure of $\angle M$ is $91°$. Which of the following could be the measure, in degrees, of $\angle O$?

A) 85

B) 89

C) 91

D) 129

14

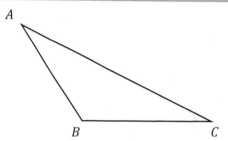

Note: Figure not drawn to scale.

An artist plans to present artwork on the front side of a wooden sculpture in the shape shown above. The base of the sculpture BC is 5 feet and sits on a table top. The height of the sculpture from point A to the table top is 4 feet. How much area, in square feet, is available to the artist?

15

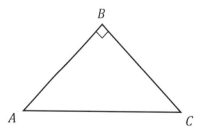

In triangle ABC, $AB = BC$ and $AC = 4\sqrt{2}$. What is the length of $\overline{AB}$?

Category 76 – Similar Triangles

Key Points
- In two similar triangles, the corresponding angles are congruent, and the corresponding sides are proportional.
  - For example, if in similar triangles ABC and DEF, the corresponding sides are AB and DE, BC and EF, and AC and DF, then $AB:DE = BC:EF = AC:DF$, $\angle A \cong \angle D$, $\angle B \cong \angle E$, and $\angle C \cong \angle F$.
- When a triangle is modified by proportionally shrinking or enlarging each side, the original and the modified triangles are similar. The perimeter and area of the modified triangle will change, and all the three sides will proportionally decrease or increase in length. However, the corresponding angles measure the same, and the corresponding sides maintain the proportion. For example, see the side lengths of the triangles in Fig. 3 below.

How to Solve
See below for similar triangle figures and how to identify them. It is important to identify the correct corresponding sides in similar triangles.

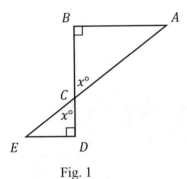

Fig. 1
Three angles are congruent

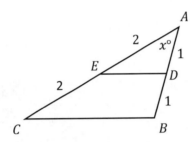

Fig. 2
Two sides are in proportion and share the same angle

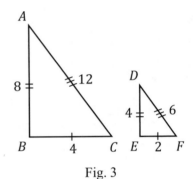

Fig. 3
Three sides are in proportion

- When all the three angles of two given triangles are congruent, then the two triangles are similar.

  In Fig. 1, ABC and EDC are right triangles. Angles x, ACB and ECD, are congruent vertical angles, and the right angles B and D are congruent. Since the sum of three angles of any triangle is $180°$, the third angle (angle A in a triangle ABC and angle E in triangle EDC) must also be congruent. Hence, the two triangles are similar.

  The corresponding sides are between the corresponding angles. BC and CD are between angles $x°$ and $90°$. Hence, they are corresponding sides. Similarly, AB and DE, and AC and CE are corresponding sides.

- When two given triangles have two sides in proportion and share the same angle between these sides, then the two triangles are similar.

  In Fig. 2, ABC and ADE are two triangles. The ratios $AB:AD$ (2:1) and $AC:AE$ (4:2 = 2:1) are the same, and the sides share the same angle x. Hence, the two triangles are similar.

  Since triangle ADE is within triangle ABC, the shared sides are the corresponding sides. Hence, AB and AD are corresponding sides and AC and AE are corresponding sides. The remaining sides BC and DE must be the third set of corresponding sides.

- When two given triangles have all three sides in proportion, then the two triangles are similar.

  In Fig. 3, the three sides of triangles ABC and DEF are in proportion. The ratios $AB:DE$ (8:4 = 2:1), $BC:EF$ (4:2 = 2:1), and $AC:DF$ (12:6 = 2:1) are the same. Hence, the two triangles are similar.

  Note that in these types of similar triangles, the question will give the corresponding vertices of the two triangles so the corresponding sides can be matched. For example, the question will mention that in triangles ABC and DEF, vertices A, B, and C correspond to vertices D, E, and F, respectively.

  The corresponding sides are between the corresponding vertices. Hence, the corresponding sides are AB and DE, BC and EF, and AC and DF.

Example 1:

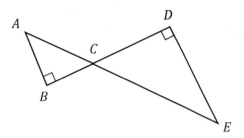

Note: Figure not drawn to scale.

In the figure above, ABC and EDC are right triangles. If $AB = 6$, $DE = 21$, and $CE = 35$, what is the length of segment AE?

Step 1: Identify similar triangles

It is given that both triangles have a right angle. Angles ACB and DCE are congruent vertical angles. Hence, triangles ABC and EDC are similar triangles with corresponding sides in proportion, $AB:DE = BC:CD = AC:CE$.

Step 2: Set up a proportion for the corresponding sides

$$AE = AC + CE = AC + 35$$

The length of AC can be determined by setting up the following proportion.

$$\frac{AB}{DE} = \frac{AC}{CE} \rightarrow \frac{6}{21} = \frac{AC}{35} \rightarrow$$

$$21 \times AC = 6 \times 35 \rightarrow 21 \times AC = 210 \rightarrow AC = 10$$

Hence,

$$AE = 10 + 35 = 45$$

The correct answer is **45**.

Example 2:

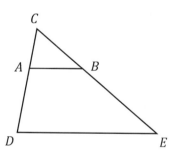

Note: Figure not drawn to scale.

In the figure above, $\overline{AB}$ is parallel to $\overline{DE}$. If $AB = 5$, $DE = 20$, and $CE = 32$, what is the length of segment BC?

Step 1: Identify similar triangles

Since AB is parallel to DE, angles CAB and CDE and angles CBA and CED are corresponding angles. Hence, triangles ABC and DEC are similar triangles with corresponding sides in proportion, $AB:DE = BC:CE = AC:CD$.

Step 2: Set up proportion for corresponding sides

$$\frac{AB}{DE} = \frac{BC}{CE} \rightarrow \frac{5}{20} = \frac{BC}{32} \rightarrow \frac{1}{4} = \frac{BC}{32} \rightarrow$$

$$4 \times BC = 32 \rightarrow BC = 8$$

The correct answer is **8**.

Category 76 – Practice Questions

1

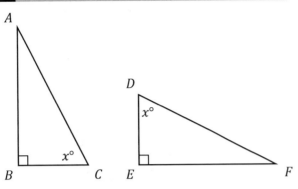

Note: Figure not drawn to scale.

The figure above shows two identical right triangles. Which of the following is equivalent to the ratio of $\frac{AB}{AC}$?

A) $\frac{DE}{EF}$

B) $\frac{EF}{DF}$

C) $\frac{DE}{DF}$

D) $\frac{EF}{DE}$

2

Triangles ABC and DEF are congruent triangles where vertices A, B, and C correspond to vertices D, E, and F, respectively. If each side of triangle ABC is four times the length of the corresponding side of triangle DEF, which of the following statements is NOT true?

A) Angle C is congruent to angle F.

B) The sum of the measures of all the angles of triangle ABC and the sum of the measures of all the angles of triangle DEF is the same.

C) The measure of angle B is four times the measure of angle E.

D) The length of $\overline{AB}$ is four times the length of $\overline{DE}$.

3

In right triangle ABC, angle B is the right angle and $AC = 9$ inches. Point D lies on line segment AB, and point E lies on line segment BC. Line segment DE is formed by joining the points D and E, and is parallel to line segment AC. If the length of line segment BE is double the length of line segment CE, what is the length of line segment DE, in inches?

4

Triangle XYZ is proportionally shrunk to form a new triangle ABC. Each side of triangle ABC is half the length of the corresponding side of triangle XYZ and vertices A, B, and C correspond to vertices X, Y, and Z, respectively. In triangle ABC, angle B measures $70°$, and angle C measures $32°$. If the difference in the degree measures of angle X and angle Z is a, what is the value of a?

5

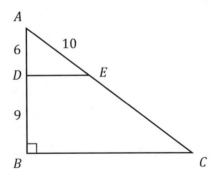

Note: Figure not drawn to scale.

In the figure above, $\overline{BC}$ and $\overline{DE}$ are parallel. If $AD = 6$, $BD = 9$, and $AE = 10$, what is the length of line segment BC?

Category 77 – Squares and Cubes

Key Points
- A square has four equal sides and four 90° angles (Fig. 1). For a square of side s, see the following formulas.
  - Perimeter = $4s$.
  - Area = s^2.
  - Diagonal = $s\sqrt{2}$.
- A cube is a three-dimensional figure bounded by 6 square faces and 12 sides (Fig. 2). Each angle is 90°. For a cube of side s, see the following formulas.
  - Surface area = $6s^2$.
  - Surface area of each square face = s^2.
  - Volume = s^3.
  - Diagonal = $s\sqrt{3}$.

Fig. 1

Fig. 2

How to Solve
Apply the appropriate formula. Note that a side may be referred to as an edge.

Example 1:
The surface area of a cube is 54 square feet. What is the volume of the cube, in cubic feet?

Step 1: Determine the length of a side
$$6s^2 = 54 \;\to\; s^2 = 9 \;\to\; s = 3$$

Step 2: Determine the volume
$$s^3 = 3^3 = 27$$

The correct answer is **27**.

Example 2:
The perimeter of a square is x inches. The function f gives the area of the square, in square inches. Which of the following defines f?

A) $f(x) = x^2$
B) $f(x) = (0.25x)^2$
C) $f(x) = (4x)^2$
D) $f(x) = 2x$

Step 1: Determine the side length:
$$\text{side} = s = \frac{\text{perimeter}}{4} = \frac{x}{4} = 0.25x$$

Step 2: Determine the area (function f):
$$f(x) = s^2 = (0.25x)^2$$

The correct answer choice is **B**.

Category 77 – Practice Questions

1

The surface area of a cube is 96 square feet. Which of the following is the volume of the cube, in cubic feet?

A) 12
B) 16
C) 32
D) 64

2

The volume of a cube, in cubic centimeters, of side length 5 centimeters is how much greater than the volume of a cube, in cubic centimeters, of side length 2 centimeters?

A) 27
B) 81
C) 117
D) 120

3

The area of a square is $\frac{b^2}{4}$, where b is a positive constant. Which of the following is the perimeter of the square in terms of b?

A) $2b$
B) b
C) $\frac{b}{2}$
D) $\frac{b}{4}$

4

The perimeter of square A is x centimeters. The perimeter of Square B is 76 centimeters greater than the perimeter of Square A. The function f gives the area of Square B, in square inches. Which of the following defines f?

A) $f(x) = x^2$
B) $f(x) = 2x^2$
C) $f(x) = (0.25x + 19)^2$
D) $f(x) = (x + 76)^2$

5

The surface area of a cube is $6\left(\frac{1}{2}\right)^2$ square inches. What is the surface area of one face of the cube, in square inches?

6

If the diagonal of a cube is $5\sqrt{3}$ inches, what is the surface area of the cube, in square inches?

7

The volume of a cube is 64 cubic feet. The area of one face of the cube is how many square feet less than the surface area of the cube?

8

If the surface area of a cube is 150 square centimeters, what is the volume of the cube, in cubic centimeters?

Category 78 – Rectangles and Right Rectangular Prisms

Key Points
- A rectangle has four sides and four 90° angles (Fig. 1). The opposite facing sides of a rectangle are equal. For a rectangle with length l and width w, see the following formulas.
  - Perimeter $= 2(l + w)$.
  - Area $= lw$.
- A right rectangular prism is a three-dimensional rectangle, such as a box (Fig. 2). Each angle is 90°. It has 6 rectangular faces and 12 sides. The opposite faces are equal. For a right rectangular prism with length l, width w, and height h, see the following formulas.
  - Surface area $= 2(lw + lh + wh)$.
  - Volume $= lwh$. This can also be written as: area of the rectangular base $lw \times$ height h.

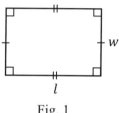
Fig. 1

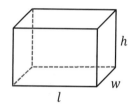
Fig. 2

How to Solve
Apply the appropriate formula.

Example 1:
A right rectangular prism has a length of 14 inches, a width of 10 inches, and a height of 4 inches. Which of the following is the volume of the prism, in cubic inches?

A) 64
B) 83
C) 158
D) 560

Step 1: Determine the volume
$l = 14$. $w = 10$. $h = 4$.
$$lwh = 14 \times 10 \times 4 = 560$$
The correct answer choice is **D**.

Example 2:
Jasper dug a 7 feet by 5 feet by 2 feet rectangular flower bed in his garden. What is the surface area of the rectangular flower bed, in square feet?

Step 1: Determine the surface area
$l = 7$. $w = 5$. $h = 2$.
$$2(lw + lh + wh) = 2((7 \times 5) + (7 \times 2) + (5 \times 2)) =$$
$$2(35 + 14 + 10) = 2 \times 59 = 118$$
The correct answer is **118**.

Category 78 – Practice Questions

1

The dimensions of a right rectangular prism are 8 inches by 5 inches by 3 inches. Which of the following is the surface area of the prism, in square inches?

A) 63
B) 120
C) 158
D) 179

2

The area of a rectangular courtyard is 147 square meters. The length of the courtyard is 3 times the width. How much shorter is the width of the courtyard than the length of the courtyard, in meters?

A) 14
B) 21
C) 37
D) 49

3

The width of rectangle Z is 9.2 times its length l, in feet. The function $f(l) = 20.4l$ gives the perimeter of rectangle Z, in feet. Which of the following is the best interpretation of $f(45) = 918$?

A) When the length of rectangle Z is 45 feet, the width of rectangle Z is 918 feet.
B) When the length of rectangle Z is 45 feet, the perimeter of rectangle Z is 918 feet.
C) When the width of rectangle Z is 45 feet, the perimeter of rectangle Z is 918 feet.
D) When the width of rectangle Z is 45 feet, the length of rectangle Z is 918 feet.

4

Naniya must paint the entire surface area of a right rectangular box for her art project. The length of the box is 7 inches, the width is 5 inches, and the height is 2 inches. What is the surface area Naniya must paint, in square inches?

A) 59
B) 118
C) 140
D) 145

5

The width, length, and height of two identical right rectangular prisms are $1.2x$ inches, $2.5x$ inches, and 8 inches, respectively. If the two prisms are glued together along a rectangular base, which of the following expressions represents the surface area of the resulting prism, in inches, in terms of x?

A) $6x^2$
B) $12x^2 + 8$
C) $6x^2 + 118.4x$
D) $12x^2 + 118.4x$

6

The length l of a right rectangular prism, in inches is two times the height h, in inches, and the height, in inches, is three times the width w, in inches. The function f models the volume of the prism, in cubic inches. Which of the following defines f?

A) $f(w) = 5w^2$
B) $f(w) = 18w^3$
C) $f(w) = 5w$
D) $f(w) = 12w$

Digital SAT Math Manual and Workbook

Category 79 – Trapezoids and Parallelograms

Key Points
- A trapezoid is a quadrilateral with one pair of opposite sides parallel (Fig. 1).
  - The area of a trapezoid is $\frac{1}{2}(a+b)h$, where a and b are the two parallel bases and h is the height (the perpendicular distance between the two parallel sides) of the trapezoid.
- A parallelogram is a quadrilateral with opposite sides parallel and equal in length (Fig. 2).
  - The area of a parallelogram is bh, where b is the base and h is the height (the perpendicular distance between two parallel sides where one of the sides is the base) of the parallelogram.

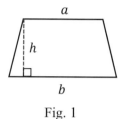
Fig. 1

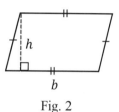
Fig. 2

How to Solve

When the height of a trapezoid or a parallelogram is not given, it can most likely be determined using the ratios of Pythagorean triples, 30°-60°-90° triangles, or 45°-45°-90° triangles.

Example 1:

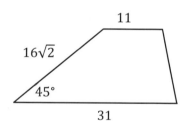

Note: Figure not drawn to scale.

What is the area of the trapezoid shown in the figure above?

Step 1: Determine the height of the trapezoid

The two bases are given but the height is unknown. See the figure below to determine the height AC.

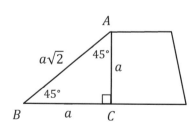

A perpendicular line from point A forms a right angle at point C. Since angle $ACB = 90°$ and angle $ABC = 45°$, angle BAC must be 45°. Hence, triangle ABC is a 45°-45°-90° triangle with side ratio as follows.

$$BC:AC:AB = a:a:a\sqrt{2}$$

It is given that $AB = 16\sqrt{2}$, Hence,

$$a\sqrt{2} = 16\sqrt{2} \rightarrow a = 16$$

Height $= AC = a = 16$

Step 2: Determine the area of the trapezoid

$$\frac{1}{2}(11 + 31)16 = 42 \times 8 = 336$$

The correct answer is **336**.

Category 79 – Practice Questions

1

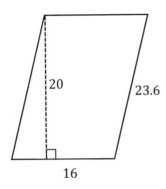

Note: Figure not drawn to scale.

The above figure shows the length of the sides and height of a parallelogram, in inches. What is the area of the parallelogram, in square inches?

2

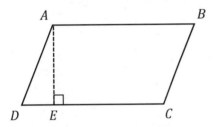

Note: Figure not drawn to scale.

In the above parallelogram, $AE = 24$ centimeters and $DE = 10$ centimeters. If the perimeter of the parallelogram is 162 centimeters, what is the length of $\overline{AB}$, in centimeters?

3

The area of a trapezoid is 110 square feet, and the lengths of the two bases are 6.5 feet and 15.5 feet. What is the height, in feet, of the trapezoid?

4

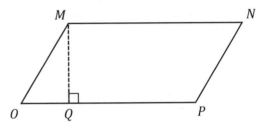

Note: Figure not drawn to scale.

In the above parallelogram, angle MOQ is 60°, the length of $\overline{MQ}$ is $3\sqrt{3}$ feet, and the length of $\overline{QP}$ is 9 feet. What is the length of $\overline{MN}$, in feet?

5

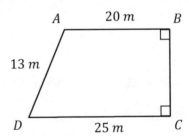

Note: Figure not drawn to scale.

A playground is designed in the form of a trapezoid, as shown in the figure above. What is the area of the playground, in square meters? (m = meters).

Category 80 – Volume of Cylinders, Spheres, Cones, Pyramids, Prisms

Key Points

- The volume of a right cylinder is $\pi r^2 h$, where r is the radius and h is the height of the cylinder (Fig. 1).
  - The volume can also be written as area of the circular base $(\pi r^2) \times h$.
- The volume of a sphere is $\frac{4}{3}\pi r^3$, where r is the radius of the sphere (Fig. 2).
- The volume of a right circular cone is $\frac{1}{3}\pi r^2 h$, where r is the radius and h is the height of the cone (Fig. 3).
  - The volume can also be written as $\frac{1}{3} \times$ area of the circular base $(\pi r^2) \times h$.
- The volume of a right pyramid with a rectangular base is $\frac{1}{3}lwh$, where l is the base length, w is the base width, and h is the height of the pyramid (Fig. 4).
  - The volume can also be written as $\frac{1}{3} \times$ area of the rectangular base $(lw) \times h$. If the base is a square, then l and w will be the same.
- The volume of a right triangular prism is the area of the triangular base $\times\, l$, where l is the base length of the prism (Fig. 5).

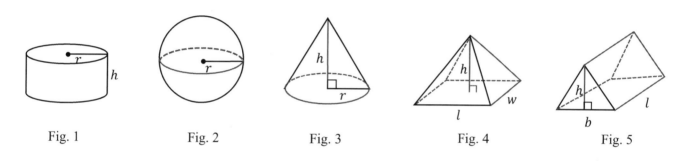

Fig. 1 Fig. 2 Fig. 3 Fig. 4 Fig. 5

How to Solve

Apply the appropriate formula.

In a right triangular prism, if the triangle is an isosceles right triangle, then use the 45°-45°-90° triangle side relationship to determine the base and height of the triangle. If the triangle is an equilateral triangle, then the area of the triangle can be directly determined using the area formula of an equilateral triangle.

Example 1:

The area of the base of a right circular cone is 9π square centimeters, and the volume is 60π cubic centimeters. What is the height of the cone, in centimeters?

Step 1: Determine the height of the cone

Volume = 60π. Area of circular base = $\pi r^2 = 9\pi$.

$$\text{volume} = \frac{1}{3}\pi r^2 h \;\rightarrow\; 60\pi = \frac{1}{3} \times 9\pi \times h \;\rightarrow\; 60 = 3h \;\rightarrow\; h = 20$$

The correct answer is **20**.

Example 2:

The area of the base of a right cylindrical container is 14 square inches. If the height of the cylindrical container is 7 inches, what is the volume of the cylindrical container, in cubic inches?

A) 14
B) 21
C) 52
D) 98

Step 1: Determine the volume of the cylinder

$h = 7$. Area of circular base $= \pi r^2 = 14$.

$$\pi r^2 h = 14 \times 7 = 98$$

The correct answer choice is **D**.

Example 3:

The volume of a pyramid with a rectangular base is 72 cubic inches. The length and width of the rectangular base are 3 inches and 6 inches, respectively. What is the height of the pyramid, in inches?

Step 1: Determine the height of the rectangular pyramid

Volume $= 72$. $l = 3$. $w = 6$.

$$\text{volume} = \frac{1}{3} lwh \;\rightarrow\; 72 = \frac{1}{3} \times 3 \times 6 \times h \;\rightarrow\; 72 = 6h \;\rightarrow\; h = 12$$

The correct answer is **12**.

Example 4:

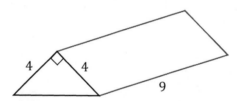

Note: Figure not drawn to scale.

What is the volume, in cubic units, of the right triangular prism shown above?

Step 1: Determine the area of the triangular base

See the figure below of the prism base. Since AB and BC form a right angle, they are the two legs of a right triangle.

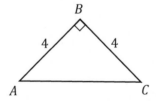

$$\text{area} = \frac{1}{2} \times \text{leg1} \times \text{leg2} = \frac{1}{2} \times 4 \times 4 = 8$$

Step 2: Determine the volume of the prism

$$\text{area of triangular base} \times 9 = 8 \times 9 = 72$$

The correct answer is **72**.

Category 80 – Practice Questions

1

A manufacturing company produces right cylindrical cones in several sizes. The company conducted research to determine the size of the cone in highest demand. The results showed that the cone with a height three times the size of the radius is in highest demand. Which of the following expresses the volume V in terms of the radius r of the cone that is highest in demand?

A) $V = \frac{1}{3}\pi r^3$

B) $V = \pi r^3$

C) $V = \pi r^2$

D) $V = 3\pi r^2$

2

A right circular cone has a volume of $\frac{1}{6}\pi$, and the radius of the cone is twice its height. Which of the following is the height of the cone?

A) $\frac{1}{2}$

B) $\frac{2}{3}$

C) $\sqrt{4}$

D) $3\sqrt{4}$

3

The volume of a right cylindrical pipe is $1,728\pi$ cubic inches, and the radius is 6 inches. What is the height of the pipe, in inches?

A) 12

B) 19

C) 48

D) 96

4

Isa is finalizing the dimensions of a cone for her school project. She wants the height of the cone to be 12 inches, the diameter to be between 7 to 10 inches inclusive, and the volume to be less than or equal to 64π cubic inches. Based on the above dimensions, which of the following can NOT be the radius of the cone, in inches?

A) 3.5

B) 3.7

C) 3.9

D) 4.1

5

Cory has two right cylindrical containers of different sizes. The volume of the smaller container is x cubic inches, and the volume of the larger container is y cubic inches. If the radius and height of the larger container, in inches, are twice of the smaller container, what is $\frac{x}{y}$?

A) $\frac{1}{4}$

B) $\frac{1}{8}$

C) 2

D) 4

6

A circular cone of volume 6π cubic inches has a height of 2 inches. If the radius and height of the circular cone are doubled to create a new circular cone, which of the following statements is true when the volume of the new cone is compared with the volume of the original cone?

A) The volume of the new cone increases 2 fold.

B) The volume of the new cone increases 4 fold.

C) The volume of the new cone increases 8 fold.

D) The volume of the new cone decreases 4 fold.

Digital SAT Math Manual and Workbook

7

The triangular base of the right triangular prism shown in the above figure is an equilateral triangle. What is the volume, in cubic units, of the right triangular prism?

A) 9
B) 12
C) $8\sqrt{3}$
D) $24\sqrt{3}$

8

Suman bought an inflatable ball that has a diameter of 6 inches when fully inflated. How many cubic inches of air must be filled in the ball for it to fully inflate, rounded to the nearest whole number?

9

When a 6 centimeters high right cylindrical bottle is placed on a flat surface, it occupies 7 square centimeters of the surface area. What is the volume of the bottle, in cubic centimeters?

10

Fred built a wooden sculpture in the shape of a right pyramid with a square base. The perimeter of the base is 12 inches and the volume of the pyramid is 42 cubic inches. What is the height, in inches, of the pyramid Fred built?

11

Jasmine has several right cylindrical containers with a height twice the length of the radius, in inches. If one such container has a volume of 54π cubic inches, what is the height of the container, in inches?

12

The volume of a right cylindrical cone is $27\pi h$ cubic inches, where h is the height of the cone in inches. What is the radius, in inches, of the cone?

13

The volume of a sphere is $\frac{32}{3}\pi$ cubic feet. What is the diameter of the sphere, in feet?

14

The volume of a pyramid with a rectangular base is 32 cubic feet. The height of the pyramid is 6 feet. What is the area of the rectangular base, in square feet?

Category 81 – Mass, Volume, and Density Relationship

Key Points
- The relationship is defined by the following formula.

$$\text{density} = \frac{\text{mass}}{\text{volume}}$$

How to Solve

Example 1:
The density of a metal sample in the shape of a cube is 10 kilograms per cubic centimeters, and the mass of the metal sample is 80 kilograms. What is the length of each side of the metal sample, in centimeters?

A) 0.1
B) 0.8
C) 2
D) 8

Step 1: Determine the volume
Density = 10. Mass = 80.

$$\text{density} = \frac{\text{mass}}{\text{volume}} \rightarrow 10 = \frac{80}{\text{volume}} \rightarrow \text{volume} = \frac{80}{10} = 8$$

Step 2: Determine the length of each side of the cube

$$\text{volume} = s^3 = 8 = 2^3 \rightarrow s = 2$$

Hence, the length of each side $= s = 2$.
The correct answer choice is **C**.

Category 81 – Practice Questions

1

A sample of wood in the form of a right rectangular prism has a density of 562 kilograms per cubic meter. The length, width, and height of the wood sample are 0.75 meters, 0.65 meters, and 0.95 meters, respectively. Which of the following is closest to the approximate mass, in kilograms, of the wood sample?

A) 239
B) 260
C) 562
D) 822

2

A right rectangular pyramid created from a certain metal has a density of 1.05 grams per cubic centimeter and mass of 0.84 grams. The area of the base of the pyramid is 3 square centimeters. What is the height, in centimeters, of the pyramid?

A) 0.8
B) 1.2
C) 2.6
D) 4.9

Digital SAT Math Manual and Workbook

Category 82 – Combined Geometric Figures

Key Points

- A geometric figure may be comprised of one or more geometric shapes. A geometric shape may be adjacent to another, sharing a common side (for example, a semicircle and a rectangle with a common side, a triangle and a square with a common side, tangent circles, and so on), or may be contained within another (for example, triangle in a circle, square in a circle, rectangle in a square, rectangle in a semicircle, and so on).
- See a few examples below that are good to remember.
    - A regular hexagon is comprised of six congruent equilateral triangles. The total area of a hexagon is the sum of the areas of the six equilateral triangles (Fig. 1).
    - A rectangle is made up of two equal right triangles with a common diagonal (Fig. 2).
    - A triangle formed within a circle with two sides as radii is an isosceles triangle (Fig. 3).
    - A triangle formed within a circle with one side as the diameter of the circle and other two sides as chords has a right angle where the two chords meet (Fig. 4).
    - An angle formed by the radius of a circle and a line segment tangent to the circle is a right angle (Fig. 5).
    - Two line segments tangent to a circle form a quadrilateral. See quadrilateral $ABCO$ in Fig. 5 below. The tangent sides AB and BC are of equal length, and opposite angles AOC and ABC are supplementary angles. A line segment from point O (center) to the opposite point B divides the quadrilateral into two equal triangles.

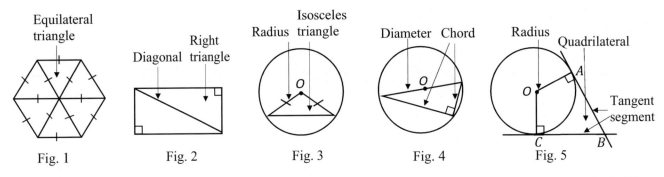

Fig. 1   Fig. 2   Fig. 3   Fig. 4   Fig. 5

How to Solve

It is important to determine an approach before solving the questions on combined geometric shapes.

Example 1:

What is the perimeter of a regular hexagon with an area of $24\sqrt{3}$?

Step 1: Determine the approach

The area of each equilateral triangle of the hexagon is the total area of the hexagon divided by 6. Using the equilateral triangle area formula, the length of a side can be determined. The perimeter will be $6 \times$ length of a side.

Step 2: Determine the length of each side of the equilateral triangle

$$\text{area of each equilateral triangle} = \frac{24\sqrt{3}}{6} = 4\sqrt{3}$$

Hence,

$$\frac{\sqrt{3}}{4}a^2 = 4\sqrt{3} \rightarrow a^2 = 4 \times 4 = 4^2 \rightarrow a = 4$$

Step 3: Determine the perimeter

$$6 \times 4 = 24$$

The correct answer is **24**.

Example 2:

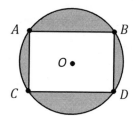

Note: Figure not drawn to scale.

In the figure above, point O is the center of the circle. Points A, B, C, and D lie on the circle and form the inscribed rectangle $ABCD$. The diagonals AD and BC (not shown) of the rectangle $ABCD$ pass through the point O and each measure 10 inches. If the width of the rectangle BD is 6 inches, what is the area of the shaded region, in square inches, rounded to the nearest tenth?

A) 12.2

B) 30.5

C) 48.0

D) 78.5

Step 1: Determine the approach

$$\text{area of the shaded region} = \text{area of the circle} - \text{area of the rectangle}$$

See the figure below for the approach to determine the length of the rectangle and radius of the circle.

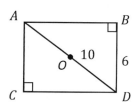

Rectangle: The diagonal AD divides the rectangle $ABCD$ into two equal right triangles. Either of these triangles can be used to determine the length of the rectangle.

In the triangle ABD, AB is the length of the rectangle and BD is the width of the rectangle. The length of BD is given but AB is unknown. Since the lengths of BD and AD are the ratio of the Pythagorean triple $6:8:10$, the length of AB can be determined.

Circle: The diagonal of the rectangle AD passes through the center of the circle. Hence, AD is the diameter of the circle $= 10$. The radius will be half of the diameter.

Step 2: Determine the area of the rectangle

$$BD:AB:AD = 6:AB:10 = 6:8:10 \rightarrow AB = 8$$
$$\text{area} = lw = AB \times BD = 8 \times 6 = 48$$

Step 3: Determine the area of the circle

Since diameter $= 10$, radius $= 5$.

$$\pi r^2 = \pi \times 5 \times 5 = 25\pi = 25 \times 3.14 = 78.5$$

Step 4: Determine the area of the shaded region

$$\text{area of the circle} - \text{the area of the rectangle} = 78.5 - 48 = 30.5$$

The correct answer choice is **B**.

Category 82 – Practice Questions

1

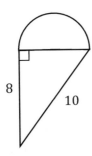

Note: Figure not drawn to scale.

An ice cream company is redesigning the company logo as shown in the figure above. The design consists of a semicircle on top of a right triangle. The lengths of two sides of the triangle, in inches, are given in the above figure. Which of the following is the area of the semicircle, in square inches?

A) 4.5π

B) 5.0π

C) 9.0π

D) 10.5π

2

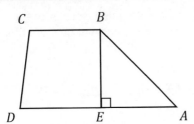

Note: Figure not drawn to scale.

A building architect is designing a roof in the form of the trapezoid $ABDC$ shown above. If $AE = BE$, what is the sum of the degree measures of angles ABE and CBE?

A) 100

B) 110

C) 125

D) 135

3

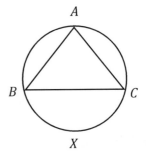

Note: Figure not drawn to scale.

In the figure above, triangle ABC is inscribed in a circle. Arcs AB and AC are congruent, and the degree measure of arc BXC is 160°. What is the degree measure of angle B?

A) 20

B) 50

C) 80

D) 120

4

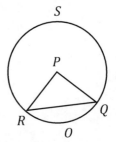

Note: Figure not drawn to scale.

Point P is the center of the circle shown above and angle PQR is 40°. Arc QOR is what fraction of arc QSR?

A) $\dfrac{1}{4}$

B) $\dfrac{2}{5}$

C) $\dfrac{5}{13}$

D) $\dfrac{5}{18}$

Digital SAT Math Manual and Workbook

5

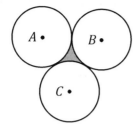

Note: Figure not drawn to scale.

In the figure above, the congruent circles A, B, and C, each have a radius of 6 inches, and are tangent to each other. What is the area of the shaded region, in square inches?

A) $9\pi(\sqrt{3} - 2\pi)$

B) $18(2\sqrt{3} - \pi)$

C) $9\sqrt{3} - 2\pi$

D) $24\sqrt{3} - \pi$

6

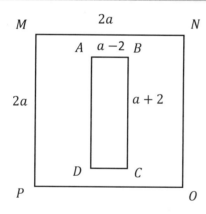

In the figure above, rectangle $ABCD$ is inscribed in square $MNOP$. The dimensions of the rectangle are $(a-2)$ by $(a+2)$, and each side of the square is $2a$. In context of the given dimensions, what could $3a^2 + 4$ represent, where a is a constant greater than 0?

A) The perimeter of the square.

B) The perimeter of the inscribed rectangle.

C) The combined area of the square and inscribed rectangle.

D) The area of the square not covered by the inscribed rectangle.

7

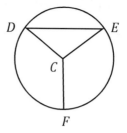

Note: Figure not drawn to scale.

Point C is the center of the circle shown in the figure above. Angle $CDE = 30°$, and points D, E, and F lie on the circumference of the circle. If the length of $\overline{CF}$ is 4 inches, what is the area of triangle CDE, in square inches?

A) $\sqrt{3}$

B) $4\sqrt{3}$

C) 3

D) 16

8

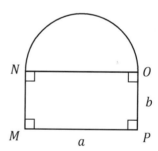

Note: Figure not drawn to scale.

The figure above shows a wall design in the shape of a rectangle with a semicircle on top. The length a of the rectangle is twice the width b. If the radius of the semicircle is 2 feet, what is the total area of the rectangle, in square feet?

9

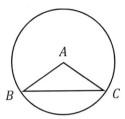

In the figure above, A is the center of the circle, and points B and C lie on the circumference of the circle. If angle A is $\frac{5}{9}\pi$ and the degree measure of angle B is x, what is x?

10

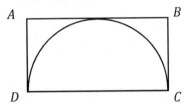

The figure above shows a semicircle inscribed in the rectangle $ABCD$. $\overline{CD}$ is the diameter of the semicircle and the length of the rectangle. If the area of the semicircle is 18π, what is the area of the rectangle?

11

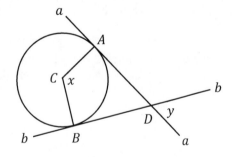

Note: Figure not drawn to scale

In the figure above, point C is the center of the circle, and lines a and b are tangent to the circle at points A and B, respectively. If the measures of angles x and y are in degrees, and $x = 120$, what is y?

12

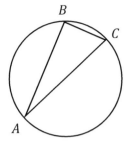

Note: Figure not drawn to scale.

In the figure above, $\overline{AC}$ passes through the center of the circle. The length of chord BC is 10 units, and the radius of the circle is 13 units. What is the area of triangle ABC, in square units?

13

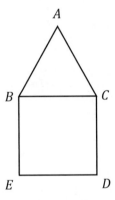

In the figure above, ABC is an equilateral triangle with an area of $16\sqrt{3}$ square yards, and $BCDE$ is a square. What is the perimeter of the square, in yards?

Digital SAT Math Manual and Workbook

Category 83 – Geometric Figures in the xy-plane

Key Points
- The (x, y) coordinates of the two end points of a line segment determine its length.
- In a vertical line segment, the x-coordinates of the two end points are the same. The length of the line segment is the difference between the y-coordinates of the two end points.
- In a horizontal line segment, the y-coordinates of the two end points are the same. The length of the line segment is the difference between the x-coordinates of the two end points.
- The length of a slanting line segment can be determined using the distance formula. If (x_1, y_1) and (x_2, y_2) are the two end points, then the length can be determined as

$$\sqrt{(x_2 - x_1)^2 + (y_2 - y_1)^2}$$

How to Solve
Look out for the ratios of Pythagorean triples, or the side ratios of 45°-45°-90° and 30°-60°-90° triangles.

Example 1:

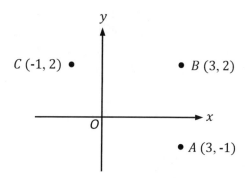

In the xy-plane, the points A, B, and C shown in the figure above are the coordinates of triangle ABC. What is the perimeter of triangle ABC?

Step 1: Determine the length between points

Calculate $\overline{AB}$: $A = (3, -1)$ and $B = (3, 2)$. AB is a vertical line segment.
$$AB = 2 - (-1) = 3$$
Calculate $\overline{BC}$: $B = (3, 2)$ and $C = (-1, 2)$. BC is a horizontal line segment.
$$BC = 3 - (-1) = 4$$
Calculate $\overline{AC}$: Since the vertical line segment AB and horizontal line segment BC meet at point B, angle ABC is 90° and triangle ABC is a right triangle.

$AB: BC = 3: 4$ is the ratio of the Pythagorean triple $3: 4: 5$. Hence,
$$AB: BC: AC = 3: 4: 5$$
$$AC = 5$$
Alternatively, the distance formula can be used to determine AC.

Step 2: Determine the perimeter
$$AB + BC + AC = 3 + 4 + 5 = 12$$
The correct answer is **12**.

Category 83 – Practice Questions

1

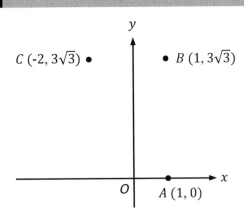

Note: Figure not drawn to scale.

In the xy-plane, points A, B, and C shown in the figure above are coordinates of triangle ABC. What is the measure of angle BAC, in radians?

A) 2π

B) $\frac{\pi}{2}$

C) $\frac{2\pi}{3}$

D) $\frac{\pi}{6}$

2

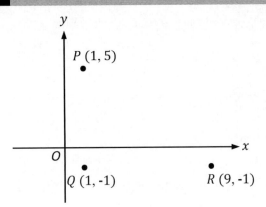

Note: Figure not drawn to scale.

In the xy-plane, points P, Q, and R shown in the above figure form a triangle. What is the perimeter of the triangle?

A) 9

B) 12

C) 24

D) 26

3

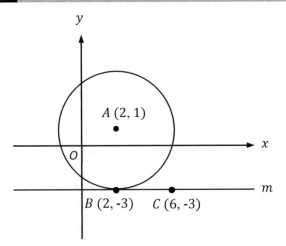

Note: Figure not drawn to scale.

In the xy-plane, a circle with center A is shown above. Line m is tangent to the circle at point B, and point C lies on line m. If points A, B, and C are joined to form triangle ABC, which of the following is the degree measure of angle ACB?

A) 30

B) 45

C) 50

D) 60

4

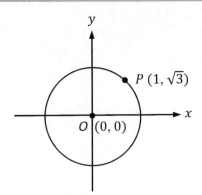

Note: Figure not drawn to scale.

In the figure above, O is the center of a circle in the xy-plane, and point P lies on the circle. What is the diameter of the circle?

Digital SAT Math Manual and Workbook

Category 84 – Geometric Figures and Percent

Key Points
- An increase or decrease in one or more dimensions of a geometric figure will result in percent change of the area or the volume of the figure.

How to Solve
Refer to Section 9 for further details on calculating the percent change.

Example 1:
If the length of a rectangle is decreased by 25% and the width is increased by 20%, which of the following statements are true?

A) The area of the rectangle will decrease by 5%.
B) The area of the rectangle will increase by 5%.
C) The area of the rectangle will decrease by 10%.
D) The area of the rectangle will increase by 20%.

Step 1: Determine the area

Area before change: Let length $= l$ and width $= w$.
$$\text{area} = lw$$

Area after change:
Length: 25% decrease $= 1 - 0.25 = 0.75$. Hence, the decreased length is $0.75l$.
Width: 20% increase $= 1 + 0.2 = 1.2$. Hence, the increased width is $1.2w$.
$$\text{area} = 0.75l \times 1.2w = 0.9lw$$

Step 2: Determine the percent change in the area
$$\text{area after change} - \text{area before change} = 0.9lw - lw = -0.1lw = 10\% \text{ reduction}$$
The correct answer choice is **C**.

Example 2:
Each side of Square A measures 15 inches. Square B is created by reducing each side of Square A by 20%. By how many square inches is the area of Square B less than the area of Square B?

Step 1: Determine the area of Square A
Side $= s = 15$.
$$\text{area} = s^2 = 15^2 = 225$$

Step 2: Determine the area of Square B
Each side of Square B is reduced by 20% of side length of Square A. Hence each side of Square B is 80% of 15.
$$\text{side} = s = 15 \times 0.8 = 12$$
$$\text{area} = s^2 = 12^2 = 144$$

Step 3: Determine the difference in the areas of Square A and Square B
$$\text{area of Square A} - \text{area of Square B} = 225 - 144 = 81$$
Correct answer is **81**.

Category 84 – Practice Questions

1

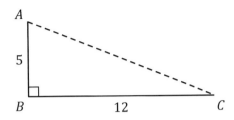

Note: Figure not drawn to scale.

The figure above shows the driving route Adriane takes to work each weekday, Monday through Friday. Adriane drives 5 miles from point A to B and then 12 miles from point B to C. If a bypass is built from point A to point C that allows Adriane to directly drive from point A to point C, what will be the percent change in the number of miles driven by Adriane each day to work, rounded to the nearest tenth?

A) 8.5%
B) 23.5%
C) 26.2%
D) 47.5%

2

A landscape architect initially designed a square shaped garden with an area of x square meters. In the final design, the landscape architect increased the area by 30%, resulting in a square with each side measuring 8 meters. Which of the following ranges could contain the length of each side, in meters, of the square garden initially designed by the architect?

A) 6.1 to 6.2
B) 6.8 to 6.9
C) 7.0 to 7.1
D) 8.0 to 8.1

3

Johnathan designed a circular garden of radius 4 yards in his backyard. The following year, Jonathan increased the radius of the circular garden by 50%. What is the percent change in the area of the circular garden after the 50% increase in radius?

A) 50%
B) 100%
C) 125%
D) 150%

4

If all the sides of a square are proportionally increased by 40%, which of the following is the approximate percent change in the area of the square?

A) 25%
B) 40%
C) 80%
D) 96%

5

If the length of a rectangle is increased by 10% and the width is decreased by 20%, which of the following statements is true?

A) The area of the rectangle will decrease by 12%.
B) The area of the rectangle will increase by 12%.
C) The area of the rectangle will decrease by 10%.
D) The area of the rectangle will be unchanged.

Category 85 – Ratio of Linear Side Length to Area or Volume

Key Points

- In two similar two-dimensional figures, such as rectangles, the ratio of their area is the square ratio of their corresponding linear side lengths.
- In two similar three-dimensional figures, such as right rectangular prisms, the ratio of their volume is the cube ratio of their corresponding linear side lengths.

How to Solve

Example 1:

The area of rectangle $ABCD$ is 16 square inches. The area of a similar rectangle $MNOP$ is 144 square inches. $\overline{MN}$ is 6 inches and corresponds to $\overline{AB}$. What is the length of $\overline{AB}$, in inches?

Step 1: Determine the square ratio of the areas

$$\text{area of } ABCD : \text{area of } MNOP = 16:144 = 1:9 = 1^2:3^2$$

Note that 9 is a perfect square $= 3^2$, and the square of 1 is also 1.

Hence, the ratio of the corresponding sides (linear length) of $ABCD$ to $MNOP$ is $1:3$.

$$AB:MN = 1:3$$

Step 2: Set up a proportion

$$AB:MN = 1:3 = AB:6 \quad \rightarrow \quad AB = 2$$

The correct answer is **2**.

(If a question gives the volume of two similar three-dimensional figures, then determine the cube ratio of the volumes, and proceed as shown above.)

Category 85 – Practice Questions

1

Trapezoid K is similar to trapezoid L. The length of the shortest side of trapezoid K is 2 feet. The length of the corresponding side of trapezoid L is 5 feet. The area of trapezoid K, in feet, is what percent of the area of trapezoid L, in feet?

A) 4%
B) 16%
C) 40%
D) 125%

2

The volume of a right rectangular prism is 1,000 cubic feet, and the height is 4 feet. The volume of a similar right rectangular prism is 64 cubic feet, and the height is h feet. What is the value of h?

A) 1.6
B) 4.6
C) 16.0
D) 20.0

Digital SAT Math Manual and Workbook

Section 13 – Review Questions

1

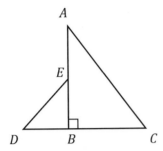

Note: Figure not drawn to scale.

In the figure above, $AC = 10$, $BC = 6$, $AB = 2BE$, and $BD = BE$. The area of triangle DBE is what fraction of the area of triangle ABC?

A) $\frac{1}{4}$

B) $\frac{1}{3}$

C) $\frac{1}{2}$

D) $\frac{3}{5}$

2

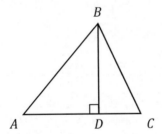

Note: Figure not drawn to scale.

If x is the area of triangle ABC shown above and $BD = 10$, which of the following represents $\overline{AC}$ in terms of x?

A) $\frac{x}{5}$

B) $\frac{x}{2}$

C) $2x$

D) $5x$

3

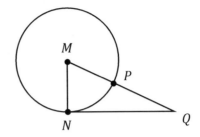

Note: Figure not drawn to scale.

In the figure above, M is the center of the circle and $\overline{NQ}$ is tangent to the circle at point N. If $MN = 1$ and $NQ = \sqrt{3}$, which of the following is the ratio of the length of minor arc PN to the circumference of the circle?

A) $1:3$

B) $1:4$

C) $1:6$

D) $1:8$

4

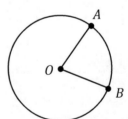

Note: Figure not drawn to scale.

In the circle above, angle AOB is a central angle, the minor arc AB is 2π, and the radius is 5. What is the value of angle AOB, in degrees?

A) 60

B) 72

C) 90

D) 116

5 — Desmos

In the xy-plane, a circle with center $(3, -4)$ is tangent to the x-axis. Which of the following is an equation of the circle?

A) $(x - 3)^2 + (y + 4)^2 = 4$
B) $(x + 3)^2 + (y - 4)^2 = 4$
C) $(x - 3)^2 + (y + 4)^2 = 16$
D) $(x + 3)^2 + (y - 4)^2 = 16$

6

An advertising company hired an artist to create a new company logo in a rectangular shape. The dimensions of the rectangle proposed by the artist are a feet by b feet. The company manager suggested to double the length of a and decrease the length of b by half. Based on the suggestion of the company manager, how will the area of the rectangle, in square feet, change when compared to the proposal by the artist?

A) The area of the rectangle will double.
B) The area of the rectangle will be half.
C) The area of the rectangle will be the same.
D) The area of the rectangle will be four times more.

7

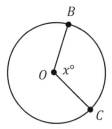

Note: Figure not drawn to scale.

In the circle shown above, the center is point O, $x = 120°$, and the area of the sector enclosed by angle x is 12π. What is the radius of the circle?

8

If the length of a rectangle is increased by 25% and the width is decreased by 20%, which of the following statements is true?

A) The area of the rectangle will decrease by 5%.
B) The area of the rectangle will increase by 5%.
C) The area of the rectangle will decrease by 20%.
D) The area of the rectangle will be unchanged.

9

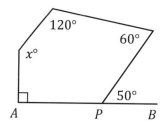

Note: Figure not drawn to scale.

In the figure above, point P lies on line segment AB. What is the value of x?

A) 60
B) 100
C) 130
D) 140

10 — Desmos

In the xy-plane, the equation of a circle is $(x - 6)^2 + (y + 1)^2 = 9$. Which of the following points lies on the circumference of the circle?

A) $(3, -2)$
B) $(3, 1)$
C) $(6, 2)$
D) $(7, 4)$

11

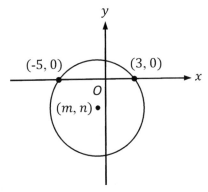

Note: Figure not drawn to scale.

In the figure above, a circle of radius 5 has its center at (m, n) in the xy-plane. Which of the following are the coordinates of (m, n)?

A) $(-1, -4)$
B) $(-1, -3)$
C) $(-1, -1)$
D) $(-1, 3)$

12 Desmos

In the xy-plane, the equation of a circle is $(x)^2 + (y - 14)^2 = 18$. Line p is tangent to this circle at the point $(3, 11)$. Which of the following points also lies on line p?

A) $(-25, -14)$
B) $(-15, -7)$
C) $(-3, 17)$
D) $(14, 18)$

13

A rectangle with length l meters and width $(5 + l)$ meters has an area of 36 square meters. What is the width of the rectangle, in meters, where l is a positive constant?

14

Rectangles $ABCD$ and $MNOP$ are similar. The length of each side of $ABCD$ is one-fourth the length of the corresponding side of $MNOP$. The area of $MNOP$ is 864 square units. What is the area, in square units, of $ABCD$?

15

In triangle ABC, line segment AB is the base of the triangle, $AC = 4$, and $BC = 5$. Point D extends from point C on side BC, and point E extends from point C on side AC such that line segment DE is parallel to line segment AB. If $CE = 10$, what is the length of line segment BD?

16

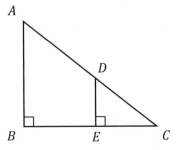

Note: Figure not drawn to scale.

In the figure above, $AB = 7$, $CD = 5$ and $DE = 3$. What is the length of $\overline{BE}$, rounded to the nearest tenth?

17

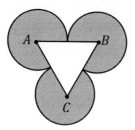

Note: Figure not drawn to scale.

In the figure, three congruent circles A, B, and C are tangent to each other. Points A, B, and C are the center of circles A, B, and C, respectively, and form equilateral triangle ABC. If the area of triangle ABC is $4\sqrt{3}$, what is the radius of each circle?

18 — Desmos

The graph of $x^2 + 4x + y^2 + 10y = 71$, in the xy-plane, is a circle. What is the diameter of the circle?

19

A right rectangular prism has a length of l inches, a width of w inches, and a height of h inches. If $lw = 5$, $hw = 6$, and $lh = 30$, what is the volume, in cubic inches, of the prism?

20

Raj glued one complete exterior side of a box to a piece of cardboard. He plans to use the remaining exterior surface of the box for artwork. Each side of the box is in the shape of a square, and the volume of the box is 1,331 cubic units. How much exterior surface area of the box, in square units, is available to Raj for artwork?

21

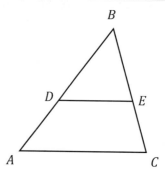

Note: Figure not drawn to scale.

In the figure above, $\overline{AC}$ is parallel to $\overline{DE}$. If angle BDE measures $52°$, angle ACB measures $80°$, and angle ABC measures $x°$, what is x?

22

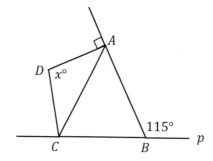

Note: Figure not drawn to scale.

In the figure above, points B and C are on line segment p, $AB = AC$, and $AD = CD$. What is the value of x?

23

If each side of a cube of volume 64 cubic feet is reduced by 25%, what is the surface area of the cube after reduction, in square feet?

Section 14 – Trigonometry

Category 86 – Right Triangles and Trigonometry
Category 87 – Unit Circle and Trigonometry

Category 86 – Right Triangles and Trigonometry

Key Points
- The three main trigonometric functions are the sine (sin), the cosine (cos), and the tangent (tan).

$$\tan = \frac{\sin}{\cos}$$

- The trigonometric functions are based on the right triangles. A right triangle has one of the angles as 90°, also known as the right angle. Each of the other two angles is less than 90°, also known as an acute angle. The sum of the two acute angles is 90°. In the figure below, triangle ABC is a right triangle with angle B as the right angle. For acute angle x, AB is the opposite side, BC is the adjacent side, and AC is the hypotenuse.
- The definitions of the trigonometric functions can be remembered as follows:
    - SOH: <u>S</u>ine equals <u>O</u>pposite over <u>H</u>ypotenuse. For angle x,

    $$\sin x = \frac{\text{opposite}}{\text{hypotenuse}}$$

    - CAH: <u>C</u>osine equals <u>A</u>djacent over <u>H</u>ypotenuse. For angle x,

    $$\cos x = \frac{\text{adjacent}}{\text{hypotenuse}}$$

    - TOA: <u>T</u>angent equals <u>O</u>pposite over <u>A</u>djacent. For angle x,

    $$\tan x = \frac{\text{opposite}}{\text{adjacent}}$$

    This is same as

    $$\tan x = \frac{\sin x}{\cos x} = \frac{\text{opposite}}{\text{hypotenuse}} \div \frac{\text{adjacent}}{\text{hypotenuse}} = \frac{\text{opposite}}{\text{hypotenuse}} \times \frac{\text{hypotenuse}}{\text{adjacent}} = \frac{\text{opposite}}{\text{adjacent}}$$

- For the acute angles x and y in a right triangle, the following facts are helpful to remember.
    - $\sin x° = \cos y°$ and $\sin y° = \cos x°$ (sine of one acute angle equals the cosine of the other acute angle and vice versa).
    - $\sin x° = \cos(90° - x°)$ and $\sin y° = \cos(90° - y°)$ (sine of an angle equals to the cosine of its complement).
    - $\cos x° = \sin(90° - x°)$ and $\cos y° = \sin(90° - y°)$ (cosine of an angle equals to the sine of its complement).
    - tan of one acute angle is the inverse of the other acute angle. For example, if $\tan x = \sqrt{3}$, then $\tan y = \frac{1}{\sqrt{3}}$.
- In similar right triangles, the sine, cosine, and tangent of the corresponding vertices are the same. For example, in similar right triangles ABC and XYZ, if vertex A corresponds to vertex X, then $\sin A = \sin X$, $\cos A = \cos X$, and $\tan A = \tan X$. The same is true for the other two vertices.

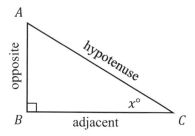

How to Solve
If a question does not give a figure, it can be helpful to draw one. Look out for the side ratios of a right triangle. They may be the ratio of Pythagorean triples, or the ratio of a 45°-45°-90° and 30°-60°-90° triangles. (See Section 12 Category 71 for further details on this.)

Example 1:

In a right triangle ABC, angle B is the right angle.

Question 1

If $\cos A = \frac{5}{13}$, what is the value of $\sin A$?

A) $\frac{5}{12}$

B) $\frac{7}{12}$

C) $\frac{5}{13}$

D) $\frac{12}{13}$

Step 1: Determine the ratio of sides

See the figure below.

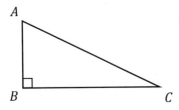

$$\sin A = \frac{\text{opposite}}{\text{hypotenuse}} = \frac{BC}{AC}$$

Determine AC and BC as shown below.

It is given that $\cos A = \frac{5}{13}$. Hence,

$$\cos A = \frac{\text{adjacent}}{\text{hypotenuse}} = \frac{AB}{AC} = \frac{5}{13}$$

$AB: AC = 5: 13$ is the ratio of Pythagorean triple $5: 12: 13$. Hence,

$$AB: BC: AC = 5: BC: 13 = 5: 12: 13$$
$$BC = 12$$

Step 2: Determine $\sin A$

$$\sin A = \frac{BC}{AC} = \frac{12}{13}$$

The correct answer choice is **D**.

Question 2

If $\cos A = \frac{5}{13}$, what is the value of $\sin(90° - A)$?

A) $\frac{5}{12}$

B) $\frac{7}{12}$

C) $\frac{5}{13}$

D) $\frac{12}{13}$

There is no need to solve since $\cos A = \sin(90° - A)$. See key points.

The correct answer choice is **C**.

Example 2:

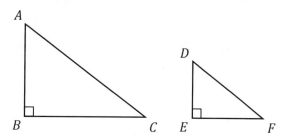

Note: Figure not drawn to scale.

In the figure above, ABC and DEF are similar triangles with vertices A, B, and C corresponding to vertices D, E, and F, respectively.

Question 1

If $\sin A = 0.8$, which of the following is the value of $\sin F$?

A) $\dfrac{5}{4}$

B) $\dfrac{4}{5}$

C) $\dfrac{3}{5}$

D) $\dfrac{4}{3}$

Step 1: Determine the ratio of sides

The question asks to determine $\sin F$ in triangle DEF but gives information on $\sin A$ in triangle ABC.

Since the two right triangles are similar, the value of sin at the corresponding vertices will be the same. Since the question gives the value of $\sin A$, use triangle ABC to determine $\sin C = \sin F$ as shown below.

It is given that $\sin A = 0.8 = \dfrac{8}{10}$. Hence,

$$\sin A = \dfrac{\text{opposite}}{\text{hypotenuse}} = \dfrac{BC}{AC} = \dfrac{8}{10}$$

$BC : AC = 8 : 10 = 2(4 : 5)$ is the ratio of Pythagorean triple $2(3 : 4 : 5)$. Hence,

$$AB : BC : AC = AB : 8 : 10 = 6 : 8 : 10$$
$$AB = 6$$

Step 2: Determine $\sin F$

$$\sin F = \sin C = \dfrac{\text{opposite}}{\text{hypotenuse}} = \dfrac{AB}{AC} = \dfrac{6}{10} = \dfrac{3}{5}$$

The correct answer choice is **C**.

Question 2

If $\cos F = \dfrac{4}{5}$ and $BC = 12$, what is the length of $\overline{AC}$?

Step 1: Determine the side proportion

Since the two right triangles are similar, the corresponding sides are in proportion and $\cos F = \cos C$. Hence,

$$\cos F = \cos C = \dfrac{\text{adjacent}}{\text{hypotenuse}} = \dfrac{BC}{AC} = \dfrac{4}{5}$$

It is given that $BC = 12$. This is three times of 4. Hence AC is three times of 5.

$$AC = 3 \times 5 = 15$$

The correct answer is **15**.

Digital SAT Math Manual and Workbook

Category 86 – Practice Questions

1

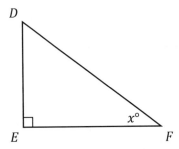

Note: Figure not drawn to scale.

In right triangle DEF shown above, $EF = 12$. If $\tan x$ is 0.75, which of the following is the length of $\overline{DE}$?

A) 3
B) 4
C) 7
D) 9

2

$$LM = 48$$
$$MN = 36$$
$$LN = 60$$

The side lengths of triangle LMN are given above. Triangle PQR is similar to triangle LMN, where vertices L, M, and N correspond to vertices P, Q, and R, respectively. Which of the following is the value of $\tan R$?

A) $\frac{3}{5}$
B) $\frac{3}{4}$
C) $\frac{4}{3}$
D) 3

3

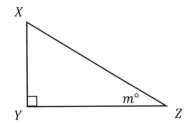

Note: Figure not drawn to scale.

In right triangle XYZ shown above, the tangent of $m°$ is $\frac{1}{\sqrt{3}}$. What is the degree measure of m?

A) 30
B) 40
C) 45
D) 60

4

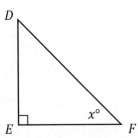

Note: Figure not drawn to scale.

In right triangle DEF above, the tangent of $x°$ is 1 and $DE = 5$. What is the length of $\overline{DF}$?

A) 1
B) 5
C) $\sqrt{2}$
D) $5\sqrt{2}$

5

In a right triangle, a and b are the two acute angles. If $\sin a = \frac{3}{5}$, which of the following is the value of $\cos(90 - a)$?

A) $\frac{3}{5}$
B) $\frac{4}{5}$
C) $\frac{3}{4}$
D) 1

6

Triangle ABC has a right angle at B. If the tangent of one of the acute angles is $\frac{1}{\sqrt{2}}$, what is the tangent of the other acute angle?

A) $\sqrt{3}$
B) $\sqrt{2}$
C) $\frac{3}{5}$
D) $\frac{5}{12}$

7

In a right triangle, the tangent of one of the acute angles is $\frac{5}{12}$. What is the cosine of the other acute angle?

A) $\sqrt{1}$
B) $\frac{5}{12}$
C) $\frac{5}{13}$
D) $\frac{12}{13}$

8

In a right triangle, x and y are the two acute angles. If the sine of angle y is 0.8, what is the tangent of x?

9

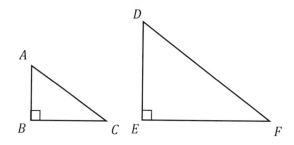

Note: Figure not drawn to scale.

In triangle ABC above, $\sin C = \frac{6}{10}$. Triangle DEF is a similar triangle, where vertices D, E, and F correspond to vertices A, B, and C, respectively. If $EF = 20$, what is the length of $\overline{DF}$?

10

In a right triangle, one of the acute angles has a degree measure of b. If $\sin b = \frac{4}{5}$, what is the value of $\cos(90° - b°)$?

11

Triangles ABC and XYZ are similar triangles, where vertices A, B, and C correspond to vertices X, Y, and Z, respectively. Each side of triangle ABC is half the length of the corresponding side of triangle XYZ. In triangle ABC, the measure of angle B is $90°$, $\tan C = \frac{3}{4}$, and $BC = 8$ inches. What is the length of $\overline{XZ}$, in inches?

12

In a right triangle, one of the acute angles is k. If $\sin(k + 20)° = \cos(3k + 10)°$, what is the value of k?

13

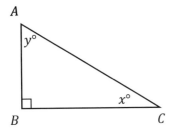

Note: Figure not drawn to scale.

In the figure above, if $x = 30°$ and $y = 60°$, which of the following is NOT true?

A) $\sin x = \cos y$
B) $\sin y = \cos x$
C) $\sin x = \cos 90° - x$
D) $\sin y = \cos 90° - x$

14

Right triangles ABC and XYZ are congruent triangles where vertices A, B, and C correspond to vertices X, Y, and Z, respectively, and angle $B = 90°$. If $AB \neq BC$, which of the following is NOT true?

I. $\sin A = \cos Z$
II. $\tan C = \tan X$
III. $\sin (90° - X) = \cos A$

A) I only
B) II only
C) I and II only
D) I and III only

15

In right triangle ABC, angle B is the right angle and x is one of the acute angles. If $\sin x° = k$, which of the following must be true for all values of k?

A) $\cos (x^2)° = k$
B) $\sin (x^2)° = k$
C) $\cos (90° - x°) = k$
D) $\tan (90° - x°) = k$

16

Note: Figure not drawn to scale.

In the figure above, triangles DEF and DGH are right triangles and $\tan F = 1.6$. $\overline{DG}$ is what fraction of $\overline{GH}$?

A) $\frac{8}{5}$
B) $\frac{4}{3}$
C) $\frac{5}{4}$
D) $\frac{16}{15}$

17

In the xy-plane, points A, B, and C form a right triangle at point B. If the (x, y) coordinates of point A are $(4, 2)$, point B are $(1, 2)$, and point C are $(1, 6)$, what is the value of $\sin A$ (as a decimal or fraction)?

18

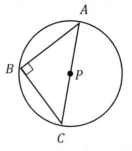

Note: Figure not drawn to scale.

Triangle ABC is inscribed in a circle with center P. Line segment $AB = 12$ and $\sin A = 0.6$. What is the radius of the circle?

Category 87 – Unit Circle and Trigonometry

Key Points

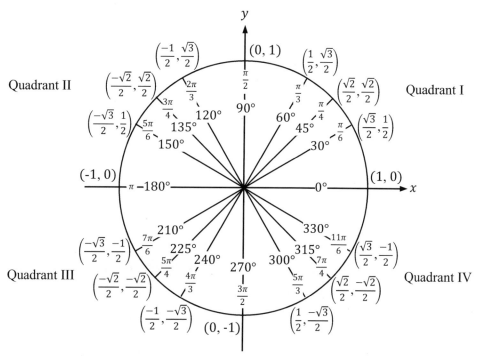

- A unit circle is a circle that has a radius of 1, and the center at origin (0, 0).
- For an angle θ starting from the origin on the positive x-axis and moving in the counterclockwise direction, the (x, y) coordinates of the endpoint on the unit circle are $(\cos\theta, \sin\theta)$. See the figure above.
- For the angles shown in the above figure, $(\cos\theta, \sin\theta)$ are a combination of positive and negative values of $\frac{1}{2}, \frac{\sqrt{3}}{2}$, and $\frac{2}{\sqrt{2}}$.
- One or more 360° (or 2π radians) rotations of an angle from the same origin have the same endpoints on a unit circle. For example, 420° is one 360° rotation of 60° angle (60° + 360° = 420°). Since 60° and 420° have the same endpoint, their $(\cos\theta, \sin\theta)$ coordinates are the same. Such angles are known as coterminal angles.
- The equation of a unit circle is $x^2 + y^2 = 1$.

How to Solve

It is best to use a calculator for solving questions on unit circle.

*Several questions in this category can be partly solved using the Desmos graphing calculator.

- Desmos displays the coordinates as numbers and decimals, not as fractions shown in the figure above. The easiest approach when using Desmos is to evaluate each answer choice by converting the fraction from an answer choice to a decimal, as shown in Example 1.
- An additional tip is to eliminate answer choices by evaluating the (x, y) coordinates in a quadrant. For example, if a question asks for the value of sin 45° or cos 60°, any negative answer choice(s) can be eliminated as (x, y) is positive in the first quadrant.
- When typing an angle in degrees, make sure in "Settings" (wrench icon) that Desmos is set to "Degrees", and when typing an angle in radians, make sure in "Settings" (wrench icon) that Desmos is set to "Radians"

Digital SAT Math Manual and Workbook

Example 1:

What is the value of $\cos \frac{3\pi}{4}$?

A) $\frac{-\sqrt{3}}{2}$

B) $\frac{-\sqrt{2}}{2}$

C) $\frac{\sqrt{3}}{2}$

D) $\frac{\sqrt{2}}{2}$

Step 1: Determine the coordinates on the unit circle

A student who knows the $(\cos \theta, \sin \theta)$ coordinates of a unit circle (as shown in the figure on the previous page) will know that the correct answer choice is B.

If a student is not familiar with the $(\cos \theta, \sin \theta)$ coordinates of a unit circle or does not remember them, then use a graphing calculator. See the approach below using the Desmos graphing calculator.

*Desmos Graphing Calculator Solution

Type $\cos \frac{3\pi}{4}$ in Desmos graphing calculator (make sure Desmos is to Radians). Its value will appear to the right in the same row. See the first row below.

Note that $\frac{3\pi}{4}$ is 135°. In the second quadrant, x-coordinates are negative. Hence, $\cos \frac{3\pi}{4}$ is negative. This eliminates answer choices C and D.

Type the remaining answer choices and match with the value in the first row.

See the second row. Answer choice A does not match with the value in the first row.

See the third row. Answer choice B matches with the value in the first row.

The correct answer choice is **B**.

Category 87 – Practice Questions

1

What is the value of tan 45° ?

A) $\frac{\sqrt{2}}{2}$

B) $\sqrt{2}$

C) 0

D) 1

2

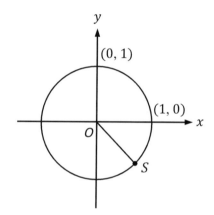

In the figure above, S is a point on the circumference of a circle with the origin at $(0, 0)$. If the x-coordinate of point S is $\frac{\sqrt{2}}{2}$, which of the following is the y-coordinate of point S?

A) $\frac{-\sqrt{3}}{2}$

B) $\frac{-\sqrt{2}}{2}$

C) $\frac{1}{2}$

D) $\frac{\sqrt{3}}{2}$

3

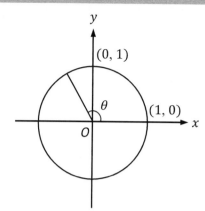

The figure above shows an angle θ. If $\cos\theta = \frac{-1}{2}$, what is the value of $\tan\theta$?

A) $-\sqrt{3}$

B) $\frac{-1}{2}$

C) $\frac{\sqrt{3}}{2}$

D) $\frac{\sqrt{2}}{2}$

4

In the xy-plane, a circle with center $(0, 0)$ has a radius of 1. Which of the following is a possible value of $\sin\frac{1}{3}\pi$?

A) $\frac{-\sqrt{3}}{2}$

B) $\frac{-\sqrt{2}}{2}$

C) $\frac{\sqrt{3}}{2}$

D) 1

5

What is the value of $\tan\frac{111\pi}{18}$?

A) $\frac{1}{2}$

B) $\frac{\sqrt{3}}{2}$

C) $\frac{1}{\sqrt{3}}$

D) $\sqrt{3}$

This page is intentionally left blank

Note from the author

My mission is to provide students preparing for the SAT math with resources that will improve their score while maximizing study time. See below the complete suite of books to prepare for the digital SAT math.
I wish good luck to all the students preparing for the SAT!!

Step 1: Go for the quick wins
Check out the type of questions that can be quickly solved using the Desmos graphing calculator.
Learn from 60 use cases.
Practice 60 questions.

Step 2: Complete your study
Learn to maximize time and build confidence.
Cover all required topics, with 200+ examples.
Practice 800+ questions.

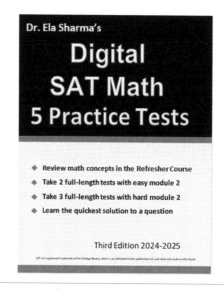

Step 3: Test yourself
Assess your preparedness.
Experience the type of questions you will see on the day of the test on the easy and hard modules.

Made in the USA
Middletown, DE
13 August 2024